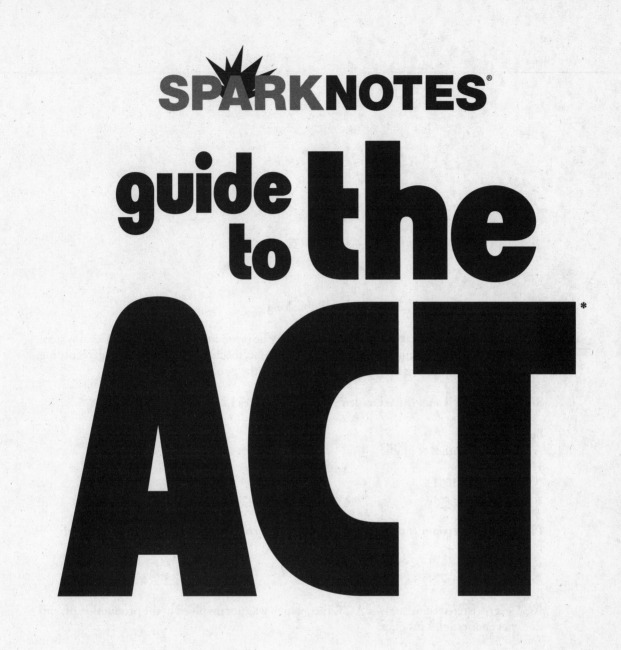

SPARKNOTES®

guide to the ACT*

SPARK PUBLISHING

Spark Publishing
A Division of Barnes & Noble
120 Fifth Avenue
New York, NY 10011
www.sparknotes.com

Please submit all comments and questions or report errors to www.sparknotes.com/errors.

ISBN-13: 978-1-4114-0245-4
ISBN-10: 1-4114-0245-6

Printed and bound in Canada.

14 13 12 11

Contents

Orientation

ACT English Review

ACT Math Review

ACT Reading Review

ACT Science
Reasoning Review

Practice Tests

Orientation

Introduction to the ACT

Chapter Contents

Each year, more than a million students take the ACT (officially called the ACT Assessment), spending 175 grueling minutes poring over a multiple-choice test that colleges and universities use to help them decide which students to admit. And most students will also spend 30 additional minutes taking the "optional" writing test that the ACT tacks on to the end of the exam.

As the ACT plays such an obvious role in the college admissions process, students often get headaches as soon as those three little letters come up. We wrote this book to try to dispel the fears surrounding the ACT while teaching the topics and study methods that will help you score your best. Ideally, we'd like you to relax and see the ACT for what it really is: a three-hour test covering the basics of a high-school education. It is not a test that will determine your future happiness. The questions on the ACT are probably easier than the questions you regularly encounter on tests in high school. It's a test that you can easily study and prepare for, if you approach it in the proper way.

In this chapter, we will put the ACT into context. We'll explain the ACT's relation to the SAT, what topics the ACT covers, how it's formatted and organized, how it's scored, and why colleges use it to evaluate prospective students. Most important, we'll begin to discuss how you should approach the ACT to minimize anxiety and maximize your score.

3

The "Optional" ACT Writing Test

The ACT Writing Test presents an issue pertinent to high school students and then asks examinees to describe their opinion on the issue. Students can write their essay in support of one of the given perspectives or develop their own. They have 30 minutes.

Optional, you say? Yes, optional, but make sure you read the fine print closely: The test is optional in the sense that institutions have the option of requiring it. You might not necessarily have the option of not taking it. The only way for you to get out of taking the writing section is to know well in advance that you won't be applying to a school that requires it for admission. If there's even a chance that you'll want to apply to a school that requires the writing test, then you should spend the extra 30 minutes taking it. Either way, this book will show you how to ace the writing test. Check out the chapter at the end of the English Review.

The ACT versus the SAT

The SAT dominates the national discussion of standardized testing; the ACT seldom gets mentioned. However, each year, nearly the same number of students take each test. Traditionally, American colleges used the SAT, rather than the ACT, as the standard-bearer in college admissions. But recently an increasing number of colleges around the country have begun to accept ACT scores from applicants, either in addition to SAT scores or in lieu of them. For you, the important question is which of the two tests should you take?

You should do the following two things when deciding whether to take the ACT or the SAT:

1. Find out whether the colleges to which you are applying require one test rather than the other.

2. If it doesn't matter which test you take, decide which test is better suited to your skills (i.e., the test on which you'll score better).

College Requirements

The majority of colleges in the U.S., particularly those on the East and West Coasts, still require an SAT score as part of the application. But depending on the schools to which you are applying, you may have a choice between the ACT and the SAT, so be aware of your options. Given the varying preferences at American colleges, you should carefully examine your application requirements before registering for either test. Beware of tricky wording as well: when the writers of the

ACT tell you that most U.S. colleges and universities "accept" ACT results, don't be fooled into thinking that those schools will take the ACT in place of the SAT—many are merely willing to look at your ACT score in addition to your SAT score. In order to avoid confusion (and possibly despair) near application deadline time, make sure you know which scores schools want.

Also remember that the writing section is an optional requirement. Some schools will require it and others won't, so make sure you know each institution's requirements. Note that if you do choose to take the writing test, your writing scores will be sent to all schools regardless of whether or not they require the writing test. Schools must specifically request not to be sent the writing scores, which is fairly unlikely.

Choosing the Right Test for You

The ACT and the SAT are both meant to test your knowledge of the fundamentals of a high school education in the United States. Yet the writers of the two tests are guided by very different philosophies, and the two exams have different formats and test different subject matter. These differences are significant enough that you might feel much more comfortable taking one test over the other. We will describe these differences below.

Differences in Testing Philosophy

ACT	SAT
The ACT strives to assess the knowledge you've acquired, meaning that the test focuses on subjects and skills taught in high school.	The SAT tries to assess "innate ability." It does so using tricky and confusing phrasing to determine your test-taking skills (i.e., your performance under pressure and your ability to identify what's being asked).

You should consider your strengths in comparison with the subjects tested by both tests. The ACT may appear more difficult than the SAT because it tests a broader range of subjects, but keep in mind that a weakness in one subject may not be as damaging on the ACT as on the SAT. You should also keep in mind that although the SAT may deal with simpler topics than the ACT, the SAT questions are often deliberately worded to confuse the test taker. In addition, you can study actual subject matter to improve your ACT score, while improving your SAT score requires you to understand test-taking tricks.

Differences in Format

	The ACT	The SAT
Total Time	175 minutes (plus 30 minute optional writing tests)	225 minutes (plus 25 minute experimental section)
Total Number of Sections	4 (plus the optional writing test)	3 (plus 1 experimental section)

The differences in format are not terribly significant.

Taking Both Tests

If time and money allow, you may want to consider taking both the ACT and the SAT. That way, you can have your choice of the two scores when applying to colleges. If you're applying to a mix of schools, some of which accept the SAT and some the ACT, you're covered on all sides. While we emphasized the differences between the two tests, studying for both tests actually would overlap a great deal. Both the ACT and the SAT ultimately test your ability to think, and both cover the basics of a high school education.

The Content and Structure of the ACT

The ACT consists of four multiple-choice "Subject Tests" covering English, Math, Reading, and Science Reasoning. As we've already mentioned, there is also an "optional" writing section at the very end of the test. These Subject Tests will always appear on the ACT in the order in which we just named them. In this chapter, we'll give you brief introductions to the subject tests and the material they cover. First, though, we'll briefly discuss the unvarying content of the test.

The writers of the ACT pride themselves on the regularity and predictability of their tests. They claim that every test has the same breakdown of question types. For example, every English Subject Test will contain ten punctuation questions, and every Math Subject Test will contain four trigonometry questions. The ACT writers believe that it is very important to maintain these numbers exactly. They will not vary.

The essentially unchanging content of the ACT means you can be thoroughly prepared for the test. The ACT doesn't want to trick you. They want to tell you exactly what will be on the test and give you every chance in the world to prepare for the test. The ACT wants to test your knowledge, and it makes sense that the best way to do that is to let you know precisely what you need to know and then see how well you can learn it. You won't be caught off guard by unfamiliar material on test day.

You can also take advantage of the regularity of the ACT to help you pinpoint your weaknesses on the test by using practice tests. We explain how to use practice tests as a powerful study tool in the chapter called "Practice Tests Are Your Best Friends," which is located just before the practice tests at the back of this book.

The English Subject Test (75 Questions, 45 Minutes)

The English Subject Test contains five reading passages laced with grammatical and stylistic errors. Each passage is accompanied by fifteen questions. You are given 45 minutes to answer these 75 questions. The questions ask you to make corrections to the text through your multiple-choice options.

The English Test assesses your understanding of the basic grammar of the English language, as well as your grasp of the tools and strategies a writer can use to put sentences together to form paragraphs and arguments. The ACT calls grammar "Usage/Mechanics" and essay writing skills "Rhetorical Skills." The English Subject Test includes 40 questions on Usage/Mechanics and 35 on Rhetorical Skills. These two types of question can be further broken down into the following categories:

Subject	Number of Questions
Usage/Mechanics	**40**
Punctuation	10
Basic Grammar and Usage	12
Sentence Structure	18
Rhetorical Skills	**35**
Strategy	12
Organization	11
Style	12
Total	**75**

Perhaps the only category that isn't self-explanatory is Strategy, which tests your understanding of a writer's strategic decisions in putting together a passage; the rest of the categories should be fairly obvious. All the above categories are covered in great detail in our chapter on the English Test.

What the English Test Really Tests

The English Test assesses your *sense* of correct English writing. You do not have to memorize esoteric grammatical terminology in order to do well on this Subject Test.

You do not need to know, for example, an appositive from a prepositional phrase. However, though you don't need to know precise grammatical terms and definitions, a good intuitive grounding in grammar is important for doing well on this Subject Test. For that reason, in "The ACT English Test," we provide you with a grammar refresher course that is tailored to the grammar you'll encounter on the ACT.

The Optional Writing Test (1 Essay Question, 30 Minutes)

In a nutshell, you are given 30 minutes to construct an essay based on a given issue. The issue will be relevant to your life as a high school student. You can either choose to support the perspective given on the issue or relate one of your own. Two "raters" will score your essay on a scale of 1–6. These raters have been trained and certified to evaluate your writing specifically for this test. The two scores from the raters are then added together to make up your subscore, ranging from 2–12. If the two raters come to a substantially different score, a third rater will be brought in.

Your score on the writing section will be incorporated into your English subject score. You will also see a writing subscore separate from the English score on your test results. Your essay will be scanned and made available online so schools can look up and see exactly what you wrote (and how bad your handwriting is). For more information on how to beat the writing test, look at the section at the end of the English Review section.

The Math Test (60 Questions, 60 Minutes)

The Math Subject Test covers six areas of high school math: pre-algebra, elementary algebra, intermediate algebra, coordinate geometry, plane geometry, and trigonometry. The test will cover those topics according to the following breakdown:

Subject	Number of Questions
Pre-Algebra	14
Elementary Algebra	10
Intermediate Algebra	9
Coordinate Geometry	9
Plane Geometry	14
Trigonometry	4
Total	**60**

As you can see, the majority of questions deal with pre-algebra, elementary algebra, and plane geometry, which are topics usually covered at the beginning of high school.

The other three topics—intermediate algebra, coordinate geometry, and trigonometry—constitute only 22 of the 60 questions on the test. You should learn these more difficult topics by the end of junior year in high school. If you have not learned trigonometry by that time, don't sweat it: there are only four trig questions on the test, and four questions won't ruin your score. Our chapter on the Math Test includes an in-depth review of all of these topics.

The Math Test differs from the other Subject Tests in two significant ways:

1. Calculator use is allowed.

2. There are five answer choices for each question, rather than four.

Later in the guide, we'll discuss how these differences should affect your strategy on the Math Test.

The Reading Test (40 Questions, 35 Minutes)

The Reading Test consists of four passages, each approximately 750 words long. The passages cover Prose Fiction, Social Science, Humanities, and Natural Science. These passages always appear in the above order, and they are given equal weight in scoring. Each passage is accompanied by ten questions of varying levels of difficulty. You are given 35 minutes to read the four passages and answer the 40 questions.

Unlike the English and Math Tests, the Reading Test evaluates a set of skills you've acquired rather than subjects you've learned. As the name of this Subject Test implies, these skills are your ability to read and to comprehend different types of passages. The Reading Test assesses these skills through a variety of questions that ask you to:

1. Identify details and facts

2. Draw inferences from given evidence

3. Make character generalizations

4. Identify the main idea of a section or the whole passage

5. Identify the author's point of view

6. Identify cause-effect relationships

7. Determine the meaning of words through context

8. Make comparisons and analogies

The Science Reasoning Test (40 Questions, 35 Minutes)

Despite its intimidating name, Science Reasoning doesn't test your understanding of any scientific field. Instead, the Subject Test assesses your ability to "reason like a scientist" or to test your ability to understand and think about data. All of the information you need to know for the Science Reasoning Test will be presented in the questions. You just have to dig it out.

The Science Reasoning Test consists of seven passages that contain a mixture of graphs, charts, and explanatory text. Each passage is followed by five to seven questions. You will encounter three different types of passages on the test:

- **Data Representation Passages.** The three Data Representation passages are each accompanied by five corresponding questions. These passages ask you to understand and use information presented in graphs or tables.

- **Research Summaries Passages.** The three Research Summaries passages each come with six questions. These passages put scientific data in the context of an experiment; the questions are similar to those in Data Representation, but they demand a greater degree of analysis from you. They require you to evaluate an experimental design.

- **Conflicting Viewpoints Passage.** The one Conflicting Viewpoints passage is accompanied by seven questions. This type of passage presents you with two or three alternative theories on a natural phenomenon. The questions test your understanding of the differences between the viewpoints and ask you to evaluate the soundness of the arguments.

You are given 35 minutes to read the seven passages and answer the 40 questions.

Science Reasoning "Content"

The ACT says that the Science Reasoning passages cover biology, earth/space sciences, chemistry, and physics. This is true, but the subject matter of the passages is largely irrelevant to what you're trying to accomplish. In "The Science Reasoning Test," we will teach you how to see through the confusing scientific terminology and strike at the heart of the matter—the data.

ACT Scoring and the Score Report

The way the ACT is scored might be the most confusing aspect of the test. The number of different scores a single ACT test produces is mind-boggling.

- First, you receive **four raw scores**, one for each Subject Test, in addition to **raw subscores** for subsections of the Subject Test (for example, Usage/Mechanics and Rhetorical Skills are the two subsections of the English Test).

- Those raw scores are converted into **four scaled scores** for the subject tests and **scaled subscores** for the subsections.

- The four scaled scores are averaged, producing the **Composite Score**.

- Finally, every single score is assigned a corresponding **percentile ranking**, indicating how you fared in comparison to other test takers.

The two scores that will matter most to you and to colleges are the Composite Score and the overall percentile ranking. You will receive these two numbers, plus your scaled scores and subscores, in a score report about four to seven weeks after you take the test.

Raw Scores

Although you will never see a raw score on your score report, you should know how the raw score is computed. All raw scores are based on the number of questions you answered correctly. To compute the raw score of a Subject Test, simply count up the number of questions you answered correctly in that Subject Test. For each correct answer, you receive one point. Your raw score is the total number of points you receive. There are no point deductions for wrong answers.

Raw Subscores

Each subject test contains component subsections, each of which is assigned a raw subscore. For example, the English Subject Test breaks down into Usage/Mechanics and Rhetorical Skills. Let's say you correctly answered 32 Usage/Mechanics questions and 21 Rhetorical Skills questions. Your raw scores for those two subsections would be 32 and 21, respectively.

Scaled Scores

Scaled scores account for disparities among different versions of the ACT. Without scaled scores, you wouldn't be able to compare your score on a particular test with the score that someone else received on a different test taken on a different date. One version of the test might be more difficult than another, affecting the overall raw scores received.

The makers of the ACT don't reveal the formula used to convert raw scores into scaled scores, but we provide you with conversion charts that mimic the ACT conversion formula, so you can get an idea of your scaled performance. These conversion charts are located with the practice tests at the back of this book.

Scaled Subscores

To add to the confusion, the subscores of a Subject Test are not scaled according to the same curve as the entire Subject Test of which they are a part: adding together scaled subscores will not necessarily produce a Subject Test's scaled score. For example, if you receive scaled subscores of 14 on Usage/Mechanics and 15 on Rhetorical Skills, your English scaled score will not necessarily be 29. More likely, it will be either 27 or 28.

If you want to take and score a practice test at home, it pretty much stinks that the ACT uses these different scale conversions. The makers of the ACT use computers and programs—to which you don't have access—to compute their scaled scores. For this reason, when we provide you with a conversion key to compute your scaled scores on practice tests, we skip the step of scaling the subsections separately. This means that the scores you receive on our practice tests will be very close to the scores you would get on an ACT, but they will not always be exact. Any test preparation book that implies the scores you receive on its practice test are exactly right isn't telling you the truth.

Use of Scaled Scores

When you receive your score report, you will see both your scaled scores and scaled subscores. Colleges will care primarily about your scaled scores for Subject Tests.

Your scaled subscores will come in handy if you plan to take the test again. They can help you identify your weak and strong areas so you can better focus your studying.

ACT Scores and the Optional Writing Test

The writing test will be graded on a scale of 1 to 6. Two raters will grade your essay, and their scores will be added for a final subscore between 2–12. This subscore will then be combined with the English score to create a "Combined English/Writing score," on a 1–36 scale. This score, along with the writing test subscore, is listed on your score report in addition to the regular battery of scores. Also, the Writing Test answer sheet will be scanned and made available for download, so institutions will be able to read exactly what you wrote.

SPECIAL NOTE: If you take the writing test, all scores, including the Combined English/Writing score and Writing subscore, will be sent to all the institutions you requested to receive your scores during the registration process. *This is regardless of whether or not those schools require the writing test.* A school must specifically request not to receive the results of the writing test or they will be sent to them automatically.

Percentile Rankings

Percentile rankings indicate how you performed compared to the other students in the nation who took the same test you did. A percentile ranking of 75 means that 74 percent of test takers scored worse than you and 25 percent scored the same or better.

The percentile rankings that matter most are the ones given for each Subject Test and the one accompanying the Composite Score (the chart below gives a sampling of percentile rankings and their corresponding Composite Scores). You will receive these percentiles on your score report.

The Composite Score

The Composite Score is the big one. It is the score your parents will tell their friends and the one your curious peers will want to know. More precisely, it is the average of your scaled scores for the four Subject Tests. So, if you got a 28 on the English Test, a 26 on the Math Test, a 32 on the Reading Test, and a 30 on the Science Reasoning Test, your composite score will be:

$$\frac{28 + 26 + 32 + 30}{4} = \frac{116}{4} = 29$$

On your score report, look for the Composite Score at the bottom of the page.

Correspondence of Composite Score, Percentile Rank & Correct Answers

The chart on the following page shows a sample of Composite Scores and how they correspond to percentile rankings and percentages of questions answered correctly. This chart should give you some context for understanding the relative levels of achievement indicated by these Composite Scores:

Composite Score	ACT Approximate Percentile Rank	Percentage of Correct Answers
31	98%	89%
26	86%	76%
23	70%	66%
20	49%	55%
17	26%	44%

Who Receives the Scores? Not You.

That heading is a little misleading, but we thought we'd draw your attention to a bizarre aspect of the test. If you follow the ACT's registration instructions, you probably *won't* receive your score directly—your high school guidance counselor and any colleges you list (see "Sending Scores to Colleges," below) will get it first, and then you must retrieve your score from your guidance counselor. But there are ways around this bureaucracy.

If you want to receive the report directly at home rather than through a third party at your high school, you can do one of two things:

1. Have your high school give ACT permission to send your score to your home.

2. Leave the High School Code blank when you sign up for the test.

Option 2 is less complicated than Option 1, and there are no repercussions from leaving the Code blank. Although ACT won't explicitly tell you about Option 2, it will work.

Early Score by Web

Now you are able to view your ACT score report 10 to 15 days after you take the test, and well before 4 to 7 weeks it normally takes them to mail the scores to you. Simply log on to **actstudent.org** and locate Early Scores by Web. Of course there is a cost involved, as with most things related to the ACT, and satisfying your need to know will cost you $8. Note that it is $8 each time you view your scores, not a flat $8 fee, so make sure you print that score report page the first time you view it. Also, this feature is only available on certain test dates.

Sending Scores to Colleges

In the moments before you take the ACT, the test administrators will give you a form allowing you to submit a list of up to six colleges that will receive your score directly from the company that makes the test. Don't submit a list unless you feel extremely confident that you will achieve your target score on the exam. After all, once you receive your score report and *know* you got the score you wanted, you can always order score reports to be sent to colleges. True, this service of forwarding your scores costs a small fee after the first three reports, but the security it provides is worth it.

There is only one reason why you should opt to have your score sent directly to colleges. If you take the test near college application deadlines, you will probably have to choose this service to ensure that your scores arrive at the colleges on time.

Canceling the Score Report

If you choose to send your score report directly to colleges, but then have a really horrible day at the test center, don't panic. You have several days to cancel your score report. To do this, call ACT at (319) 337-1270. You have until noon, Central Standard Time, on the Thursday immediately following your test date to cancel your score.

Taking the ACT Twice (or Three Times)

If you have a really horrible day at the test center but you *didn't* choose to send your score report directly to colleges, don't cancel the report. No matter how many times you take the ACT, the colleges you apply to will see only one of your scores—the one you pick. If you don't score as well as you want to the first time, you can take the test again (and again and again) with impunity until you receive a score with which you are happy.

You have a good opportunity to improve your ACT score on the second try. More than half of second-time test takers increase their scores. Taking the test a third or a fourth time probably won't make much difference in your score unless something went seriously awry on your previous tries.

What an ACT Score Means

You've taken the test and received your score; now what happens? If you're still in your junior year of high school, your ACT score can help you determine which colleges to apply to. Numerous publications each year publish reports on college profiles. Both these reports and your high school guidance counselor should help you determine your safety, 50/50, and reach schools, based on your ACT score, high school GPA, and other factors such as recommendations and extracurricular activities. While an applicant's total package is what counts, a good ACT score will never hurt your chances of getting into the schools you want. If you scored better than you expected, your score may help your applications at schools that you previously considered reaches.

How Your ACT Score Fits into Your Application Package

You may be wondering why a standardized test score matters in your college application. Let's compare two students, Megan and Chloe. Megan and Chloe are straight-A students at their respective high schools. These grades reflect the girls' relative standings at their schools (unless everyone at these two schools gets As), but how can college administrator Tim use these grades to compare Megan and Chloe? It seems like we're leading you to answer, "ACT scores!" Well, that's not entirely true. The truth is that Tim will look at a number of things to differentiate between the two girls. He'll carefully consider extra-curricular activities, the girls' essays, and their recommendations. He'll also look at course descriptions to see whether Megan has long been acing Advanced Number Theory and Sanskrit while Chloe has been queen of her Shop class.

So where does the ACT fit into this? Well, it's just another way of confirming relative standing among applicants. Tim may have access to course descriptions, but that curious college administrator is always on the lookout for other means of comparison. The ACT provides that means: it is a national standard by which colleges can evaluate applicants.

The ACT is merely one factor in your total application package, but it is an important factor that should not be overlooked or slighted. Although many schools hesitate to admit it, the fact is that your ACT score is one of the first things that stands out to someone reading your application. That person will eventually get around to reading teacher recommendations and your personal essay, but your ACT score is an easily digestible piece of information that will allow an admissions staff to form an early impression of your academic achievement. We're telling you this not to scare you, but to give you an honest assessment of what the ACT means to your college application.

That said, you should think of the ACT not as an adversary but as a tool that will help you get into college. For example, if Chloe is really a class-A student, but her high school doesn't give her the opportunity to extend her talents beyond Shop class, the ACT provides an opportunity for her to show Tim she isn't a flake. If you approach the ACT pragmatically and don't hope for a knockout score you can't achieve, and if you study with some vigor, you can control your ACT destiny and get the score you need in order to get into the colleges of your choice.

When to Take the Test

Most people take the ACT at the end of junior year or the beginning of senior year. We recommend taking it at the end of junior year for a number of reasons:

1. Taking the test junior year will give you time to retake it if necessary.

2. You will have covered most of the material on the ACT by the end of junior year, and it will be fresh in your mind.

3. You are likely to forget some material during the summer before your senior year.

Ultimately, when you choose to take the test depends on only one thing: you. If you don't feel comfortable taking it junior year, spend some time during the summer reviewing and take the test during the fall of your senior year. If you are applying for regular admission to colleges, you will probably have a couple of test dates with which to work during your senior year, but take the earliest possible test if you are applying for early admission.

Registering for the ACT

To register for the ACT, you must first obtain an ACT registration packet. Your high school guidance counselor will probably have these packets available for you. If you can't get the packet through your high school, you can write or call ACT at:

ACT Registration
P.O. Box 414
Iowa City, IA 52243-0414
(319) 337-1270

You can also register for the test by visiting ACT's website (**actstudent.org**) or, if your high school has it, by using ACT's software program College Connector. If you have taken the ACT within the last two years, you may reregister over the phone for an additional fee. You must make a VISA or Mastercard payment if you register on the Web, through College Connector, or by phone.

Regular, Late, and Standby Registration

There are three types of registration: regular, late, and standby.

- **Regular registration** deadlines are approximately five weeks before the test date. The basic fee is $29 in most of the U.S., and $49 for students testing internationally. In addition to the basic fee, the optional Writing Test is $14 for all students.

- **Late registration**, which costs you an additional $19, ends three weeks before the test date.

The ACT registration packet will contain the exact dates for regular and late registration deadlines.

- **Standby registration** is for those students who missed the late registration deadline and need to take the test by a certain date. Standby registration occurs on the day of the test. It costs an additional $39, and it does not guarantee you a seat or a test booklet. Standby registration is a last resort. If you must use standby registration, make sure to bring a completed registration folder, fee payment, and appropriate personal identification to the test center.

The ACT Admission Ticket

If you have registered for the ACT using regular or late registration, you will receive an admission ticket in the mail. This ticket will tell you when and where the test will be administered. It will also list the information you submitted to ACT, such as any colleges that will receive your score directly. You should read the admission ticket carefully to make sure there are no mistakes. If you find a mistake, follow the instructions on the back of the ticket for correcting information.

Test Dates

ACT test dates usually fall in October, December, February, April, and June. Certain states also have a September test date. Double-check your test dates by going to ACT's student website at **actstudent.org**.

SparkNotes Online Test Prep

You didn't think SparkNotes would forget about the Web, did you? The Internet access card that's bound into this book comes with a code that grants you access to SparkNotes Online Test Prep for the ACT. SparkNotes ACT website provides the following features:

- An essay-grading service that offers a grade and analysis for the essay questions contained in this book. SparkNotes will grade your first essay for free.

- The two practice tests in this book, backed by diagnostic software that immediately analyzes yoru results and directs your study for efficiency and effectiveness.

- The entire book, fully searchable, with all the latest updates to keep you up to speed.

In addition to the ACT, SparkNotes Online Test Prep also coveres the SAT and the most popular SAT Subject Tests. And once you've bought this book, you can get access to the test prep for any of those other tests for $4.95, about ten dollars less than it would cost you to buy the book.

General Strategies for Taking the ACT

I MAGINE TWO CHILDREN PLAYING TAG IN the forest. Who will win—the girl who never stumbles because she knows the placement of every tree and all the twists and turns and hiding spots, or the kid who keeps falling down and tripping over roots because he doesn't pay any attention to the landscape? The answer is obvious. Even if the other kid is faster and more athletic, the girl will win because she knows how to navigate the territory and use it to her advantage.

This example of tag in the forest is extreme, but it illustrates a point. The structure of the ACT is the forest. Taking the test is the game of tag. And no one likes to lose at tag.

In this chapter, you'll learn how to take advantage of the ACT's structure to achieve the score you want. You'll learn basic rules for taking the ACT, as well as pacing and preparation strategies. These are the general test-taking strategies that you should use in all sections of the test. There are, of course, specific strategies for each of the individual Subject Tests. We'll cover those in the chapters devoted to each Subject Test.

Seven Basic Rules for Taking the ACT

These seven rules apply to every section of the ACT. They really are just common-sense guidelines, but it's amazing how the pressure and time constraints of the ACT can warp and mangle common sense. We list them here because you should always have these rules of test taking resting gently in your mind as you take the test. You don't need to focus on them obsessively, but you should be sure not to forget them. They will help you save time and cut down on careless errors.

1. Know the Instructions for Each Subject Test

Since you'll need all the time you can get, don't waste time reading the Subject Test instructions during the actual test. Learn the instructions beforehand by taking practice tests and reading our chapters on the Subject Tests.

2. Use Your Test Booklet as Scratch Paper

Some students seem to think their test booklet has to look "pretty" at the end of the test. Don't be one of those students. A pristine test booklet is a sad test booklet. In the Math Test, the ACT writers even give you "figuring" space for drawing diagrams and writing out solutions. The Math Test isn't the only place where you can benefit from marginal scribbling, though. Making margin notes alongside the Reading and Science Reasoning passages can help you stay on track when answering the subsequent questions. In addition, if you want to skip a question and come back to it later, you should make a distinctive mark next to it, so you won't miss it on your second pass through the questions.

3. Answer Easy Questions before Hard Questions

This is a crucial strategy for the ACT. Since all questions within a Subject Test are worth the same number of points, there's no point slaving away over a difficult question if doing so requires several minutes. In the same amount of time, you probably could have racked up points by answering a bunch of easy, less time-consuming questions.

In summary, answer the easy and moderate questions first. That way you'll make sure that you get to see all the questions on the test that you have a good shot of getting right, while saving the leftover time for the difficult questions.

4. Don't Get Bogged Down by a Hard Question

This rule may seem obvious, but many people have a hard time letting go of a question. If you've spent a significant amount of time on a problem (in ACT world, a minute and a half is a lot of time) and haven't gotten close to answering it, just let it go. Leaving a question unfinished may seem like giving up or wasting time you've already spent, but you can come back to the problem after you've answered the easy ones. The time you spent on the problem earlier won't be wasted. When you come back to the problem, you'll already have done part of the work needed to solve it.

This strategy goes hand in hand with Rule 3. After all, the tough question that's chewing up your time isn't worth more to the computer grading your answer sheet than the easy questions nearby.

5. Avoid Carelessness

There are two kinds of carelessness that threaten you as an ACT test taker. The first kind is obvious: making mistakes because you are moving too quickly through the questions. Speeding through the test can result in misinterpreting a question or missing a crucial piece of information. You should always be aware of this kind of error because the ACT writers have written the test with speedy test takers in mind: they often include tempting "partial answers" among the answer choices. A partial answer is the result of some, but not all, of the steps needed to solve a problem. If you rush through a question, you may mistake a partial answer for the real answer. Students often fall into the speeding trap when they become confused, since confusion brings nervousness and fear of falling behind. But those moments of confusion are precisely the moments when you should take a second to slow down. Take a deep breath, look at the question, and make a sober decision about whether or not you can answer it. If you can, dive back in. If you can't, skip the question and go on to the next one.

The second kind of carelessness arises from frustration or lack of confidence. Don't allow yourself to assume a defeatist attitude toward questions that appear to be complex. While some of these questions may actually be complex, some of them will be fairly simple questions disguised in complex-sounding terms. You should at least skim every question to see whether you have a feasible chance of answering it. Assuming you can't answer a question is like returning a present you've never even opened.

6. Be Careful Bubbling In Your Answers

Imagine this: you get all the right answers to the ACT questions, but you fill in all the wrong bubbles. The scoring computer doesn't care that you did the right work; all it cares about are the blackened bubbles on the answer sheet, and the wrong answers that they indicate.

Protect yourself against this terrifying possibility with careful bubbling. An easy way to prevent slips on the ACT answer sheet is to pay attention to the letters being bubbled. Odd-numbered answers are lettered **A, B, C, D** (except on the Math Test, where they are **A, B, C, D, E**), and even-numbered answers are lettered **F, G, H, J** (except on the Math Test, where they are **F, G, H, J, K**).

You may also want to try bubbling in groups (five at a time or a page at a time) rather than answering one by one. Circle the answers in the test booklet as you go through the page, and then transfer the answers over to the answer sheet as a group. This method should increase your speed and accuracy in filling out the answer sheet. To further increase your accuracy, say the question number and the answer in your head as you fill out the grid: "Number 24, **F**. Number 25, **C**. Number 26, **J**."

7. Always Guess When You Don't Know the Answer

We will discuss guessing below in "The Meaning of Multiple Choice," but the basic rule is: always guess! You're much better off guessing than leaving an answer blank because there is no penalty for wrong answers.

The Meaning of Multiple Choice

As we've suggested throughout this chapter, the multiple-choice format of the ACT should affect the way you approach the questions. In this section, we'll discuss exactly how.

Only the Answer Matters

A machine, not a person, will score your test. This scoring machine does not care how you came to your answers; it cares only whether your answers are correct and readable in little oval form. The test booklet in which you worked out your answers gets thrown in the garbage, or, if your proctor is conscientious, into a recycling bin.

On the ACT, no one looks at your work. If you get a question right, it doesn't matter whether you did impeccable work. In fact, it doesn't even matter whether you knew the answer or guessed. The multiple-choice structure of the test is a message to you from the ACT: "We only care about your answers." Remember, the ACT is your tool to get into college, so treat it as a tool. It wants right answers? Give it right answers, as many as possible, using whatever strategies you can.

Multiple Choice: You've Already Got the Answers

When you look at any ACT multiple-choice question, the answer is already right there in front of you. Of course, the ACT writers don't just *give* you the correct answer; they hide it among a bunch of incorrect answer choices. Your job on each question is to find the right answer. Because the answer is right there, begging to be found, you have two methods you can use to try to get the correct answer:

1. Look through the answer choices and pick out the one that is correct.

2. Look at the answer choices and eliminate wrong answers until there's only one answer left.

Both methods have their advantages: you are better off using one in some situations and the other in others. In a perfect scenario in which you are sure how to answer a question, finding the right answer immediately is clearly better than chipping away at the wrong answers. Coming to a conclusion about a problem and then picking the single correct choice is a much simpler and quicker process than going through every answer choice and discarding the four that are wrong.

However, when you are unsure how to solve the problem, eliminating wrong answers becomes more attractive and appropriate. By focusing on the answers to problems that are giving you trouble, you might be able to use the answer choices to lead you in the right direction, or to solve the problem through trial and error. You also might be able to eliminate answer choices through a variety of strategies (these strategies vary by question type; we'll cover them in the chapters dedicated to each type of question). In some cases, you might be able to eliminate all the wrong answers. In others, you might only be able to eliminate one, which will still improve your odds when you attempt to guess.

Part of your preparation for the ACT should be to get some sense of when to use each strategy. Using the right strategy can increase your speed without affecting your accuracy, giving you more time to work on and answer as many questions as possible.

Guessing and the ACT

We've said it once, but it's important enough to bear repetition: whenever you can't answer a question on the ACT, you must guess. You are not penalized for getting a question wrong, so guessing can only help your score.

Random Guessing and Educated Guessing

There are actually two kinds of guesses: random and educated. Random guesser Charlie Franklin will always guess **C** or **F** because he really, really likes those letters. Using this method, Charlie has a pretty good chance of getting about 25 percent of the questions right, yielding a Composite Score of about 11. That's not too shabby, considering Charlie expended practically no intellectual energy beyond identifying **C** and **F** as the first letters of his first and last names.

But what about educated guesser Celia? Instead of immediately guessing on each question, she works to eliminate answers, always getting rid of two choices for each question. She then guesses between the remaining choices and has a 50 percent chance of getting the correct answer. Celia will therefore get about half of the questions on the test correct. Her Composite Score will be about a 19, which is an average score on the ACT.

The example of these two guessers should show you that while blind guessing can help you, educated guessing can *really* help you. For example, let's say you know the correct answer for half of the questions and you guess randomly on the remaining half. Your score will probably be a 22—three points higher than the score you'd get leaving half of the answers blank. Now let's say you know the correct answer for half of the questions and you make educated guesses on the remaining half, narrowing the choices to two. You can probably score a 26 with this method, landing you in the 90th percentile of test takers. This is a good score, and to get it you only need to be certain of half the answers.

"Always guess" really means "always eliminate as many answer choices as possible and then guess."

A Note to the Timid Guesser

Some students feel that guessing is like cheating. They believe that by guessing, they are getting points they don't really deserve. Such a belief might be noble, but it is also mistaken, for two reasons.

First, educated guessing is actually a form of partial credit on the ACT. Let's say you're taking the ACT and come upon a question you can't quite figure out. Yet while you aren't sure of the definite answer, you are sure that two of the answer choices *can't* be right. In other words, you can eliminate two of the four answer choices, leaving you with a one in two chance of guessing correctly between the remaining two answer choices. Now let's say someone else is taking the same test and gets to the same question. But this person is completely flummoxed. He can't eliminate *any* answer choices. When this person guesses, he has only a one in four chance of guessing correctly. Your extra knowledge, which allowed you to eliminate some answer choices, gives you better odds of getting this question right, exactly as extra knowledge should.

Second, the people who made the ACT thought very hard about how the scoring of the test should work. When they decided that they wouldn't include a penalty for wrong answers, they knew that the lack of a penalty would allow people to guess. In other words, they built the test with the specific understanding that people would guess on every question they couldn't answer. The test *wants* you to guess. So go ahead and do it.

Pacing

The ACT presents you with a ton of questions and, despite its three-hour length, not that much time to answer them. As you take the test, you will probably feel some pressure to answer quickly. As we've already discussed, getting bogged down on a single question is not a good thing. But rushing isn't any good either. In the end, there's no real difference between answering very few questions and answering lots of questions incorrectly: both will lead to low scores. What you have to do is find a happy medium, a groove, a speed at which you can be both accurate and efficient, and get the score you want. Finding this pace is a tricky task, but it will come through practice and strategy.

Setting a Target Score

The ACT is your tool to get into college. Therefore, a perfect score on the ACT is not a 36, it's the score that gets you into the colleges of your choice. Once you set a target score, your efforts should be directed toward achieving *that* score and not necessarily a 36.

In setting a target score, the first rule is to be honest and realistic. Base your target score on the schools you want to attend, and use the results from your practice tests to decide what's realistic. If you score a 20 on your first practice test, your target score probably should not be a 30. Instead, aim for a 23 or 24. Your scores will likely increase on your second test simply because you'll be more experienced than you were the first time, and then you can work on getting several extra problems right on each Subject Test.

Your Target Score Determines Your Strategy and Pace

Your target score should affect your overall approach to the test. Cathy, whose target score is 31, is going to use a different strategy and pace from Elvie, whose target score is 20. Cathy must work quickly without becoming careless to get 90 percent of her questions right. Elvie, on the other hand, can afford to work more slowly; to get a 20, she needs to answer approximately half of the questions correctly. Elvie can focus her energy on carefully answering about 60 percent of the questions, allowing for some wrong answers; then she can guess on the remaining questions. Cathy needs to focus on every question to get her 90 percent. Also allowing for some wrong answers, she should aim to answer all the questions correctly.

Of course, this is all a bit like the chicken and the egg conundrum. Cathy's target score is probably higher than Elvie's because she is a faster and better test taker than Elvie. Elvie needs the extra time to spend on each problem because she is a slower worker than Cathy. It's not as though Elvie generates a lot of extra time in which she can doodle or draw elaborate diagrams by concentrating on a smaller number of questions. All of that extra time per question is being put to use by Elvie because she needs it in order to get the right answer.

The point of this anecdote: Adjust your pacing to the score you want, but also be honest with yourself about what pace you can maintain. The following charts will give you an idea of the number of questions you need to get right in order to receive certain scaled scores on the ACT. Use these charts to determine the number of correct answers you need in order to achieve your target score.

English		Math	
Target Score	# Right	Target Score	# Right
36	75	36	60
30	69–70	30	53–54
26	60–62	26	44–45
23	52–54	23	38–39
20	44–46	20	32–33
17	36–38	17	23–25
11	19–21	11	7–8

Reading		Science Reasoning	
Target Score	# Right	Target Score	# Right
36	40	36	40
30	35	30	37
26	30–31	26	32–33
23	26–27	23	27–28
20	22	20	22–23
17	18	17	16–17
11	9–10	11	7

The first target score you set doesn't have to be your last. If you reach your initial target score, set a new, higher score and try increasing the pace at which you work. In setting preparatory target scores, focus on improving a couple points at a time. In the end, incremental change will work better than a giant leap.

The White Rabbit Syndrome: Watching the Clock

Because the ACT is a timed test, you should always be aware of the time. The proctor at the test center will strictly enforce the time limits for each Subject Test. Even if you have only one question left to answer, you won't be allowed to fill in that bubble.

As you take the test, watch the clock. You shouldn't be checking it every two minutes, since you will only waste time and give yourself a headache. But you should check occasionally to make sure you are on pace to achieve your target score. If you're Cathy, aiming to answer 90 percent of the questions correctly, you'll be in trouble if you've answered only 40 of the 75 English questions in 30 minutes (the English Test is

45 minutes long). If you're Elvie, aiming for 60 percent of the questions, answering 40 English questions in 30 minutes is a pretty good pace.

Preparing for the ACT

Preparation is the key to success on the ACT. When the ACT is lurking sometime far in the future, it can be difficult to motivate yourself to study. Establishing an organized study routine can help keep you on track as you approach the test date.

Setting Up a Study Schedule

Rather than simply telling yourself to study each week, you might want to write down an actual schedule, just as you have a schedule of classes at school. Keep this schedule where you'll see it every day, and consider showing it to a parent who will nag you incessantly when you don't follow it. (You might as well use your parents' nagging capabilities to your own advantage for once.)

You should allot at least a few hours a week to studying, depending on how much time you have before the test date. If you start preparing five weeks in advance, you might consider studying one subject per week, with the last week left over for light review. Our chapters on the individual tests will give you a solid review of the material you need to know.

To complement your studying, take at least part of a practice test each week. We've given you two practice tests at the back of this book. You don't necessarily have to take a full practice test each week, but, if you're preparing for English one week, take a practice English Test to help focus your studying. We explain how practice tests can function as powerful study tools in the chapter called "Practice Tests Are Your Best Friends."

The Day of the Test

You must bring the following items to the test center on the day of the test:

1. Your admission ticket

2. Photo ID or a letter of identification

Unless a test proctor recognizes you, you will not be allowed in the test room without appropriate identification. We also suggest that you bring the following:

3. Number Two pencils

4. A calculator. You should bring the calculator you normally use (preferably with an extra battery). You don't want to get stuck searching frantically for the right buttons on an unfamiliar calculator.

5. A watch. Your test room may not have a clock, or the clock may not be visible from where you're sitting. Since the test proctors only call out the time five minutes before the end of each section, you have to rely on yourself to know how much time remains.

6. A snack, to keep up that energy.

7. Lucky clothes. Why not?

ACT English Review

The ACT English Test

THE ACT ENGLISH TEST ASSESSES YOUR knowledge of English grammar and writing. On the test, you will have 45 minutes to answer 75 questions. That may seem like a large number of questions and relatively little time, but the English Test, more than any other ACT Subject Test, assesses what you already know, rather than what you can figure out if you are given certain information. Essentially, this means you can be completely prepared for the English Test if you study all the material it covers. This section will teach you exactly that material.

Instructions for the English Test

You should learn the instructions for the English Test long before you arrive at the test center. In fact, your first step in preparing for the ACT should be learning the instructions for all four Subject Tests. On the actual test, the Subject Test instructions are time-consuming obstacles, which you can remove by learning them in advance. You can also benefit from them while you study because they contain valuable information about ACT questions and how to answer them.

At the start of each chapter on an individual Subject Test, we've given you a complete summary of the Subject Test instructions. Read through each set of instructions several times until you know them all like the back of your hand. The English Test instructions are particularly long, so you'll save yourself time on the test by learning them now.

Instructions: There are five passages on this subject test. You should read each passage once before answering the questions on it. In order to answer correctly, you may need to read several sentences beyond the question.

There are two question formats within the passages. In one format, you will find words and phrases that have been underlined and assigned numbers. These numbers will correspond with sets of alternative words/phrases, given in the right-hand column of the test booklet. From the sets of alternatives, choose the answer choice that works best in context, keeping in mind whether it employs standard written English, whether it gets across the idea of the section, and whether it suits the tone and style of the passage. You will usually be offered the option "NO CHANGE," which you should choose if you think the version found in the passage is best.

In the second format, you will see boxed numbers referring to sections of the passage or to the passage as a whole. In the right-hand column, you will be asked questions about or given alternatives for the sections marked by the boxes. Choose the answer choice that best answers the question or completes the section.

After choosing your answer choice, fill in the corresponding bubble on the answer sheet.

These instructions will seem much clearer to you after you've seen the sample English Test questions in the following sections.

The Format of the English Test

The five passages on the English Test contain two question formats: underlines and boxes. Both the underlines and the boxes will be numbered so you can find the corresponding multiple-choice answers in the right-hand column of the test booklet.

Below you'll find a sample English Test paragraph, illustrating both question formats:

[1] That summer my parents <u>buy</u> me my first
                                17
bike—my first true love. [2] One day, I crashed

into a tree and broke my leg. [3] Unfortunately,

my control of the bike was not as great as my

enthusiasm for it. [4] I spent all my afternoons

speeding around the neighborhood blocks. 18

17. **A.** NO CHANGE
     B. bought
     C. have bought
     D. buys

18. Which of the following
     provides the most logical
     ordering of the sentences
     in Paragraph 3?
     F. 3, 2, 1, 4
     G. 3, 1, 4, 2
     H. 1, 4, 3, 2
     J. 1, 4, 2, 3

Question 17 demonstrates the underline format on the English Test. In this example, the word "buy" is underlined and numbered 17, indicating that you can replace "buy" with answer choices **B**, **C**, or **D**, or keep it by selecting answer choice **A** ("NO CHANGE"). Decide which answer choice makes the sentence grammatically correct, and fill in the corresponding bubble on your answer sheet. (The correct answer is **B**.)

Question 18 is an example of a Rhetorical Skills question indicated by a boxed number. The boxed number indicates that the question will deal with a large section of the passage, not just a few words. This question asks you to reorganize the sentences of the paragraph in a logical manner. Once you've arrived at an answer, fill in the corresponding bubble on your answer sheet. (The correct answer to this question is **H**.)

Don't worry about the answers to these questions now. We'll deal with the specific question types and the grammar covered on the English Subject Test later on in this chapter.

The Content of the English Test

There are actually two types of content on the English Test: the content of the passages and the content of the questions. Question content is the more important of the two.

When we say "the content of the passages," we mean the subjects covered by the five English Test passages. The passages usually cover a variety of subjects, ranging from historical discussions to personal narratives. Don't worry about passage content for now; it is important when answering certain Rhetorical Skills questions, which we'll discuss toward the end of this chapter, but the grammar of the passage is generally more important.

"The content of the questions" refers to the two kinds of material covered by the English Test: Usage/Mechanics and Rhetorical Skills. The majority of this section is devoted to explaining the question content on the English Test. For now, we'll give you a brief summary of the material.

Usage/Mechanics Questions

The 40 Usage/Mechanics questions on the test deal with the proper use of standard written English. You can think of them as the "technical" aspect of the test because they ask you to apply the rules of standard English to sections of the passages. Questions covering usage and mechanics are almost always presented as underlined sections of the passages. Usage/Mechanics questions test your understanding of the following categories:

1. **Punctuation (10 questions):** Punctuation questions ask you to identify and correct any misplaced, misused, or missing punctuation marks. The punctuation marks most commonly tested on the ACT are, in order of decreasing frequency, commas, apostrophes, colons, and semicolons.

2. **Basic Grammar and Usage (12 questions):** Basic Grammar and Usage questions usually target a single incorrect word that violates the conventional rules of English grammar. These questions frequently test your knowledge of agreement issues and pronoun forms and cases.

3. **Sentence Structure (18 questions):** Sentence Structure questions tend to deal with the sentence as a whole. They test you on clause relationships, parallelism, and placement of modifiers.

If some of these Usage/Mechanics issues sound unfamiliar or confusing to you, don't worry—later, in the "Usage/Mechanics Questions on the English Test" chapter, we'll review all of the material you need to know for these questions.

Rhetorical Skills Questions

The 35 Rhetorical Skills questions test your ability to refine written English. If the Usage/Mechanics questions are the technical aspect of the test, then the Rhetorical Skills questions are the intuitive aspect—but they require an intuition you can develop through practice. The boxes you encounter on the test will deal with Rhetorical Skills questions; some underlined sections may deal with Rhetorical Skills as well.

Rhetorical Skills questions break down into the following categories:

1. **Writing Strategy (12 questions):** Writing Strategy questions are concerned with a passage's effectiveness. These questions require that you understand the point, purpose, and tone of a passage. When answering these questions, you must decide the best way to support a point with evidence, to introduce and conclude paragraphs, to make a transition between paragraphs, or to phrase a statement.

2. **Organization (11 questions):** Organization questions can deal with individual sentences, individual paragraphs, or the passage as a whole. They will ask you either to restructure the passage or paragraph or to decide on the best placement of a word or phrase within a sentence.

3. **Style (12 questions):** Style questions focus on effective word choice. They will ask you to eliminate redundancy and to select the most appropriate word or phrase. In order to answer style questions correctly, you need

to understand the tone of a passage, and you need to have a good eye for clear written English.

Because Rhetorical Skills questions require a sense of good English writing, they tend to be more difficult than Usage/Mechanics questions, which primarily require that you understand grammatical rules. This sense for good writing can be developed through review and practice. You'll have a chance for both in the "Rhetorical Skills Questions on the English Test" chapter.

Memorization and the Content of the English Test

The ACT writers emphasize that the English Test is not a test of memorization. It would be more accurate to say that the test does not *explicitly* test your memorization of rules of the English language.

You will not be tested on vocabulary on the English Test (unlike on the SAT Verbal, which is largely a vocabulary memorization test), but having a decent vocabulary is important in answering style and strategy questions. Those questions often ask you to choose the most effective word or phrase. If you don't know what some of the words mean, you may not be able to make the right choice.

Technically, the test does not ask you to memorize grammar rules, but it should be obvious that doing well on the test requires that you know the conventional rules of grammar. You won't be asked to state the definition of a gerund, but you'll be in trouble if you can't make your subjects and verbs agree or if you think a comma splice is something tasty in your spice rack.

Obviously, you need to understand grammatical rules for the English Test. While knowing these rules does not explicitly require memorization, most people begin to learn grammar by memorizing its rules.

Strategies for the English Test

Although the English Test is relatively straightforward, you should use certain strategies to improve your speed and efficiency and to avoid any traps the ACT writers may have included. This section covers both broad strategies for approaching the English Test as well as specific tips for eliminating multiple-choice answers.

Skim the Entire Passage before Answering the Questions

Don't immediately jump to the questions. Instead, first read quickly through the passage you're working on; then begin answering the accompanying questions.

While reading the passage once through before getting to the questions may seem like extra work, it will prevent you from making unnecessary errors. The English Test instructions warn that you may need to read beyond a question in order to answer it correctly. By being familiar with the entire passage, you can avoid the problem of not having read far enough ahead. Reading the entire passage will also help you with Rhetorical Skills questions by giving you an understanding of the passage's purpose, argument, and tone.

English Strategies

If you need further convincing, the following sample English Test question demonstrates why reading beyond the underlined section is necessary:

her dogs <u>has</u> sleek, brown hair
14

14. **F.** No change
    G. are
    H. have
    J. do not have

Seems pretty easy, doesn't it? "Ah, a simple subject-verb agreement problem," you're probably thinking. "The answer, obviously, is **H.**" But what if we show you the whole sentence?

The girl walking her dogs <u>has</u> sleek, brown hair
14

14. **F.** No change
    G. are
    H. have
    J. do not have

Reading the rest of the sentence reveals that the sleek, brown hair belongs to a girl rather than a pack of dogs. The question was about subject-verb agreement, but the words directly next to the underlined phrase misled you into thinking that the subject was "her dogs" and not "the girl." If you had read the passage first, you would have realized that the correct answer is **F.**

Admittedly, this example exaggerates the case for reading beyond the question, but it gets our point across. Ultimately, if you quickly read through the passage before tackling the questions, you'll avoid unnecessary mistakes without sacrificing much time.

Answer the Questions in the Order They Appear

Answer ACT English questions in the order in which they appear. This suggestion is really just common sense. After all, the questions appear in a certain order for a reason: a question at the beginning deals with the beginning of the passage, a question in the middle deals with the middle of the passage, and so on. An organization question in the middle of a passage won't ask you to reorganize the entire passage or a faraway section of the passage. It will ask you to reorganize the material directly to the left of the question. Rhetorical Skills questions on the passage as a whole appear at the end of the passage, and what better time to answer those questions that deal with the entire passage than at the end?

Organization of Usage/Mechanics and Rhetorical Skills Questions

Questions on the English Test do not appear in order of difficulty. On many passages, you tend to see easy Usage/Mechanics questions near the beginning and

English Strategies

relatively difficult Rhetorical Skills questions at the end, but there is no set rule about the order of their appearance.

Guess

If you come to a question you can't answer, you can either draw a mark next to it so you can return later, or you can guess right away, leaving the question behind forever. On the English Test, and only on the English Test, we suggest guessing and moving on. As we stated earlier, the questions on the English Test assess what you already know rather than what you can figure out, so if you don't get the answer right off the bat (or a few seconds off the bat), you're not likely to get it by intense wriggling and head scratching. With that in mind, marking the question in order to come back later seems like a needless waste of time—you might as well take your shot right away and move on to more fruitful English territory.

Following this strategy, you should not move on to a new passage without answering all the questions from the previous one. Needless to say, if you follow our suggestion and guess when you don't know the answer, you won't encounter this problem. But if you do decide to return to a question you skipped, do so before moving on to the next passage; otherwise, you're likely to forget crucial details from the passage.

Eliminate Answer Choices

Educated guessing is always better than blind guessing. Whenever you guess, try first to eliminate some of the multiple-choice answers to improve your odds of guessing correctly. Take a look at these sample answers:

    A.   When I swung the bat I knew, I had hit a home run.
    B.   When I swung the bat, I knew I had hit a home run.
    C.   When I swing the bat I will know I always hit a home run.
    D.   When, I swung the bat I knew, I had hit a home run.

You can probably figure out from these answer choices that there is a comma placement error. Choices **A**, **B**, and **D** all give versions of the same sentence with different comma placement. Choice **C**, attempting to lure you off the right track, offers a comma-less version of the sentence with nonsensically altered verb tenses.

Can you eliminate any of these answer choices? Well, choice **C** looks like a prime candidate for elimination because it makes little sense. Choice **D** also looks like it can go because of the comma placed after "When," which leaves the word dangling at the beginning of the sentence. If you can eliminate either or both of these, you greatly increase the chance that you'll pick the correct answer, which is **B**.

English Strategies

Eliminating Answer Choices for Questions with Multiple Errors

Quite often, you will encounter questions that involve more than one error. While these questions may seem harder to answer than single-error questions, you can benefit from the multiple errors when trying to eliminate answer choices: if you can't spot one error, you might spot the other.

Instead of tackling all the errors at once, you'll have an easier time picking them off one by one. Let's use the following example:

    A.   Cathys' friends left they're bags in the room.
    B.   Cathy's friends left there bags in the room.
    C.   Cathys friends left their bags in the room.
    D.   Cathy's friends left their bags in the room.

These sentences contain two variations. If you focus on Cathy and her friends, you realize that you should eliminate choices **A** and **C** for incorrect apostrophe placement. Now you've narrowed your options to **B** and **D**, which respectively use "there" and "their" as possessive pronouns. If you don't know the difference between the two, you have a 50 percent chance of guessing the right answer. If you do know the difference (and you will, after you read the Usage/Mechanics chapter), you know that "there bags" is incorrect and that the correct answer is therefore **D**.

Avoid Being Influenced by the Answer Choices

Be wary of answer choices that try to trick you into overcorrecting the problem. You shouldn't be fooled into finding additional "errors" by an answer choice that has completely made over the original. The correct answer to a question is not necessarily the one that has changed the most elements of the underlined phrase.

Choose "NO CHANGE"

In fact, the correct answer to a question is not necessarily one that has changed anything at all. All Usage/Mechanics questions and some Rhetorical Skills questions offer you "NO CHANGE" as an answer choice. Do not overlook "NO CHANGE" as a possible answer to the problem. It is correct approximately 20 percent of the time it's offered.

If your gut tells you there's nothing wrong with the underlined phrase, don't change the phrase.

If the Phrase Doesn't Fit, You Must "OMIT"

You will often see the answer choice "OMIT the underlined portion." By choosing it, you can remove the entire underlined portion from the passage.

When an answer choice allows you to "OMIT the underlined portion," think hard about that option. "OMIT," when it appears as an answer, is correct approximately 25 percent of the time. We don't suggest that you go through the test ticking off "OMIT" for every possible question, but we do want you to consider it as an answer.

"OMIT" is an attractive (and often correct) answer because it eliminates redundant or irrelevant statements. (For more on redundancy, see the "Style" section under "Rhetorical Skills Questions on the English Test.") For example,

The bag was free. <u>I didn't have to pay for it.</u>
21

21. A. NO CHANGE
B. I paid five dollars for it.
C. I paid almost nothing for it.
D. Omit the underlined portion

The ACT writers want your edits to make the passage as concise as possible. A statement like the one above should strike you as redundant because you clearly don't need to pay for something that's free—so why say the same thing twice? If you choose choice **A**, you keep the redundant sentence in the passage and get the answer wrong. Choices **B** and **C** don't make much sense because they have you paying for the free bag. Choice **D** is the correct answer because it omits an unnecessary statement. Without the second sentence, a reader still understands that the free bag didn't cost anything.

When deciding whether to omit, read the passage or sentence without the underlined portion and see whether the new version of the sentence makes as much, if not more, sense to you as the original. If it does, go ahead and choose "OMIT." If the passage or sentence loses something in the omission, then turn to the other answer choices.

English Strategies

Usage/Mechanics Questions on the English Test

Chapter Contents

IN ORDER TO DO WELL ON THE ENGLISH Test, you need to know the basic rules of grammar. Specifically, you need to know the rules of grammar most often tested by the ACT. This section will teach you the grammar you need to know for the test. These Usage/Mechanics topics are:

1. Punctuation

2. Basic Grammar and Usage

3. Sentence Structure

Punctuation

Punctuation shows you how to read and understand sentences. For instance, the period at the end of the last sentence indicated that the sentence had come to an end and that the next sentence would begin a new thought. We could go on and on like this, but you get the point.

The ACT English Test requires that you know the rules for the following types of punctuation:

1. Commas

2. Apostrophes

3. Semicolons

4. Colons

5. Parentheses and Dashes

6. Periods, Question Marks, and Exclamation Points

Not all of these punctuation types are tested on every English Test. However, you can definitely expect to find questions dealing with the first four items of the list on the English Test you take.

Commas

Misplaced, misused, and missing commas are the most frequent punctuation offenders on the English Test. Commas can serve several functions within sentences:

Commas Separate Independent Clauses Joined by a Conjunction

An independent clause contains a subject and a verb (an independent clause can be as short as "I am" or "he read"), and it can function as a sentence on its own. When you see a conjunction (*and*, *but*, *for*, *or*, *nor*, *yet*) joining independent clauses, a comma should precede the conjunction. For example,

> An independent clause contains a subject and a verb, *and* it can function as a sentence on its own.

> Lesley wanted to sit outside, *but* it was raining.

> Henry could tie the shoe himself, *or* he could ask Amanda to tie his shoe.

In each example, the clauses on both sides of the comma could stand as sentences on their own. With the addition of the comma and conjunction, the two independent clauses become one sentence.

Commas Delineate a Series of Items

A series contains three or more items separated by commas. The items in a series can be either nouns (such as "dog") or verb phrases (such as "get in the car"). Commas are essentially the structural backbone of a series. For example,

> The hungry girl devoured *a chicken, two pounds of pasta, and a chocolate cake*.

When he learned his girlfriend was coming over, Nathaniel *took a shower, brushed his teeth, and cleaned his room*.

The comma follows all but the last item in the series. When using a conjunction, such as "and" or "or," at the end of the series, remember to precede it with a comma (". . . brushed his teeth, *and* cleaned his room").

Commas Separate Multiple Nonessential Adjectives Modifying a Noun

When two or more nonessential adjectives modify a noun, they should be separated by a comma. Of course, the key to figuring out whether there should be a comma separating two adjectives is being able to determine whether the adjectives are essential or nonessential. Luckily, there's a simple rule that can help you: the order of nonessential adjectives is interchangeable. For example,

Rebecca's new dog has *long, silky* hair.

The *loud, angry* protesters mobbed the building.

These two sentences would make equal sense if you switched the order of the adjectives: "Rebecca's new dog has *silky, long* hair" and "The *angry, loud* protesters mobbed the building."

The case is different if you have an essential adjective modifying the noun. Essential adjectives specify the nouns they modify; they are bound to the noun, so that the noun loses meaning if separated from its adjective. A noun modified by an essential adjective should be treated as a single noun. If you come across two adjectives modifying a noun, and one is essential, you should *not* use a comma between them. For example,

My mother hates *noisy electronic music*.

"Electronic music" functions as an indivisible noun; "electronic" specifies the type of music the mother hates. "Noisy" is a nonessential adjective modifying the noun "electronic music." Changing the order of "noisy" and "electronic" ("My mother hates electronic noisy music") would not make sense. If you can't change the order of two adjectives preceding a noun, you know the adjective nearest the noun is essential, so you should not use a comma.

Commas Set Off Dependent Phrases and Clauses from the Main Clause of a Sentence

Unlike independent clauses, dependent phrases and clauses are not sentences in themselves; rather, they serve to explain or embellish the main clause of a sentence. When they appear at the beginning of a sentence, they should be set off from the main clause by a comma. For example,

Scared of monsters, Tina always checked under her bed before going to sleep.

After preparing an elaborate meal for herself, Anne was too tired to eat.

Usage/Mechanics Questions

The first example shows a dependent clause ("Scared of monsters") acting as an adjective modifying "Tina." The second example shows a dependent clause acting as an adverb. Since the adverbial clause is at the beginning of the sentence, it needs to be set off from the main clause by a comma. Adverbial clauses should also be set off by commas if they appear in the middle of a sentence. However, if an adverbial clause appears at the end of a sentence, you do not need to use a comma. For example,

Anne was too tired to eat *after preparing an elaborate meal for herself.*

Commas Set Off Nonessential Phrases and Clauses

Nonessential phrases are like nonessential adjectives in that they embellish nouns without specifying them. Nonessential phrases should be set off from the rest of the sentence by commas. For example,

Everyone voted Carrie, *who is the most popular girl in our class,* prom queen.

The decrepit street sign, *which had stood in our town since 1799,* finally fell down.

When you use nonessential phrases like the two above, you assume that "Carrie" and "the decrepit street sign" do not need any further identification. If you remove the nonessential phrases, you should still be able to understand the sentences.

Restrictive phrases, on the other hand, are not set off by commas because they are necessary to understand the modified noun and the sentence as a whole. For example,

The girl *who is sick* missed three days of school.

The dog *that ate the rotten steak* fell down and died.

If you removed the restrictive phrases ("who is sick" and "that ate the rotten steak") from these sentences, you would be left wondering "which girl?" and "which dog?" These restrictive phrases are used to identify exactly which girl missed school and exactly which dog died. Setting off "who is sick" in commas would assume that the girl's identity is never in doubt; there is only one girl who possibly could have missed school. In this case, we know the identity of the girl only because the restrictive phrase specifies "the girl who is sick."

Commas Set Off Appositives

Appositives are similar to nonessential phrases. An appositive is a phrase that renames or restates the modified noun, usually enhancing it with additional information. For example,

Everyone voted Carrie, *the most popular girl in school,* prom queen.

The dog, *a Yorkshire Terrier,* barked at all the neighbors.

In these two examples, "the most popular girl in school" and "a Yorkshire Terrier" are appositives used to explain the nouns they modify. You should be able to draw an imaginary equal sign between the noun and the appositive modifying it: Carrie = the most popular girl in school, the dog = a Yorkshire Terrier. Because they are equal, you should be able to swap them and retain the meaning of the sentence: "Everyone voted the most popular girl in school, Carrie, prom queen."

Apostrophes

Apostrophes are the second most commonly tested punctuation mark on the English Test. Apostrophes primarily indicate possession, but they also take the place of omitted letters in contractions (for example, "was not" becomes "wasn't" and "it is" becomes "it's"). You will be tested chiefly on your knowledge of the apostrophe's possessive function.

The Possessive and Singular Nouns

A singular noun (for example: Simon, the dog, the bottle) can be made possessive by adding an apostrophe followed by an "s". For example,

Simon's teacher was in the room.

My mom forgot the *dog's* food.

We removed the *bottle's* label.

The apostrophe follows directly after the noun. If you move the apostrophe after the "s" (for example, if you write "dogs'" rather than "dog's"), you will change the meaning of the sentence (see "The Possessive and Plural Nouns" below). If you forget the apostrophe altogether, you will render the sentence meaningless.

The Possessive and Plural Nouns

Most plural nouns (for example: the boys, the dogs, the bottles) can be made possessive by adding only an apostrophe. For example,

The *boys'* teacher was in the room.

My mom forgot the *dogs'* food.

We removed the *bottles'* labels.

The apostrophe directly follows plural nouns that end in "s" to make them possessive.

But for plural nouns that do not end in "s" (for example, "women"), you should treat the plural form as a singular noun (i.e., add an apostrophe followed by an "s"). For example,

The *women's* locker room needs to be cleaned.

The Possessive and Multiple Nouns

Sometimes you'll want to indicate the possessive of more than one noun (Nick and Nora, Dan and Johann). The placement of the apostrophe depends on whether the possessors share the possession. For example,

> *Nick and Nora's* dog solves crimes.

> *Dan's and Johann's* socks are dirty.

In the example of Nick and Nora, the dog belongs to both of them, so you treat "Nick and Nora" as a single unit, followed by a single apostrophe and "s." In the second example, both Dan and Johann have dirty socks, but they don't share the same dirty socks, so you treat Dan and Johann as separate units, giving each an apostrophe and "s."

The Possessive and Pronouns

Unlike nouns and proper nouns, the possessive case of pronouns does not use an apostrophe. The following chart gives you nominative pronouns (the ones you use as subjects) and the corresponding possessive pronouns:

Nominative Pronoun	Possessive Pronoun
I	my
you *(s.)*	your
she	her
he	his
we	our
you *(pl.)*	your
they	their
it	its
who	whose

For example,

> The dog chewed on *its* tail.

> You should give him *your* wallet.

Don't confuse the "its" and the "your" above with "it's" and "you're." This mistake is frequently tested on the English Test (see below).

Its/It's, Their/They're

The ACT will test you on your ability to distinguish between "its" and "it's." "Its" is the possessive form of "it." "It's" is the contraction of "it is." This can be tricky to remember, since you are normally trained to associate apostrophes with possession. But when you're dealing with "its" versus "it's," the apostrophe signals a contraction. The same is true for "their/they're/there," "your/you're," and "whose/who's." Make sure you are aware of these exceptions to the apostrophe rule of possession.

Try the following practice problem:

<u>Your face</u> is red. 9	9. (**A.**)	NO CHANGE
	B.	You're face
	C.	Your nose
	D.	OMIT the underlined portion.

You can eliminate choices C and D immediately: C changes the meaning of the sentence for no particular reason, and D leaves you without a complete sentence. The decision comes down to "Your" and "You're." If you don't know the correct answer, try replacing "You're" with "You are." The resulting sentence is "You are face is red"—an odd remark. The correct answer is **A**, "NO CHANGE." You can employ this replacement technique whenever you don't know the answer to a possessive-or-contraction question. Once you replace the contraction with the full phrase, your ear will tell you which choice is right.

Semicolons

You'll usually find several questions dealing with semicolons on the English Test. The main functions of a semicolon that you should know for the English Test are its ability to join related independent clauses and its use in a series.

The Semicolon and Two Independent Clauses

Semicolons are commonly used to separate two related but independent clauses. For example,

> Julie ate five brownies; Eileen ate seven.

> Josh needed to buy peas; he ran to the market.

In these cases, the semicolon functions as a "weak period." It suggests a short pause before moving on to a related thought, whereas a period suggests a full stop before moving on to a less-related thought. Generally, a period between these independent clauses would work just as well as a semicolon, so the ACT won't offer you a choice between period or semicolon on the English Test. But you may see the semicolon employed as a weak period in an answer choice; in that case, you should know that it is being used correctly.

Frequently, you will see two independent clauses joined by a semicolon and a transitional adverb (such as *consequently, however, furthermore, indeed, moreover, nevertheless, therefore,* and *thus*). For example,

> Julie ate five brownies; *however,* Eileen ate seven.

Usage/Mechanics Questions

Josh needed to buy peas; *thus* he ran to the market.

These sentences function similarly to those joined by a comma and a conjunction. Here, the semicolon replaces the comma, and the transitional adverb replaces the conjunction. Most transitional adverbs should be followed by a comma, but for short adverbs such as "thus," the comma should be omitted.

The Semicolon and the Series: When the Comma's Already Taken

The semicolon replaces the comma as the structural backbone of a series if the items already contain commas. For example,

The tennis tournament featured the surprise comeback player, Koch, who dropped out last year due to injuries; the up-and-coming star Popp, who dominated the junior tour; and the current favorite, Farrington, who won five of the last six tournaments.

If you used commas rather than semicolons in the above sentence, anyone reading the sentence would feel pretty confused. The semicolons in this example function exactly as commas do in a series, but they allow you to avoid overpopulating the sentence with commas.

Colons

You'll probably be tested on your knowledge of colons a couple of times on the English Test. The ACT writers want to be sure that you know how colons introduce lists, explanations, and quotations.

The Colon and Expectation

Colons are used after complete sentences to introduce related information that usually comes in the form of a list, an explanation, or a quotation. When you see a colon, you should know to expect elaborating information. For example,

The wedding had all the elements to make it a classic: *the elegant bride, the weeping mother, and the fainting bridesmaids.*

In this example, the colon is used to introduce a list of classic wedding elements. Without the list following the colon, the sentence can stand alone ("The wedding had all the elements to make it a classic"). By naming the classic elements of a wedding, the list serves mainly to explain and expand upon the independent sentence that precedes it.

Check out this example of another way to use colons:

The wedding had all the elements to make it a classic: *the elegant bride beamed as her mother wept and as the bridesmaids fainted.*

Here, the clause following the colon also has an explanatory function. In this case, the colon joins two independent clauses, but the clause following the colon is used to explain and expand the first.

Usage/Mechanics Questions

Colons can also be used to introduce quotations. For example,

> The mother's exclamation best summed up the wedding: *"If only the bridesmaids hadn't fainted!"*

Here, the colon is used to introduce the mother's exclamation. Make sure the quotation following the colon is related to the sentence.

Colon Problems

You should learn the following rules in order to avoid erroneous colon use on the English Test:

A Colon Should Always Be Preceded by an Independent Clause.

WRONG: The ingredients I need to make a cake: flour, butter, sugar, and icing.

RIGHT: I need several ingredients to make a cake: flour, butter, sugar, and icing.

In the "WRONG" example, a fragment of a sentence precedes the list of items. The sentence should be reworked to create an independent clause before the colon.

There Should Never Be More Than One Colon in a Sentence.

WRONG: He brought many items on the camping trip: a tent, a sleeping bag, a full cooking set, warm clothes, and several pairs of shoes: sneakers, boots, and sandals.

RIGHT: He brought many items on the camping trip: a tent, a sleeping bag, a full cooking set, warm clothes, sneakers, boots, and sandals.

If you see a sentence that contains more than one colon, the sentence needs to be rephrased. Lists within lists or explanations within explanations do not work in standard written English.

Other ACT Punctuation

The English Test rarely tests punctuation marks other than the ones listed above. But in the odd case that the test writers do throw in some other punctuation errors, you should know what to expect. The ACT officially states that it covers, in addition to the punctuation mentioned above, the following punctuation marks:

Parentheses and Dashes

Parentheses usually surround words or phrases that break a sentence's train of thought but provide explanatory information for it. For example,

> Their road trip *(which they made in a convertible)* lasted three weeks and spanned fourteen states.

Similarly, parenthetical sentences can be inserted between other sentences, adding additional information to them without diverting their flow. For example,

> Their road trip lasted three weeks and spanned fourteen states. *(The one they took two years ago lasted two weeks and covered ten states.)* When they got home, they were exhausted.

In this example, the parenthetical information about the previous road trip is interesting but not completely relevant to the other sentences. Note that when an entire sentence is enclosed within parentheses, the period should be inside them as well.

Dashes function similarly to parentheses. Dashes indicate either an abrupt break in thought or an insertion of additional, explanatory information.

> He walked so slowly—*with his lame leg he couldn't go much faster*—that even his neighbor's toddler eventually overtook him.

> I don't have the heart to refuse a friend's request for help—*do you?*

Periods, Question Marks, and Exclamation Points

These are the least common forms of punctuation tested by the ACT. The ACT writers probably realized that these sentence enders are easier to grasp than other forms of punctuation because they basically have only one function each:

> The sentence ends here.

> Does the sentence end here?

> Hooray, the sentence ends here!

The period in the first example indicates that the sentence has ended. In the second example, the question mark indicates that a question is being asked. The third example is an exclamatory statement marked by an exclamation point. Exclamation points should be used sparingly to indicate statements made with great emotion (for example, anger, excitement, or agitation).

Basic Grammar and Usage

As you've probably already gathered, the English Test will never *explicitly* ask you to name a grammatical error. But in order to identify and fix errors, you should know what they are. While you'll often be able to rely on your ear to detect errors, many of the questions will ask you to fix phrases that are fine for spoken English but not for formal written English.

In the following section, we'll cover these grammar issues, which appear on the English Test:

1. Subject-Verb Agreement

2. Pronoun-Antecedent Agreement

3. Pronoun Cases

4. Verb Tenses

5. Adverbs and Adjectives

6. Idioms

7. Comparative and Superlative Modifiers

Subject-Verb Agreement

Singular verbs must accompany singular subjects, and plural verbs must accompany plural subjects.

SINGULAR: The *man wears* four ties.

His favorite *college is* in Nebraska.

Matt, along with his friends, *goes* to Coney Island.

PLURAL: The *men wear* four ties each.

His favorite *colleges are* in Nebraska.

Matt and his friends go to Coney Island.

In the first example with Matt, the subject is singular because the phrase "along with his friends" is isolated in commas. But in the second example with Matt, his friends join the action; the subject becomes "Matt and his friends," calling for the change to a plural verb.

Subject-verb agreement is a simple idea, but ACT writers will make it tricky. Often, they'll put the subject at one end of the sentence and the verb a mile away. Try the following example:

An audience of thousands of expectant

people who have come from afar to listen

to live music in an outdoor setting <u>seem</u>
17

terrifying to a nervous performer.

17. **A.** NO CHANGE
B. seems
C. have seemed
D. to seem

To solve this problem, cross out the junk in the middle that separates the subject, "an audience," from the verb "seem." You're left with:

Usage/Mechanics Questions

> An audience *seem* terrifying to a nervous performer.

Now you can see what the verb should be:

> An audience *seems* terrifying to a nervous performer.

So the correct answer is **B**. Double-check by eliminating choices **C** and **D** because they are grammatically incorrect (and because they don't make much sense in the sentence).

As long as you can isolate the subject and verb, handling subject-verb agreement is relatively simple. But certain cases of subject-verb agreement can be tricky. The ACT writers like to test you on several of these difficult types of subject-verb agreement.

Collective Nouns

Collective nouns (such as *committee, family, group, number,* and *team*) can be either singular or plural. The verb depends on whether the collective noun is being treated as a single unit or as divided individuals. For example:

> SINGULAR: The number of people living in Florida varies from year to year.
>
> PLURAL: A number of people living in Florida wish they had voted for Gore.
>
> SINGULAR: The committee decides on the annual program.
>
> PLURAL: The committee have disagreed on the annual program.

You can often determine whether a collective noun is singular or plural by examining the article ("the" or "a") that precedes it. As in the first example, "*The* number" is generally singular, while "*A* number" is generally plural. This difference is demonstrated in the first example above. "*The* number" of people in Florida is a single entity—even though it comprises multiple individuals—so it takes a singular verb, "varies." "*A* number" of people, on the other hand, behave as multiple individuals—even though they wish for the same thing, they act independently of each other—so these people require a plural verb, "wish."

Looking to the article preceding a noun is a useful trick when deciding whether the noun is singular or plural, but it doesn't always work. In the second example, "*The* committee" can be both singular and plural. How the committee behaves (do they act together or apart?) decides whether the verb is singular or plural. If the committee does something as a unified whole ("*decides* on the annual program"), then the verb is singular. If the committee are divided in their actions ("*have disagreed* on the annual program"), then the verb is plural.

Indefinite Pronouns

Indefinite pronouns refer to persons or things that have not been specified. Matching indefinite pronouns with the correct verb form can be tricky because some indefinite pronouns that seem to be plural are in fact singular. Questions dealing with singular indefinite pronouns are popular with ACT writers, so you'd be wise to memorize a few of these pronouns now. The following indefinite pronouns are always singular, and they tend to appear on the English Test:

Another	Everybody	Nobody
Anybody	Everyone	One
Anyone	Everything	Somebody
Anything	Each	Someone

All the indefinite pronouns in the list above should be followed by singular verbs. For example,

> *Anyone* over the age of 21 *is* eligible to vote in the United States.

> *Each has* its own patch of grass.

If you're used to thinking these pronouns take plural verbs, these sentences probably sound weird to you. Your best bet is to memorize the list above (it's not very long!) and to remember that those pronouns take singular verbs.

You should also be aware that not all indefinite pronouns are singular. Some (for example, *all*, *any*, *none*, and *some*) can be either singular or plural depending on the context of the sentence. Other indefinite pronouns (for example, *both*, *few*, *many*, and *several*) are always plural. The differences between these indefinite pronouns can be very confusing; determining what's right often requires an astute sense of proper English (or good memorization). If you're struggling to remember the different indefinite pronouns, take comfort in these two things:

1. The most commonly tested indefinite pronouns are the singular ones in the list we gave you.

2. You probably won't come across more than a couple of indefinite pronouns on the English Test you take.

Compound Subjects

Most compound subjects (subjects joined by "and") should be plural:

> *Kerry and Vanessa live* in Nantucket.

> *The blue bike and the red wagon need* repairs.

The reasoning behind this rule is fairly simple: you have multiple subjects, so you need a plural noun. Thus "Kerry and Vanessa *live*" and the "bike and wagon *need*."

"There Is" or "There Are"?

Whether to use "there is" or "there are" depends on the singularity or plurality of the

Usage/Mechanics Questions

noun that the phrase is pointing out. If you have five grapes, you should say: "There *are* five grapes." If you have a cat, you should say: "There *is* a cat." The "is" and the "are" in these sentences are the main verbs, so they must agree with the noun.

"Or" and "Nor"

If you have singular subjects joined by an "or" or "nor," the sentence always takes a singular verb. For example,

> *Either Susannah or Caitlin is* going to be in trouble.

If one of the subjects is plural and the other is singular, the verb agrees with the subject closer to it. For example,

> *Neither the van nor the buses were* operating today.

> *Either the dogs or the cat is* responsible for the mess.

Both of these examples contain a singular and a plural subject. The main verb of the sentence is determined by the subject nearest it: in the first example, "buses" is closer to the verb, so the verb is plural, and in the second example, "cat" is closer to the verb, so the verb is singular.

Mathematics, News, Dollars, Physics

These and other words look plural but are singular in usage:

> Today's *news was* full of tragic stories.

Trust your gut instinct with these words. You'll probably know they're singular from everyday usage. "Dollars" is an exceptional case—it's singular when you're talking about an amount of money ("ninety dollars *is* a big chunk of change") but plural when you're discussing a particular group of bills ("the dollars in my pocket *are* green").

Pronoun-Antecedent Agreement

The ACT writers usually include several pronoun-antecedent agreement errors on the English Test. An antecedent is a word to which a later pronoun refers back. For example, in the sentence "Richard put on his shoes," "Richard" is the antecedent to which "his" refers. When the pronoun does not agree in gender or number with its antecedent, there's an agreement error. For example:

> *WRONG:*   Already late for the show, *Mary* couldn't find *their* keys.

> *RIGHT:*   Already late for the show, *Mary* couldn't find *her* keys.

Unless another sentence states that the keys belong to other people, the possessive pronoun should agree in gender and number with "Mary." As far as we can tell, Mary is a singular, feminine noun, so the pronoun should be too.

The example of Mary contained a fairly obvious example of incorrect agreement, but sometimes the agreement error isn't as obvious on the ACT. In everyday speech, we tend to say "someone lost *their* shoe" (wrong) rather than "someone lost *his* shoe" (correct) or "someone lost *her* shoe" (also correct) because we don't want to exclude either gender and because "someone lost *his* or *her* shoe" sounds cumbersome. The common solution? We attempt gender neutrality and brevity by using "their" instead of "his" or "her." In informal speech, such a slip is okay. But if you see it on the test, it's an error.

You will also run into agreement errors where the antecedent is unclear. In these cases, the pronoun is ambiguous. We use ambiguous pronouns all the time in everyday speech, but on the test (you guessed it) they're wrong.

> *WRONG:*   Trot told Ted that *he* should get the mauve pants from the sale rack.

This sentence is wrong because we don't know to whom "he" refers. Should Ted get the pants, or should Trot? Or should neither, because mauve pants are never a good idea? You should restate the original sentence so all the pertinent information is relayed without confusion or multiple meanings.

Pronoun Cases

The ACT writers will definitely include some questions on pronoun cases. Pronoun case refers to the role of the pronoun in a sentence. There are three cases: nominative, objective, and possessive. You don't need to know the names of these cases, but you do need to know the differences between them (and knowing the names doesn't hurt). Here, we'll briefly describe each case.

The Nominative Case

The nominative case should be used when a pronoun is the subject of a sentence—for example, "*I* went to the store" and "*They* walked to the park." You should also use a nominative pronoun after any form of *to be*:

> *WRONG:*   It was *me* on the phone.

> *RIGHT:*   It was *I* on the phone.

The right sentence may sound awkward to you, but it's the correct use of the nominative. The people who laid down the rules of grammar considered *to be* a grammatical equal sign, so when you have a sentence like "It was I on the phone," you should be able to do this "It" = "I." If that equation holds true, "I" should be able to take the place of "It" in the sentence: "I was on the phone."

Pronoun Comparisons

The nominative also follows comparative clauses that usually begin with "as" or "than." When a pronoun is involved in a comparison, it must match the case of the other pronoun involved. For example,

WRONG: I'm fatter than *her*, so I'll probably win this sumo wrestling match.

RIGHT: I'm fatter than *she*, so I'll probably win this sumo wrestling match.

In this sentence, "I" is being compared to "her." Obviously, these two pronouns are in different cases, so one of them must be wrong. Since only "her" is in question, it must be wrong, and therefore "she" is the correct answer.

Another way to approach comparisons is to realize that comparisons usually omit words. For example, it's grammatically correct to say, "Alexis is stronger than Bill," but that's an abbreviated version of what you're really saying. The long version is, "Alexis is stronger than Bill is." That last "is" is invisible in the abbreviated version, but you must remember that it's there. Now let's go back to the sumo sentence. As in our Alexis and Bill example, we don't see the word "is" in the comparison, but it's implied. If you see a comparison using a pronoun and you're not sure if the pronoun is correct, add the implied "is." In this case, adding "is" leaves us with "I'm fatter than her is." That sounds wrong, so we know that "she" is the correct pronoun in this case.

The Objective Case

As may be obvious from its name, the objective case should be used when the pronoun is the object of another part of speech, usually a preposition or a transitive verb (a verb that takes a direct object):

PREPOSITION: She handed the presents *to them*.

               Olivia made a cake *for* Emily, Sarah, and *me*.

               Between whom did you sit?

TRANSITIVE VERB: Harry *gave me* the tickets.

               Call me!

               Did you *take him* to the movies?

In the second preposition example, two names appear between "for" and "me." If this confuses you, eliminate "Emily, Sarah, and" to get "Olivia made a cake *for me*." Then you'll see that "me" is the correct pronoun case, not "I" (as in "Olivia made a cake for I"). This strategy of crossing out intervening words also works in spotting the correct case for an object of a transitive verb.

In informal, spoken English, you will not hear "whom" used frequently, but in written English (particularly written ACT English), you must remember the all important "m." As in the third preposition example, "between whom" is correct; "between who" is not. A good way to figure out if you should use "who" or "whom" in a sentence is to see whether the sentence would use "he" or "him" (or "they" or "them") if it were rearranged a little. If the sentence takes "he" or "they," you should use "who"; if it takes "him" or "them," you should use "whom."

If you rearrange "Between whom did you sit?" you get:

> Did you sit between them?

Now you can see that you need to use "whom" in the original sentence.

The Possessive Case

You already know to use the possessive case when indicating possession of an object (see "The Possessive and Pronouns" under "Apostrophes"):

> *My* car

> *Her* dress

> *Its* tail

> *Whose* wheelbarrow

You should also use the possessive case before a gerund, a verb form that usually ends with "ing" and is used as a noun. For example,

> When it comes to *my studying* for the ACT, "concentration" is my middle name.

> Despite hours of practice, *her playing* is really terrible.

You can think of gerunds as turncoat verbs that are now nouns, so they need to be preceded by the same possessive pronouns that precede noun objects.

The following chart shows you all the pronoun cases we've just discussed:

Nominative Case	Objective Case	Possessive Case
I	me	my
you (s.)	you	your
she	her	her
he	him	his
we	us	our
you (pl.)	you	your
they	them	their
it	it	its
who	whom	whose

Usage/Mechanics Questions

Now that you know something about pronoun cases, try the following sample problem:

<u>Me and Jesse</u> went to Cosmic Bowling 4 Night at the Bowladrome.	4.	F. NO CHANGE G. Jesse and me H. Jesse and I J. I and Jesse

Knowing when to use "I" and when to use "me" can be difficult, especially within compound nouns. If you're not sure which is correct, use the crossing-out trick: cross out "and Jesse" and see what you have left.

> *Me* went to Cosmic Bowling Night at the Bowladrome.

Unless you're doing your Ralph Wiggum imitation, that sentence sounds (and is) wrong. The correct sentence?

> *Jesse and I* went to Cosmic Bowling Night at the Bowladrome.

So the answer to the problem is **H**. Choice J, which also contains the correct pronoun "I," is wrong because the conventional rules of grammar require that you show a little deference in forming sentences involving yourself. "I" should always come after the other people involved in the activity.

Verb Tenses

Most verb tense errors on the English Test will be pretty easy to spot, since we don't often make tense errors in everyday speech. When you read a tense error on the test, it will most likely sound wrong to you. Your ear is your most reliable way of spotting tense errors.

Different Verb Tenses in One Sentence

Nowhere is it written that you must use the same tense throughout a sentence. For example, you can say, "I used to eat chocolate bars exclusively, but after going through a conversion experience last year, I have broadened my range and now eat gummy candy too." That sentence has tense switches galore, but they are logical: the sentence uses past tense when it talks about the past, and present tense when it talks about the present, and the progression from past to present makes sense. For another acceptable example,

> They *are* the best team in baseball, and I think they *will triumph* over what *could have been* devastating injuries.

But you can't throw in different tenses willy-nilly. They have to make sense. You can't say:

> Next year, I *was* on an ocean voyage.

"Next year" refers to the future, and "was" refers to the past. The sentence doesn't make any sense unless you're doing some time travel. Your most powerful weapon against tense switch questions is logic. We could prattle on for paragraph after paragraph about present tense, simple past, general present, and present perfect, but remembering the millions of different tense forms, and when to use which, is both difficult and unnecessary. For the English Test, if you don't hear an error the first time you read a sentence, and you don't see a pronoun problem, check out the tenses and figure out whether they're OK.

Tricky Verbs You're Likely to See on the ACT

By tricky verbs, we mean those verbs that never sound quite right in any tense—like "to lie," or "to swim." When do you lay and when do you lie? When do you swim and when have you swum? Unfortunately, there's no easy memory trick to help you remember when to use which verb form. The only solution is to learn and remember.

> You LIE down for a nap.
>
> You LAY something down on the table.
>
> You LAY down yesterday.
>
> You SWIM across the English Channel.
>
> You SWAM across the Atlantic Ocean.
>
> You HAD SWUM across the bathtub as a child.

"To lie" and "to swim" aren't the only two difficult verbs. Below, you'll find a table of difficult verbs in their infinitive, simple past, and past participle forms. You don't have to memorize all of these forms; you'll probably only see one tricky-verb question. Still, it is well worth your time to read the list below carefully, and especially to make sure you understand those verbs that you've found confusing before.

Infinitive	Simple Past	Past Participle	Infinitive	Simple Past	Past Participle
Arise	Arose	Arisen	Lead	Led	Led
Become	Became	Become	Lie (to recline)	Lay	Lain
Begin	Began	Begun	Lie (tell fibs)	Lied	Lied
Blow	Blew	Blown	Put	Put	Put
Break	Broke	Broken	Ride	Rode	Ridden
Choose	Chose	Chosen	Ring	Rang	Rung
Come	Came	Come	Rise	Rose	Risen

Usage/Mechanics Questions

Infinitive	Simple Past	Past Participle	Infinitive	Simple Past	Past Participle
Dive	Dived/dove	Dived	Run	Ran	Run
Do	Did	Done	See	Saw	Seen
Draw	Drew	Drawn	Set	Set	Set
Drink	Drank	Drunk	Shake	Shook	Shaken
Drive	Drove	Driven	Shine	Shone	Shone
Drown	Drowned	Drowned	Shrink	Shrank	Shrunk
Dwell	Dwelt/dwelled	Dwelt/dwelled	Shut	Shut	Shut
Eat	Ate	Eaten	Sing	Sang	Sung
Fall	Fell	Fallen	Sink	Sank	Sunk
Fight	Fought	Fought	Sit	Sat	Sat
Flee	Fled	Fled	Speak	Spoke	Spoken
Fling	Flung	Flung	Spring	Sprang	Sprung
Fly	Flew	Flown	Sting	Stung	Stung
Forget	Forgot	Forgotten	Strive	Strove/strived	Striven/strived
Freeze	Froze	Frozen	Swear	Swore	Sworn
Get	Got	Gotten	Swim	Swam	Swum
Give	Gave	Given	Swing	Swung	Swung
Go	Went	Gone	Take	Took	Taken
Grow	Grew	Grown	Tear	Tore	Torn
Hang (a thing)	Hung	Hung	Throw	Threw	Thrown
Hang (a person)	Hanged	Hanged	Wake	Woke	Woke/woken
Know	Knew	Known	Wear	Wore	Worn
Lay	Laid	Laid	Write	Wrote	Written

The ACT writers are going to get a little sneaky and use the tenses we *do* get wrong when we talk. One notoriously annoying trick is the difference between "lie" and "lay" and all their variations. Here are the rules:

LIE: to recline or to disguise the truth

RIGHT: We *lie* down on the hammocks when we want to relax.

I *lie* to my mother about eating the cookies.

LAY:	to place
RIGHT:	Just *lay* down that air hockey table over there.
	I *lay* the book on the table.

The tricky part is that the past tense of "lie" is "lay."

> She *lay* down yesterday, and today she'll *lie* down again.

The past tense of "lay" is "laid."

> She *laid* down the law with an iron fist.

The Conditional

Another thorny tense issue arises with something called the conditional. The conditional is the verb form we use to describe something uncertain, something that's conditional upon something else. You can memorize the conditional formula; it goes "If . . . were . . . would." Look at this sentence:

WRONG:	If I were running for president, my slogan *will be* "I'll Fight for Your Right to Party."

The use of "will be" in this sentence is wrong because you're not certain you're going to run for president (as suggested by "If I were"); consequently, the word "will" is too strong. "Will" implies you're definitely going to campaign for president. You should use "would" instead—the conditional form of "will"—to indicate that running is still only a possibility.

RIGHT:	If I were running for president, my slogan *would be* "I'll Fight for Your Right to Party."

Notice also that the correct form is "If I *were*" not "If I *was*." You'll often hear people use "was" incorrectly in "If . . ." phrases like this, but now you'll know better. Sentences beginning with "If . . ." call for the subjunctive form of the verb. In English, the subjunctive is often the same as the regular past tense verb, but in certain cases, notably *to be*, the forms are irregular:

> If I were, *you* were, *s/he* were, *we* were, *they* were, *who* were, *it* were

Adverbs and Adjectives

The ACT writers will test you once or twice on your ability to use adjectives and adverbs correctly in sentences. To describe a noun, you use an adjective. To describe a verb, adjective, or adverb, you use an adverb. Look at the following example:

WRONG:	My mom made a *well* dinner.
RIGHT:	My mom made a *good* dinner.

Since "dinner" is a noun, the descriptive word modifying it should be an adjective.

Now look at this example:

WRONG: My mom made dinner *good*.

RIGHT: My mom made dinner *well*.

Here, the word modified is "made," a verb, so the descriptive word modifying it should be an adverb. Don't let the placement of the adverb fool you: just because it's next to the noun "dinner" doesn't mean that "dinner" is the word modified. Often, though, you *will* find the modifier next to the modified word:

WRONG: I didn't do *good* in the game last night.

RIGHT: I didn't do *well* in the game last night.

In the example above, how the athlete did (a verb) is being described, so you need an adverb ("well") rather than an adjective ("good").

Adverb/adjective errors are pretty common in everyday speech, so don't rely entirely on your ear.

WRONG: She shut him up *quick*.

RIGHT: She shut him up *quickly*.

WRONG: I got an A *easy*.

RIGHT: I got an A *easily*.

The wrong examples above may sound familiar to you from everyday speech, but they are incorrect in written English.

Idioms

You *should* trust your ear when you're being tested on idioms. Idioms are expressions and phrasings that are peculiar to a certain language—in the ACT's case, the English language. They include odd expressions like "through the grapevine" and "rain check" as well as simple ones like "bring up" (meaning "raise"). Idiom questions on the English Test will often ask you to identify the correct prepositions used in certain expressions. This task is difficult because there are no laws governing idioms. You have to be able to read a sentence and think, "That sounds plain old wrong." Fortunately, you probably won't encounter more than a few idiom errors on the English Test you take. Take a look at this idiom error:

WRONG: We spent days *wading into* the thousands of pages of reports.

"Wading into" sounds wrong. Instead, we say:

RIGHT: We spent days *wading through* the thousands of pages of reports.

Why do we use some prepositions instead of others? That's just the way it is. The following is a list of proper idiomatic usage:

He can't *abide by* the no-spitting rule.

She *accused me of* stealing.

I *agreed to* eat the broccoli.

I *apologized for* losing the hamsters in the heating vent.

She *applied for* a credit card.

My mother pretends to *approve of* my boyfriend.

She *argued with* the bouncer.

I *arrived at* work at noon.

You *believe in* ghosts.

I can't be *blamed for* your neuroses.

Do you *care about* me?

He's *in charge of* grocery shopping.

Nothing *compares to* you.

What is there to *complain about*?

He can always *count on* money from his mommy.

Ice cream *consists of* milk, fat, and sugar.

I *depend on* no one.

That's where cats *differ from* dogs.

It's terrible to *discriminate against* parakeets.

I have a plan to *escape from* this prison.

There's no *excuse for* your behavior.

You can't *hide from* your past.

It was all he'd *hoped for*.

I must *insist upon* it.

It's impossible to *object to* her lucid arguments.

I refuse to *participate in* this discussion.

Pray for me.

Protect me from evil.

Provide me with plenty of Skittles.

She stayed home to *recover from* the flu.

I *rely on* myself.

She *stared at* his chest.

He *subscribes to* several trashy magazines.

I *succeeded in* fooling him.

Wait for me!

Work with me, people!

Comparative and Superlative Modifiers

Comparative modifiers compare one thing to another, while superlative modifiers tell you how one thing compares to everything else. For example:

COMPARATIVE: My boyfriend is *hotter* than yours.

That purple-and-orange spotted dog is *weirder* than the blue cat.

Dan paints *better* than the other students.

SUPERLATIVE: My boyfriend is the *hottest* boy in the world.

That purple-and-orange spotted dog is the *weirdest* pet on the block.

Of all the students, Dan paints *best*.

You will probably see only one or two comparative and superlative modifier questions on the English Test, and they will likely ask you to distinguish between the two types of modifiers. Remember that comparative modifiers are used in relative statements; in other words, they compare one thing to another. Just because my boyfriend is *hotter* than yours, it doesn't mean that my boyfriend is hotter than Sue's. However, if I used the superlative and told you that my boyfriend is the *hottest* boy in the world, then there's no way that Sue's boyfriend is hotter than mine, unless, as is probably the case, I'm exaggerating.

Comparative statements always require a comparison with something else. Simply saying "my boyfriend is hotter" may get your meaning across in a heated dispute with your friends, but in proper English you need to finish that sentence with a "than" phrase: "my boyfriend is hotter *than Jude Law*" or "my boyfriend is hotter *than your dog*."

Sentence Structure

Sentence structure is the Big Deal when it comes to Usage/Mechanics problems. Of the 40 Usage/Mechanics questions, almost half of them (18 to be exact) will test you on your knowledge of sentence structure, the topics of which include:

1. Connecting and Transitional Words

2. Subordinate or Dependent Clauses

3. Sentence Fragments

4. Comma Splices

5. Run-on Sentences

6. Misplaced Modifiers

7. Parallelism

Connecting and Transitional Words

We've already mentioned coordinating conjunctions (*and, but, for,* etc.) and transitional adverbs (*however, nevertheless, moreover,* etc.) in "Punctuation." Here you'll learn more about these and other transitional words.

Coordinating Conjunctions

Coordinating conjunctions (*and, but, or, nor, for, yet*) connect words, phrases, and independent clauses of equal importance in a sentence.

> *WORDS:*   You can hand the bottle to Seamus *or* Bea.
>
> Liz *and* Amanda got down on the dance floor.

PHRASES:	To get there, you must drive over a bridge *and* through a farm.
	We walked by the park *but* not by the river.
CLAUSES:	Tim can go to the store, *or* Jen can go instead.
	It's only ten o'clock, *yet* I feel really sleepy.

When joining two words or phrases, you should not use a comma, but (as demonstrated in "Commas") if you have a list of more than two words or phrases, commas should separate them and precede the conjunction. A comma also needs to precede the coordinating conjunction when it joins two independent clauses.

Transitional Adverbs

Like coordinating conjunctions, these adverbs (*however, also, consequently, nevertheless, thus, moreover, furthermore*, etc.) can join independent clauses. When they do, they should be preceded by a semicolon (see "Semicolons") and followed, most of the time, by a comma. Short adverbs, such as "thus," do not need a comma. Here are some examples of transitional adverbs in action:

Joe always raves about soccer; *however,* he always refuses to watch a match.

If you can't go to the prom with me, let me know as soon as possible; *otherwise,* I'll resent you and your inability to communicate, for the rest of my life.

You need to remember that transitional adverbs must be accompanied by semicolons. If you see a transitional adverb on its own or preceded by a comma on the English Test, you should immediately know there's an error.

Subordinating Conjunctions

When you have two independent clauses, but you feel that one is more important than the other, you can use a subordinating conjunction to connect them. In other words, you use a subordinating conjunction (*because, when, since, after, until, although, before*, etc.) to make one clause dependent on the other. By subordinating one clause, you show the reader the relationship between the two clauses. For example, take the following two sentences:

I ate a rotten egg.

I became violently ill.

It seems likely that eating the rotten egg caused the violent illness. To make that relationship grammatically clear, you can rephrase the sentences as:

Because I ate a rotten egg, I became violently ill.

Let's try another example:

I found out my dog was really a rat.

I called the exterminator.

Put them through the subordinating conjunction transformation machine:

After I found out my dog was really a rat, I called the exterminator.

I called the exterminator *after* I found out my dog was really a rat.

In these examples, "I found out my dog was really a rat" becomes subordinate to "I called the exterminator." You can base your decision on which clause to subordinate by determining the relationship between the clauses. In the example above, the discovery about the "dog" leads to the call; in other words, the discovery is the cause and calling the exterminator the result. Subordinating the cause to the result often makes the most sense when forming these sentences. For further discussion of this topic, move on to the next section.

Subordinate or Dependent Clauses

When you're tested on subordinate conjunctions, you'll need to select the most appropriate conjunction and place it correctly within the sentence. When you're tested on subordinate and dependent clauses, you'll need to decide how to form the whole sentence correctly. As touched upon above, not all clauses deserve the same emphasis in a sentence. Equality is a good thing, but in the writing world you've got to give preference to some clauses over others.

You can run into problems if you're too liberal with your coordinating conjunctions and transitional adverbs (the adverbs that link independent clauses). These adverbs assume that the clauses being connected deserve equal weight in a sentence. Take a look at this sentence:

Everyone regards Ginger as the most promising student in the class, and she gets the highest grades; also, she is the president of the student council.

This sentence doesn't read very well. Subordinating some of the clauses will improve the flow of the sentence:

Everyone regards Ginger as the most promising student in the class *because* she gets the highest grades and is the president of the student council.

This new sentence explains why Ginger is "the most promising student" by subordinating the clauses that cite her high grades and student council presidency.

Sentence Fragments

Sentence fragments are incomplete sentences that tend to look like this on the English Test:

We didn't go outside. *Even though the rain had stopped.*

Tommy could not pay for his lunch. *Having spent his last dollars on sunglasses.*

Always a bit shy. She found herself unable to talk to the other kids.

The sentence fragments above are not sentences on their own. They can be attached to the independent clauses next to them to form complete sentences:

We didn't go outside, *even though the rain had stopped.*

Having spent his last dollars on sunglasses, Tommy could not pay for his lunch.

Always a bit shy, she found herself unable to talk to the other kids.

The answer choices on English Test questions will often make clear whether you should incorporate a fragment into a neighboring sentence. For example:

We didn't go <u>outside. Even</u> though the rain
                       17
had stopped.

17. **A.** NO CHANGE
    B. outside;
    C. outside; even
    D. outside, even

Notice how choices **B**, **C**, and **D** all give you the option of combining two sentences into one. That should give you a good clue as to what's required. The variation between the last three choices occurs in punctuation. If you agree that **A** is incorrect, you can rely on your punctuation skills to decipher the correct answer. The answer, by the way, is **D** because **B** and **C**, with their use of the semicolon, continue to isolate the sentence fragment from the sentence.

Other sentence fragment questions on the English Test will ask you to turn a fragment into its own full sentence rather than simply to incorporate it into a different sentence. Again, you'll be able to tell from the answer choices what the ACT writers want:

We didn't go outside. <u>While the</u> rain continued
                              18
to fall.

18. **F.** NO CHANGE
    G. Although the
    H. The
    J. Since the

Answers **F**, **G**, and **J** don't solve the sentence fragment problem. Choosing those, you still end up with a subordinate clause posing as a sentence (**G** and **J** simply replace one subordinating conjunction with another). But by getting rid of the subordinating conjunction altogether, you form a real sentence: "The rain continued to fall." The correct answer is **H**.

Most sentence fragments on the English Test will be subordinate or dependent clauses trying to be complete sentences. By studying your subordinate and dependent clauses and learning what they look like, you'll be able to catch them committing sentence fragment crime.

Usage/Mechanics Questions

Comma Splices

The ACT writers may test your ability to weed out illegal comma splices. A comma splice occurs when two independent clauses are joined together by a comma with no intervening conjunction. For example,

> Bowen walked to the *park, Leah* followed behind.

The comma between "park" and "Leah" forms a comma splice. Although reading the sentence may sound correct because the comma demands a short pause between the two related clauses, the structure is wrong in written English. Instead, two sentences are necessary:

> Bowen walked to the *park. Leah* followed behind.

Or, if you explicitly want to show the relationship between the clauses, you can write:

> Bowen walked to the *park, while* Leah followed behind.

> *OR*

> Bowen walked to the *park, and* Leah followed behind.

Inserting "while" subordinates the "Leah" clause to the "Bowen" clause. In the second sentence, the "and" joins the two clauses on equal footing.

Think about the comma splice in construction terms: the comma (a wimpy nail) is too weak a punctuation mark to join together two independent clauses (two big heavies). In order to join them, you have to add a conjunction (super glue) to the comma or use a period (a bolt) instead.

Run-on Sentences

You can think of run-on sentences as comma splices minus the commas. For example:

> Joan runs every day she is preparing for a marathon.

> John likes to walk his dog through the park Kevin doesn't.

To fix run-on sentences, you need to identify where they should be split. The first example should be broken into two parts: "Joan runs every day" and "she is preparing for a marathon." These are two independent clauses that can stand on their own as sentences:

> Joan runs every day. She is preparing for a marathon.

Alternatively, you may choose to show the relationship between these sentences by subordinating one to the other:

> Joan runs every day *because* she is preparing for a marathon.

The second example, when split, becomes: "John likes to walk his dog through the park" and "Kevin doesn't." The following sentences are correct alternatives to the original run-on:

> John likes to walk his dog through the park. Kevin doesn't.

> John likes to walk his dog through the park, *but* Kevin doesn't.

> John likes to walk his dog through the park; *however,* Kevin doesn't.

These are just a few ways you can join the two clauses. We could go on and on, showing different relationships between the two clauses (but we won't).

Misplaced Modifiers

Does the following sentence sound odd to you?

> Having eaten six corn dogs, nausea overwhelmed Jane.

Nausea didn't eat six corn dogs. Gluttonous Jane did. However, the sentence above says that nausea was the one "having eaten six corn dogs." This is a case of a misplaced modifier. When you have a modifier like "having eaten six corn dogs," it must come either directly before or directly after the word that it is modifying.

> *Having eaten six corn dogs,* Jane was overwhelmed by nausea.

> Jane, *having eaten six corn dogs,* was overwhelmed by nausea.

These two sentences make it clear that Jane was the one wolfing down the corn dogs.

Modifiers are not necessarily phrases like the one above. They can be adverbial phrases, adverbial clauses, or single-word adverb modifiers. You've already seen how adverbial-phrase modifiers work in the example above. The simple rule for phrase modifiers is to *make sure phrase modifiers are next to the word(s) they modify.* The same rule applies to clause modifiers. Misplaced clause modifiers look like this:

> Bill packed his favorite clothes in his suitcase, *which he planned to wear on vacation.*

Now do you really think this guy is planning to wear his suitcase on vacation? Well, that's what the sentence says. It'll be a pretty heavy outfit too, since the suitcase is packed with clothes. If Bill decides to wear his clothes instead of his suitcase, you should say:

> Bill packed his favorite clothes, *which he planned to wear on vacation,* in his suitcase.

Of course, he'll be a slightly more conventional dresser, but the clothes will probably fit better than the suitcase.

The placement of single-word adverbs is slightly trickier than that of clause and phrase modifiers. You need to make sure that adverb modifiers (such as *just, almost,*

Usage/Mechanics Questions

barely, *even*, and *nearly*) are modifying the word you intend them to modify. If they aren't, the sentence will probably still make sense, but it will have a different meaning than you intended.

Take the sentence "Jay walked a half hour to the grocery store." Now add to that sentence the adverbial modifier "only." The placement of "only" within the sentence will alter the meaning of the sentence:

> *Only Jay* walked a half hour to the grocery store.

The sentence above means that no one but Jay made the walk.

> Jay *only walked* a half hour to the grocery store.

Here, "only" modifies the verb "walked," and the sentence means that Jay did nothing but walk—he didn't run, and he didn't swim—to the store.

> Jay walked *only a half hour* to the grocery store.

Hey, the walk to the grocery store isn't too bad. According to the sentence above, it took Jay only a half hour to get there.

> Jay walked a half hour to *only the grocery store*.

Now we find out that Jay's single destination was the grocery store (and we were about to accuse him of having ulterior motives for taking that walk).

Parallelism

When you see a list underlined on the English Test, look for a parallelism error. Parallelism errors occur when items in a list are mismatched. For example, if you have a list of verbs, then all items in the list must be verbs of the same tense. For example,

> *WRONG:*   In the pool area, there is no *spitting*, no *running*, and *don't throw* your cigarette butts in the water.

The first two forbidden activities end in "ing" (they're called gerunds, though that doesn't really matter), and because of that, the third activity must also end in "ing".

> *RIGHT:*   In the pool area, there is no *spitting*, no *running*, and no *throwing* your cigarette butts in the water.

By simply converting the final verb to gerund form, you have parallel structure. Parallelism is also important when you have expressions linked by the verb *to be*. Because you should think of *to be* as an equal sign, the words on either side of the sign must be parallel. For example:

> *WRONG:*   *To grow* tired of London is *growing* tired of life.

> *RIGHT:*   *To grow* tired of London is *to grow* tired of life.

Usage/Mechanics Questions

| WRONG: | *Growing* tired of London is *to grow* tired of life. |
| RIGHT: | *Growing* tired of London is *growing* tired of life. |

The examples above are not parallel when the verb forms are different on either side of "is." You can make them parallel by simply changing the form of one verb to the form of the other.

If you have a list of nouns, you must also maintain parallel construction. For example,

The personal ad said that she likes "*books*, good *food*, and *to take* long walks on the beach."

She apparently *doesn't* like parallelism. "Books" and "food" are nouns, but "to take" is a verb infinitive. If she's hoping to get a call from the grammarian of her dreams, she should rewrite her ad to look like this:

The personal ad said that she likes "*books*, good *food*, and long *walks* on the beach."

Now that's one grammatically correct lady.

Rhetorical Skills Questions on the English Test

Chapter Contents

T HE ACT WRITERS BREAK RHETORICAL Skills questions into three categories:

1. Writing Strategy

2. Organization

3. Style

Some people may find these questions more challenging than the Usage/Mechanics questions because there are no rules that strictly determine the Rhetorical Skills answers. Others may find them easier for that very reason—there's little to memorize. In any case, to answer Rhetorical Skills questions correctly you must develop an intuitive sense for good English writing. We'll show you how below.

Read the Whole Passage

Yes, we already gave you this advice in the "Strategies" section earlier in the book. But we think it's such good advice that we'll give it again: you should read (or at least skim) the whole passage. You may want to underline key phrases or transitions that help you decode the passage and that help you understand how its parts fit together. This strategy is particularly important for answering Rhetorical Skills questions. Quite a few Rhetorical Skills questions demand that you have a good understanding of the passage's content, tone, and purpose. You won't have that understanding if you haven't read (or at least skimmed) the entire passage.

Writing Strategy Questions

Writing strategy involves improving the effectiveness of a passage through careful revision and editing. Frequently, strategy questions will ask you to choose the most appropriate topic or transitional sentence for a paragraph. Almost as frequently, you will have to choose the best option for strengthening an argument by adding information or evidence. In other questions, you may also have to choose which sections of an argument can be deleted. You will also have to identify the purpose of a passage—its audience, its message—in other strategy questions.

The following strategy topics are covered in this section:

1. Transitions and Topic Sentences

2. Additional Detail and Evidence

3. Big Picture Purpose

Transitions and Topic Sentences

These questions ask you to figure out the best way to open or conclude paragraphs within a passage. Here's an example of a strategy question:

[2]

Victorian novelists were often

concerned with issues of character, plot,

and the Victorian social world. Dickens's

novels, for example, were several-

hundred-page-long works documenting

the elaborate interweaving of his

characters.

[3]

47 Their "modernist" novels tended

47. The writer wishes to begin Paragraph 3 with a sentence that

Rhetorical Skills Questions

to focus on the characters' inner lives,

which they depicted through a stylistic

technique called "stream of

consciousness." Several of the best-

known modernist novels were written

in this stream-of-consciousness

style. 48

strengthens the focus of the
paragraph, while providing a
transition from Paragraph 2.
Which of the following would be
the best choice?

A. In the early twentieth century,
novelists began to reject the
Victorian emphasis on social context
and look for a new focus for the
novel.

B. Victorian novels ended with the
Victorian era.

C. In the early twentieth century,
novelists further developed this
emphasis on characters' inner lives

D. World War I significantly affected
British culture in the twentieth
century.

Question 47 asks you to choose a sentence that will simultaneously serve as a topic sentence ("a sentence that strengthens the focus of the paragraph") for Paragraph 3 and as a transition sentence between the two paragraphs ("while providing a transition from Paragraph 2"). In order to answer this question correctly, you need to understand what the two paragraphs are saying. We suggest that you reread Paragraph 3 first. By developing a good sense of what that paragraph says, you can eliminate answer choices that clearly do not work as topic sentences. After you've eliminated any choices, make sure that you understand Paragraph 2. From the remaining choices, you can identify the best transition sentence.

Done that? We hope that you immediately eliminated choices **B** and **D** from your list of possible topic sentences. Choice **B** talks exclusively about the Victorian novel, making it an inappropriate topic sentence for a paragraph on modernist novels. Choice **D** doesn't talk specifically about novels at all. Its focus is World War I, which is not mentioned elsewhere in the paragraph. So now you've narrowed the selection down to **A** and **C**. These sentences have similar constructions, but they say radically different things: choice **A** claims that twentieth-century novelists rejected Victorian ideas, while choice **C** claims that they embraced and developed Victorian ideas. In order to figure out which one of these claims is true, you need to have read Paragraph 2 in addition to Paragraph 3. Paragraph 2 tells you that Victorian novelists were primarily concerned with the social world. In Paragraph 3, you discover that modernist novelists were primarily concerned with characters' thoughts and inner lives. Thus Paragraph 3 describes a *change* in novel writing that occurred between the Victorian era and the early twentieth century. The correct answer to the question is **A**.

The example above is fairly typical of transition and topic sentence questions you will encounter on the English Test. Sometimes you'll be asked to select only a topic sentence or only a transition sentence from the answer choices. Those questions are usually less complex than the example above because you have to perform one fewer step. You may also be asked to choose a concluding sentence for a paragraph. These questions are similar to transition questions because a good concluding sentence tends to be one that easily and sensibly makes the transition to the next paragraph.

Additional Detail and Evidence

These questions ask you to flesh out a paragraph by selecting the answer choice that provides the best additional detail or evidence. For example,

[3]

47 Their "modernist" novels tended to focus on the characters' inner lives, which they depicted through a stylistic technique called "stream of consciousness." Several of the best-known modernist novels were written in this stream-of-consciousness style. 48

48. The writer wishes to add information here that will further support the point made in the preceding sentence. Which of the following sentences will do that best?

F. Today, this style is not as popular as it once was.

G. However, there are many famous early twentieth-century works not written in this style.

H. Joyce's *Ulysses*, for example, was written in this style, and it is widely considered one of the most important books of the century.

J. Ford's *The Good Soldier*, although less read today, is a great example of this style.

This question asks for additional information to support the point of the preceding sentence ("Several of the best-known modernist novels were written in this stream-of-consciousness style"). To answer this question correctly, you need to understand the point being made, so read the sentence carefully. You should be able to eliminate choices **F** and **G** immediately. Choice **F** talks about the popularity of this style among contemporary authors—an issue that the preceding sentence does not address. You can eliminate choice **G** almost immediately because it starts with "however," which indicates that it is going to make a statement that attempts to contradict, not support, the previous point. Now you've successfully limited the answer choices to **H** and **J**. Both would provide the paragraph with an example of a stream-of-consciousness work. The key to deciding which of these sentences is correct lies in the preceding sentence, which talks about the "best-known modernist novels." On the one hand, choice **J** tells you that *The Good Soldier* is "less read today" and also, presumably, less well known. On the other hand, choice **H** tells you that *Ulysses* is "widely considered one of the most important books of the century." This statement suggests that the novel is famous, so choice **H** is the best answer to the question.

Big Picture Purpose

On each English Test, you'll probably encounter a few Big Picture Purpose questions. These questions always come at the end of a passage. We call them Big Picture Purpose questions because they ask you to look at the big picture and identify a passage's main point, intended purpose, or intended audience.

These questions in many ways resemble some of the questions on the Reading Test. BPP questions do, after all, test your comprehension of the passage—and comprehension is also what the Reading Test assesses. Because these questions test your overall comprehension, they are difficult to prepare for outside the context of a whole passage. That said, we suggest you prepare for these questions by studying our Reading Test chapter.

Before you start flipping through the book, we'll give you an idea of how these questions look on the English Test. They will often be phrased like this:

> Suppose the writer has been assigned to write an essay explaining the development of the British novel from 1799 to 1945. Would this essay successfully fulfill the assignment?

The answer choices to these questions come in two parts: the first part will respond either "No" or "Yes" to the question, and the second part will give an explanation for this answer. For example,

- **A.** No, because the essay restricts its focus to the American novel from 1850 to 1945.
- **B.** No, because the essay omits mention of famous poets.
- **C.** Yes, because the essay focuses on the novel's birth in the eighteenth century.
- **D.** Yes, because the essay describes changes in novel writing from the end of the French Revolution to the end of World War II.

Without reading the entire passage, you're probably unable to answer a definite "No" or "Yes" to this question, but you can eliminate an incorrect answer or two because of

Rhetorical Skills Questions

irrelevant or nonsensical explanations. In this example, you can immediately cross off choice **B** because the explanation calls for a discussion of famous poets in the essay. Famous poets, however, do not necessarily belong in an essay on the novel's development. You can also cross off choice **C**. It claims that the passage *successfully* fulfills the essay requirements because it discusses the novel's birth in the eighteenth century. However, the assignment calls for a discussion of the novel starting in 1799 (the end of the eighteenth century), so choice **C** cannot be correct. By reading and understanding the passage, you'll be able to choose from the two remaining answers. If the passage indeed focuses on the American novel, choice **A** is correct, and the essay does not succeed; if the essay describes the novel from the end of the French Revolution (1799) to the end of the World War II (1945), choice **D** is correct, and the essay does succeed.

Organization

Organization questions deal with the logical structuring of the passage on the level of the sentence, the paragraph, and the passage as a whole. These questions ask you to organize sections to maximize their coherence, order, and unity. It does this by asking three types of questions:

1. Sentence Reorganization

2. Paragraph Reorganization

3. Passage Reorganization

Sentence Reorganization

Sentence reorganization questions often involve the placement of a modifier within a sentence. Your ability to reorder a sentence correctly will depend on how well you have absorbed your grammar lessons above—specifically the "Misplaced Modifiers" section. For example,

Austen wrote about a society of manners, in

which love triumphs over a rigid social hierarchy

despite confinement to her drawing room.
43

43. **A.** NO CHANGE
B. (Place after *love*)
C. (Place after *Austen*)
D. (Place after *society*)

You probably guessed that the underlined phrase does not modify "hierarchy," "love," or "society." The pronoun "her" in the underlined phrase should tip you off that "Austen" is being modified. If you read "Misplaced Modifiers" in the previous chapter, you should already know the cardinal rule of placing the modifier next to the modified word. So the correct answer is **C** because the underlined part modifies "Austen."

Approximately half of the organization questions on the English Test will ask you to reorder sentences. All of these sentence reorganization problems will look similar to the one above. Study up on your modifier placement in order to get them right.

Paragraph Reorganization

A couple of questions will ask you to reorder sentences within a paragraph. They will look much like this:

[1] In April, I'm usually in a bad mood because

of my debilitating pollen allergies. [2] In

November, despite the graying trees and the

short days, I'm elated because I can

celebrate both Thanksgiving and my birthday.

[3] My mood changes with the months.

[4] In the summer months I feel happy

from days spent in the sun. 61

61. Which of the following provides the most logical ordering of the sentences in the preceding paragraph?
   A. 1, 4, 3, 2
   B. 3, 4, 2, 1
   C. 3, 1, 4, 2
   D. 2, 1, 4, 3

The best way to approach these questions is to decide which sentence should come first, and then to eliminate incompatible answer choices. Ask yourself: which sentence logically comes first in this sequence? Sentence 3 makes a good topic sentence because it provides a general argument that can be followed and supported by examples. By deciding that Sentence 3 should come first, you can immediately eliminate choices **A** and **D** because they do not begin with Sentence 3. Now you can move on to arranging the rest of the paragraph. Each of the remaining sentences talks about a different time of year: April, summer, and November. The three sentences should fall in that chronological order (April, summer, November), as this is the most logical arrangement in this example. Therefore, the correct answer is **C**.

If you are totally lost on a paragraph reorganization question, you can often look to the answer choices for clues. You can look at the first sentences given to you by the answer choices and see whether any of them sound like topic sentences. If you can identify a topic sentence, you're well on your way to getting the correct answer.

Passage Reorganization

These appear at the end of passages. They will ask you either to insert a sentence where it best belongs in the passage or to move a paragraph to a different location in the passage. Questions that ask you to insert a sentence will generally look like this:

> **72.** The writer wishes to include the following sentence in the essay: "That summer, I spent so much time on the beach that I could smell only a combination of sand and seaweed when I finally returned to school." That sentence will fit most smoothly and logically into Paragraph:
>
> **F.** 2, before the first sentence.
> **G.** 3, after the last sentence.
> **H.** 4, before the first sentence.
> **J.** 5, after the last sentence.

This question is basically a strategy question disguised as an organization question. It asks you to identify the sentence provided as an appropriate topic or concluding sentence for Paragraphs 2, 3, 4, or 5. When the answer choice calls for the sentence to be placed "before the first sentence," then it would become the topic sentence of the paragraph. When the answer choice calls for the sentence to be placed "after the last sentence," then it would become the concluding sentence.

Questions that ask you to relocate a paragraph will generally look like this:

> **74.** For the sake of the unity and coherence of this essay, Paragraph 4 should be placed:
>
> **F.** where it is now.
> **G.** after Paragraph 1.
> **H.** after Paragraph 2.
> **J.** after Paragraph 5.

To answer this question, look at (and perhaps underline) the topic sentences of each paragraph. These topic sentences, removed from the passage, should follow a logical chain of thought. For example, look at these topic sentences:

Topic Sentence 1:	Seasonal variations affect many aspects of my life.
Topic Sentence 2:	This April, the sight of leaves and the sounds of returning birds cheered me so much that I hugged a tree.
Topic Sentence 3:	The return of the warm weather also meant that I got some much-needed exercise after being stuck indoors all winter.
Topic Sentence 4:	My mood changes with the months.
Topic Sentence 5:	The weather's effect on my mood and my fitness always reminds me of the undeniable connection between people and nature.

Rhetorical Skills Questions

Even without reading the whole passage, you can take an educated stab at the correct answer. Consider the logical organization of an essay: introduction, supporting paragraphs, and conclusion. According to this structure, Topic Sentence 1 should present the passage's argument, and it should be followed by three paragraphs supporting the argument and a final paragraph presenting a conclusion.

Now take a look at Topic Sentence 4, our representative from Paragraph 4. Topic Sentence 4 makes a general argument about the weather's effect on the author's mood. Ask yourself where the paragraph best fits into the passage: is it a supporting paragraph or a conclusion? It's unlikely that Paragraph 4 is a conclusion because it narrows the focus of the essay to talk about the author's mood, while other paragraphs in the essay discuss the author's physical condition. If it's a supporting paragraph, then where does it belong? Eliminating choice J (which would make it the conclusion) leaves you with three options for a supporting paragraph.

Your next step should be to take a look at the remaining Topic Sentences. Topic Sentence 2 also discusses the weather's effect on the author's mood, but it deals specifically with April weather. Topic Sentence 3 discusses the weather's effects on the author's physical health. If you choose Choice **F** and keep Paragraph 4 where it is, the passage will be ordered like this: introduction, weather/mood, weather/health, weather/mood, conclusion. This order doesn't make much sense because it inexplicably divides the weather/mood discussions. Choices **G** and **H** place the weather/mood paragraphs side by side. Choice **G** puts Paragraph 4 (general weather/mood) before Paragraph 2 (April weather/mood), while choice **H** puts 2 before 4. When writing an essay, moving from the general to the specific makes more sense than moving in the opposite direction because you want to support your claims with specific evidence. So by using good writing strategy, you will arrive at the correct answer: **G**.

Style

Style questions generally concern effective word choice. They often ask you to choose the most appropriate word for a sentence in terms of its tone and clarity. Other times, they'll ask you to eliminate redundant words or phrases. In the next section, we discuss the following style topics:

1. Redundancy

2. Appropriate Word Choice and Identifying Tone

Redundancy

The ACT writers will test you on your ability to spot redundant statements. Redundant statements say the same thing twice, and you should always avoid redundancy on the English Test (in life too, if possible). For example,

WRONG: The diner closes at 3 a.m. in the morning.

RIGHT: The diner closes at 3 a.m.

"In the morning" is redundant because it is implied in "a.m." Here's another example of a redundant statement:

WRONG: In my opinion, I think we should go get some food.

"I think" and "In my opinion" mean the same thing, so you can eliminate one of the phrases from the sentence:

RIGHT: In my opinion, we should go get some food.

ALSO RIGHT: I think we should go get some food.

Either one of those phrases gets the point across; using both merely makes the sentence cumbersome.

Redundancy questions almost always give you the option to "OMIT the underlined portion." If you spot a phrase or word that means the same thing as the underlined portion, then you should always choose to "OMIT." (For more on "OMIT," refer to "If the Phrase Doesn't Fit, You Must 'OMIT'" on p. 41.)

Appropriate Word Choice and Identifying Tone

Identifying the appropriate word choice can be as simple as figuring out whether a sentence should use the word "their," "there," or "they're." But word choice can also be more complicated, involving many words working together to create a tone. For example, the sentence "Lloyd George rocks!" probably does not belong in an essay on World War I. It doesn't fit because it's written in a casual, slangy tone, and history essays are generally neither casual nor slangy. The sentence might belong, however, in a passage on your awesome new friend, Lloyd George.

The content of a passage will generally give you a clue about the appropriate tone. Essays on history and culture will probably be written in a fairly formal style—a style that omits youthful slang, casual contractions, and familiar personal pronouns (such as "I" and "you"). A personal essay on your experiences driving a bulldozer, on your great-grandmother, or on your new skateboard calls for a relatively informal style of writing. These personal essays can exhibit varying degrees of informality. An essay by a young writer may be more colloquial and relaxed than an essay by a mature writer recalling past experiences.

Tone is one of the most important elements in correctly answering word choice questions. You will encounter quite a few questions that look like this:

Rhetorical Skills Questions

During the Great War, the British Public believed

that Lloyd George <u>rocks!</u> He was widely admired
                        7

for his ability to unify the government and thus

to unify Britain.

7. **A.**   NO CHANGE
    B.   rocked!
    C.   was an effective political leader.
    D.   had the ability to unify
             the government and thus to unify
             Britain.

Because we already told you that informality does not belong in a history essay, you can immediately eliminate choices **A** and **B**, even though **B** correctly changes the verb tense. If you read the section above, you should also be able to eliminate **D** because it is redundant—it repeats the information given in the next sentence. That leaves the correct answer, **C**.

The ACT
Writing Test

A "GREAT ACT ESSAY" AND A "GREAT ESSAY" are *not* the same thing. Truly great essays take hours or even days to plan, research, and write. The ACT essay can't take more than 30 minutes. That means you've got to write an essay that convinces your genius in less time than it takes to watch *The Simpsons*, right? Wrong.

The ACT knows that 30 minutes isn't enough time for anyone, anywhere, to write a genius essay. Forget genius. Forget about trying to write an essay that changes the world. When the ACT says to you, "Here's 30 minutes, write an essay," what they mean is: "Write a *standard* essay that does exactly what we want."

To give the ACT what it wants, you need to have a very firm essay-writing strategy in place before you sit down to take the test. You then need to apply that strategy to whatever question the ACT essay poses. In this chapter, we'll teach you a strategy for writing a great ACT essay that will work every time, on any topic. It all starts with fast food.

The Fast Food Essay

One of the best things about fast food is not just that it's quick, it's *consistent*. Walk into a McDonald's in Tosserdorf, Germany, and a Big Mac is still a robust, comforting Big Mac, just like at home. What makes fast food so consistent? Restaurants like McDonald's use the same ingredients and preparation methods at every location.

In this chapter, we'll show you how to apply the concept behind fast food to the process of writing the ACT essay. That way you'll be able to write a top-notch ACT essay every time. To make it happen, you need to know three key things, just like all the fast food chains:

- Know Your Customers

- Know Your Ingredients

- Know How to Put the Ingredients Together

Know Your Customers

After you finish taking the ACT, two "raters" will score your essay. These raters are trained and certified specifically for grading the ACT essay. Each rater is instructed to give every essay a score on a scale of 1–6. The two grades are then added together to make up your entire essay subscore, which will range from 2–12. If the two raters come to wildly different scores for an essay, like a 2 and a 5, a third rater will be brought in.

So the essay graders are your *customers*, and you want to give them an essay that tastes just like what they're expecting. How are *you* supposed to know what *they're* expecting? You can learn exactly what ACT essay-raters expect by looking at the actual ACT essay directions.

The ACT Essay Directions

Read the directions now and make sure you understand them:

<u>Assignment:</u>

In your essay, take a position on this question. You may write about either one of the two points of view given, or you may present a different point of view on this question. Use specific reasons and examples to support your position.

We've expanded upon these directions and created a list of Dos and Don'ts in order to make the rules of great ACT writing easy to grasp:

DO	DON'T
Write only on the given topic.	Write on a topic that relates vaguely to the one given.
Take a clear position on the topic.	Take a wishy-washy position or try to argue two sides.
Write persuasively to convince the rater.	Write creatively or ornately just to show off.
Include reasons and examples that support your position.	Include examples not directly related to your position.
Write with correct grammar and spelling.	Forget to proof your work for spelling and grammar mistakes.
Write as clearly as possible.	Use too many fancy vocabulary words or overly long sentences.
Write specifically and concretely.	Be vague or use generalizations.
Write about five paragraphs.	Put more importance on length than on quality.
Write only on the given lined paper.	Make your handwriting too large (or you'll sacrifice space).
Write as neatly as possible in print.	Write in cursive. Print is much easier to read.

The Rater's Instructions

The raters must refer to a set-in-stone list of criteria when evaluating each essay and deciding what grade (1 through 6) it deserves. We thought you might appreciate having the scoring criteria spelled out and explained by the ACT right before your very eyes. They address a student's ability:

- To take and articulate a perspective on an issue
- To maintain a clear focus on the perspective throughout the essay
- To explain a position by using supportive evidence and logical reasoning
- To organize ideas logically
- To communicate clearly in writing

And here's how they separate the good from the bad:

SCORE	CHARACTERISTICS
4-6	Writers will show a clear understanding of the purpose of the essay by articulating their perspective and developing their ideas. Most generalizations will be developed with specific examples to support the writer's perspective. A clear focus will be maintained throughout the essay. The paper will show competent use of language. Although there may be some errors, these will only occasionally distract the rater and will not interfere with the rater's ability to understand the writer's meaning.
1-3	Writers will not clearly articulate a perspective on the issue. The writing will usually demonstrate some development of ideas, but the development may be very general or repetitious. Most papers will maintain focus on the general topic identified in the prompt, but they may not maintain focus on the specific issue. Except for the weakest papers, the essay will use a clear but simple organizational structure. The language will be understandable for the most part, but errors will distract the rater and possibly interfere with understanding.

Now you know your customers, and you know what they want. We'll spend the rest of this chapter teaching you precisely how to give it to them.

Know Your Ingredients

To write a tasty ACT essay, you've got to know the necessary ingredients. The different grades of 1–6 are based on the quality of your essay in four fundamental categories:

1. **Positioning**: The strength and clarity of your stance on the given topic

2. **Examples**: The relevance and development of the examples you use to support your argument

3. **Organization**: The organization of each of your paragraphs and of your essay overall

4. **Command of Language**: Sentence construction, grammar, and word choice

1. Positioning

ACT essay topics will address issues that pertain to high school students. A typical ACT topic will give you a statement that addresses ideas like *dress codes*, *block scheduling*, *justice*, *the definition of success*, or *the importance of learning from mistakes*. Though this list may sound overwhelming at first, the broadness of the topics means that with a little thought you can come up with plenty of examples to support your position on the topic.

Philosophers take years to write volumes on the topics of *justice* or *success*. On the ACT, you get 30 minutes. Given these time constraints, the key to writing a great ACT essay is taking a strong position on an extremely broad topic. A solid position requires you to employ two strategies:

- Rephrase the Prompt

- Choose Your Position

Here's a sample prompt with the directions you will find on the test:

> Many successful adults recall a time in their life when they were considered a failure at one pursuit or another. Some of these people feel strongly that their previous failures taught them valuable lessons and led to their later successes. Others maintain that they went on to achieve success for entirely different reasons. In your opinion, can failure lead to success? Or is failure simply its own experience?

> Assignment:

> In your essay, take a position on this question. You may write about either one of the two points of view given, or you may present a different point of view on this question. Use specific reasons and examples to support your position.

Rephrase the Prompt

Rephrase the prompt in your own words and make it more specific. If you rephrase the question:

> "In your opinion, can failure lead to success?"

you might come up with a sentence like:

> "Failure can lead to success by teaching important lessons that help us avoid repeating mistakes in the future."

Putting the ACT essay question in your own words makes it easier for you to take a position confidently since you'll be proving your own statement, rather than the more obscure version put forth by the ACT.

Choose Your Position

Agree or disagree. When you choose an argument for a paper in school, you often have to strain yourself to look for something original, something subtle. Not here. Not on the 30-minute, fast food essay. Once you've rephrased the topic, agree or disagree with it. It's that simple.

At this point, you may be thinking, "I could argue the 'agree' side pretty well, but I'm not sure that I totally believe in the agree side because . . ." Drop those thoughts. Remember, you're not going to have a week to write this essay. You need to keep it simple. Agree or disagree, then come up with the examples that support your simple stand. And don't take a position that straddles both sides of the issue.

2. Examples

To make an ACT essay really shine, you've got to include excellent examples. There are two things that make excellent ACT examples stand out from the crowd:

- Specific Examples
- Variety of Examples

Specific Examples

Strong examples discuss specific events, dates, or measurable changes over time. Another way to put this is: You have to be able to talk about things that have happened in detail.

Let's say you're trying to come up with examples in support of the position that "Learning the lessons taught by failure is a sure route to success." Perhaps you might come up with the example of the American army during the Revolutionary War, which learned from its failures in the early years of the war how it needed to fight the British. Awesome! That's a *potentially* great example. To make it *actually* great, though, you have to be able to say more than just, "The American army learned from its mistakes and then defeated the British Redcoats." You need to be specific: Give dates, mention people, battles, tactics. If you use the experience of the American Army in the Revolutionary War as an example, you might mention the signing of the Treaty of Paris in 1783, which officially granted the Americans independence and gave the United States all lands east of the Mississippi river.

Don't be intimidated if you can't instantly recall the dates of pivotal historical events. Any descriptive details that you can provide will strengthen your argument, whether they are personal examples or historical facts. Just make sure to choose examples that you know a lot about in order to be specific. Knowing that the Americans defeated the British is the start of a great example, but you need to show specifically how the American victory answers the question, "In your opinion, can failure lead to success?" What failures on the part of the British government and army led to the Americans' success? (Morale issues, leadership differences, inadequate soldiers and supplies, the Battle of Yorktown, and so on.) The one-two punch of a solid example and details that use the example to prove your argument make the difference between a good ACT example and a great one.

The Variety of Your Examples

The other crucial thing about ACT Essay examples is how much ground they cover. Sure, you could come up with three examples from your personal life about how you learned from failure. But you're much more likely to impress the raters and write a better essay if you use a broad range of examples from different areas: history, art, politics, literature, and science, as well as your own life. That means when you're thinking up examples, you should consider as wide a variety as possible, as long as all of your examples work to prove your argument.

To answer the question, "In your opinion, can failure lead to success?" you might choose one example from history, literature, and business or current events. Here are three examples that you might choose from those three areas:

- **History:** The Americans' victory over the British in the Revolutionary War

- **Literature:** In spite of David Copperfield's difficult childhood, he eventually found personal and professional happiness.

- **Business or Current Events:** The JetBlue airline succeeding by learning from the mistakes of its competitors

A broad array of examples like those will provide a more solid and defensible position than three examples drawn from just one or two areas.

3. Organization

No matter what topic you end up writing about, the organization of your essay should be the same. Whether you're asked to answer "Can failure lead to success?" or "Does progress always come at a cost?," the *structure* of your essay should be almost identical. The ACT is looking for those standard ingredients, and the structure we're about to explain will make sure those ingredients stand out in your essay.

So what's this magical essay structure? Well, it's back to the trusty fast food analogy: A good ACT essay is a lot like a triple-decker burger.

The ACT Writing Test

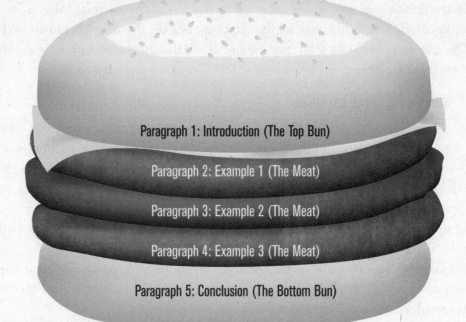

Paragraph 1: Introduction (The Top Bun)

Paragraph 2: Example 1 (The Meat)

Paragraph 3: Example 2 (The Meat)

Paragraph 4: Example 3 (The Meat)

Paragraph 5: Conclusion (The Bottom Bun)

No matter what the topic is, how you feel about it, or which examples you choose, you should always follow this five-paragraph structure on your ACT essay. The first and last paragraphs are your essay's introduction and conclusion; each of the middle three paragraphs discuss an example that supports and illustrates your argument. That's it.

Just as important as the organization of your entire essay is the organization within each of the five paragraphs. Let's take a closer look at each paragraph next.

The Top Bun: Introduction

The introduction to an ACT essay has to do three things:

- Grab the rater's attention

- Explain your position on the topic clearly and concisely

- Transition the rater smoothly into your three examples

To accomplish these three goals, you need three to four sentences in your introduction. These three to four sentences will convey your thesis statement and the overall map of your essay to the rater.

The Thesis Statement: The thesis statement is the first sentence of your essay. It identifies where you stand on the topic and should pull the raters into the essay. A good thesis statement is strong, clear, and definitive. A good thesis statement for the essay prompt, "In your opinion, can failure lead to success?" is:

Learning from the lessons taught by failure is a sure route to success.

This thesis statement conveys the writer's position on the topic boldly and clearly. In only a few words, it carves out the position that the essay will take on the very broad, vague topic: learning from failure yields success.

The Essay Summary: After the thesis statement, the rest of the first paragraph should serve as a kind of summary of the examples you will use to support your position on the topic. Explain and describe your three examples to make it clear how they fit into your argument. It's usually best to give each example its own sentence. Here's an example:

> *The United States of America can be seen as a success that emerged from failure: by learning from the weaknesses of the Articles of Confederation, the founding fathers were able to create the Constitution, the document on which America is built. Google Inc., the popular Internet search engine, is another example of a success that arose from learning from failure, though in this case Google learned from the failures of its competitors. Another example that shows how success can arise from failure is the story of Rod Johnson, who started a recruiting firm that rose out of the ashes of Johnson's personal experience of being laid off.*

Three sentences, three examples. The rater knows exactly what to expect from your essay now and is ready to dive in.

The Meat: 3-Example Paragraphs

Each of your 3-example paragraphs should follow this basic format:

- 4–5 sentences long

- The first sentence should be the **topic sentence**, which serves as the thesis statement of the paragraph. It explains what your example is and places it within the context of your argument.

- The next 3–4 sentences are for **developing your example**. In these sentences you show through specific, concrete discussion of facts and situations just how your example supports your essay thesis statement.

Below we've given you an example of a strong meat paragraph:

> *The United States, the first great democracy of the modern world, is also one of the best examples of a success achieved by studying and learning from earlier failures. After just five years of living under the Articles of Confederation, which*

established the United States of America as a single country for the first time, the states realized that they needed a new document and a stronger government. In 1786, the Annapolis convention was convened. The result, three years later, was the Constitution, which created a more powerful central government while also maintaining the integrity of the states. By learning from the failure of the Articles, the founding fathers created the pivotal document of a country that has become both the most powerful country in the world and a beacon of democracy.

The best Meat paragraphs on the ACT essay are specific. The ACT's essay directions say it loud and clear: "Use specific reasons and examples to support your position." In its topic sentence, this paragraph states that the United States is one of the great examples of "a success achieved by studying and learning from earlier failures." It then uses the specific example of the Articles of Confederation, the Annapolis convention, and the Constitution to prove its position. It's specific throughout and even includes a few dates.

Transitions Between Meat Paragraphs Your first meat paragraph dives right into its thesis statement, but the second and third Meat paragraphs need transitions. The simplest way to build these transitions is to use words like *another* and *finally*. That means your second Meat paragraph should start off with a transitional phrase such as, "Another example . . ."

A slightly more sophisticated way to build transitions is to choose examples from different sources, such as history and business. If the first paragraph is about a political instance of learning from failure and the second is from business, make that fact your transition: "As in politics, learning from failure is a means to gaining success in business as well. Take the case of . . ."

The Bottom Bun: Conclusion

The conclusion of your essay should accomplish two main goals:

- Recap your argument, while broadening it a bit.

- Push a little further. Look to the future.

To accomplish these two goals, your conclusion should contain three to four sentences.

The Recap: The recap is a one-sentence summary of what you've already argued. As in the thesis statement, the recap should be straightforward, bold, and declarative. By "broadening" your argument, we mean that you should attempt to link your specific examples to other fields, such as politics, business, and art. Here's a recap example:

The examples of the Constitution, *Google, and Rod Johnson make it clear that in the realms of politics and business, the greatest successes arise from careful considerations of the lessons of failure.*

Expand on Your Position: The last two or three sentences of the essay should take the argument you just recapped and push it a little further. One of the best ways to push your argument further is to look to the future and think about what would happen if the position that you've taken in your essay could be applied on a broader scale. Here's an example:

> *Failure is often seen as embarrassing, something to be denied and hidden. But as the examples of the U.S. Constitution , Google, and Rod Johnson prove, if an individual, organization, or even a nation is strong enough to face and study its failure, then that failure can become a powerful teacher. As the examples of history and business demonstrate, if everyone had the courage and insight to view failure as a surefire way to learn from mistakes, success would be easier to achieve.*

The Bottom Bun wraps up the entire ACT essay. And there you have it! If you follow the template we have just provided, and break down the essay into its core ingredients, your ACT essay will be strong, clear, and easy to write.

The Universal ACT Essay Template

To make sure you really get the essay organization we're suggesting, we'll sum it all up. Here's the ACT essay outline you should use, no matter what topic you get or what position you take:

	Length	Purpose
The Introduction		
Thesis Statement	1 sentence	Describe your position clearly and concisely.
The Essay Summary	3 sentences	Lay out the three examples you will use to support your thesis statement.
Example Paragraph #1		
Topic Sentence	1 sentence	Describe your example and fit it into the context of your overall thesis statement.
Example Development	3–4 sentences	Show how your example supports your argument. Be as specific as possible.
Example Paragraph #2		
Topic Sentence	1 sentence	Describe your example and fit it into the context of your overall Thesis. Provide a transition from the previous example paragraph.

The ACT Writing Test

	Length	Purpose
Example Development	3–4 sentences	Show how your example supports your example. Be as specific as possible.

Example Paragraph #3

	Length	Purpose
Topic Sentence	1 sentence	Describe your example and fit it into the context of your overall thesis. Provide a transition from the previous paragraph.
Example Development	3–4 sentences	Use specific facts to show how your example supports your example. Be as specific as possible.

The Conclusion

	Length	Purpose
Recap	1 sentence	Summarize your argument and examples, and link the examples to broader things like politics, history, art, business, etc.
Broaden Your Argument	2–3 sentences	Expand your position by contemplating what would happen in the world if other groups followed the argument you make in your essay.

4. Command of Language

Taking a clear position and defending it with solid detailed examples is a strong start to a successful ACT essay. But the ACT-raters also care about the mechanics of your writing, which we call your "command of language." Think of your command of language as your fast food essay's Special Sauce—it's the coating of perfect word choice, grammar, sentence structure, and spelling that oozes through your entire essay. An ACT essay with a clear position and strong examples won't get a perfect score without the Special Sauce, so pay close attention to these three facets of your essay:

- Variation in Sentence Structure

- Word Choice

- Grammar and Spelling

Variation Sentence Structure

Sentence structure is very important. Sentence structure, if done well, can keep your readers engaged and help make your essay exciting and easier to read. Sentence structure, if it is monotonous and unchanging, can make your essay sound boring and unsophisticated. Sentence structure is important on the ACT essay. Sentence structure is also important in essays you write for school.

Did you notice how dull that entire last paragraph became after the first two sentences? That's because every one of those sentences not only started in the same way, but also they all had the same predictable plodding rhythm.

Now go back and look at the earlier sample Meat paragraph on the Constitution. Notice how the various sentences start differently and also have different internal rhythms. These variations in sentence structure keep the writing vibrant and interesting. Focus on changing the structure of your sentences as you write the essay. You don't have to invert every clause, but you should be careful not to let a few sentences in a row follow the same exact structure. You've got to mix it up. Here's the boring first paragraph of this section rewritten with varied sentence structure:

> *Sentence structure is very important. Varying the structure of your sentences keeps your reader engaged and makes your writing easier to read and more exciting. Monotonous and repetitive sentence structure can make your essay sound boring and unsophisticated. Mixing up your sentence structure is crucial on the ACT essay—it's also important to consider when writing essays for school.*

Much easier to read and far less repetitive, right?

Transitions Between Sentences: One great way to vary your sentence structure while increasing the logical flow of your essay is to use transitions. Transitions provide the context necessary to help readers understand the flow of your argument. They're words, phrases, or sentences that take readers gently by the hand, leading them through your essay. Here are some examples of different kinds of transitions you can use to spice up your sentence structure:

- **Showing Contrast:** *Katie likes pink nail polish.* In contrast, *she thinks red nail polish looks trashy.*

- **Elaborating:** *I love staying up late.* Even more than that, *I love sleeping in until noon.*

- **Providing an Example:** *If you save up your money, you can afford pricey items.* For example, *Patrick saved up his allowance and years later purchased a sports car.*

- **Showing Results:** *Manuel ingested nothing but soda and burgers every day for a month.* As a result, *he gained ten pounds.*

- **Showing Sequence:** *The police arrested Bob at the party.* Soon after, *his college applications were all rejected, and* eventually *Bob drifted into a life of crime.*

The ACT Writing Test

Overly Complex Sentences: Sometimes students think writing long complicated sentences will impress teachers. Maybe, but it won't impress ACT essay-raters. Keep your sentences short and simple. Complex sentences are difficult to understand, and your ACT essays should be as clear and easy to read as possible.

We could fill an entire book with rules about creating simple and succinct prose. Instead, we'll give you two handy rules to simplify the sentences that you write on the ACT essay:

1. Never write a sentence that contains more than three commas. Try to avoid sentences with more than two commas. (Unless you need to include a list.)

2. Never write a sentence that takes up more than three lines of ACT-essay paper.

Those rules are certainly not foolproof, but abiding by them will keep you from filling your ACT essay with overly complex sentences and will ultimately make your essay easier to understand.

Word Choice

When students see that "word choice" plays a part in their essay score, they often think they have to use tons of sophisticated vocabulary words in order to score well. That belief is wrong and potentially damaging to your ACT essay score. If you're straining to put fancy words into your essay, you're bound to end up misusing those words. And misusing a sophisticated word is a worse offense than not using one at all.

Word choice doesn't mean that you have to go for the big word every time. It means you should go for the *proper* word, the best word, the word that makes your essay as clear as possible. Let's look at part of the paragraph about the Constitution:

The United States, the first great democracy of the modern world, is also one of the best examples of a success achieved by studying and learning from earlier failures. After just five years of living under the Articles of Confederation, which established the United States of America as a single country for the first time, the states realized that they needed a new document and a stronger government. In 1786, the Annapolis convention was convened. The result, three years later, was the Constitution, which created a more powerful central government while also maintaining the integrity of the states. By learning from the failure of the Articles, the founding fathers created the pivotal document of a country that has become both the most powerful country in the world and a beacon of democracy.

This is 6-level writing, but it isn't teeming with five-syllable words. What the passage does do is use every single word correctly. When it includes an uncommon word, like *beacon*, it uses the word appropriately and effectively. Now *that's* good word choice.

So don't try to use a word unless you know what it means. Don't go throwing around tough words in the hope that you'll impress your reader. The likelihood is that you're going to use the word incorrectly and give the rater a bad impression. Instead, keep it simple, and stick to words you know well.

Grammar and Spelling

A few grammar or spelling mistakes throughout your essay will not destroy your score. The ACT understands that you're bound to make minor mistakes in a rushed 30-minute essay.

Raters are instructed to look for *patterns* of errors. If a rater sees that your punctuation is consistently wrong, that your spelling of familiar words is often incorrect, or that you write run-on sentences again and again, that's when your score will suffer.

You need to be able to write solid grammatical sentences to score well on the essay. As for learning the grammar, well, you're in luck. We cover all the important grammar you need to know in "Beat Identifying Sentence Errors" and "Beat Improving Sentences."

Know How to Put the Ingredients Together

By now you know all of the ingredients you should use and the template you should follow to write a great ACT essay. Next you need to learn the writing process. Follow the five steps we describe below and you'll be on your way to a "6."

Five Steps to a "6"

STEP 1:	Understand the prompt and take a position.	1 MINUTE
STEP 2:	Brainstorm examples.	2–3 MINUTES
STEP 3:	Create an outline.	3–4 MINUTES
STEP 4:	Write the essay.	15 MINUTES
STEP 5:	Proof the essay.	2 MINUTES

Step 1. Understand the prompt and take a position. (1 minute)

The first thing you must do before you can even start to think about your essay is read the prompt very carefully. Here's the sample topic we will use throughout this section:

> Many successful adults recall a time in their life when they were considered a failure at one pursuit or another. Some of these people feel strongly that their previous failures taught them valuable lessons and led to their later successes. Others maintain that they went on to achieve success for entirely different reasons. In your opinion, can failure lead to success? Or is failure simply its own experience?
>
> Assignment:
>
> In your essay, take a position on this question. You may write about either one of the two points of view given, or you may present a different point of view on this question. Use specific reasons and examples to support your position. =

Make sure you understand the topic thoroughly by making it your own. To do that, use the two steps we discussed in the Ingredients section:

- **Rephrase the prompt.** "Failure can lead to success by teaching important lessons that help us avoid repeating mistakes in the future."

- **Choose Your Position.** (In our example, we agree with the first question.)

That's it. One step down, four to go.

Step 2. Brainstorm examples. (4–5 minutes)

You believe the answer to the question, "In your opinion, can failure lead to success?" is yes. Terrific.

Brainstorming, or thinking up, examples to support your position is the crucial next step. Plenty of ACT–takers will succumb to the temptation to plunge straight from Step 1 into writing the essay (Step 4). Skipping the brainstorming session will leave you with an opinion on the topic but with no clearly thought-out examples to prove your point. You'll write the first thing that comes to mind, and your essay will probably derail. So even though you feel the time pressure, don't skip brainstorming.

Brainstorming seems simple. You just close your eyes and scrunch up your face and THINK REALLY HARD until you come up with some examples. But, in practice, staring at a blank page under time pressure can be intimidating and frustrating. To make brainstorming less daunting and more productive, we've got two strategies:

Brainstorm by Category: The best examples you can generate to support your ACT essay topic will come from a variety of sources, such as science, history, politics, art, literature, business, and personal experience. So, brainstorm a list split up by category in order to organize your thoughts. Here's the list we brainstormed for your agreement with the question, "In your opinion, can failure lead to success?"

Current Events	failure of 9/11 security heightened security at airports
Science	babies learn to walk only after trying and failing time and time again.
History	can't think of one
Politics	the U.S. Constitution was only written after the failure of the Articles of Confederation
Art	can't think of one
Literature	James Joyce became a writer only after failing as a singer
Personal Experience	Rod Johnson (your uncle), realized the need for a placement agency in South Carolina after getting laid off
Business	Through watching the failures of its competitors, Google learned how to create a successful search engine

Let's say you took four minutes and came up with a list of eight categories like our's, and got examples for five of them. That's still great. That means your next step is to choose the top three of your five potential examples.

Prepare Ahead of Time: If you want to put in the time, you could also do some brainstorming ahead of time. Brainstorming ahead of time can be a great method, because it gives you time to do more than just brainstorm. You can actually prepare examples for each of the eight categories we've brainstormed above in our chart. You could, for instance, read about various scientists, learning about their successes, their failures, the impact of their discoveries (positive and negative) and memorizing dates, events and other facts.

The risk inherent in planning ahead is that you can get stuck with a topic on the ACT in which all your knowledge about scientists just isn't applicable. But while this is somewhat of a risk, since the ACT essay topics are so broad, you can often massage your examples to fit. Still, if you don't want to risk wasting your time with advance preparation, don't.

Choose Your Top Three: When you go through your brainstormed and preprepared examples to decide which three you should actually use, you need to keep three things in mind:

1. Which examples can you be most specific about?

2. Which examples will give your essay the broadest range?

3. Which examples are not controversial?

The first two reasons are pretty straightforward: Specificity and variety in your examples will help you write the strongest essay. The point about controversy is a bit more subtle. Staying away from very controversial examples ensures that you won't accidentally offend or annoy your rater, who might then be more inclined to lower your grade. For instance, the 9/11 example from our brainstormed list should be cut. The event just is too full of unresolved issues to serve as a suitable essay topic, and the last thing you want to do is upset anyone.

Here's another example. Let's say that you're not so certain if that story about James Joyce being a singer is even really true, and you think lots of people might select the babies walking example. That would mean you decide to keep the examples about the Constitution, Google, and the story of Rod Johnson.

Now that you've narrowed down your brainstormed topics to the top three, it's time to move on. Next up: Outlining.

Step 3. Create an outline. (5-6 minutes)

After brainstorming comes the essay writing step that students tend to dread most—writing an outline. We're here to encourage you to embrace the outline. Love the outline! Live the outline! At the very least, *write* the outline. Organizing your ideas in outline form and then sticking to that outline is crucial. Though you may feel that you're wasting your time, the five or six minutes that you invest in writing out an outline will *definitely* be paid back when you write the essay.

Writing the Outline: Since your outline is a kind of bare-bones "map" of your essay, the outline should follow our Universal ACT Essay Template. Here's a summary of the template:

PARAGRAPH #	PURPOSE	WHAT IT SHOULD CONTAIN
1.	Introduction	Thesis Statement; State Examples
2.	Example 1	Topic Sentence for Example 1; Explain Example 1
3.	Example 2	Topic Sentence for Example 2; Explain Example 2
4.	Example 3	Topic Sentence for Example 3; Explain Example 3
5.	Conclusion	Thesis rephrased in a broader way; a look into the future

As you write the outline, remember that conveying your ideas clearly is what matters most. Your outline need not be articulate, or even comprehensible to anyone other than you. However, it must contain all the essential raw material that will become your thesis statement, topic sentences, and your concluding statement when you write your essay.

As you sketch out your outline, consider where you want each example to go. We suggest that you put what you consider to be your strongest example first, followed by the second strongest, and then the least strong. We suggest this because the essay is a timed section, and if you run out of time and can only fit two example paragraphs between your intro and conclusion, they should be your best two examples. Here's a sample outline we've written based on the topic and examples we have already discussed. Notice that we've placed our examples in strongest to weakest order starting in Paragraph 2.

PARAGRAPH 1: INTRODUCTION	Failure can lead to success teaching lessons, learning mistakes. Three examples: 1) U.S. Constitution and Articles failure 2) failed dot coms lead to better more successful online businesses 3) guy who started successful recruiting business after getting laid off
PARAGRAPH 2: EXAMPLE 1 (BEST)	U.S. Constitution developed by studying the failures of previous document, Articles of Confederation. By studying failures the U.S. became true revolutionary democracy.
PARAGRAPH 3: EXAMPLE 2 (NEXT BEST)	Google studied competitors' struggles, then came up with better technological solution and better business model. Since failure is good teacher, intelligent companies look for failure everywhere, even in rivals, to learn and evolve.
PARAGRAPH 4: EXAMPLE 3 (NEXT BEST)	Johnson founded job placement agency based on difficulties finding a new job after getting laid off. Studied his failure; found problems lay with system, not with him
PARARAPH 5: CONCLUSION	Failure often seen as embarrassing. People try to hide it. But if you or society take responsibility for it and study it, history shows failure leads to success for everyone.

Your outline does not have to be written in complete sentences. Notice how in the example above we drop articles and pronouns and write in a note-taking style. Write just enough to convey to yourself what you need to be able to follow during the actual writing of your essay. Once you have the outline down on paper, writing the essay becomes simply a job of polishing language and ideas, rather than creating them from scratch.

The ACT Writing Test

Step 4. Write the essay. (15 minutes)

Writing the essay consists of following your outline and plugging in what's missing. Your outline should already contain a basic version of your thesis statement, one topic sentence for each of your three examples, and a conclusion statement that ties everything together. The final product will be about ten more sentences than what you've jotted down in your outline. So, all together your essay should be about fifteen to twenty sentences long.

As you write, keep these three facets of your essay in mind:

- Organization

- Development

- Clarity

Following your outline will make sure you stick to the Universal ACT Essay organization template. That means *organization* shouldn't be a problem.

As far as *development* goes, you should make sure that every sentence in the essay serves the greater goal of proving your thesis statement, as well as the more immediate purpose of building on the supporting examples you present in the introduction and in each example paragraph's topic sentence. You should also make sure that you are being *specific* with your examples: give dates, describe events in detail, and so on.

By *clarity*, we mean the simplicity of the language that you use. That involves spelling and grammar, but it also means focussing on varying sentence length and structure, as well as including a few well-placed vocabulary words that you definitely know how to use correctly.

Do not break from your outline. Never pause for a digression or drop in a fact or detail that's not entirely relevant to your essay's thesis statement. You're serving fast food, and fast food always sticks to the core ingredients and the universal recipe.

If You Run Out of Time: If you're running out of time before finishing the introduction, all three example paragraphs, and the conclusion, there's still hope. Here's what you should do: Drop one of your example paragraphs. You can still get a decent score, possibly a 4 or 5, with just two. Three examples is definitely the strongest and safest way to go, but if you just can't get three, take your two best examples and go with them. Just be sure to include an introduction and a conclusion in every ACT essay.

The Finished Essay: Our Example: Here is an example of a complete ACT essay. It's based strictly on the outline we built in Step 3 of our Five Steps to a "6" with a focus on clear simple language and the occasional drop of special sauce.

> Learning the lessons taught by failure is a sure route to success. The United States of America can be seen as a success that emerged from failure: by learning from the

weaknesses of the *Articles of Confederation*, the founding fathers were able to create the *Constitution*, the document on which America is built. Google Inc., the popular Internet search engine, is another example of a success that arose from learning from failure, though in this case Google learned from the failures of its competitors. Another example that shows how success can arise from failure is the story of Rod Johnson, who started a recruiting firm that rose out of the ashes of Johnson's personal experience of being laid off.

The United States, the first great democracy of the modern world, is also one of the best examples of a success achieved by studying and learning from earlier failures. After just five years of living under the Articles of Confederation, which established the United States of America as a single country for the first time, the states realized that they needed a new document and a stronger government. In 1786, the Annapolis convention was convened. The result, three years later, was the Constitution, which created a more powerful central government while also maintaining the integrity of the states. By learning from the failure of the Articles, the founding fathers created the pivotal document of a country that has become both the most powerful country in the world and a beacon of democracy.

Unlike the United States, which had its fair share of ups and downs over the years, the Internet search engine company, Google, has suffered few setbacks since it went into business in the late 1990s. Google has succeeded by studying the failures of other companies in order to help it innovate its technology and business model. Google identified and solved the problem of assessing the quality of results by using the number of links pointing to a page as an indicator of the number of people who find the page valuable. Suddenly, Google's results became far more accurate and reliable than those from other companies, and now Google's dominance in the field of Internet search is almost absolute.

The example of Rod Johnson's success also show how effective learning from mistakes and failure can be. Rather than accept his failure after being laid off, Johnson decided to study it. After a month of research, Johnson realized that his failure to find a new job resulted primarily from the inefficiency of the local job placement agencies, not from his own deficiencies. A month later, Johnson created Johnson Staffing to correct this weakness in the job placement sector. Today Johnson Staffing is the largest job placement agency in South Carolina, and is in the process of expanding into a national corporation.

Failure is often seen as embarrassing, something to be denied and hidden. But as the examples of the *U.S. Constitution*, Google, and Rod Johnson prove, if an individual, organization, or even a nation is strong enough to face and study its failure, then that failure can become a powerful teacher. The examples of history and business demonstrate that failure can be the best catalyst of success, but only if people have the courage to face it head on.

In the Practice Essay section at the end of this chapter, we'll provide analysis to explain more fully why we think this essay deserves a "6." For now, it's time to move on to the final step of our Five Steps to a "6"—proofing your essay.

Step 5. Proof your essay. (3 minutes)

Proofing your essay means reading through your finished essay to correct mistakes or to clear up words that are difficult to read. If you don't have three minutes after you've finished writing the essay (Step 4), spend whatever time you do have left proofing. Read over your essay and search for rough writing, bad transitions, grammatical errors, repetitive sentence structure, and all that special sauce stuff. You should also be on the lookout for instances in which bad handwriting makes it look as if you've made a grammatical or spelling mistake.

If you're running out of time and you have to skip a step, proofing is the step to drop. Proofing is important, but it's the only one of the Five Steps to a "6" that isn't absolutely crucial.

A Sample ACT Essay—Up Close

Here's the sample prompt again:

> Many successful adults recall a time in their life when they were considered a failure at one pursuit or another. Some of these people feel strongly that their previous failures taught them valuable lessons and led to their later successes. Others maintain that they went on to achieve success for entirely different reasons. In your opinion, can failure lead to success? Or is failure simply its own experience?

> Assignment:

> In your essay, take a position on this question. You may write about either one of the two points of view given, or you may present a different point of view on this question. Use specific reasons and examples to support your position.

Below is our example of the "6" essay. As you read, note that we have marked certain sentences and paragraphs to illustrate where and how the essay abides by our Universal ACT Essay Template.

A "6" Essay

Learning the lessons taught by failure is a sure route to success. (THESIS STATEMENT) The United States of America can be seen as a success that emerged from failure: by learning from the weaknesses of the *Articles of Confederation*, the founding fathers were able to create the *Constitution*, the document on which America is built. (BEST SUPPORTING EXAMPLE [#1]) Google Inc., the popular Internet search engine, is another example of a success that arose from learning from failure, though in this case Google learned from the failures of its competitors. (NEXT BEST SUPPORTING EXAMPLE [#2]) Another example that shows how success can arise from failure is the story of Rod Johnson, who started a recruiting firm that rose out of the ashes of Johnson's personal experience of being laid off. (NEXT BEST SUPPORTING EXAMPLE [#3])

The United States, the first great democracy of the modern world, is also one of the best examples of a success achieved by studying and learning from earlier failures. (TOPIC SENTENCE FOR EXAMPLE #1) After just five years of living under the Articles of Confederation, which established the United States of America as a single country for the first time, the states realized that they needed a new document and a stronger government. In 1786, the Annapolis convention was convened. The result, three years later, was the

Constitution, which created a more powerful central government while also maintaining the integrity of the states. By learning from the failure of the Articles, the founding fathers created the pivotal document of a country that has become both the most powerful country in the world and a beacon of democracy. (FOUR DEVELOPMENT SENTENCES TO SUPPORT EXAMPLE #1)

Unlike the United States, which had its fair share of ups and downs over the years, the Internet search engine company, Google Inc., has suffered few setbacks since it went into business in the late 1990s. (TOPIC SENTENCE FOR EXAMPLE #2) Google has succeeded by studying the failures of other companies in order to help it innovate its technology and business model. Google identified and solved the problem of assessing the quality of search results by using the number of links pointing to a page as an indicator of the number of people who find the page valuable. Suddenly, Google's search results became far more accurate and reliable than those from other companies, and now Google's dominance in the field of Internet search is almost absolute. (THREE DEVELOPMENT SENTENCES TO SUPPORT EXAMPLE #2)

The example of Rod Johnson's success as an entrepreneur in the recruiting field also shows how effective learning from mistakes and failure can be. (TOPIC SENTENCE FOR EXAMPLE #3) Rather than accept his failure after being laid off, Johnson decided to study it. After a month of research, Johnson realized that his failure to find a new job resulted primarily from the inefficiency of the local job placement agencies, not from his own deficiencies. A month later, Johnson created Johnson Staffing to correct this weakness in the job placement sector. Today Johnson Staffing is the largest job placement agency in South Carolina, and is in the process of expanding into a national corporation. (FOUR DEVELOPMENT SENTENCES TO SUPPORT EXAMPLE #3)

Failure is often seen as embarrassing, something to be denied and hidden. But as the examples of the *U.S. Constitution* , Google, and Rod Johnson prove, if an individual, organization, or even a nation is strong enough to face and study its failure, then that failure can become a powerful teacher. (THESIS STATEMENT REPHRASED IN BROADER WAY THAT PUSHES IT FURTHER) The examples of history and business demonstrate that failure can be the best catalyst of success, but only if people have the courage to face it head on.

Why This Essay Deserves a "6"

First, we need to assess whether this essay contains the four essential ingredients of a great ACT essay. Here they are, just to refresh your memory:

1. **Positioning.** The strength and clarity of the position on the given topic

2. **Examples.** The relevance and development of the examples used to support your argument

3. **Organization.** The organization of each paragraph and of the essay overall

4. **Command of Language.** Sentence construction, grammar, and word choice

This essay serves up all four ACT essay ingredients. It takes a strong and clear stance on the topic in the first sentence and sticks to it from start to finish. It uses three examples from a diverse array of disciplines—Internet technology to history and politics to a profile of an entrepreneur—and it never veers from using these examples to support the thesis statement's position. The organization of the essay follows our Universal ACT Essay Template perfectly, both at the paragraph level (topic sentences and development sentences) and at the overall essay level (intro, three meaty example paragraphs, a strong conclusion). The command of language remains solid throughout. The writer does not take risks with unfamiliar vocabulary but instead chooses a few out of the ordinary words like *beacon*, *deficiencies*, and *innovate* that spread just the right amount of special sauce throughout the essay. Sentence structure varies often, making the entire essay more interesting and engaging to the rater. Finally, no significant grammar errors disrupt the overall excellence of this ACT essay.

Here's a quick-reference chart that takes a closer look at this "6" essay based on the ACT's evaluation criteria for raters and based on our Universal ACT Essay Template.

ACT CRITERIA FOR "6" ESSAYS	YES OR NO?
Takes and articulates a perspective on an issue	YES
Maintains a clear focus on the perspective throughout the essay	YES
Explains a position by using supportive evidence and logical reasoning	YES
Organizes ideas logically	YES
Communicates clearly in writing	YES
OUR UNIVERSAL ACT ESSAY TEMPLATE CRITERIA	**YES OR NO?**
Thesis statement in first sentence of paragraph 1	YES
Three examples listed in paragraph 1 in order from best to worst	YES
Topic Sentence for example in Paragraph 2	YES
3-4 development sentences to support Paragraph 2's example	YES
Topic Sentence for example in Paragraph 3	YES
3-4 development sentences to support Paragraph 3's example	YES
Topic Sentence for example in Paragraph 4	YES
3-4 development sentences to support Paragraph 4's example	YES
Conclusion paragraph contains rephrased thesis statement	YES
About 15 sentences total	YES

The ACT Writing Test

ACT Math Review

The ACT Math Test

On the ACT Math Test, you are given 60 minutes to answer 60 questions. In terms of time allotted per question, the Math Test ranks the highest among the subject tests, averaging one minute per question. The drawback is that the Math Test is relatively difficult for most people. It tests you on knowledge that you've *learned*, not just intuited.

The Math Test covers the material taught in your middle school and high school math classes. Those classes covered a lot of ground, and in order to do well on this test, you have to have a good fundamental grasp of all of those topics.

Instructions for the Math Test

You should memorize the instructions for the Math Test before you arrive at the test center. These instructions are long, and you should not waste a second even glancing in their direction on test day. So here they are—get to know them:

> After solving each problem, pick the correct answer from the five given and fill in the corresponding oval on your answer sheet. Solve as many problems as you can in the time allowed. Do not worry over problems that take too much time; skip them if necessary and return to them if you have time.
>
> Calculator use is permitted on the test. Calculators can be used for any problem on the test, though calculators may be more harm than help for some questions.
>
> Note: unless otherwise stated on the test, you should assume that:

1.   Figures accompanying questions are not drawn to scale.

2.   Geometric figures exist in a plane.

3.   When given in a question, "line" refers to a straight line.

4.   When given in a question, "average" refers to the arithmetic mean.

The Format of the Math Test

The format of the ACT Math Test is straightforward. ACT simply lumps all the problems into one big list of math questions. The only visible quirk in formatting is that all the questions are printed in the left half of the page, while the right half is reserved for "your figuring." We'll discuss this empty space and what you should do with it in the Strategies section of this chapter. There are two other aspects of Math Test questions that you should keep in mind. We'll describe them to you below.

Five, Not Four, Multiple Choice Answers

Unlike the three other ACT Subject Tests, the Math Test offers you five, not four, multiple choice answers. You should be aware of this fact when filling in the bubbles on the answer sheet. If you are answering choices D or J, don't automatically fill in the last bubble in the row because you'll really be filling in E or K. Again, this is just another reason to verbalize to yourself which blank you want to be filling in as you actually fill it in.

Guessing with the Extra Answer Choice

The additional answer choice will also affect your chances of guessing the right answer. If you plan to guess blindly on a math problem, your odds of getting the correct answer are one in five, or 20 percent. On the other Subject Tests, your chances are higher: one in four, or 25 percent. This difference of 5 percent really isn't that big of a deal and shouldn't change your guessing strategy. You should still guess on any question you can't answer. Guess blindly if you have no clue about how to answer the question. But your best bet is always to eliminate whatever answer choices you can and then guess.

Question Types: Basic Problems and Word Problems

There are two kinds of questions on the ACT Math Test: basic problems and word problems. Word problems tend to be more difficult than basic problems simply because they require the additional step of translating the words into a numerical problem that you can solve. Of course, a basic problem on a complex topic will still likely be more difficult for you than a word problem on a very easy topic.

Basic Problems

Basic math problems are exactly how they sound: basic. You won't see any complicated wording or context in these problems. They simply present you with a math problem in a no-frills fashion. If you encounter a basic math problem that asks you to calculate what two plus two is (you won't), the question would look like this:

$2 + 2 = ?$

That's pretty straightforward; you shouldn't have a problem figuring out what this question wants you to do.

Word Problems

Word problems are so named because they use words to describe a math problem. These questions are by nature more complicated than basic math problems because you have to sort through the words to figure out the math problem beneath them. In essence, you have two steps: figuring out what the math problem is and then solving it.

For example, if you were asked for the same calculation of two plus two as a word problem, it might look something like this:

Jane has two green marbles, and Beth has two red marbles. Together, how many marbles do Jane and Beth have?

This question isn't exactly complicated, but it is certainly more complicated than the basic version of the problem. The setting of the problem, rather than elucidating the question, only adds to its complexity. Your job on this and all word problems is to sort through the muck and translate the words into a straightforward math problem. A question like "Together, how many marbles do Jane and Beth have?" really means "Jane's marbles plus Beth's marbles equals what?" or ultimately "Two plus two equals what?"

The Content of the Math Test

The ACT Math Test covers a broad array of topics, from simple topics like pre-algebra to more difficult ones such as trigonometry. You shouldn't assume that the pre-algebra questions will be a thousand times easier than the trig questions, though. To compensate for their relative difficulty, ACT usually uses the basic format to ask you questions on trig. Pre-algebra questions, on the other hand, run the gamut of difficulty, so don't slight them in your math review.

Below, we'll run through the entire content of the ACT Math Test, listing topics according to mathematical subject area. We won't bother describing the topics here because the majority of this section is devoted to reviewing all the concepts in depth. Don't panic about the length of this list: its length actually benefits you. Because the Math Test covers many topics, it can't devote more than one or two questions to most of them. So if you completely blank on the rules for perpendicular lines, you won't lose a significant number of points—especially if you guess well.

Pre-Algebra		**Coordinate Geometry**	
1.	Number Problems	1.	Number Lines & Inequalities
2.	Multiples, Factors, & Primes	2.	The (x, y) Coordinate Plane
3.	Divisibility and Remainders	3.	Distance and Midpoints
4.	Percentages	4.	Slope
5.	Ratios and Proportions	5.	Parallel & Perpendicular Lines
6.	Mean, Median, & Mode	6.	Graphing Equations
7.	Probability	7.	Conic Sections
8.	Absolute Value	**Plane Geometry**	
9.	Exponents and Roots	1.	Angles
10.	Series	2.	Triangles
Elementary Algebra		3.	Polygons
1.	Substitution	4.	Circles
2.	Simplifying Algebraic Expressions	5.	Simple 3-D Geometry
3.	Writing Expressions & Equations	**Trigonometry**	
4.	Solving Linear Equations	1.	SOHCAHTOA
5.	Multiplying Binomials	2.	Solving Triangles
6.	Inequalities	3.	Trigonometric Identities
Intermediate Algebra		4.	Trigonometric Graphs
1.	Solving & Factoring Quadratic Equations		
2.	Solving Systems of Equations		
3.	Relationship between Sides of an Equation		
4.	Functions		
5.	Matrices		
6.	Logarithms		

Also, note that this list covers all the topics that *could*, not all the topics that *will* appear. A number of these topics will not appear on the ACT you take. That doesn't mean you shouldn't review, but it does mean that you shouldn't worry. As part of our review of ACT Math, which takes up the last two thirds of this section, we will tell you which topics appear often and which pop up only occasionally.

The ACT Math Test

Strategies for the Math Test

Chapter Contents

THE MOST IMPORTANT STRATEGY FOR doing well on the ACT Math Test is to give yourself a good deal of time to review math. In this section, we will help you to approach the Math Test, but you should not think of the strategies and methods we provide as substitutions for knowledge of math. They are meant to augment your understanding of math. Good strategies can help you put your knowledge of math and the ACT format to the best possible use. They can't replace knowledge of math.

We're not trying to discourage you. We're just trying to warn you that you really do need to review your math if you want to do well on this Subject Test. Even if you're dominating your math class this year, you'll benefit from a full review because the material covered on this test is quite broad and can reach back to the math you studied in seventh grade. Those subjects aren't hard, but they may cover minor details that you've forgotten—and which could be important on the test.

With that gentle warning in mind, you can peruse the following Strategies section for really helpful tips for taking the test. Reading and understanding these tips alone isn't going to get you a perfect score on the test, but applying them along with your math skills will definitely help you achieve your target score.

On the Math Test, a D+ Is a Pretty Good Grade

On a normal test for your high school math class, if you get two-thirds of the questions right, you'll receive something like a D-plus—not exactly a parent-impressing grade. But if you get two-thirds of the questions right on the ACT, you'll likely end up with a Math score of 24 or 25, scoring several points higher than the average test taker. Not too shabby.

Use Your Calculator Wisely

Just because calculator use is permitted on the Math Test doesn't mean you should go calculator crazy. Calculators can certainly be helpful on some problems, but on others using a calculator might actually take more time than working the problem out by hand.

Sometimes the ACT will hint that you should stay away from the calculator. You can find this hint in the answer choices. If a fraction problem gives all the answers in fraction, not decimal, form, you should not use your calculator. You'll only be wasting time converting your decimal answer to fraction form. This rule also applies to problems involving radicals, or any other answer where the answer is not worked out to some final number. There's no reason ever to touch a calculator when you're dealing with variables.

When you use your calculator on the test, it should be because you've thought about the question, you have a good sense of how to proceed, and you see how your calculator can help you. You should only use your calculator when you have a definite operation you want to perform. You should not reach for your calculator instinctively any time you run into trouble.

Questions on the ACT are designed to be answered within a minute, if that. They do not involve intense calculation. If you find yourself reaching for a calculator to work out $\sqrt{934}$, you can be certain that you've made a mistake somewhere. No calculation on the test should be that difficult.

Use the Same Old Calculator (and Make Sure the Battery Is New)

Don't purchase a fancy calculator with 500 buttons and 600 functions for the ACT. If that's the kind of calculator you always use and you feel comfortable using it, then go ahead and bring it to the test. But if you use the basic standby, you should bring that to the test.

The ACT test center is not the place to break in a new calculator, particularly if it's one with a lot of buttons. By the time you've figured out how to turn the stupid thing on and find all the buttons, the Math Test will be over.

Now imagine for a moment that we are a nosy parent. Make sure your battery is new! This advice may seem anal, but do you really want to be the person whose battery fails halfway through the test?

Encourage Your Inner Artist

ACT wants to bring out the artist in you, and we think they've got the right idea. On the right-hand side of every Math Test page, you will find a column with the header "DO YOUR FIGURING HERE." You can use this space to write formulas, graphs, drawings of triangles, or whatever else you want.

This space can be particularly useful for drawing figures that are not provided with the question. If you have a hard time visualizing shapes in your head, you can draw them in the figuring space. If a question asks you about angles in a polygon but doesn't provide a figure, you can make your own if it helps you solve the problem.

While writing out your answers can be extremely helpful, it can also be time consuming. Be careful not to write out all your work, if some of that work is merely aesthetic. Remember, no one will see your test booklet, and only the bubble answers count. Don't bother being neat or thorough in this scribble space. You should not do work as if you're trying to impress your teacher. You should do just as much work as you need to do in order to get the question right: no more, no less.

Avoid Partial Answers

For problems that have more than one step, a partial answer is the answer to one of the steps of the problem, but not to the whole problem. For example,

> On Monday, a bus carries ten girls and five boys. On Tuesday, it carries five girls and six boys. What is the average number of girls and boys on the bus over the period of Monday and Tuesday?
>
> **A.** 0
> **B.** 11
> **C.** 13
> **D.** 15
> **E.** 26

The correct answer to this question is **C**, 13 girls and boys, but you may have liked choices **B**, **D**, or **E**, which are all partial answers to this problem (choice A is just silly). Here's why you might have chosen **B**, **D**, or **E**: choice **B** is the total number of passengers on the Tuesday bus; choice **D** is the total number of passengers on the Monday bus; choice **E** is the total number of passengers riding for both days. You have to calculate each one of these numbers to get the final answer (choice **E** divided by the number of days, 2). At any point during those calculations, you may have looked down and seen that a number you had calculated matched a number in the answer choices. Then you may have assumed you found the right answer. But, no, you didn't.

Partial answers love to prey upon eager test takers who are in a hurry to get the right answer. Instead of paying careful attention to the question, these test takers get a number, see it in the answer choices, and immediately identify it as the correct answer. ACT knows about all these eager, jumpy test takers, and deliberately plants partial answers throughout the Math Test.

On word problems, the last sentence of the problem usually tells you what the question is looking for. Consider rereading this last sentence once you've formulated your answer to make sure you did what the question asked.

Order of Difficulty and the Math Test

Knowing the order of difficulty will help you shape your approach to the test. ACT claims that the Math Test is ordered roughly by increasing difficulty. We want to emphasize the adverb "roughly" so you will not be surprised to find an easy question near the end of the test or a difficult one near the beginning.

You should pace yourself according to the knowledge that an early problem on the test will be easier than a problem late in the test. With 60 minutes to solve 60 problems, you might be thinking that you should allot a minute for each problem. But easy problems should take you less than a minute to solve, while solving a difficult problem can be time-consuming. If you find yourself spending too much time on a problem early in the test, skip it and come back to it later.

That said, you should not rush through the early problems on the test to save time for the problems near the end. Remember that all questions on the ACT are worth the same to the scoring machine, so you should set a pace that allows you to answer the early problems carefully without sacrificing speed.

Approaching Math Questions

The best way to approach a math question is to initially ignore the answer choices and to come up with your own answer using the information provided in the question. By formulating an answer on your own, you can avoid being influenced in the wrong direction by incorrect but appealing answer choices.

Here's the process for answering questions:

1. Read the question without paying attention to the answer choices.

2. Make sure you understand what the question is asking, and have a plan for finding the answer.

3. Answer the question as if there were no answer choices.

4. Match your answer to the answer choices given.

5. Fill in the appropriate bubble on the answer sheet.

Following this method simply insures that you will actively engage with each problem. When you write essays, teachers often tell you to write an outline first, since a quick outline can help you organize your thoughts and actually save you time by letting you see where you need to go. Think of this method as providing you with a tiny outline for each math question. When you read the question and take a moment to make sure you know what it's asking, you are building in your head an outline of how to solve it. In the long run, this will cut down on wrong paths and dead ends, and save you time.

Going to the Answer Choices

We've told you not to look at the answers. Now we're going to amend that advice: you shouldn't look at the answers unless you've taken the time to try to understand a question, and you've come to the conclusion that going to the answers and using them to try to answer the question is your best strategy. There are two reasons why you might come to this decision:

1. You think plugging in the answer choices is the best tactic for approaching the question.

2. You're not sure exactly how to answer the question, and you think you can either eliminate all the wrong answers—or at least some of them—by working with the answer choices.

Whatever your reason, make sure you approach the answer choices critically and strategically. Don't let them influence you. Try to see how you can use them.

Take the following example:

A classroom contains 31 chairs, some of which have arms and some of which do not. If the room contains 5 more armchairs than chairs without arms, how many armchairs does it contain?

A. 10
B. 13
C. 16
D. 18
E. 21

Given this question, you could build the equations:

$$\text{total chairs } (31) = \text{armchairs } (x) + \text{normal chairs } (y)$$
$$\text{normal chairs } (y) = \text{armchairs } (x) - 5$$

Then, since $y = x - 5$ you can make the equation:

$$31 = x + (x - 5)$$
$$31 = 2x - 5$$
$$36 = 2x$$
$$x = 18$$

There are 18 armchairs in the classroom.

This approach of building and working out the equations will produce the right answer, but it takes a long time! What if you strategically plugged in the answer choices instead? Since the numbers ascend in value, let's choose the one in the middle: **C**, 16. This is a smart strategic move because if we plug in 16 and discover that it is too small a number to satisfy the equation, we can eliminate **A** and **B** along with **C**. Alternatively, if 16 is too big, we can eliminate **D** and **E** along with **C**.

So our strategy is in place. Now let's work it out. If you have 16 armchairs, then you would have 11 normal chairs and the room would contain 27 total chairs. We needed the total numbers of chairs to equal 31, so clearly **C** is not the right answer. But because the total number of chairs was too few, you can also eliminate **A** and **B**, the answer choices with smaller numbers of armchairs. If you then plug in **D**, 18, you have 13 normal chairs and 31 total chairs. There's your answer.

In this instance, plugging in the answers takes less time, and, in general, just seems easier. Notice that the last sentence began with the words "in this instance." Working backward and plugging in is not always the best method. For some questions, it won't be possible to work backward at all. For the test, you will need to build up a sense of when working backward can most help you. A good rule of thumb for deciding whether to work backward is:

- Work backward when the question describes an equation of some sort, and the answer choices are all simple numbers.

If the answer choices contain variables, working backward will often be quite difficult—more difficult than working out the problem would be. If the answer choices are complicated, with hard fractions or radicals, plugging in might prove so complex that it's a waste of time.

Math Questions and Time

As we've just discussed, there are often several ways to answer an ACT math question. You can use trial and error; you can set up and solve an equation; and, for some questions, you might be able to answer the question quickly, intuitively, and elegantly, if you can just spot how. These different approaches to answering questions vary in the amount of time they take. Trial and error generally takes the longest, while the flash-of-intuition method either happens very quickly or not at all.

Take, for example, the following problem:

> Which has a greater area, a square with sides measuring 4 cm, or a circle with a radius of the same length?

The obvious way to solve this problem is simply to plug 4 into the formula for the area of a square and the area of a circle. Let's do it: the area of a square is equal to s^2, so the area of this square = $4^2 = 16$. The area of a circle is equal to πr^2, and the area of this circle must therefore be $\pi \times 4^2 = 16\pi$. Since 16π is obviously bigger than 16, the circle must be bigger. That worked nicely. But a faster approach would have been to draw a quick to-scale diagram with the square and circle superimposed.

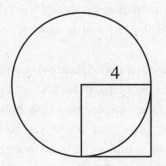

An even quicker way would have been to understand the equations of area for a square and a circle so well that it was just *obvious* that the circle was bigger, since the equation for the circle will square the radius and multiply it by π, whereas the equation for the square will only square the radius.

While you may not be able to become a math whiz and just *know* the answer, you can learn to look for a quicker route, such as choosing to draw a diagram instead of working out the equation. As with the example above, a quicker route is not necessarily a less accurate one. Making such choices comes down to practice, an awareness that those other routes are out there, and basic mathematical ability.

The value of timesaving strategies is obvious: less time spent on some questions allows you to devote more time to difficult problems. It is this issue of time that separates the students who ace the math section from those who merely do well.

Whether or not the ability to find accurate shortcuts is an actual measure of mathematical prowess is not for us to say (though we can think of arguments on either side), but the ability to find those shortcuts absolutely matters on this test.

Shortcuts Are Really Math Intuition

So we've told you all about shortcuts, but now we're going to give you some advice that might seem strange: you shouldn't go into every question searching for a shortcut. If you have to search and search for a shortcut, it might end up taking longer than the normal route. Instead of instructing you always to seek out math shortcuts, then, we just want to advise you not to get so focused and frantic about getting a question right that you miss the possibility that a shortcut exists. If you go into each question knowing there might be a shortcut and keep your mind open as you think about the question, you will find the shortcuts you need.

To some extent, you can teach yourself to recognize when a question might contain a shortcut through practice. For example, simply from the problem above, you know that there will probably be a shortcut for all those questions that give you the dimensions of two shapes and ask you to compare them: you can just draw a diagram. A frantic test taker would see the information given and then rush to the simplest route and work out the equations. But if you are a little calmer, you can see that drawing a diagram is the best idea.

Finally, the fact that we advocate using shortcuts doesn't mean you shouldn't focus on learning how to work out a problem. In fact, we can guarantee that you're not going to find a shortcut for a problem *unless* you know how to work it out the long way. After all, a shortcut is just you using your knowledge to see a faster way to answer the question. To put it another way, while we've been using the term "math shortcut," we could just as easily have used the term "math intuition." If you don't have that knowledge base from which to work, you're not going to have anything on which to base your intuition. In contrast, you might be able to figure out an answer by trial and error even if you don't see exactly how to solve the problem.

Strategy = Target Score

Your strategy in the Math Test, and particularly the extent of your efforts to find shortcuts, should be based on your target score. If you're looking to get a 23 or lower on the Math Test, there simply is no need to go looking for shortcuts. You can get a 23, or even a 25 or 26, without answering a large number of questions, so there's no need to race through the test. You should focus on getting questions right. Of course, you should remain aware that shortcuts exist and use them when you see them, but don't get upset or worried if you're not unearthing a shortcut in every other question.

Students looking to score a 27 or above on the Math Test, though, should *not* be working out every question. Finding quicker ways to answer questions must be part of your strategy, because only through these faster methods will you give yourself the time to get to and answer the last few difficult questions that can make all the difference. On these last few questions, even the best students might very well have to plow their way through using trial and error, and trial and error takes a bit of time. So you must give yourself that time by moving quickly through the earlier stages of the test.

Be wary: this advice does *not* imply that you should simply work faster; it says that you should look for the shorter but *just as accurate* route to the answer. Do not sacrifice accuracy for speed. If you can find the short but accurate route, great! But if you can't do both, it's always better to answer correctly than to answer quickly.

ACT Math Subjects

Chapter Contents

T HE ACT MATH SUBJECT TEST seeks to evaluate your knowledge of the math taught in high school. Questions can range across the following broad topics:

1. Pre-Algebra

2. Elementary Algebra

3. Intermediate Algebra

4. Coordinate Geometry

5. Plane Geometry

6. Trigonometry

This chapter provides a review of each of these six categories. We will explain the math concepts and rules on the ACT tests, and we'll also discuss *how* the ACT will likely test these topics.

Pre-Review Review

Before diving into the math on the ACT tests, we very quickly want to review the math the ACT assumes you know. The ACT will not explicitly ask questions on these topics, but since the test writers assume that you know them, many questions will indirectly test them.

Order of Operations

You must know the order of operations for the test. The best way to remember which operation gets performed before another is the acronym PEMDAS, which stands for:

Parentheses
Exponents
Multiplication
Division
Addition
Subtraction

If you come across an equation that contains all of these elements, you should first carry out the math within the parentheses, then work out the exponents, then do the multiplication and the division (working from left to right), and finally the addition and subtraction, again working from left to right. For example, take the expression:

$$\frac{(18 - 3) \times 2^2}{5} - 7 + (6 \times 3 - 1)$$

You would first work out the math in the parentheses (following PEMDAS even within the parentheses, meaning you should do multiplication before subtraction):

$$\frac{15 \times 2^2}{5} - 7 + 17$$

Then work out the exponents:

$$\frac{15 \times 4}{5} - 7 + 17$$

Then do the multiplication:

$$\frac{60}{5} - 7 + 17$$

Then the division:

$$12 - 7 + 17$$

Then the addition and subtraction:

Odd and Even Numbers

You should know about odd and even numbers and the difference between them. For this topic, however, we will provide a very quick review.

Even Numbers

Even numbers are numbers that are divisible by 2 with no remainder. Remember that 0 is included in this definition.

$$\ldots, -6, -4, -2, 0, 2, 4, 6, \ldots$$

Odd Numbers

Odd numbers are numbers that, if divided by 2, will leave a remainder of 1.

$$\ldots, -5, -3, -1, 1, 3, 5, \ldots$$

Operations and Odd and Even Numbers

There are a number of rules regarding operations and odd and even numbers that you should know instinctively.

Addition		
+	**Odd**	**Even**
Odd	Even	Odd
Even	Odd	Even

Subtraction		
−	**Odd**	**Even**
Odd	Even	Odd
Even	Odd	Even

Multiplication		
x	**Odd**	**Even**
Odd	Odd	Even
Even	Even	Even

Signed Numbers

The term "signed numbers" refers to numbers that include either a positive or negative sign, and are therefore marked as being either greater than zero (positive) or less than zero (negative). Zero has no sign.

Students who are comfortable with positive numbers sometimes get confused when dealing with negative numbers. For example, while positive numbers become larger as they move farther away from zero, negative numbers become smaller: –10 is a smaller number than –1. When dealing with negative numbers, be careful not just to see the 10 in –10 and assume that it is a larger number than –1.

Negative Numbers and Operations

Negative numbers behave differently than positive numbers when you perform the various operations on them. In terms of addition and subtraction, negative numbers invert the operations.

Adding Signed Numbers

When a negative number is added to another number, the sum will be a smaller number. In fact, adding a negative number is the same as subtracting a positive number of the same absolute value (see p. 146).

$$3 + (-2) = 1, \text{ just as } 3 - 2 = 1$$

Subtracting Signed Numbers

When a negative number is subtracted from another number, the difference will be a larger number. In fact, subtracting a negative number is the same as adding a positive number of the same value.

$$3 - (-2) = 5, \text{ just as } 3 + 2 = 5$$

Multiplying and Dividing with Negative Numbers

Negative numbers also follow sign rules when you multiply or divide them:

× or ÷	Positive	Negative
Positive	Positive	Negative
Negative	Negative	Positive

Pre-Algebra

The various pre-algebra topics are the most basic on the ACT Math Test. You probably covered much of this material in your middle school math classes. These topics are not conceptually difficult, but they do have some nuances you may have forgotten along the way. Also, since questions covering pre-algebra are often not that hard, you should make sure you review properly to get these questions right.

The topics in this section appear roughly in order of frequency on the Math Test. Number problems are usually the most common pre-algebra questions on the test, while series questions are usually the least common.

1. Number Problems

2. Multiples, Factors, and Primes

3. Divisibility and Remainders

4. Percentages, Fractions, and Decimals

5. Ratios and Proportions

6. Mean, Median, and Mode

7. Probability

8. Absolute Value

9. Exponents and Roots

10. Series

While "Multiples, Factors, and Primes" and "Divisibility and Remainders" do not explicitly appear too frequently on the test, the math behind them will help you answer number problems, so we've included them at the top of the list.

We mentioned that the above list is only roughly ordered by decreasing frequency. If it were in an exact order, percentages would share the top billing with number problems; because we wanted to keep related topics close together, we sacrificed a bit of precision.

Number Problems

On the ACT Math Test, number problems are word problems that ask you to manipulate numbers. The math in number problems is usually extremely simple. You are seldom asked to perform operations that are more complicated than basic addition, subtraction, multiplication, and division. Despite the simple operations, number problems can be confusing because of their wording and because of the multiple steps involved in answering them. Here's an example of a typical number problem on the Math Test:

> Train A travels at 90 miles per hour and covers 360 miles. Train B covers the same distance but travels at 60 miles per hour. How much longer does it take Train B than Train A to cover that distance?

The first step in answering these questions is to read carefully to make sure you know exactly what they are asking. Because of the time pressure of the test, some students feel as if the time taken to understand the question is wasted since they aren't actually doing any math. But taking a moment to ask yourself what the question is asking is *crucial*. Not only will you be more likely to get the question right if you take a moment to make sure you understand it, but that little bit of invested time will actually *save* you time later, since you will be able to proceed with an understanding of what you need to do.

The question above asks the difference in time it takes the two trains to cover the same distance. Your first step should be to figure out how long each train takes to travel 360 miles. Once you've done that, you can subtract the smaller number from the bigger number to get the difference in time.

The question gives you two pieces of information that will help you figure out the trains' times: the speed (miles per hour) and the distance (miles). If you divide the distance by the speed, you will cancel out the miles and end up with the hours:

$$\text{Time (hours)} = \frac{\text{distance (miles)}}{\text{speed (miles/hour)}}$$

Once you've done that, you'll see that Train A travels for 4 hours and Train B for 6 hours:

$$6 \text{ hours} - 4 \text{ hours} = 2 \text{ hours}$$

Multiples, Factors, and Primes

Multiples, factors, and primes appear quite frequently on the ACT Math Test. You will rarely see a non-word problem covering multiples, factors, and primes; this topic almost always appears in word problem form.

While these questions are relatively easy, they can be quite confusing simply because of the terminology they use. Below, we give you the definition for each of these three mathematical concepts.

Multiples

The multiple of a number is the product generated when that number is multiplied by an integer. The first five multiples of 7 are 7, 14, 21, 28, and 35 since $7 \times 1 = 7$, $7 \times 2 = 14$, $7 \times 3 = 21$, $7 \times 4 = 28$, and $7 \times 5 = 35$.

The Least Common Multiple

The least common multiple (LCM) is the name given to the lowest multiple that two particular numbers share. For example, the multiples of 6 and 8 are:

- **Multiples of 6:** 6, 12, 18, **24**, 30, 36, 42, **48**, 54, . . .

- **Multiples of 8:** 8, 16, **24**, 32, 40, **48**, 56, 64, 72, . . .

As the two lists show, 6 and 8 both have 24 and 48 as multiples (they also share many other multiples, such as 72, 96, etc.). Because 24 is the lowest in value of these shared multiples, it is the least common multiple of 6 and 8.

Being able to figure out the least common multiple of two numbers can prove quite handy on the ACT, especially for questions in which you have to add or subtract two fractions with unlike denominators (we'll explain when we talk about fractions).

Factors

A factor of a number is an integer that divides evenly into the number. For example, 6, 4, 3, and 2 are all factors of 12 because $12/6 = 2$, $12/4 = 3$, $12/3 = 4$, and $12/2 = 6$. Factors, then, are related to multiples. A given number is a multiple of all of its factors: 2 and 6 are factors of 12, so 12 is a multiple of both 2 and 6.

The Greatest Common Factor

The greatest common factor (GCF) of two numbers is the largest factor that the two numbers share. For example, the GCF of 18 and 24 is 6, since 6 is the largest number that is a factor of both 18 and 24.

Factorization

To find all the factors of a number, write them down in pairs, beginning with 1 and the number you're factoring. We'll factor 24 for this example. So, 1 and 24 are both factors of 24. Next, try every integer greater than 1 in increasing order. Here are the factor pairs we find for 24: 1 and 24, 2 and 12, 3 and 8, and 4 and 6.

You know you've found all the factors of a number when the increasing integer in each pair exceeds the decreasing integer. For example, after you found that 4 was a factor of 24 and 5 was not, you would see that 6, the next factor of 24, had already been included in a pair of factors. Thus, all the factors have been found.

As you might imagine, factoring a very large number can get pretty involved. But don't worry; that kind of extensive factoring won't be asked of you on the test.

Primes

A prime number is divisible by only 1 and itself (the number 1 itself is not considered prime). For example, 17 is prime because it is divisible by only 1 and 17. The first few primes, in increasing order, are:

$$2, 3, 5, 7, 11, 13, 17, 19, 23, 29, 31, 37, 41, 43, 47, 53, \ldots$$

Prime Factorization

Another form of factorization is called prime factorization. Prime factorization expresses an integer as the product of a series of prime numbers.

To find the prime factorization of a number, divide it and all of its factors until every integer remaining is prime. This group of prime numbers is the prime factorization of the original integer. Let's find the prime factorization of 36 as an example:

$$36 = 2 \times 18 = 2 \times 2 \times 9 = 2 \times 2 \times 3 \times 3$$

As you may already have noticed, there is more than one way to find the prime factorization of a number. We could have first resolved 36 into 6×6, for example, and then determined the prime factorization from there. So don't worry—you can't screw up. No matter which path you take, you will always get the same result—that is, as long as you do your arithmetic correctly.

Just for practice, let's find a couple more prime factorizations:

$$45 = 3 \times 15 = 3 \times 3 \times 5$$
$$41 = 1 \times 41$$

Since the only factors of 41 are 1 and 41, it is a prime number. In other words, 41 is its own prime factorization.

Relatively Prime Numbers

Two numbers are called relatively prime if they share no common prime factors (i.e., if their GCF is 1). This doesn't necessarily mean, however, that each number is itself prime. For instance, 8 and 15 are relatively prime, because they have no common primes in their prime factorizations ($8 = 2 \times 2 \times 2$ and $15 = 3 \times 5$), but neither number is prime. It is a good idea just to know the definition of relatively prime numbers, in case the concept pops up on the test somewhere.

Divisibility and Remainders

Divisibility and remainders are also popular subjects for pre-algebraic number problems on the ACT Math Test. As with multiples, factors, and primes, you will probably not see basic problems on divisibility and remainders, but the topic will appear in relatively complicated word problems.

A number (x) is divisible by another number (y) if, when x is divided by y, the answer is a whole number. For example, 6 is divisible by 3 because $6/3 = 2$, and 2 is a whole number. However, 6 is not divisible by 4, because $6/4 = 1\frac{2}{4}$, which is not a whole number. Another way of describing 6/4 is to say that you can make one complete division with a remainder of 2.

To check divisibility, it is always possible to do the division by hand and see whether the result is a whole number. However, if the number we are dividing is large, this becomes very difficult. There are some divisibility rules that make this task much easier—these rules allow us to determine whether a number is divisible by another number without having to carry out the division.

Divisibility Rules

1. All whole numbers are divisible by 1.

2. All numbers with a ones digit of 0, 2, 4, 6, and 8 are divisible by 2.

3. A number is divisible by 3 if its digits add up to a number divisible by 3. For example, 6,711 is divisible by 3 because $6 + 7 + 1 + 1 = 15$, and 15 is divisible by 3.

4. A number is divisible by 4 if its last two digits are divisible by 4. For example, 78,052 is divisible by 4 because 52 is divisible by 4. But 7,850 is not divisible by 4 because 50 is not divisible by 4.

5. A number is divisible by 5 if it ends in 0 or 5.

6. A number is divisible by 6 if it is even and also divisible by 3.

7. Sorry. There are no rules for 7.

8. A number is divisible by 8 if its last three digits are divisible by 8. For example, 905,256 is divisible by 8 because 256 is divisible by 8. But 74,513 is not divisible by 8 because 513 is not divisible by 8.

9. A number is divisible by 9 if its digits add up to a number divisible by 9. For example, 1,458 is divisible by 9 because $1 + 4 + 5 + 8 = 18$ and 18 is divisible by 9.

10. A number is divisible by 10 if it ends in 0.

Two Notes: (1) Because a number divided by itself always yields 1, a number is always divisible by itself. For example, 7 is divisible by 7, and 8,374 is divisible by 8,374. **(2)** No number is divisible by a number greater than itself.

Remainders

A remainder is the number that remains after x has been divided by y. If y divides evenly into x, the remainder of $x \div y$ is zero. A remainder will always be smaller than the number that is doing the dividing. For instance, if you divide 22 by 5, your answer is 4 with a remainder of 2.

Percentages, Fractions, and Decimals

Percentage problems appear frequently on the ACT Math Test. Because percentages are essentially fractions and decimals, our review of percentages will begin with a review of fractions and decimals. While questions dealing specifically with fractions and decimals *per se* are rare on the ACT Math Test, knowing more about them will aid your understanding of the more common questions about percentages.

Fractions

Although you may not see a fraction problem on the Math Test (or, at most, you'll see one or two), you should still review your knowledge of fractions, as they form the basis for percentages, a favorite topic of the ACT.

A fraction describes a part of a whole. The number on the bottom of the fraction is called the denominator, and it denotes how many equal parts the whole is divided into. The number on the top of the fraction is called the numerator, and it denotes how many of the parts we are taking. For example, the fraction ¾ denotes "three of four equal parts," 3 being the numerator and 4 being the denominator. You can also think of fractions as similar to division. In fact, ¾ has the same value as $3 \div 4$.

The ACT may indirectly test your ability to add, subtract, multiply, and divide fractions. Questions that deal more directly with fractions will probably test your ability to reduce and compare fractions.

Adding and Subtracting Fractions

There are two different types of fractions that you may have to add or subtract: those with the same denominator and those with different denominators.

If fractions have the same denominator, adding them is extremely easy. All you have to do is add up the numerators:

$$\frac{1}{20} + \frac{3}{20} + \frac{13}{20} = \frac{17}{20}$$

Subtraction works similarly. If the denominators of the fractions are equal, then you simply subtract one numerator from the other:

$$\frac{13}{20} - \frac{2}{20} = \frac{11}{20}$$

If the fractions do not have equal denominators, the process is somewhat more involved. The first step is to make the denominators the same. To set the denominators of two fractions as equal, find the least common denominator (LCD), which is simply the Least Common Multiple of the two denominators. For example, 18 is the LCD of $\frac{1}{6}$ and $\frac{4}{9}$, since 18 is the smallest multiple of both 6 and 9.

Setting the denominators of two fractions equal to one another is a two-step process. First, find the LCD. Second, write each fraction as an equivalent fraction with the LCD as the new denominator, remembering to multiply the numerator by the same multiple as the denominator. For example, if you wanted to add $\frac{5}{12}$ and $\frac{4}{9}$, you would do the following:

First, find the LCD:

1. Factor the denominators: $12 = 2 \times 2 \times 3$ and $9 = 3 \times 3$.

2. Find the LCM of the denominators: $2 \times 2 \times 3 \times 3 = 36$.

3. The LCD is 36.

Once you've found the LCD, write each fraction as an equivalent fraction with the LCD as the new denominator. Multiply the denominator of the first fraction by an integer to get the LCD. Multiply the numerator by the same integer.

$$\text{denominator} = 12 \times 3 = 36$$
$$\text{numerator} = 5 \times 3 = 15$$

The new first fraction is, therefore, $\frac{15}{36}$.

Multiply the denominator and numerator of the second fraction by an integer to get the LCD. Multiply the numerator by the same integer.

$$\text{denominator} = 9 \times 4 = 36$$
$$\text{numerator} = 4 \times 4 = 16$$

The new second fraction is, therefore, $\frac{16}{36}$.

Now that the fractions have the same denominator, you can quickly add the numerators to get the final answer: $15 + 16 = 31$, so the answer is $^{31}\!/\!_{36}$.

Multiplying Fractions

Multiplying fractions is quite easy. Simply multiply the numerators together and multiply the denominators together, as seen in the example below:

$$\frac{4}{5} \times \frac{2}{7} \times \frac{1}{3} = \frac{4 \times 2 \times 1}{5 \times 7 \times 3} = \frac{8}{105}$$

Dividing Fractions

Multiplication and division are inverse operations. It makes sense, then, that to perform division with fractions, all you have to do is invert (flip over) the dividing fraction and then multiply:

$$\frac{1}{4} \div \frac{5}{8} = \frac{1}{4} \times \frac{8}{5}$$

Note that just as multiplication by a fraction smaller than one results in a *smaller* product, division by a fraction smaller than one results in a *larger* product.

Reducing Fractions

If you encounter fractions involving large, unwieldy numbers, such as $^{18}\!/\!_{102}$, the best move is usually to see if the fraction can be reduced to smaller numbers.

The fastest way to simplify a fraction is to divide both the numerator and denominator by their greatest common factor. In the case of $^{18}\!/\!_{102}$, the GCF of 18 and 102 is 6, leaving you with $^{3}\!/\!_{17}$. With your knowledge of divisibility rules, you should be able to see that both the numerator and denominator are divisible by 6. Had you not immediately seen that 6 was the greatest common factor, you could have divided both numbers by 2 and gotten $^{9}\!/\!_{51}$. From there, it would have been pretty obvious that both the numerator and denominator are also divisible by 3, yielding $^{3}\!/\!_{17}$.

The ACT might also present you with variables in fraction form and ask you to reduce them. You can reduce these variable fractions as long as you can find like factors in both the numerator and denominator. For example, to reduce this fraction,

$$\frac{6x^2 + 2}{4x}$$

you merely have to notice that all of the terms in both the numerator and denominator contain 2 as a factor. Dividing 2 out of the fraction, you get:

$$\frac{3x^2 + 1}{2x}$$

Comparing Fractions

The rare fraction problem you see may ask you to compare two fractions. If either the denominators or the numerators of the two fractions are the same, that comparison is easy. For example, $\frac{8}{9}$ is obviously greater than $\frac{5}{9}$, just as $\frac{5}{9}$ is greater than $\frac{5}{17}$. Just remember, if the numerators are the same, the greater fraction is the one with the smaller denominator.

If the two fractions don't lend themselves to easy comparison, there is still a quick and easy method that will allow you to make the comparison: cross multiplication. To do this, multiply the numerator of each fraction by the denominator of the other. Write the product of each multiplication next to the numerator you used to calculate it. The greater product will be next to the greater fraction. For example:

$$32 = \frac{4}{7} \times \frac{5}{8} = 35$$

Since 35, the greater product, is written next to $\frac{5}{8}$, that is the greater fraction.

Decimals

Decimals are simply another way to express fractions. To get a decimal, divide the numerator of a fraction by the denominator. For example, if you take the fraction $\frac{2}{5}$ and divide 2 by 5, you get 0.4. Therefore the decimal 0.4 is equal to $\frac{2}{5}$.

Questions testing decimals almost never appear on the ACT. If decimal numbers do appear and you have to add, subtract, multiply, or divide them, the best thing to do is to use a calculator.

Percentages

Percentage problems always make an appearance on the ACT Math Test. You will probably see at least two per test. Percentages are just another way to talk about a specific type of fraction. Percent literally means "of 100." If you have 25% of all the money in the world, that means you have $\frac{25}{100}$ of the world's money.

Let's take the question "4 is what percent of 20?" This question presents you with a whole, 20, and then asks you to determine how much of that whole 4 represents in percentage form, which means "of 100." To come to the answer, you have to set up an equation that sets the fraction 4/20 equal to x/100:

$$\frac{4}{20} = \frac{x}{100}$$

If you then cross multiply to solve for x, you get $20x = 400$, meaning $x = 20$. Therefore, 4 is 20% of 20. You also might realize that instead of working out all this cross multiplication, you could simply do the following:

$$\frac{4}{20} \times 100 = 20$$

Important Percentage Terms

Percentage terminology can be a little tricky, so here is a short glossary of terms:

- **Percent more**: if one person has 50% more children than a second person, then that first person has the same amount as the second person, plus 50% of the amount the second person has.

- **Percent increase**: percent increase means the same thing as percent more. If the price of some item increases 10%, the new price is the original plus 10% of that original.

- **Percent decrease**: the opposite of percent increase. This term means you subtract the specified percent of the original value from that original.

Sometimes students see these terms and figure out what the 10% increase or decrease is, but then forget to carry out the necessary addition or subtraction. Here's a sample ACT percentage problem:

> A shirt originally cost $20, but during a sale its price was reduced by 15%. What is the current price of the shirt?
>
> A. $3
> B. $5
> C. $13
> D. $17
> E. $23

In this question, you are told the whole, $20, and the percentage, 15%, and you need to figure out the part. You can therefore quickly set up the equation (once you are comfortable with percentages you might be able to skip this step of setting up the equation and move straight to solving for x):

$$\frac{x}{20} = .15$$

You can find x by multiplying 20 by .15 to see what the change in price was:

$$x = 20 \times .15 = 3$$

Once you know the price change, you then need to subtract it from the original price, since the question asks for the reduced price of the shirt.

$$\$20 - \$3 = \$17$$

The answer is **D**. Notice that if you had only finished the first part of this solution and had looked at the answer choices, you might have seen that $3 hanging out at answer **A** like a big affirmation of correctness and been tempted into choosing it without finishing the question. You could also solve this problem in one step by realizing that if the sale price was 15% lower than the original, it was 85% of the original. Therefore, $0.85(\$20) = \$17$.

Double Percentages

Some ACT questions will ask you to determine a percent of a percent. Take this question:

The original price of a banana in a store is $2. During a sale, the store reduces the price by 25% and Joe buys the banana. Joe then meets his friend, Sam, who is almost faint with hunger. Seeing an opportunity, Joe raises the price of the banana 10% from the price at which he bought it, and sells it to Sam. How much does Sam pay?

In this question, you are asked to determine the cumulative effect of two percentage changes. The key to solving this type of problem is to realize that each percentage change is dependent on the last. In other words, you have to work out the effect of the first percentage change, come up with a value, and then use that value to determine the effect of the second percentage change.

In the problem asked above, you would first find 25% of the original price.

$$\frac{25}{100} \times \$2 = \frac{50}{100} = \$.50$$

Now subtract that $.50 from the original price.

$$\$2 - \$.5 = \$1.50$$

Then we find 10% of $1.50:

$$\frac{10}{100} \times \$1.50 = \frac{15}{100} = \$.15$$

Therefore, Sam buys the banana at a price of $1.50 + $.15 = $1.65.

When you are working on a percentage problem that involves a series of percentage changes, you should follow the same procedure you would for one single percentage change at each stage of the series. For the first percentage change, figure out what the whole is, calculate the percentage of the whole, and make sure to perform addition or subtraction, if necessary. Then take the new value and put it through these same steps for the second percentage change.

Ratios and Proportions

On the typical ACT Math Test, you'll see a couple of problems dealing with proportions or ratios.

Ratios

Ratios can look a lot like fractions, and they are related to fractions, but they differ in important ways. Whereas a fraction describes a part out of a whole, a ratio compares two separate parts of the same whole.

A ratio can be written in a variety of ways. Mathematically it can appear as 3/1 or as 3:1. In words, it should be written out as the ratio of three to one. Each of these three forms of this ratio means the same thing: there are three of one thing for every one of another. If you have three red marbles and one blue marble, then the ratio of red marbles to blue marbles is 3:1. For the ACT, you must remember that ratios compare parts to parts, rather than parts to a whole. For example:

> Of every 40 games a baseball team plays, it loses 12 games. What is the ratio of the team's losses to wins?
>
> **A.** 3:10
> **B.** 7:10
> **C.** 3:7
> **D.** 7:3
> **E.** 10:3

This ratio question is a little tricky because the information is stated in terms of whole to part, but the question asks for a part to part answer. The problem tells you that the team loses 12 of every 40 games, but it asks you for the ratio of losses to *wins*, not losses to *games*. So the first thing you have to figure out is how many times the team wins in 40 games:

$$40 - 12 = 28$$

The team wins 28 of every 40 games. So for every 12 losses, the team has 28 wins, or 12:28. You can reduce this ratio by dividing both sides by 4, to get 3 losses for every 7 wins, or 3:7. Answer **C** is correct. However, if you didn't realize that losses to games was part to whole, you might have just reduced the ratio 12:40 to 3:10, and then picked choice **A**.

Proportions

If you have a ratio of 3 red marbles to 1 blue marble, that doesn't necessarily mean that you have exactly 3 red marbles and 1 blue one. It could also mean that you have 6 red and 2 blue marbles, or that you have 240 red and 80 blue marbles. In other words, ratios compare only *relative* size. In order to determine how many of each color of marbles you actually have, you need to know how many total marbles you have in addition to knowing the ratio.

The ACT will occasionally ask questions testing your ability to figure out a quantity given the ratio between items and the total number of all the items. For example:

> You have red, blue, and green marbles in the ratio of 5:4:3, and you have a total of 36 marbles. How many blue marbles do you have?

The information given states that for each group of 5 red marbles, you have a corresponding group of 4 blue marbles and a group of 3 green marbles. The ratio therefore tells you that out of every 12 marbles (since 12 = 5 + 4 + 3), 4 of them will be blue. The question also tells you that you have 36 total marbles.

Since we know that the ratio will not change no matter how many marbles you have, we can solve this problem by setting up a proportion, which is an equation that states that two ratios are equal. In this case, we are going to equate 4:12 and x:36, with x being the number of blue marbles that we would have if we had 36 total marbles. To do math with proportions, it is most useful to set up the proportions in fraction form:

$$\frac{4}{12} = \frac{x}{36}$$

Now you just need to isolate x by cross-multiplying:

$$12x = 4 \times 36$$
$$12x = 144$$
$$x = 12$$

Mean, Median, and Mode

The arithmetic mean, median, and mode are all different ways to describe a group, or set, of numbers. On the ACT, you'll most likely see questions dealing with the arithmetic mean, but you should be prepared for median and mode questions as well.

Arithmetic Mean (a.k.a. Average)

The arithmetic mean, which is also called the average, is the most important and most commonly tested of these three mathematical concepts. The basic rules for finding an average are not very complicated. To find the average of a set of n numbers, you need to find the sum of all the numbers and divide that sum by n.

For example, the mean of the set 9, 8, 13, 10 is:

$$\frac{9 + 8 + 13 + 10}{4} = \frac{40}{4} = 10$$

Many ACT problems about mean will be straightforward, giving you a bunch of numbers and asking you to find their average. But some problems will be presented in a more roundabout fashion. For instance, the ACT might give you three numbers of a four-number set as well as the average of that set, and ask you to find the fourth number, like so:

> If the average of four numbers is 22, and three of the numbers are 7, 11, and 18, then what is the fourth number?

To solve this type of problem, you have to realize that if you know the average of a group, and also know how many numbers are in the group, you can calculate the sum of the numbers in the group. In the question asked above, you know that the average of the numbers is 22 and that there are four numbers. This means that the four numbers, when added together, must equal 4×22, which is 88. Now, from the information given in the problem and our own calculations, we know three of the four numbers in the set and the total sum of the numbers in the set:

$$7 + 11 + 18 + \text{unknown number} = 88$$

Solving for the unknown number is easy: all you have to do is subtract 7, 11, and 18 from 88 to get 52, which is the answer.

Median

The median is the number whose value is in the middle of the numbers in a particular set. Take the set 6, 19, 3, 11, 7. If we arrange the numbers in order of value, we get:

$$3, 6, 7, 11, 19$$

When we list the numbers in this way, it becomes clear that the middle number in this group is 7, making 7 the median.

The set we just looked at contained an odd number of items, but in a set with an even number of items it's impossible to isolate a single number as the median. Let's add one number to the set from the previous example:

$$3, 6, 7, 11, 15, 19$$

In this case, we find the median by taking the two numbers in the middle and finding their average. The two middle numbers in this set are 7 and 11, so the median of the set is $(7 + 11)/2 = 9$.

Mode

The mode is the number within a set that appears most frequently. In the set 10, 11, 13, 11, 20, the mode is 11 since that number appears twice and all the others appear just once. In a set where all the numbers appear an equal number of times, there is no mode.

Probability

A typical ACT Math Test asks one question on probability. To begin to deal with these questions, you first have to understand what probability is:

$$\frac{\text{chance of a particular outcome}}{\text{total number of possible outcomes}}$$

For example, let's say you're on a game show and are shown three doors. Behind one door there is a prize, while behind the other two doors sit big piles of nothing. The probability that you will choose the door with the prize is $1/3$, because out of the total three possibilities there is one chance to pick the lucrative door.

Here's an example of a probability question:

> Joe has 3 green marbles, 2 red marbles, and 5 blue marbles. If all the marbles are dropped into a dark bag, what is the probability that Joe will pick out a green marble?

There are three ways for Joe to pick a green marble (since there are three different green marbles), but there are 10 total possible outcomes (one for each marble in the bag). Therefore, the probability of picking a green marble is:

$$\text{Probability} = \frac{\text{particular outcome}}{\text{total outcomes}} = \frac{\text{green marbles}}{\text{total marbles}} = \frac{3}{10} \text{ or } 30\%$$

When you calculate probability, always be careful to divide by the total number of possible outcomes. In the last example, you may have been tempted to leave out the three chances of picking a green marble from the total possibilities, yielding the equation $P = \frac{3}{7}$. If you did that, you'd be wrong.

Absolute Value

The absolute value of a number is its magnitude, regardless of sign. Absolute value is indicated by two vertical lines that surround the number: $|5|$ and $|-5|$, for example. The absolute value of positive five is equal to five: $|5| = 5$. The absolute value of negative five is also equal to five: $|-5| = 5$. Simply remove the sign before the number to produce its absolute value

On the ACT, you will generally be asked to do a simple addition, subtraction, multiplication, or division problem using the absolute values of numbers. For example,

$$|-4| + |2| = ?$$

Remember that the vertical lines mean you simply ignore the sign, so the question actually looks like this: $4 + 2 = 6$

Exponents and Roots

At most, you'll see one problem on the ACT Math Test dealing with exponents or roots. It's quite likely you won't see any, but you're still doing yourself a favor by preparing for them.

Exponents

Exponents are a shorthand method of describing how many times a particular number is multiplied by itself. To write $3 \times 3 \times 3 \times 3 \times 3$ in exponent form, we would simply count out how many threes were being multiplied together (in this case, five), and then write 3^5. In verbal form, 3^5 is stated as "three to the fifth power."

Raising an Exponent to an Exponent

Occasionally, a question might ask you to raise a power to a power, in the following format: $(3^2)^4$. In such cases, multiply the exponents:

$$(3^2)^4 = 3^{(2 \times 4)} = 3^8$$

If you have an expression involving a variable, like $2a^2$, and you raise it to the third power, then you would write $(2a^2)^3$. To simplify this expression, you would multiply the exponents and raise 2 to the third power; the end result would be $8a^6$. Most basic calculators have an exponent or y^x function key. Be sure to know how to use this function on your calculator before the test.

Square Roots

The square root of a number is the number that, when squared (multiplied by itself), is equal to the given number. For example, the square root of 16 is 4, because $4^2 = 4 \times 4 = 16$. A perfect square is a number whose square root is an integer.

The sign denoting a square root is $\sqrt{}$. To use the previous example, $\sqrt{16} = 4$. Again, be sure to find and know how to use the square-root function, or $\sqrt{}$ key, on your calculator.

Cube Roots

The cube root of a number is the number that, when cubed (raised to the third power), is equal to the given number. The cube root of 8 is 2, because $2 \times 2 \times 2 = 8$.

The sign denoting a cube root is $\sqrt[3]{}$.

Series

Series questions are pretty rare on the ACT. Every once in a while they do pop up, though. A series is a sequence of numbers that proceed one after another, according to some pattern. Usually the ACT will give you a few numbers in a series and ask you to specify what number should come next. For example,

$$-1, 2, -4, 8, -16$$

is a series in which each number is multiplied by −2 to yield the next number; 32 is the next number in the series. This type of question asks you to be able to recognize patterns and then apply them. There isn't one tried-and-true way to find a pattern. Just think critically, and use your intuition and trial and error.

Elementary Algebra

Unlike the section on pre-algebra, we've organized this elementary algebra section in terms of increasing difficulty:

1. Substitution

2. Simplifying Algebraic Expressions

3. Writing Expressions and Equations

4. Solving Linear Equations

5. Multiplying Binomials

6. Inequalities

This is also the order of the topics in terms of *decreasing frequency* on the test, with one exception: problems involving inequalities pop up more often than problems involving binomial multiplication.

Before covering these topics, however, we will address a question brought up by the teachings of some other test prep companies.

To Algebra or Not to Algebra

There are many ways to answer most algebra problems. You can use algebra—setting up and working out equations—or you can plug numbers into equations to try and avoid using algebra. In some cases, you might even be able to solve a question by being a particularly intuitive genius and finding a magnificent shortcut.

We want to stress that none of these methods is necessarily better than another. Which method is best for you depends on your math ability and your target score. Trying to solve problems with algebra is more conceptually demanding, but can take less time. Plugging in numbers makes questions easier to understand, but will likely take more time. In general, if you are uncomfortable with algebra, you should try to use the plugging-in method. If you are comfortable with algebra, using it is probably the best way to go. Still, these suggestions are not carved in stone. If you are generally comfortable with algebra but come upon a question that is stumping you, try plugging in answers. If you usually prefer plugging in answers but come upon a question you can answer using algebra, use algebra. When you study your practice tests and look at the algebra questions you got wrong, you should think about the method you employed. Did you plug in when you should have used algebra? Did you use algebra when you should have plugged in? As for being an intuitive math genius, it just can't be taught—though we will show you how one might think.

Here's a sample algebra question:

A man flipped a coin 162 times. The coin landed with the heads side up 62 more times than it landed with tails up. How many times did the coin land heads?

A.   100
B.   104
C.   108
D.   112
E.   116

Solving by Plugging In

If you were to answer this problem by plugging in numbers, you would pick the middle number or **C**, 108, as the first number to try, since if it does not happen to be the answer, you can discard the numbers smaller than it or larger than it. If the coin came up heads 108 times, then how many times did it land tails? It landed tails $162 - 108 = 54$

times. Is 108 heads landings 62 more than 54 tails landings? No, 108 − 54 = 54. In order for the problem to work out, you need more heads landings. You can eliminate A and B as possibilities. Let's say we choose **D**, 112, as our next plug-in number: 162 − 112 = 50. Does 112 − 50 = 62? Yes. **D** is the answer.

Solving with Algebra

If you answer this question with algebra, you realize that if heads are represented by the variable x, then tails are represented by $(x − 62)$. Therefore,

$$x + (x - 62) = 162$$
$$2x - 62 = 162$$
$$2x = 224$$
$$x = 112$$

As you can see, there's simply less math to do for this problem when you use algebra. Using algebra will only take you longer than plugging in if you have trouble coming up with the equation $x + (x − 62) = 162$.

Therefore, if you can quickly come up with the necessary equation, then use algebra to solve algebra problems. If you have the feeling that it will take you a while to figure out the correct equation, then plug in.

Solving by Being an Amazing Genius

It is quite possible that you just looked at this problem and said to yourself, "Other than the 62 more heads, all the other flips were equally heads and tails. So if you take the 62 out of the total of 162, then you know that the other 100 flips were 50 heads and 50 tails. Now I can just add 62 + 50 = 112. Man, I am an amazing genius!"

The Bottom Line on Using Algebra

Hopefully, our example has convinced you that there isn't any "right way" to answer a question dealing with algebra. There are faster ways and slower ways, and it always benefits you to use the faster way if you can, but the most important thing is getting the question right. Therefore, when you come to a question, don't insist on using only one method to try to answer it. Just do what you have to do in order to answer the question correctly in as little time as possible.

Now we'll begin to cover the topics of elementary algebra tested on the ACT.

Substitution

Substitution questions are the simplest algebra problems on the ACT. These questions provide you with an algebraic expression and the value of a variable within the equation, and ask you to calculate the value of the equation. For example,

If $2y + 8x = 11$, what is the value of $3(2y + 8x)$?

You might see this question with all its variables and panic. But, in truth, this is a simple problem. Since $2y + 8x = 11$, all you have to do is substitute 11 for $2y + 8x$ in the expression $3(2y + 8x)$, and you get $3(11) = 33$.

For some substitution questions, you will have to do some simple math either before or after the substitution.

Math before Substitution

If $3x - 7 = 8$, then $23 - 3x =$

In this problem you have to find what $3x$ equals before you can substitute that value into the expression $23 - 3x$. To find $3x$, take:

$$3x - 7 = 8$$

and add 7 to both sides, getting:

$$3x = 15$$

Now we can substitute that 15 into $23 - 3x$:

$$23 - 15 = 8$$

Math after Substitution

If $a + b = 7$ and $b = 3$, then $4a =$

Here we first have to solve for a by substituting the 3 in for b:

$$a + b = 7$$
$$a + 3 = 7$$
$$a = 4$$

Once you know that $a = 4$, just substitute it into $4a$:

$$4 \times 4 = 16$$

Simplifying Algebraic Expressions

Some ACT Math questions test your ability to simplify or manipulate algebraic expressions. To master either of these skills, you must be able to see how an equation might be expressed differently without changing the value of the expression in any way. There are two primary ways to simplify an equation: factoring and combining like terms.

Factoring and Unfactoring

Factoring an algebraic expression means finding factors common to all terms in an expression and dividing them out. For example, to factor $3a + 3b$, you simply divide out the 3 to get $3(a + b)$. Below are some more examples of factoring:

1. $6y + 8x = 2(3y + 4x)$

2. $8b + 24 = 8(b + 3)$

3. $3(x + y) + 4(x + y) = (3 + 4)(x + y) = 7(x + y)$

4. $\dfrac{2x + y}{x} = \dfrac{2x}{x} + \dfrac{y}{x} = 2 + \dfrac{y}{x}$

Unfactoring involves taking a factored expression, such as $8(b + 3)$, and distributing one term to the other(s): $8b + 24$.

Combining Similar Terms

If an expression contains "like terms," you can combine those terms and simplify the equation. "Like terms" refers to identical variables that have the same exponent value. For example:

- You can combine: $x^2 + 8x^2 = 9x^2$
$$y^{13} + 754y^{13} = 755y^{13}$$
$$m^3 + m^3 = 2m^3$$

As long as two terms have the same variable and the same exponent value, you can combine them. Note that when you combine like terms, the variable doesn't change. If two terms have different variables, or the exponent value is different, the terms are not "like terms" and you cannot combine them.

- You can't combine: $x^4 + x^2$ or $y^2 + x^2$

Writing Expressions and Equations

Occasionally, the ACT will throw you a word problem that describes an algebraic expression. You will have to write out the expression in numerical form and perhaps simplify it. For example:

Mary poured g cups of water into a bucket, leaving the bucket with a total of f cups in it. Mary then removed $(g - 3)$ cups of water from the bucket. How many cups of water remain in the bucket?

To answer this question, you have to interpret the word problem. In other words, you have to figure out what is important in the word problem and how it fits into the expression you need to build. This question asks you to generate an expression that describes how many cups of water there are in the bucket *after* Mary removes $(g - 3)$

cups. It doesn't matter what g actually equals, because we don't care how much water was in the bucket before Mary added g cups.

To work out the equation, we take the original number of cups in the bucket and subtract from it what was removed:

$$f - (g - 3) = f - g + 3$$

Solving Linear Equations

The most common and foolproof way to solve linear equations is to isolate the variable whose value you are trying to determine on one side of the equation.

If you stay alert, you may also be able to find shortcuts that will greatly lower your time spent per question without affecting your accuracy. Let's look at an easy example:

If $6p + 2 = 20$, then $6p - 3 =$

This is an easy problem to solve through the normal algebraic method. First we solve for p:

$$6p + 2 = 20$$
$$6p = 18$$
$$p = 3$$

Next, we plug 3 into the second equation:

$$6p - 3 =$$
$$6(3) - 3 =$$
$$18 - 3 = 15$$

But there's a faster way to answer this question. The secret is that you don't have to solve for p at all. Instead, notice that both equations contain $6p$ and that the value of $6p$ will not change. Therefore, all you have to do in the first equation is solve for $6p$. And as you can see above, that simply means subtracting 2 from 20 to get 18. Once you know $6p$ is 18, you can plug 18 in for $6p$ in the second equation and get your answer.

When you come upon an algebra question asking you to solve an equation, you should always take a second to look for shortcuts. Look for equations that not only have the same variables, but also the same coefficients attached to that variable (such as $6p$ and $6p$). If you are able to find a good shortcut, your knowledge of algebra will save you time.

Multiplying Binomials

A binomial is an algebraic expression consisting of two terms combined by a plus or minus sign. For instance, $x + 4$ and $y - 11$ are both binomials. Multiplying binomials is not a difficult task if you remember the acronym FOIL, which stands for FIRST

OUTER INNER LAST. For example, say you are asked to multiply the binomials:

$$(x + 2)(x + 3)$$

You start by multiplying the first number in each polynomial $(x)(x)$, then the outer numbers $(x)(3)$, then the inner numbers $(2)(x)$, and finally the last numbers $(2)(3)$:

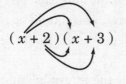

and you get:

$$x^2 + 3x + 2x + 6 = x^2 + 5x + 6$$

The only tricky part to following FOIL is remembering to pay attention to signs. For instance, if you have the polynomials $(x + 2)(x - 3)$, then the −3 comes to play an important part. You always add up the products of FOIL, but look what happens when there's a negative number involved:

$$(x + 2)(x - 3) = x^2 + 2x + (-3x) + (-6) = x^2 + 2x - 3x - 6$$
$$= x^2 - x - 6$$

There are three equations involving binomial multiplication that you should know backward and forward before you take the ACT, the most important being the first:

$$(x + y)(x - y) = x^2 - y^2$$
$$(x + y)(x + y) = x^2 + 2xy + y^2$$
$$(x - y)(x - y) = x^2 - 2xy + y^2$$

Inequalities

An equation states that the quantities on either side of the equal sign are of the same value. An inequality states that one side of the equation is greater than the other: $a < b$ states that a is less than b, and $a > b$ states that a is greater than b. In other cases, $a \le b$ means that a is less than or equal to b, while $a \ge b$ means that a is greater than or equal to b.

Solving an inequality is basically the same as solving a normal equation: all the rules of simplification and having to do the same thing to both sides still apply. The one rule that does differ when working with inequalities comes when you multiply or divide both sides by a negative. If you do so, you must flip the sign: if $x > y$, then $-x < -y$. For example, if you have $2x + 6 \ge y$ and multiply the inequality by −2, the result is $-4x - 12 \le -2y$.

Intermediate Algebra

Intermediate algebra questions are some of the toughest questions on the ACT Math Test. To compensate for the difficulty of the topic, almost all of the intermediate algebra problems will be in basic form, meaning that you don't need to sort through a mess of words to find the question. Also, you should be glad to hear that there will be only nine intermediate algebra problems on the Math Test, making them worth less than one-sixth of your math score.

In this section, we'll present the intermediate algebra topics to you in the following order:

1. Solving and Factoring Quadratic Equations

2. Solving Systems of Equations

3. Relationships between the Sides of an Equation

4. Functions

5. Matrices

6. Logarithms

The first two topics in this list appear most frequently on the ACT. You may not encounter a single example of the last four topics, particularly the last two, on a given test. Those topics do appear from time to time, though, so it pays to be prepared for them.

Solving and Factoring Quadratic Equations

This topic constitutes a major portion of the intermediate algebra questions. You will probably see about three quadratic equations questions per test. Those three questions make up a third of the intermediate algebra questions. If you can master these questions, then you're well on your way to overcoming intermediate algebra.

Definition of a Quadratic Equation

A quadratic equation is a second-degree equation with one variable and usually two solutions. If you don't understand what that means, hold on a second. A quadratic equation on the ACT will almost always appear in the following form:

$$ax^2 + bx + c = 0$$

where a and b are coefficients and $a \neq 0$. That is the standard form of a quadratic equation, and it is the form that the ACT almost always uses. In some cases, you may come across an equation that looks like this:

$$ax^2 + c = bx$$

In this case you can subtract bx from both sides of the equation to get the equation into standard form:

$$ax^2 - bx + c = 0$$

Every quadratic equation contains a variable raised to the second power. In most of the quadratic equations you'll see on the test, there'll be two solutions for this variable.

Also, the ACT almost always makes a equal to 1 to simplify solving these equations. (Note that when $a = 1$, $1x^2$ is simply written x^2.)

Solving a Quadratic Equation

Solving a quadratic equation means solving for the variable used in the equation. Almost all quadratic equations appearing on the ACT can be solved by factoring. Solving a quadratic equation by factoring is essentially the reverse of what you do when multiplying binomials. Take the following example:

$$x^2 + 9x + 18 = 0$$

Solving for x here requires a good degree of intuition, but with time and practice your intuition will become increasingly keen. Try to imagine which binomials would create the equation above. You can do this by considering the factors of 18 (1 and 18; 2 and 9; 3 and 6) and asking yourself which pair of factors adds up to 9. Done that? If so, you see that 3 and 6 add up to 9. So you can factor the equation as:

$$(x + 3)(x + 6) = 0$$

Whenever you see something in the above form, you can solve it like this:

$$x + 3 = 0 \quad x + 6 = 0$$
$$x = -3 \quad x = -6$$

Either $x = -3$ or $x = -6$ satisfies the equation.

The Quadratic Formula

Very rarely on the ACT, you may encounter a quadratic equation that cannot be solved by factoring. In that case, you can use the quadratic formula to solve the equation. The quadratic formula is:

$$x = \frac{-b \pm \sqrt{b^2 - 4ac}}{2a}$$

where a, b, and c are the same coefficients as in the quadratic equation. You simply plug in the coefficients to determine solutions for x. Just to prove to you that the equation works, we'll work out the quadratic equation whose roots we already know: $x^2 + 9x + 18 = 0$. Remember that it's in the form $ax^2 + bx + c = 0$.

$$x = \frac{-9 \pm \sqrt{9^2 - 4 \times 1 \times 18}}{2 \times 1}$$

$$x = \frac{-9 \pm \sqrt{81 - 72}}{2}$$

$$x = \frac{-9 \pm \sqrt{9}}{2}$$

$$x = \frac{-9 \pm 3}{2}$$

$$x = \frac{-6}{2} = -3 \text{ or } x = \frac{-12}{2} = -6$$

Solving Systems of Equations

A few times per test, the ACT will give you two equations and ask you to determine the value of a particular variable or some other equation or expression. For example,

If $3x + 4y = 32$ and $2y - x = 6$, then $x - y =$

The best way to answer this type of question is to use a substitution method: solve for one variable and then substitute that value into the other equation. In looking at the two equations above, it seems obvious that it would be easier to solve for x using the second equation than it would be to solve for y in either of the two equations. All it takes is a little reorganizing:

$$2y - x = 6$$
$$2y - 6 = x$$
$$x = 2y - 6$$

Next, all we have to do is plug $2y - 6$ into the value for x in the first equation:

$$3(2y - 6) + 4y = 32$$

Now we have only one variable to deal with in the equation, and we can easily solve for it:

$$6y - 18 + 4y = 32$$
$$10y = 50$$
$$y = 5$$

Once we know the value of y, we can plug that value into either equation to solve for x:

$$x = 2y - 6$$
$$x = 2(5) - 6$$
$$x = 4$$

Now we can answer the question, which asked for $x - y$. We get $4 - 5 = -1$. When you solve systems of equations questions, always be careful of a few things:

1. When you first solve for one variable, make sure you solve for it in its lowest form (solve for x rather than $2x$).

2. When you substitute, make sure you correctly apply the distributive law of multiplication: $3(2y - 6) = 6y - 18$.

3. Always answer the question the ACT asks. For example, in the sample above, the question asked for the value of $x - y$. But it's certainly possible that after doing all the work and figuring out that $x = 4$ you might forget to carry out the final simple operation of $4 - 5 = -1$, and instead incorrectly answer 4.

Systems of Equations with Infinite Solutions

Occasionally, the ACT will test your understanding of systems of linear equations by asking you to determine when two equations in a system yield an infinite number of solutions. To answer this sort of question, you only need to know one thing: a system of equations will yield an infinite number of solutions when the two equations describe the same line. In other words, the system of equations will have an infinite number of solutions when the two equations are equal and in $y = mx + b$ form. Here's an example:

> The following system of equations would have an infinite number of solutions for which of the following values of b?
>
> $$3x - 2y = 4$$
> $$12x - 4by = 16$$
>
> A. 1
> B. 2
> C. 4
> D. 8
> E. 12

To answer this question, you have to pick a value for b such that the two equations have the same formula fitting the $y = mx + b$ form. The first step in this process is to transfer $3x - 2y = 4$ into the $y = mx + b$ form:

$$3x - 2y = 4$$
$$-2y = -3x + 4$$
$$y = \frac{3}{2}x - 2$$

Then put $12x - 4by = 16$ into the same form:

$$12x - 4by = 16$$
$$-4by = -12x + 16$$
$$by = 3x - 4$$
$$y = \frac{3x}{b} - \frac{4}{b}$$

Since you know that the two equations have to be equal, you know that $(3/2)x$ must equal $3x/b$. This means that $b = 2$, so **B** is the right answer to the question.

Relationships between the Sides of an Equation

You should understand the relationship between the two sides of an equation. If you have an equation that says $w = kt^2$, where k is a constant, the equation tells you that w varies directly with the square of t; in other words, as t increases, so does w.

If, on the other hand, you have an equation that says $w = k/t^2$, where k is a constant, the equation tells you that w varies inversely with the square of t; in other words, as t increases, w decreases.

Functions

If you restated $y = ax + b$ as $f(x) = ax + b$, you would have a function, $f(x)$, which is pronounced "f of x." On the ACT, you can almost always treat $f(x)$ as you would treat y, but we want you to be aware of the different format.

Compound Functions

On rare occasions, the ACT has asked questions about compound functions, in which one function is worked out in terms of another. The notation for a compound function is $f(g(x))$, or $f \circ g$. To evaluate a compound function like $f(g(x))$, first evaluate g at x. Then evaluate f at the results of $g(x)$. Basically, work with the inner parentheses first, and then the outer ones, just like in any other algebraic expression. Try the following example:

Suppose $h(x) = x^2 + 2x$ and $j(x) = \left|\frac{x}{4} + 2\right|$. What is $j(h(4))$?

$$
\begin{aligned}
(j \circ h)(4) &= j(h(4)) \\
&= j(4^2 + 2(4)) \\
&= j(16 + 8) \\
&= j(24) \\
&= \left|\frac{24}{4} + 2\right| \\
&= |8| \\
&= 8
\end{aligned}
$$

Here's a slightly more complicated example:

Suppose $f(x) = 3x + 1$ and $g(x) = \sqrt{5x}$. What is $g(f(x))$?

This question doesn't ask you to evaluate the compound function for a given value—it asks you to express the compound function as a single function. To do so, simply plug the formula for f into the formula for g:

$$g(f(x)) = g(3x + 1)$$
$$g(f(x)) = \sqrt{5(3x + 1)}$$
$$g(f(x)) = \sqrt{15x + 5}$$

Matrices

You will seldom see a matrix problem on the ACT, and many high school math courses may not have covered matrices by the time you take the test. Still, any matrix problems on the ACT will be very straightforward and fundamental, so you really only need to know the basics of matrices in order to get the right answers. We will cover those basics here.

Adding and Subtracting Matrices

You will not be asked to do anything more advanced than adding or subtracting matrices. For example,

$$A = \begin{bmatrix} 2 & 0 \\ 3 & -5 \end{bmatrix} \qquad B = \begin{bmatrix} -4 & 1 \\ 6 & 3 \end{bmatrix}$$

What is $A + B$? To answer this question, you simply add the corresponding entries in A and B. The entries in the first row are $2 + (-4) = -2$ and $0 + 1 = 1$. The entries in the second row are $3 + 6 = 9$ and $(-5) + 3 = -2$. So the resulting matrix is:

$$A + B = \begin{bmatrix} -2 & 1 \\ 9 & -2 \end{bmatrix}$$

If the question had asked you what $A - B$ is, then you would simply subtract the entries in B from the corresponding entries in A.

Logarithms

Like matrices, logarithms rarely appear in the ACT Math Test. But they do pop up occasionally, and you should know how to handle them. Logarithmic functions are inverses of exponential functions. The exponential equation $x = a^b$ is equivalent to the logarithmic equation $\log_a x = b$.

This inverse relationship between logs and exponents is all you need to know in order to answer a logarithm question on the ACT. If you see $\log_x 16 = 4$, then you know that $x^4 = 16$. You will be able to use this second, more manageable mathematical expression to answer the question.

Coordinate Geometry

Coordinate geometry is geometry dealing primarily with the line graphs and the (x, y) coordinate plane. The ACT Math Test includes nine questions on coordinate geometry. The topics you need to know are:

1. Number Lines and Inequalities

2. The (x, y) Coordinate Plane

3. Distance and Midpoints

4. Slope

5. Parallel and Perpendicular Lines

6. The Equation of a Line

7. Graphing Equations

8. Conic Sections

Most of the questions on coordinate geometry focus on slope. About two questions on each test will cover number lines and inequalities. The other topics are usually covered by just one question, if they are covered at all.

Number Lines and Inequalities

Number line questions generally ask you to graph inequalities. A typical number line graph question will ask you:

What is the graph of the solution set for $2(x + 5) > 4$?

To answer this question, you first must solve for x.

1. Divide both sides by 2 to get: $x + 5 > 2$

2. Subtract 5 from both sides to get: $x > -3$

3. Now you match $x > -3$ to its line graph:

The circles at the endpoints of a line indicating an inequality are very important when trying to match an inequality to a line graph. An open circle at −3 denotes that x is greater than but *not* equal to −3. A closed circle would have indicated that x is greater than *or* equal to −3.

For the solution set −3 < x < 3, where x must be greater than −3 and less than 3, the line graph looks like this:

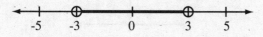

The (*x,y*) Coordinate Plane

The (x,y) coordinate plane is described by two perpendicular lines, the x-axis and the y-axis. The intersection of these axes is called the origin. The location of any other point on the plane (which extends in all directions without limit) can be described by a pair of coordinates. Here is a figure of the coordinate plane with a few points drawn in and labeled with their coordinates:

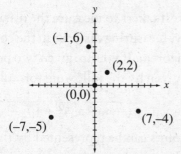

As you can see from the figure, each of the points on the coordinate plane receives a pair of coordinates: (x,y). The first coordinate in a coordinate pair is called the x-coordinate. The x-coordinate of a point is its location along the x-axis and can be determined by the point's distance from the y-axis ($x = 0$ at the y-axis). If the point is to the right of the y-axis, its x-coordinate is positive, and if the point is to the left of the y-axis, its x-coordinate is negative.

The second coordinate in a coordinate pair is the y-coordinate. The y-coordinate of a point is its location along the y-axis and can be calculated as the distance from that point to the x-axis. If the point is above the x-axis, its y-coordinate is positive; if the point is below the x-axis, its y-coordinate is negative.

The ACT often tests your understanding of the coordinate plane and coordinates by telling you the coordinates of the vertices of a defined geometric shape like a square, and asking you to pick the coordinates of the last vertex. For example:

In the standard (x,y) coordinate plane, 3 corners of a square are (2,−2), (−2,−2), and (−2,2). What are the coordinates of the square's fourth corner?

The best way to solve this sort of problem is to draw a quick sketch of the coordinate plane and the coordinates given. You'll then be able to see the shape described and pick out the coordinates of the final vertex from the image. In this case, the sketch would look like this:

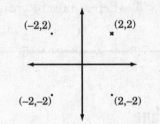

A square is the easiest geometric shape which a question might concern. It is possible that you will be asked to deal with rectangles or right triangles. The method for any geometric shape is the same, though. Sketch it out so you can see it.

Distance

The ACT occasionally asks test takers to measure the distance between two points on the coordinate plane. Luckily, measuring distance in the coordinate plane is made easy thanks to the Pythagorean theorem. If you are given two points, (x_1, y_1) and (x_2, y_2), their distance will always be given by the following formula:

$$\text{Distance} = \sqrt{(x_2 - x_1)^2 + (y_2 - y_1)^2}$$

The distance between two points can be represented by the hypotenuse of a right triangle whose legs are of lengths $(x_2 - x_1)$ and $(y_2 - y_1)$. The following diagram shows how the formula is based on the Pythagorean theorem (see p. 176).

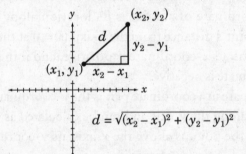

Here's a sample problem:

Calculate the distance between (4,–3) and (–3,8).

To solve this problem, just plug the proper numbers into the distance formula:

$$\text{Distance} = \sqrt{((-3) - 4)^2 + (8 - (-3))^2} = \sqrt{49 + 121} = \sqrt{170}$$

The distance between the points is $\sqrt{170}$, which equals approximately 13.04.

Finding Midpoints

Like finding the distance between two points, the midpoint between two points in the coordinate plane can be calculated using a formula. If the endpoints of a line segment are (x_1, y_1) and (x_2, y_2), then the midpoint of the line segment is:

$$\text{Midpoint} = \left(\frac{x_1 + x_2}{2}, \frac{y_1 + y_2}{2}\right)$$

In other words, the x- and y-coordinates of the midpoint are the averages of the x- and y-coordinates of the endpoints.

Here is a practice question:

What is the midpoint of the line segment whose endpoints are (6,0) and (3,7)?

All you have to do is plug the end points into the midpoint formula. According to the question, $x_1 = 6$, $y_1 = 0$, $x_2 = 3$, and $y_2 = 7$:

$$\text{Midpoint} = \left(\frac{6 + 3}{2}, \frac{0 + 7}{2}\right) = \left(\frac{9}{2}, \frac{7}{2}\right) = (4.5, 3.5)$$

Slope

The slope of a line is a measurement of how steeply the line climbs or falls as it moves from left to right. More technically, the slope is a line's vertical change divided by its horizontal change, also known as "rise over run." Given two points on a line, (x_1, y_1) and (x_2, y_2), the slope of that line can be calculated using the following formula:

$$\text{Slope} = \frac{y_2 - y_1}{x_2 - x_1}$$

The variable most often used to represent slope is m.

So, for example, the slope of a line that contains the points $(-2, -4)$ and $(6, 1)$ is:

$$m = \frac{1 - (-4)}{6 - (-2)} = \frac{5}{8}$$

Positive and Negative Slopes

You can easily determine whether the slope of a line is positive or negative just by looking at the line. If a line slopes uphill as you trace it from left to right, the slope is positive. If a line slopes downhill as you trace it from left to right, the slope is negative.

You can determine the relative magnitude of the slope by the steepness of the line.

The steeper the line, the more the "rise" will exceed the "run," and the larger $y_2 - y_1$ and, consequently, the slope will be. Conversely, the flatter the line, the smaller the slope will be.

For practice, look at the lines in the figure below and try to determine whether their slopes are positive or negative and which have greater relative slopes:

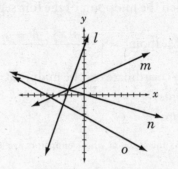

Lines l and m have positive slopes, and lines n and o have negative slope. In terms of slope magnitude, line $l > m > n > o$.

Special Slopes

It can be helpful to recognize a few slopes by sight.

- A line that is horizontal has a slope of 0. Since there is no "rise," $y_2 - y_1 = 0$, and thus $m = (y_2 - y_1)/(x_2 - x_1) = 0/(x_2 - x_1) = 0$.

- A line that is vertical has an undefined slope. In this case, there is no "run," and $x_2 - x_1 = 0$. Thus $m = (y_2 - y_1)/(x_2 - x_1) = ((y_2 - y_1)/0)$, and any fraction with 0 in its denominator is, by definition, undefined.

- A line that makes a 45° angle with a horizontal has a slope of 1 or −1. This makes sense because the "rise" equals the "run," and $y_2 - y_1 = x_2 - x_1$ or $y_2 - y_1 = -(x_2 - x_1)$.

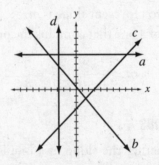

Line a has slope 0 because it is horizontal. Line b has slope −1 because it makes a 45° angle with the horizontal and slopes downward as you move from left to right. Line c

has slope 1 because it makes a 45° angle with the horizontal and slopes upward as you move from left to right. Line *d* has undefined slope because it is vertical.

Parallel and Perpendicular Lines

Parallel lines are lines that don't intersect. In other words, parallel lines are lines that share the exact same slope.

Perpendicular lines are lines that intersect at a right angle (or 90°). In coordinate geometry, perpendicular lines have negative reciprocal slopes. That is, a line with slope *m* is perpendicular to a line with a slope of $-1/m$.

In the figure below are three lines. Lines *q* and *r* both have a slope of 2, so they are parallel. Line *s* is perpendicular to both lines *q* and *r*, and thus has a slope of $-1/2$.

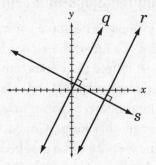

On the ACT, never assume that two lines are parallel or perpendicular just because they look that way in a diagram. If the lines are parallel or perpendicular, the ACT will tell you so. (Perpendicular lines can be indicated by a little square located at the place of intersection, as in the diagram above.)

Equation of a Line

We've already shown you how to find the slope of a line using two points on the line. It is also possible to find the slope of a line using the equation of the line. In addition, the equation of a line can help you find the *x*- and *y*-intercepts of the line, which are the locations where the line intersects with the *x*- and *y*-axes. This equation for a line is called the slope-intercept form:

$$y = mx + b$$

where *m* is the slope of the line, and *b* is the *y*-intercept of the line.

Finding the Slope Using the Slope-Intercept Form

If you are given the equation of a line that matches the slope-intercept form, you immediately know that the slope is equal to the value of *m*. However, it is more likely that the ACT will give you an equation for a line that doesn't exactly match the slope-intercept form and ask you to calculate the slope. In this case, you will have to manipulate the given equation until it resembles the slope-intercept form. For example,

What is the slope of the line defined by the equation $5x + 3y = 6$?

To answer this question, isolate the y so that the equation fits the slope-intercept form.

$$5x + 3y = 6$$
$$3y = -5x + 6$$
$$y = -\frac{5}{3}x + 2$$

The slope of the line is $-5/3$.

Finding the Intercepts Using the Slope-Intercept Form

The y-intercept of a line is the y-coordinate of the point at which the line intersects the y-axis. Likewise, the x-intercept of a line is the x-coordinate of the point at which the line intersects the x-axis. In order to find the y-intercept, simply set $x = 0$ and solve for the value of y. To find the x-intercept, set $y = 0$ and solve for x.

To sketch a line given in slope-intercept form, first plot the y-intercept, and then use the slope of the line to plot another point. Connect the two points to form your line. In the figure below, the line $y = -2x + 3$ is graphed.

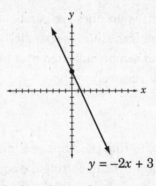

$$y = -2x + 3$$

Since the slope is equal to -2, the line descends two units for every one unit it moves in the positive x direction. The y-intercept is at 3, so the line crosses the y-axis at $(0,3)$.

Graphing Equations

For the ACT Math Test, you should know how the graphs of certain equations look. The two equations that are most important in terms of graphing are $y = x^2$ and $y = x^3$:

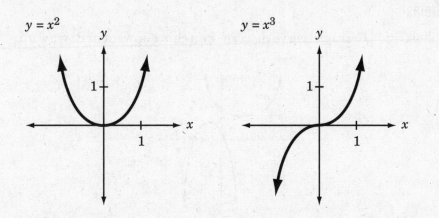

If you add lesser-degree terms to the equations, these graphs will shift around the origin but retain their basic shape. You should also keep in mind what the negatives of these equations look like:

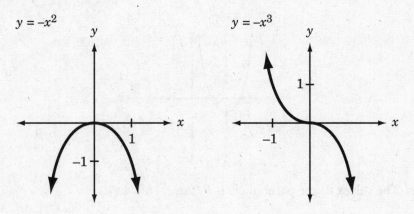

Conic Sections

Occasionally, the ACT will test your knowledge of parabolas, circles, or ellipses. These topics do not regularly appear on the ACT, but it still pays to prepare: if these topics do appear, getting them right can separate you from the crowd.

Parabolas

A parabola is a "U"-shaped curve that can open either upward or downward.

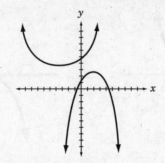

A parabola is the graph of a quadratic function, which, you may recall, follows the form $ax^2 + bx + c$. The equation of a parabola gives you quite a bit of information about the parabola.

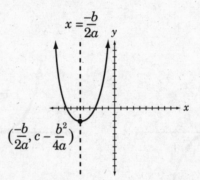

1. The vertex of the parabola is $(-b/2a, c - b^2/4a)$.

2. The axis of symmetry of the parabola is the line $x = -b/2a$.

3. The parabola opens upward if $a > 0$, and downward if $a < 0$.

4. The y-intercept is the point $(0, c)$.

Circles

A circle is the collection of points equidistant from a given point, called the center of the circle. Circles are defined by the formula:

$$(x - h)^2 + (y - k)^2 = r^2$$

where (h,k) is the center of the circle, and r is the radius. Note that when the circle is centered at the origin, $h = k = 0$, so the equation simplifies to:

$$x^2 + y^2 = r^2$$

That's it. That's all you need to know about circles in coordinate geometry. Once you know and understand this equation, you should be able to sketch a circle in its proper place on the coordinate system if given its equation. You should also be able to figure out the equation of a circle given a picture of its graph with coordinates labeled.

Ellipses

An ellipse is a figure shaped like an oval. It looks like a circle somebody sat on, but it is actually a good deal more complicated than a circle, as you can see from all the jargon on the diagram below.

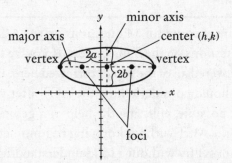

The two foci are crucial to the definition of an ellipse. The sum of the distances from the foci to any point on the ellipse is constant. To understand this visually, look at the figure below. The quantity $d_1 + d_2$ is constant for each point on the ellipse.

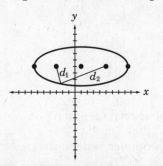

The line segment containing the foci of an ellipse with both endpoints on the ellipse is called the major axis. The endpoints of the major axis are called the vertices. The line segment perpendicularly bisecting the major axis with both endpoints on the ellipse is the minor axis. The point midway between the foci is the center of the ellipse. When you see an ellipse, you should be able to identify where each of these components would be.

The equation of an ellipse is:

$$\frac{(x - h)^2}{a^2} + \frac{(y - k)^2}{b^2} = 1$$

where $a, b, h,$ and k are constants. With respect to this formula, remember that:

1. The center of the ellipse is (h, k).

2. The length of the horizontal axis is $2a$.

3. The length of the vertical axis is $2b$.

4. If $a > b$, the major axis is horizontal and the minor axis is vertical; if $b > a$, the major axis is vertical and the minor axis is horizontal.

Plane Geometry

Plane geometry problems account for 14 questions on the ACT Math Test—that's almost a quarter of the questions on the Subject Test. If you've taken high school geometry, you've probably covered all of the topics reviewed here. If you haven't taken high school geometry, you should consider taking the ACT after you've taken a geometry course, or, if that's not possible, enlisting the help of a geometry teacher. While you can probably get by on the ACT without knowing trigonometry or intermediate algebra very well, you cannot get by without a solid understanding of plane geometry, because these questions constitute such a significant part of the test.

In this section, we'll cover these plane geometry topics in the following order:

1. Angles and Lines

2. Triangles

3. Polygons

4. Circles

5. Simple Three-Dimensional Geometry

Key topics, such as area and perimeter, will be covered in the relevant sections. For instance, areas of triangles are covered in the section on triangles.

Angles and Lines

An angle is a geometric figure consisting of two rays with a common endpoint:

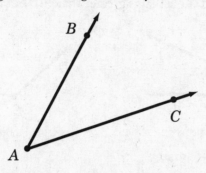

The common endpoint of the rays is called the vertex of the angle. In this case, the vertex is point A, which is a part of the ray $\overrightarrow{AB}$ as well as the ray $\overrightarrow{AC}$. The angle can be called either $\angle CAB$ or $\angle BAC$. The only rule in naming an angle is that the vertex *must* always be the middle "initial" of the angle.

Measuring Angles

Angles are measured in degrees, sometimes denoted by the symbol °. There are 360° in a complete rotation around a point; a circle therefore has 360°.

Consider two intersecting lines. The intersection of these lines produces four angles:

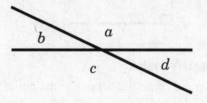

From the diagram below, you should see that the four angles together encompass one full revolution around the two lines' point of intersection. Therefore, the four angles produced by two intersection lines total 360°; angles $a + b + c + d = 360°$.

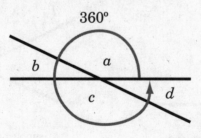

Types of Angles

There are many different types of angles, all categorized by the number of degrees they have.

Acute and Obtuse Angles

As shown in the diagram below, an acute angle is an angle that is smaller than 90°, while an obtuse angle is an angle that is greater than 90° but less than 180°.

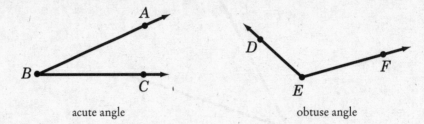

acute angle   obtuse angle

Right Angles

An angle with a measure of 90° is called a right angle. Notice that a right angle is symbolized by a square drawn in the corner of the angle. Whenever you see that little square, you know that you are dealing with a right angle. You also know that the lines that meet at the right angle are perpendicular.

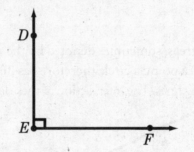

Complementary and Supplementary Angles

Special names are given to pairs of angles whose sums equal either 90° or 180°. Two angles whose sum is 90° are called complementary angles. If two angles add up to 180°, they are called supplementary angles.

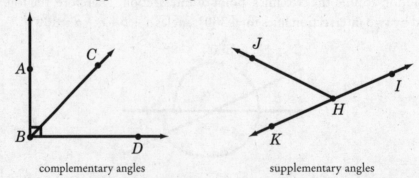

complementary angles   supplementary angles

Angles *ABC* and *CBD* are complementary, whereas angles *KHJ* and *JHI* are supplementary.

It is important to remember that these terms are only relative. An angle is only supplementary or complementary to *another specific angle*. A single angle, when considered alone, can be neither supplementary nor complementary—it can only take on one of these properties when considered as part of a pair of angles.

Vertical Angles

When two lines (or segments) intersect, the angles that lie opposite each other, called vertical angles, are always equal.

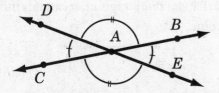

Angles *DAC* and *BAE* are vertical angles and are therefore equal to each other. Angles *DAB* and *CAE* are also vertical (and equal) angles.

Parallel Lines Cut by a Transversal

Occasionally on the ACT, you will run into a problem in which two parallel lines are cut by a third straight line, known as a transversal. The eight angles created by these two intersections have special relationships with one another.

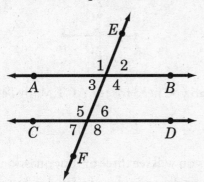

Angles 1, 4, 5, and 8 are all equal to each other. So are angles 2, 3, 6, and 7. Also, the sum of any two adjacent angles, such as 1 and 2 or 7 and 8, equals 180°. From these rules, you can make justified claims about seemingly unrelated angles. For example, since angles 1 and 2 add up to 180°, and since angles 2 and 7 are equal, the sum of angles 1 and 7 also equals 180°, based on the substitution principle of addition.

Lines

You may see a problem on the ACT that asks you about lines. In order to understand these questions, there is some vocabulary that you need to know.

- **Line.** A line is a set of infinite points that runs straight. If you have two points, the line will run straight through them and extend infinitely in both directions.

- **Line Segment.** A line segment consists of two points (endpoints) and all the points on a straight line between them. If you have a line segment that stretches from point A to point B, the line segment will be referred to as $\overline{AB}$.

- **Ray.** A ray is a line that has one endpoint; it extends infinitely in the direction without the endpoint.

- **Midpoint.** A midpoint is the point exactly halfway between the two endpoints of a line segment.

- **Bisect (verb).** Anything that bisects a line segment cuts the line segment exactly in half, at the midpoint. Line $\overrightarrow{CD}$ bisects line segment $\overline{AB}$.

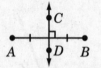

And that's all the line vocab you need for the ACT Math Test.

Triangles

On each ACT Math Test, you will see three or four questions on triangles. These questions tend to deal with the angles and sides of triangles, but you may also see questions about their areas and perimeters.

Triangles are closed figures containing three angles and three sides. There are a number of important rules about these angles and sides which, if mastered, will take you a long way on the ACT.

- The sum of the three angles in a triangle will always equal $180°$. Thus, if you know the measure of two angles in a triangle, you can calculate the measure of the third angle.

- The exterior angle of a triangle is always equal to the sum of the remote interior angles (i.e., the angles that are not adjacent to the exterior angle). In the figure, the exterior angle, x, is equal to $140°$, which is the sum of the two remote interior angles.

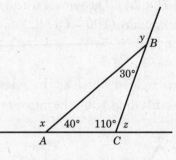

- The sum of the exterior angles of a triangle will always equal 360°, therefore $\angle x + \angle y + \angle z = 360°$.

- The longest side of a triangle is always opposite the largest angle; the second-longest side is opposite the second-largest angle; the shortest side is opposite the smallest angle. Therefore, in the triangle above, $\angle ACB$ is the largest angle, because its opposite side $\overline{AB}$, is the longest side.

- No side of a triangle can be as long as the sum of the other two side lengths. Therefore, in the triangle above, $\overline{AB} < \overline{BC} + \overline{CA}$.

- If you know that a triangle has sides of length 4 and 6, you know the third side is shorter than 10 and longer than 2. This can help you eliminate possible answer choices on multiple-choice questions.

There are a number of specialized types of triangles. We'll discuss them below.

Isosceles Triangles

Isosceles triangles have two equal sides, in this case sides a and b (the little marks on those two sides mean that the sides are congruent, which means equal). The angles opposite the congruent sides, in this case angles A and B, are also equal.

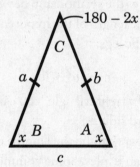

Because these two angles are equal, and the sum of a triangle's angles is always 180°, if you know the value of one of the two equal angles, let's say angle A, you know the value of all the angles in the triangle. Angle B is equal to A. Angle C is equal to $180 - 2A$

(since A and B are equal, $A + B = 2A$). The same is true if you start with the measure of angle C: angles A and B each measure $(180 - C) / 2$.

Equilateral Triangles

An equilateral triangle is a triangle in which all the sides and all the angles are equal. Since the angles of a triangle must total $180°$, the measure of each angle of an equilateral triangle must be $60°$.

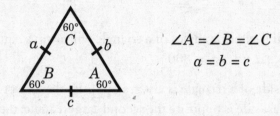

Right Triangles

A triangle with a right angle ($90°$) is called a right triangle. Because the angles of a triangle must total $180°$, the nonright angles (angles A and B in the diagram below) in a right triangle must add up to $90°$. The side opposite the right angle (side c in the diagram below) is called the hypotenuse.

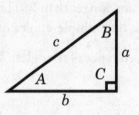

The Pythagorean Theorem

The Pythagorean theorem defines the relationship between the sides of every right triangle. The theorem states that the length of the hypotenuse squared is equal to the sum of the squares of the lengths of the legs:

$$c^2 = a^2 + b^2$$

If you are given any two sides of a right triangle, you can use the Pythagorean theorem to calculate the length of the third side.

Certain groups of three integers can be the lengths of a right triangle. Such groups of integers are called Pythagorean triples. Some common Pythagorean triples include $\{3, 4, 5\}$, $\{5, 12, 13\}$, $\{8, 15, 17\}$, $\{7, 24, 25\}$, and $\{9, 40, 41\}$. Any multiple of one of these groups is also a Pythagorean triple. For example, $\{9, 12, 15\} = 3\{3, 4, 5\}$. If you know these basic Pythagorean triples, they can help you quickly determine, without calculation, the length of a side of a right triangle in a problem that gives you the length of the other two sides.

Special Right Triangles

There are two kinds of special right triangles for which you don't have to use the Pythagorean theorem because their sides always exist in the same distinct ratios. This is not to say that you *can't* use the Pythagorean theorem when dealing with these triangles, just that you don't have to, since you can work out problems very quickly if you know the ratios. The two types of triangles are called 30-60-90 and 45-45-90 right triangles.

A 30-60-90 triangle is, as you may have guessed, a triangle with angles of 30°, 60°, and 90°. What makes it special is the specific pattern that the side-length of 30-60-90 triangles follow. Suppose the short leg, opposite the 30° angle, has length x. Then the hypotenuse has length $2x$, and the long leg, opposite the 60° angle, has length $x\sqrt{3}$. Study the following diagram, which shows these ratios:

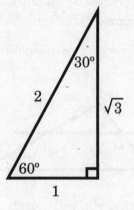

A 45-45-90 triangle is a triangle with two angles of 45°, and one right angle. This type of triangle is also known as an isosceles right triangle, since it's both isosceles and right. Like the 30-60-90 triangle, the lengths of the sides of a 45-45-90 triangle also follow a specific pattern that you should know. If the legs are of length x (they are always equal), then the hypotenuse has length $x\sqrt{2}$. Take a look at this diagram:

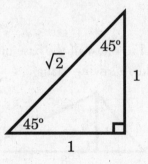

Similarity in Triangles

In reference to triangles, the word similar means "shaped in the same way." Two triangles are similar if their corresponding angles are equal. If this is the case, then the lengths of corresponding sides will be proportional to each other. For example, if triangles *ABC* and *DEF* are similar, then sides $\overline{AB}$ and $\overline{DE}$ correspond to each other, as do $\overline{BC}$ and $\overline{EF}$, and $\overline{CA}$ and $\overline{FD}$.

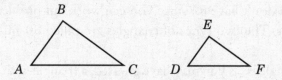

The proportionality of corresponding sides means that:

$$\frac{AB}{DE} = \frac{BC}{EF} = \frac{CA}{FD}$$

The properties of similarity will almost definitely be tested on the ACT. Let's say you come across the following question:

Triangles *ABC* and *DEC* are similar, and line *l* is parallel to segment $\overline{AB}$. What is the length of $\overline{CE}$?

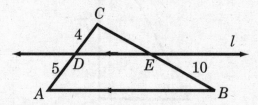

If you know the rule of similarity, you will quickly realize that the ratio $\overline{CD}:\overline{CA}$ is 4:9 and that $\overline{CE}:\overline{CB}$ must have the same ratio. Since $\overline{EB}$ is equal to 10, the only possible length of $\overline{CE}$ is 8, since 8:18 is equivalent to 4:9.

Two triangles are similar if they have two pairs of corresponding angles and one pair of sides that are equal, or if one pair of angles is equal and the two pairs of adjacent sides are proportional.

Area of a Triangle

The area of a triangle is equal to one-half the base of the triangle times the height, or (½)*bh*. For example, given the following triangle,

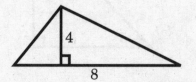

the area equals $(\frac{1}{2})(4 \times 8) = 16$. If you know the length of one leg of a triangle and can determine the height of the triangle (using that leg as a base), then you can plug those two numbers into the area formula.

Perimeter of a Triangle

The perimeter of a triangle is equal to the sum of the lengths of the triangle's three sides. If a triangle has sides of length 4, 6, and 9, then its perimeter is $4 + 6 + 9 = 19$.

Polygons

Polygon questions on the Math Test tend to deal with perimeters and areas, so you should pay particular attention to those sections below.

By definition, a polygon is a two-dimensional figure with three or more straight sides. Under that definition, triangles are a type of polygon. However, since triangles are such an important part of the ACT, we gave them their own section. This section will deal with polygons of four sides or more.

Perimeter of Polygons

As with triangles, the perimeter of a polygon is equal to the sum of the length of its sides. Perimeter problems on the ACT usually involve unconventional polygons like this one:

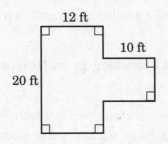

If you saw this polygon on the ACT, you would probably be asked to determine its perimeter. These questions can be tricky because of the number of sides involved and the number of sides the ACT decides to label. Wouldn't it have been easier if all the sides were labeled? Yes, it would have been easier, which is why the ACT didn't label them. Still, if you think about it, this question isn't hard. In fact, if you flipped the lines out in the upper-right and lower-right corners, you would have a rectangle:

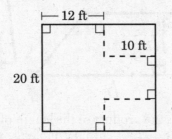

The ACT writers were kind enough to give you the height of the rectangle (20 ft), and you can figure out the width of the rectangle by adding 12 ft and 10 ft to get 22 ft. So the perimeter of this normal rectangle masquerading as a weird polygon is $2 \times l + 2w$ or $2 \times 20 + 2 \times 22 = 84$ ft.

Parallelograms

A parallelogram is a quadrilateral whose opposite sides are parallel.

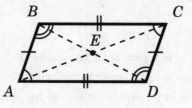

In a parallelogram,

1. Opposite sides are equal in length; $\overline{BC} = \overline{AD}$ and $\overline{BA} = \overline{CD}$.

2. Opposite angles are equal; $\angle A = \angle C$; $\angle B = \angle D$.

3. Adjacent angles are supplementary.

4. The diagonals bisect each other; therefore, $\overline{BE} = \overline{ED}$ and $\overline{AE} = \overline{EC}$.

5. Each diagonal splits a parallelogram into two congruent triangles; $\triangle AEB \cong \triangle CED$.

6. Two diagonals split a parallelogram into two pairs of congruent triangles.

Area of a Parallelogram

To calculate the area of a parallelogram, we must introduce a new term: altitude. The altitude of a parallelogram is the line segment perpendicular to a pair of opposite sides with one endpoint on each side. Below are various parallelograms and their altitudes.

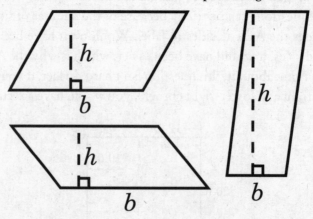

The area of a parallelogram is the product of the length of its altitude and the length of a side that contains an endpoint of the altitude. This side is called the base of the parallelogram. Any side can become a base of a given parallelogram: all you need to do is draw an altitude from it to the opposite side. A common way to describe the area of a parallelogram is the base times the height, where the height is the altitude:

$$A = b \times h$$

Rectangles

A rectangle is a specialized parallelogram whose angles all equal 90°. All the rules that hold for parallelograms hold for rectangles. A rectangle has further properties, however:

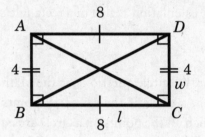

In a rectangle,

1. The angles are all equal to 90°.

2. The diagonals are equal in length; $\overline{BD} = \overline{AC}$.

Area of a Rectangle

The area of a rectangle is equal to its length multiplied by its width:

$$A = lw$$

In the case of the rectangle pictured above, the area equals $4 \times 8 = 32$ square units.

Squares

A square is a specific kind of rectangle where all of the sides are of equal length.

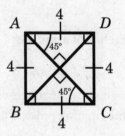

In a square,

1. All sides are of equal length.

2. All angles are equal to 90°.

3. The diagonals bisect each other at right angles; $\overline{BD} \perp \overline{AC}$.

4. The diagonals bisect the vertex angles to create 45° angles. (This means that the two diagonals break the square into four 45-45-90 triangles.)

5. The diagonals are equal in length; $\overline{BD} = \overline{AC}$.

Area of a Square

The area of a square is equal to the square of the length of a side:

$$A = s^2$$

In the case of the square above, the area is **16**. Notice that the calculation for a square's area is essentially the same calculation as that of a rectangle's area (length times width).

Circles

You may encounter one or two circle questions on the Math Test. As we said in the co-ordinate geometry section, a circle is the set of all points equidistant from a given point. The point from which all the points on a circle are equidistant is called the center, and the distance from that point to the circle is called the radius.

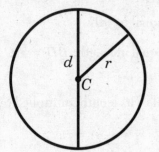

The circle above has its center at point C and a radius of length r. All circles also have a diameter. The diameter of a circle is a line segment that contains the center and whose endpoints are both on the circle. The length of the diameter is twice that of the radius.

Circumference of a Circle

The formula to find the circumference of a circle is:

$$C = 2\pi r$$

where r stands for the length of the radius. Because two times the radius is also equal to a circle's diameter, the formula for the circumference of a circle can also be written as πd.

Area of a Circle

The area of a circle is the radius squared multiplied by π:

$$A = \pi r^2$$

Simple Three-Dimensional Geometry

Solids are three-dimensional shapes. You probably will not see any questions on solids on the Math Test. When these questions do show up, they almost always cover rectangular solids, which are the easiest solids with which to work.

A rectangular solid is a six-faced, three-dimensional shape with six rectangular faces.

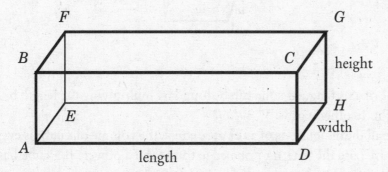

Just as squares are specialized rectangles, cubes are specialized rectangular solids. For a cube, the length, width, and height are all equal.

Surface Area

The surface area of a solid is the area of its outermost skin. A cardboard box, for example, is made up of a bunch of rectangles fastened together. The sum of the areas of those rectangles is the surface area of the cardboard box.

To calculate the surface area of a rectangular solid, all you have to do is find the area of each of the sides and sum them. In fact, your job is even easier than that. The six sides of a rectangular solid can be divided into three pairs of two. If you look at the solid diagrammed above, you should see that panel *ABFE = DCGH, BCDA = FGHE*, and *BCGF = ADHE*. Therefore, you only have to calculate the areas of one of each of the three pairs, sum those areas, and multiply that answer by two.

With a cube, finding the surface area is even easier. By definition, each side of a cube will always be the same, so to calculate the surface area, find the area of one side and multiply by six.

There is one property of surface area of which you should be aware. Imagine a rectangular solid that has a length of 8, a width of 4, and a height of 4. Now image a giant cleaver that comes and cuts the solid into two cubes, each of which has a length, width, and height of 4. Do the two cubes have a bigger combined surface area, a smaller combined surface area, or a combined surface area equal to the original solid? The answer is that the two cubes have a bigger surface area. Think about the cleaver coming down: it cuts the original solid in half, meaning it creates two new faces that are now on the surface. Whenever something is cut in half, or in pieces, its surface area increases (although its volume is unchanged).

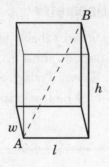

Volume

The volume of a rectangular solid can be found by multiplying the length by the width by the height. In other words, $V = lwh$.

Because all the dimensions of a cube are equal, the volume of a cube is even easier to calculate: just raise the length of one edge to the third power. If a cube has a length, width, and height of 3, the volume equals $3^3 = 27$.

Diagonal Length

The diagonal of a rectangular solid is the line segment whose endpoints are at opposite corners. Each rectangular solid has four diagonals, all with the same length, which connect each pair of opposite vertices.

The formula for the length of a diagonal is:

$$d = \sqrt{l^2 + w^2 + h^2}$$

where l is the length, w is the width, and h is the height.

You can think of this formula as the Pythagorean theorem in three dimensions. In fact, you can derive this formula using the Pythagorean theorem. First, find the length of the diagonal along the base. This is $\sqrt{l^2 + w^2}$. Then use the Pythagorean theorem again, incorporating height to find the length of the diagonal from one corner to the other: $d^2 = (\sqrt{l^2 + w^2})^2 + h^2$. Thus $d^2 = l^2 + w^2 + h^2$ and $d = \sqrt{l^2 + w^2 + h^2}$.

Trigonometry

At last we've arrived at everyone's favorite part of the Math Test. At least, it's our favorite. We're not sure what all the fuss is about when it comes to ACT trig. Many students are a little scared of trig, but the ACT seems to overcompensate for that fact by testing trig in an extremely straightforward way. ACT trig is basically all about right triangles. If you felt comfortable in the triangle section above, trig will be a breeze. If you didn't feel too comfortable, learning a bit of trig can help you. When it comes down to it, you only have to be comfortable with the most basic aspects of trig to do well on the ACT trig questions.

Finally, there will only be four trig questions on the Math Test, so even if you aren't comfortable with trig, it won't destroy your Math score. The topics of trigonometry covered by the ACT are:

1. SOHCAHTOA

2. Solving Triangles

3. Trigonometric Identities

4. Trigonometric Graphs

SOHCAHTOA: Sine, Cosine, and Tangent

If you can remember the acronym SOHCAHTOA, you'll do really well on the trig questions. Yup, it's as easy as that. This acronym captures almost everything you'll need to know to answer ACT trig questions. It means:

SOH: Sine   (Opposite over Hypotenuse)

CAH: Cosine   (Adjacent over Hypotenuse)

TOA: Tangent   (Opposite over Adjacent)

All of this opposite-adjacent-hypotenuse business in the parentheses tells you how to calculate the sine, cosine, and tangent of a right triangle. Opposite means the side facing the angle; adjacent means the side that's next to the angle, but isn't the hypotenuse (the side opposite the 90° angle). Say you have the following right triangle:

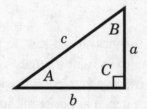

If you want to find the sine of A just think of SOH, and you know you have to divide a, the opposite side, by c, the hypotenuse of the triangle. Get the idea? So in the above:

$$\sin A = \frac{a}{c} \quad \sin B = \frac{b}{c}$$

$$\cos A = \frac{b}{c} \quad \cos B = \frac{a}{c}$$

$$\tan A = \frac{a}{b} \quad \tan B = \frac{b}{a}$$

There are some values for the sine, cosine, and tangent of particular angles that you should memorize for the ACT. ACT trig questions often test these angles, and if you have the trig values memorized, you can save a great deal of time.

Angle	Sine	Cosine	Tangent
0°	0	1	0
30°	1/2	$\sqrt{3}/2$	$\sqrt{3}/3$
45°	$\sqrt{2}/2$	$\sqrt{2}/2$	1
60°	$\sqrt{3}/2$	1/2	$\sqrt{3}$
90°	1	0	undefined

Solving Triangles

Once you understand the trigonometric functions of sine, cosine, and tangent, you should be able to use these functions to "solve" a triangle. In other words, if you are given some information about a triangle, you should be able to use the trigonometric functions to figure out the values of other angles or sides of the triangle. For example,

What is the length of $\overline{BC}$ in the triangle below?

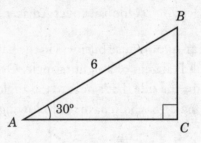

In this problem, you are given the measure of $\angle A$, as well as the length of $\overline{AB}$. The image also shows that this triangle is a right triangle. You can use this information to solve for $\overline{BC}$ if you can figure out which trigonometric function to use. You have to find the value of side $\overline{BC}$, which stands opposite the angle you know. You also know the value of the hypotenuse. To figure out $\overline{BC}$, then, you need to use the trig function that uses both opposite and hypotenuse, which is sine. From the chart of the values of critical points, you know that sin 30° = ½.

To solve:

$$\sin 30° = \frac{x}{6}$$
$$\frac{1}{2} = \frac{x}{6}$$
$$x = 3$$

Another favorite ACT problem is to combine the Pythagorean theorem with trig functions, like so:

What is the sine of $\angle A$ in right triangle ABC below?

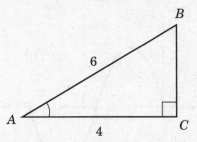

To find the sine of $\angle A$, you need to know the value of the side opposite $\angle A$ and the value of the hypotenuse. The figure gives the value of the hypotenuse, but not of the opposite side. However, since the figure *does* provide the value of $\overline{AC}$, you can calculate the value of the opposite side, $\overline{BC}$, by using the Pythagorean theorem.

$$AB^2 = AC^2 + BC^2$$
$$6^2 = 4^2 + x^2$$
$$36 = 16 + x^2$$
$$x^2 = 20$$
$$x = \sqrt{20} = 2\sqrt{5}$$

Now that you know the value of $\overline{BC}$, you can solve for sine A:

$$\sin A = \frac{2\sqrt{5}}{6}$$
$$\sin A = \frac{\sqrt{5}}{3}$$

Trigonometric Identities

A trigonometric identity is an equation involving trigonometric functions that holds true for all angles. For the ACT test, trigonometric identities, on those few occasions when they come up, will be helpful in situations when you need to simplify a trigonometric expression. The two identities you should know are:

1. $\tan\theta = \dfrac{\sin\theta}{\cos\theta}$

2. $\sin^2\theta + \cos^2\theta = 1$

ACT Math Subjects

If you see an expression that contains either $(\sin\theta)/(\cos\theta)$ or $\sin^2\theta + \cos^2\theta$, you should immediately substitute in its identity.

Trigonometric Graphs

The ACT will include one or two questions covering the graphs of the trigonometric functions. You should be able to match each graph with each function, and you should know when the different functions reach their highest point and lowest point.

Graph of $y = \sin x$

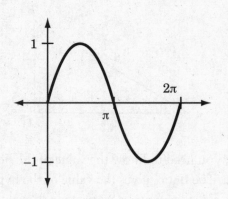

Graph of $y = \cos x$

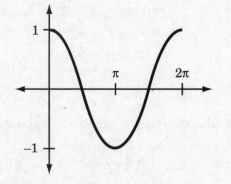

Graph of $y = \tan x$

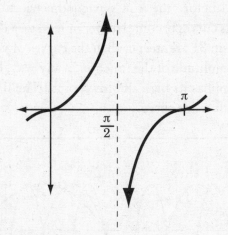

Stretching the Trigonometric Graphs

In addition to knowing the graphs of the trigonometric functions, you should also know how the graphs can be stretched vertically or horizontally. Vertical stretches affect the graph's amplitude, while horizontal stretches change the period.

Stretching the Amplitude

If a coefficient is placed in front of the function, the graph will stretch vertically: its highest points will be higher and its lowest points will be lower. Whereas the function $y = \sin x$ never goes higher than 1 or lower than -1, the function $y = 3\sin x$ has a high point of 3 and a low point of -3. Changing the amplitude of a function does not change the value of x at which the high and low points occur. In the figure below, for example, $y = \sin x$ and $y = 3\sin x$ both have their high points when x equals $-3\pi/2$ and $\pi/2$.

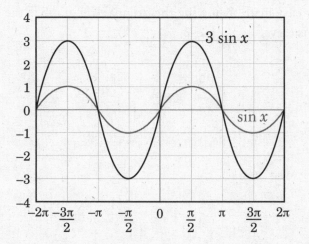

The amplitude of a trigonometric function is equal to the absolute value of the coefficient that appears before the function. The amplitude of $y = 2\cos x$ is 2, the amplitude of $y = \frac{1}{2}\sin x$ is $\frac{1}{2}$, and the amplitude of $y = -2\sin x$ is 2.

Stretching the Period

If a coefficient is placed before the x in a trigonometric function, the function is stretched horizontally: its curves become steeper or less steep depending on the coefficient. The curves of $y = \sin 3x$ are steeper than the curves of $y = \sin(\frac{1}{2})x$. This coefficient doesn't affect the amplitude of the function in any way, but it does affect *where* on the x-axis the function has its high and low points. The figure below shows how changing the period affects a sine curve.

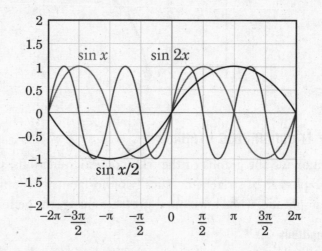

The ACT may test your knowledge of period by presenting you with a trig function that has a period coefficient and asking you for the smallest positive value where the function reaches its maximum value. For example:

What is the smallest positive value for x where $y = \cos 2x$ reaches its maximum value?

To answer this question, you need to know the original cosine curve and be able to carry out some very easy math. Knowing the original trig graph is the crucial thing; the math, as we said, is easy.

ACT Reading Review

The ACT Reading Test

Chapter Contents

T HE ACT READING TEST GIVES YOU 35 minutes to read four rather lengthy passages and answer 40 questions on the passages. Because you have little time to do a lot of work, time is really of the essence on the Reading Test. Becoming familiar with the format and content of this Subject Test before you actually have to take it will help you use your time efficiently and effectively.

Instructions for the Reading Test

There's no reason to waste a single minute (or even a fraction of one) glancing at the instructions during the test. Do yourself a favor and learn them before test day. You should know the drill by now: read, repeat, remember. Rinse only after your test date.

> **Instructions:** On this test, you will have 35 minutes to read four passages and answer 40 questions (ten questions on each passage). Each set of ten questions appears directly after the relevant passage. You should select the answer choice that best answers the question. There is no time limit for work on the individual passages, so you can move freely between the passages and refer to each as often as you'd like.

Got that? These directions are pretty straightforward. If you do feel any confusion, rest assured it will be gone by the time you finish this chapter and are familiar with the layout of the test. Let's move on.

The Format of the Reading Test

The Reading Test has two main components: the passages and the questions.

The Passages

Each of the four passages is approximately 750 words long and presented in two columns. They'll basically look like this (except they'll be longer and have words other than "blah"):

This is a sample passage.

Blah blah blah blah blah blah blah blah blah blah blah blah blah blah blah
blah blah blah blah blah blah blah blah blah blah blah blah blah blah blah
blah blah blah blah blah blah blah blah blah blah blah blah blah blah blah
blah blah blah blah blah blah blah blah blah blah blah blah blah blah blah
5   blah blah blah blah blah blah blah blah blah blah blah blah blah blah blah
blah blah blah blah blah blah blah blah blah blah blah blah blah blah blah
blah blah.
Blah blah blah blah blah blah blah blah blah blah blah blah blah blah blah
blah blah blah blah blah blah blah blah blah blah blah blah blah blah blah
10   blah blah blah blah blah blah blah blah blah blah blah blah blah blah blah
blah blah blah blah blah blah blah blah blah blah blah blah blah blah blah
blah blah blah blah blah blah blah blah blah blah blah blah blah blah blah
blah blah blah blah blah blah blah blah blah blah blah blah blah blah blah
blah blah.
15   Blah blah blah blah blah blah blah blah blah blah blah blah blah blah blah
blah blah blah blah blah blah blah blah blah blah blah blah blah blah blah
blah blah blah blah blah blah blah blah blah blah blah blah blah blah blah
blah blah blah blah blah blah blah blah blah blah blah blah blah blah blah
blah blah blah blah blah blah blah blah blah blah blah blah blah blah blah
20   blah blah blah blah blah blah blah blah blah blah blah blah blah blah
blah blah.

The numbers along the left side of the column are line numbers (the "5" means that you're reading the fifth line of the passage, the "15" means you're reading the fifteenth line, etc.). Line numbers appear on every fifth line of the passage. They are useful primarily to refer to specific sections addressed by some questions.

The Questions

Each passage is directly followed by 10 questions of varying difficulty, making a total of 40 questions on the Reading Test. The ACT includes a number of different types of questions in each batch of 10. We'll cover each type in the following "Content" section, and provide in-depth examples in the section featuring sample passages and questions.

The ACT Reading Test

The Content of the Reading Test

When we say "the content of the Reading Test," we are actually referring to two different things. The first type of content refers to the subject matter of the passages. The second type refers to the sorts of questions asked about the passages.

The Passages

The Reading Test consists of four passages: Prose Fiction, Social Science, Humanities, and Natural Science—always appearing in that order. Prose Fiction is the only fiction passage on the test; the other three are nonfiction. All four passages are given equal weight in scoring.

Later in this chapter, we will present and analyze sample passages covering the four content areas. For now, read below for brief descriptions of each passage type.

Prose Fiction

The Prose Fiction passage is the only fiction piece on the Reading Test. Prose Fiction passages are usually excerpts from novels or short stories. You should approach this passage as you would an assignment for your high school English class, not as you would a book you read in your spare time. When you read fiction for pleasure, you may be tempted to read simply for the story. Yet while the plot is an important element of most fiction, and one on which the questions will test you, it is certainly not the only element.

In addition to the plot of the passage, pay attention to character development. Since plot and character are usually essential to a story, your ability to identify and comprehend them are probably pretty strong already. You should also pay attention to tone, style, and mood when reading the passage. Ask yourself questions like: "Who is the narrator?" "Does the narrator exhibit any sympathies or biases?" "What are the relationships between the characters?" These questions will help you keep on top of the passage as you read.

Social Science

The Social Science passage can cover a variety of subjects ranging from anthropology to economics to politics. All of the subjects that appear in the Social Science passage essentially deal with the ways societies and civilization work, and most of them have a political context.

When reading the passage, you should pay attention to the key names, dates, and concepts mentioned, and you want to underline this information as you read over the passage. Because the subject of this passage is often historical, you should also pay attention to cause-effect relationships and the chronology of events.

Social Science writing is often research-based and, as a result, relatively formal in tone. Despite the relative objectivity implied by words like "research" and "science," the authors of Social Science passages often express strong and controversial views on their subjects. You should try to decipher the author's standpoint—if he or she has one—from the general argument of the passage and individual statements.

Humanities

Humanities passages cover cultural matters, particularly art and literature. These passages tend to be written analytically or journalistically. On rare occasions, you might encounter a Humanities passage that is an excerpt from a personal essay.

In some respects, the Humanities passage closely resembles the Social Science passage. They both deal with either historical or contemporary figures and events, so they are both full of specific information. The difference between the two types of passages lies in their emphasis. Whereas the Social Science passage usually provides a political context for figures and events, the Humanities passage focuses on their artistic or literary significance.

As in the Social Science passage, the writer of the Humanities passage will often have a slant or bias, and your reading of the passage should be sensitive to that.

Natural Science

Natural Science passages discuss, wildly enough, scientific topics. These passages present scientific arguments or experiments and explain the reasoning behind them and their significance.

These passages are usually heavy on facts and scientific theories. You should keep an eye out for cause-effect relationships and comparisons when reading Natural Science passages.

The Questions

The 40 questions found on the Reading Test can be broken down into several types according to what they test. Most broadly, the questions can be categorized by the way in which they force you to interact with the passage. One type will ask you to deal with the passage in a very straightforward way, and to identify details, facts, and specific information that is clearly stated in the passage. The second type will ask you to take a further step, and to use the information in the passage to figure out larger issues such as main idea, relationships, point of view, etc.

More specifically, the different types of questions test your ability to:

1. Identify specific details and facts

2. Determine the meaning of words through context

3. Draw inferences from given evidence

4. Understand character and character motivation

5. Identify the main idea of a section or the whole passage

6. Identify the author's point of view or tone

7. Identify cause-effect relationships

8. Make comparisons and analogies

Some of the question types apply primarily—and sometimes solely—to certain passages. For instance, understanding character questions appear only on the Prose Fiction passage, since it's the only passage that will have characters. On the other hand, you won't find a main idea question on the Prose Fiction passage, since works of fiction generally don't present arguments.

The list above is designed to give you a general impression of the questions asked on the Reading Test. We will cover each question type in far more detail later in the section, when we provide sample passages and questions.

Strategies for the Reading Test

O
F THE FOUR SUBJECT TESTS, IT CAN BE the most difficult to prepare for the Reading Test. Doing well on the Reading Test is not a matter of having tricks up your sleeve. When you come to a question that asks about a passage's main point, you can't rely on some handy main-point trick to figure out the answer—either you know it or you don't.

That said, you can use a general strategy to improve your performance on the test. We like to think of this general strategy as a macro approach to the entire Subject Test, rather than micro tips to get you from question to question. The crux of the strategy is your ability to read well—that is, with speed and without sacrificing comprehension.

Read!

Before we go on to discuss specific strategies for the Reading Test, we want to give you this piece of advice: reading during the months and weeks before the ACT is the best preparation for the Reading Test. The Reading Test assesses one main thing: your reading comprehension skills. Every time you read, regardless of *what* you read, you exercise your reading comprehension skills. And the more you read, the better you'll become at quickly and thoroughly comprehending what's written. So it makes sense that the best practice for the Reading Test is reading.

While reading this SparkNotes book will have you well on your way toward ACT success, we encourage you to improve your score and your mind by reading other things in your spare time. Newspapers, novels, and homework assignments provide good reading material. You may particularly want to focus on reading science articles in a newspaper or scientific magazine, as many students have less familiarity with this type of material. The more challenging the material, the more exercise your brain will get, so don't just read comic books and cereal boxes.

Order of Difficulty, the Reading Test, and You

Neither the passages nor the questions on the Reading Test are ordered by difficulty. Different students find different passages of the Reading Test difficult. Some people can't make heads or tails of Prose Fiction, while others get bogged down by the slew of facts in the Natural Science passage. Similarly, different students have difficulty with different types of questions on the Reading Test. Some students may find it difficult to remember facts, while others may become confused drawing inferences.

Beating yourself silly trying to master all the Reading Test passages and questions is not necessarily the best method of preparation. In an ideal world, you'd know how to answer all the questions correctly. But in ACT world, being aware of your abilities and using that awareness strategically will get you as far as you need to go.

Using Practice Tests

Practice tests are your most useful tool for spotting your weaknesses. Take a practice Reading Test before you begin studying and then another after you've done some preparation. On the answer sheets accompanying each test in the back of this book, we've provided the question type for each question. When you score your practice tests, you'll be able to see how you did on each type of question, so you can pinpoint your weak and strong areas for focused study.

Using Your Abilities to Develop a Test-Taking Strategy

Knowing your strong and weak points is essential for developing a simple but effective Reading Test strategy. On the actual test, play to your strong points and play down your weak ones. For example, after all your studying, if you're still incapable of correctly answering cause-effect questions, don't waste valuable time struggling with them on the actual test. Instead, guess on those questions or save them for a second pass through the test. Play the percentages: concentrate on questions you're more likely to get right to achieve your optimum score.

The Perfect Balance: Optimizing Your Time

As is probably abundantly clear to you by now, the Reading Test demands a little extra something from you: in addition to answering its questions, you must digest approximately 3,000 words worth of information. In order to be effective on this test, you must achieve an optimum balance between the time you spend reading the passages and the time you spend answering the questions. For instance, if you sweat over the first passage, painstakingly making sure you know its every little detail, you'll probably run out of time before you get to the last passage. On the flip side, if you breeze through the passages, registering a word here and there, you'll probably have a hard time answering the questions. The lesson here is that you need to find the perfect balance.

There's no formula for this perfect balance; in fact, what's "perfect" varies from person to person. Below, we'll give you some general strategies for rationing your time on the Reading Test. We think these strategies work well for most people, but ultimately it's up to you to decide what works best. Our strategies can help you, but you should complement them by taking timed practice Reading Tests. By practicing frequently, you can determine your ideal reading speed—the speed that allows you to get through the passages quickly while understanding what's being said.

Reading the Reading Test

Because the Reading Test quizzes you on your understanding of general themes and specific information in each passage, your instinct is probably to read the entire passage carefully, making sure you don't miss anything that can be covered in the questions. If you had unlimited time, this method of reading would probably make sense, but you don't have unlimited time; in fact, you have extremely limited time.

There are only ten questions accompanying each passage. These ten questions cannot cover the entire content of a passage, so reading for every detail is a waste of time. When reading an ACT passage, read carefully to understand general elements: the topic, theme, argument, etc. When you see details that seem important, don't fuss painstakingly over those details. Instead, lightly note them in your mind and perhaps make a quick mark in the margin. This way, you'll reduce wasted time and gain a good enough comprehension of the passage to answer questions that cover general aspects of the passage correctly. You'll also have a good enough sense of the passage's layout, so that when the passage asks about specific information, you'll be able to go back quickly to the passage, check the information, and choose the correct answer.

Reading Strategies

Achieving the Perfect Balance

You may be thinking that finding the perfect balance is easier said than done. Well, yes, that's probably true. But there are methods you can use to find this balance.

Read the Passage First, Then Answer the Questions

We suggest that you read the passage first and save the questions until you're done reading. Read the passage quickly and lightly for a general understanding. Pay active attention to what's going on, but don't get bogged down trying to assimilate every detail. By the end of your first reading, you should understand the themes of the passage and the argument, if there is one. We definitely don't mean that you should ignore the meat of paragraphs and focus only on their first sentences; if you do that, you won't understand the passage.

Reading for a general understanding means you don't have to memorize all the specific facts of the passage. The author uses specific facts to support an argument, but as you read, you should be more concerned with their cumulative effect (i.e., the larger argument) than with the specific facts themselves. If you get to a point in a passage where the author lists a bunch of facts to support an idea, you can make a quick note of the list in the margin for future reference (for more on this, see "Scribble, Doodle, Underline").

The only time you should slow down and go back is if you lose the flow of the passage—if you realize you don't know what's happening, what's being argued, or what in the world that entire last paragraph was about.

Read the passage with an awareness of the general questions you might be asked. What is the author's goal in writing the passage? What are the tone, themes, major points, and so on of the passage? When you finish a passage, you should be able to answer these questions and also have a sense of the passage's layout. Reading on the ACT is like taking a tour of a room—you have to know the layout of the room, but you don't have to know the location of every knicknack.

After you finish the passage, go to the questions. Since you read the passage with the big picture in mind, you should be able to answer the general questions dealing with main points, point of view, tone, etc. When you get to a question on a specific detail, don't immediately look at the answer choices to avoid being influenced by "trick" answers. Instead, articulate to yourself exactly what the question is asking. Then quickly go back to the passage and come up with your own answer to the question. Finally, choose the answer that best matches yours.

If you get to a question that is very hard and threatens to take a lot of time, place a mark next to it, skip it, move on to the next question, and come back if you have time. You should *not*, however, move on to the next passage while leaving a blank question behind you. Answer all questions dealing with a passage while the passage is still fresh in your mind.

Why "Passage First, Questions After" Is a Good Strategy

Some test prep books advise you to look at the questions first to find key words, and then to read the passage with an eye to answering the questions. While this strategy seems good on paper, it's really quite difficult in practice, especially in high-pressure situations like taking the ACT. Imagine trying to remember what 10 questions ask while reading an unfamiliar passage, simultaneously trying to get the gist of it and looking for possible answers to the questions. That's like trying to chew gum while patting your head, rubbing your stomach, and singing "The Star Spangled Banner." In addition, because some of the questions ask for specific details, you'll feel pressured to pay close attention to the passage line by line, which takes too much time. Ultimately, the "questions first, passage after" strategy can be extremely confusing as well as extremely difficult to execute.

"Passage first, questions after" is really just common sense. Using this method, you can avoid the confusion caused by other strategies. Again, think about the passage as a room and the answers to the questions as objects within the room. If you follow the other test books' strategy of "questions first," you'll be left groping helplessly for the objects in a completely dark room. If you follow our strategy (in other words, if you use common sense), you'll have turned on the lights first, making the objects much easier to find.

Scribble, Doodle, Underline

Once upon a time, you learned that a pristine ACT test booklet is a sad ACT test booklet. Here, on the Reading Test, you have an opportunity to give your friendly test book a happy buzz by scribbling and underlining away in it. You won't be doing all this scrawling simply for the benefit of the ACT booklet, though; any marking you do will help you when it's time to answer the questions.

You're probably wondering how you'll know what to underline without having read the questions. Indeed, that does seem like the tricky part. But the point of underlining is not to pinpoint specific answers to questions; in fact, if you could underline answers, you'd be wasting time underlining them when you could be filling in a bubble on the answer sheet.

The point of underlining, then, is not to highlight correct answers, but to assist you when you refer back to the passage for those answers. You can use your underlines and notes as a map through the passage, so you don't waste time covering passage territory for a second time. As long as scribbling and underlining don't take up a significant amount of time (you should not be drawing straight lines or printing neatly), any marginal notes and underlines will help and guide you when you answer the questions.

Underlining the topic sentence of each paragraph (it's not always the first sentence) will help you keep on top of the argument's direction. These underlines will serve as handy reference tools when you need to refer back to the passage. Because you're reading for the general point of a passage and its component paragraphs, you do not need to know every single illustrative example. When you encounter a sentence or a section that looks like it will enumerate examples to support a point, you can quickly glance at the section, then scribble "eg" or "ex" or some other mark in the margin to let you know that this is an example. If a question asks you for specific evidence that demonstrates a certain point, you can refer back to the relevant passage by glancing at your notes and then moving down to the section marked "eg" or "ex." You can also use numbers to mark items in an extended list. Underlining key phrases that help relate parts of the passage, such as "subsequently," "on the other hand," and "in contrast" will also help you map your way through the passage.

Take a practice Reading Test and exercise your wrists making marginal notes and underlines. Soon you should be able to develop a scribbling system that works for you.

Passages and Questions on the Reading Test

IN THE FOLLOWING SECTION, YOU'LL GET AN in-depth look at the passages on the Reading Test through four sample passages covering each topic area. You should read these sample passages to gain familiarity with the types of passages on the test.

Our four sample passages are accompanied by descriptions of the question types you're likely to encounter, along with examples of these questions and methods for answering the sample questions. Our goal in offering you these descriptions and examples is to increase your familiarity with the types of questions on the test. These descriptions are usually not heavy on suggested strategy. As we've said before, there aren't many strategies you can use to answer individual questions on the Reading Test. The best thing you can do to prepare is to know what the test will ask you.

We've divided this section into two parts: Prose Fiction first, and the other three tests second. We've made this division because the Prose Fiction passage differs the most from the others in terms of how you read it and what you're reading it for.

The Prose Fiction Passage

As we've stated before, you should not read the ACT Prose Fiction passage as you would a novel that you casually pick up on a Saturday afternoon. Treat the Prose Fiction passage as you would an English homework assignment. In addition to understanding the story behind the passage, you should also strive to understand the passage's use of style and tone.

The Sample Passage

The following sample is adapted from James Joyce's short story "Grace" in Dubliners.

She was an active, practical woman of middle age. Not long before she
had celebrated her silver wedding and renewed her intimacy with her
husband by waltzing with him to Mr. Power's accompaniment. In her days
of courtship, Mr. Kernan had seemed to her a not ungallant figure: and she
5 still hurried to the chapel door whenever a wedding was reported and,
seeing the bridal pair, recalled with vivid pleasure how she had passed out
of the Star of the Sea Church in Sandymount, leaning on the arm of a jovial
well-fed man, who was dressed smartly in a frock-coat and lavender
trousers and carried a silk hat gracefully balanced upon his other arm. After
10 three weeks she had found a wife's life irksome and, later on, when she was
beginning to find it unbearable, she had become a mother. The part of
mother presented to her no insuperable difficulties and for twenty-five
years she had kept house shrewdly for her husband. Her two eldest sons
were launched. One was in a draper's shop in Glasgow and the other was
15 clerk to a tea-merchant in Belfast. They were good sons, wrote regularly
and sometimes sent home money. The other children were still at school.

Mr. Kernan sent a letter to his office next day and remained in bed. She
made beef-tea for him and scolded him roundly. She accepted his frequent
intemperance as part of the climate, healed him dutifully whenever he was
20 sick and always tried to make him eat a breakfast. There were worse
husbands. He had never been violent since the boys had grown up, and she
knew that he would walk to the end of Thomas Street and back again to
book even a small order.

Two nights after, his friends came to see him. She brought them up to
25 his bedroom, the air of which was impregnated with a personal odor, and
gave them chairs at the fire. Mr. Kernan's tongue, the occasional stinging
pain of which had made him somewhat irritable during the day, became
more polite. He sat propped up in the bed by pillows and the little color in
his puffy cheeks made them resemble warm cinders. He apologized to his
30 guests for the disorder of the room, but at the same time looked at them a
little proudly, with a veteran's pride.

He was quite unconscious that he was the victim of a plot which his
friends, Mr. Cunningham, Mr. M'Coy and Mr. Power had disclosed to Mrs.
Kernan in the parlor. The idea had been Mr. Power's, but its development
35 was entrusted to Mr. Cunningham. Mr. Kernan came of Protestant stock

and, though he had been converted to the Catholic faith at the time of his
marriage, he had not been in the pale of the Church for twenty years. He
was fond, moreover, of giving side-thrusts at Catholicism.

40   Mr. Cunningham was the very man for such a case. He was an elder
colleague of Mr. Power. His own domestic life was not very happy. People
had great sympathy with him, for it was known that he had married an
unpresentable woman who was an incurable drunkard. He had set up house
for her six times; and each time she had pawned the furniture on him.

45   Everyone had respect for poor Martin Cunningham. He was a
thoroughly sensible man, influential and intelligent. His blade of human
knowledge, natural astuteness particularized by long association with cases
in the police courts, had been tempered by brief immersions in the waters
of general philosophy. He was well informed. His friends bowed to his
opinions and considered that his face was like Shakespeare's.

50   When the plot had been disclosed to her, Mrs. Kernan had said:
"I leave it all in your hands, Mr. Cunningham."

    After a quarter of a century of married life, she had very few illusions
left. Religion for her was a habit, and she suspected that a man of her
husband's age would not change greatly before death. She was tempted

55 to see a curious appropriateness in his accident and, but that she did not
wish to seem bloody-minded, would have told the gentlemen that Mr.
Kernan's tongue would not suffer by being shortened. However, Mr.
Cunningham was a capable man; and religion was religion. The scheme
might do good and, at least, it could do no harm. Her beliefs were not

60 extravagant. She believed steadily in the Sacred Heart as the most
generally useful of all Catholic devotions and approved of the sacraments.
Her faith was bounded by her kitchen, but, if she was put to it, she could
believe also in the banshee and in the Holy Ghost.

The Questions

Below, we'll give you a rundown of the questions you're most likely to find on the
Prose Fiction passage and how to answer them. All of the examples below pertain to
the above passage.

Identify Specific Details and Facts

Specific detail questions are perhaps the most straightforward questions you'll encounter anywhere on the test. As the name suggests, these questions ask you to find
specific details within the passage. They are very common on the Prose Fiction passage
and throughout the rest of the test. You'll probably see three or four specific detail
questions accompanying the Prose Fiction passage.

    Here's an example of a relatively easy specific detail question:

    According to his friends, Mr. Cunningham resembles:

A.   Mr. Kernan.
B.   a policeman.
C.   Shakespeare.
D.   Mr. Power.

If you know the answer to this question, you're all set. If you don't, you probably remember there was a section near the end of the passage that discussed Mr. Cunningham and his background. To answer this question, you should first look in that section because the answer is probably there. Have you looked yet? Well, the answer *is* there, on line 49 ("his face was like Shakespeare's"). The correct answer is **C**.

That question was fairly simple, partly because it had a one-word answer, but specific detail questions can be more confusing when the answers are longer. Try another question about Mr. Cunningham:

> According to the passage, people feel sorry for Mr. Cunningham because:
>
> **A.** he is sensible, influential, and intelligent.
> **B.** he was the victim of a plot by his friends.
> **C.** he has a long association with police courts.
> **D.** he is married to a drunkard.

While this question is not too difficult, it is slightly more confusing than the previous one simply because the answers are longer. If you've read the passage reasonably carefully and you've quickly double-checked the answer in the passage, you can correctly identify **D** as the answer. Choices **A** and **C** are actually given as reasons why Mr. Cunningham is *respected* by his acquaintances, and choice **B** applies not to Mr. Cunningham but to Mr. Kernan.

While specific-detail questions are generally straightforward, they can try to trick you by leading you to give an answer that seems correct if you read one sentence, but is revealed as incorrect by another. For example,

> How many children do the Kernans have?
>
> **A.** None
> **B.** One
> **C.** Two
> **D.** More than two

If you remembered that the Kernans' children were mentioned in the first paragraph, you'd look there, and perhaps your eye would fall on the sentence, "Her two eldest sons were launched." A quick glance at this sentence may miss the word "eldest," which indicates that there are younger children, so you may decide that there are only two children in the Kernan family and the answer is **C**. But the word "eldest" and the last sentence of the paragraph, "The other children were still at school," indicate that there are other children in the family and that the correct answer is **D**.

Draw Inferences

Inference questions ask for implied information. They want you to take a piece of information given in the passage and use it to figure out something else. Because the answers are not given explicitly within the passage, these questions are often significantly more difficult than specific detail questions. But they are just as common, so you need to get a handle on them.

You can usually spot an inference question from a mile away. Inference questions frequently use verbs such as "suggest," "infer," "imply," and "indicate."

As with specific detail questions, some inference questions are easier than others. Sometimes, the ACT writers will feel extra nice and refer you to a specific portion of the passage. For example,

> The second paragraph (lines 17–23) suggests that the Kernans' marriage is characterized primarily by:
>
> A.   Mr. Kernan's violent behavior toward his wife.
> B.   Mrs. Kernan's patience with her husband.
> C.   Mr. Kernan's fondness for his wife's beef-tea.
> D.   Mr. Kernan's willingness to go to the store for his wife.

In some ways, this inference question resembles a specific detail question. Elements of all the answer choices are mentioned in the paragraph. Your job is to figure out which answer choice *best* answers the question. Perhaps choice **A** characterized the marriage at one point in time, but the narrator notes that Mr. Kernan "had never been violent since the boys had grown up," so **A** is wrong. Nowhere in the paragraph does it mention that Mr. Kernan likes the beef-tea his wife makes for him, so you can rule out **C**. Choice **D** seems to be a true statement, since the last sentence of the paragraph states, "she knew that he would walk to the end of Thomas Street and back again to book even a small order." But does this willingness adequately *characterize* their marriage? Not really. The specificity of the act makes it an unlikely candidate to be a characteristic. If choice **D** had said, "Mr. Kernan's courtesy to his wife" or "Mr. Kernan's consideration for his wife," the choice would have a little more promise as a characteristic (but then its validity would come into question). That leaves us with choice **B**. Although we eliminated the other answer choices, it doesn't hurt to make sure that **B** fits the bill. The key sentence in the paragraph that suggests B is the correct answer is the third one (lines 18–20): "She accepted his frequent intemperance as part of the climate, healed him dutifully whenever he was sick and always tried to make him eat a breakfast." Words such as "accepted" and "dutifully" don't suggest that Mrs. Kernan takes care of her husband because she thinks it's fun; rather, these words suggest a patient resignation to her life and duties. So you can safely choose **B** as the correct answer.

Less direct inference questions will ask you to draw out character or plot details from the information given in the passage. These inference questions can be more difficult to answer than the one given above. Here's an example of a character inference question:

It can be reasonably inferred from this passage that Mrs. Kernan's attitude toward religion is:

A.   fervently pious.
B.   practical but faithful.
C.   skeptical.
D.   nonexistent.

If you read effectively, you'll remember that the last paragraph contains a description of Mrs. Kernan's brand of religious faith. There are several key phrases in this passage that should help you choose the correct answer: "Religion for her was a habit"; "Her beliefs were not extravagant"; "She believed steadily in the Sacred Heart as the most generally useful of all Catholic devotions"; "Her faith was bounded by her kitchen, but, if she was put to it, she could believe also in the banshee and in the Holy Ghost." We can't provide you with a strategy for interpreting this information. You must be able to comprehend the writing in order to get this question right. No matter what your understanding is, you'll probably realize that **D** is wrong because the existence of the phrases indicates that Mrs. Kernan has some kind of attitude toward religion. If you understand what's being said in the phrases above, you can eliminate choice **A** (because "Her beliefs were not extravagant") and choice **C** (because "she could also believe in the banshee and in the Holy Ghost"). So the correct answer is **B**, "practical but faithful," which is exactly what those phrases imply.

Now try this plot inference question:

One can reasonably infer from this passage that the goal of the friends' plan, mentioned in line 32, is to:

A.   make Mr. Kernan a good, practicing Catholic.
B.   cure Mr. Kernan of his alcohol abuse.
C.   turn Mr. Kernan into a better husband.
D.   go to Thomas Street for Mrs. Kernan while her husband recovers.

The nice thing about inference questions is that they do the inferring for you. If you have no idea what the friends are plotting for Mr. Kernan, don't worry: the ACT writers have given you the right answer already—along with three wrong answers. The best way to approach this question, and any like it, is to read the sentences around the provided section (line 32, in this case). For this question, the information following line 32 will help you decide on the correct answer. The rest of the paragraph is devoted primarily to Mr. Kernan's religious background and his attitude toward Catholicism, and it should give you a good clue that the answer is probably **A**. If you've gotten to this point but feel uncomfortable committing yourself to the answer, consider the other answer choices and how well they work. Choice **B** suggests that the friends want Mr. Kernan to stop drinking; however, there is no mention of his drinking habit after line 24 (in fact, there is only one reference to it in this passage), so it is most likely not the answer. Choice **C** suggests the vague goal of turning Mr. Kernan into a better husband.

While this may be a consequence of the desired change in his behavior, it doesn't seem to be the right answer because there is no mention of it in the passage; in fact, Mrs. Kernan seems reasonably content with their relationship. Choice **D**, which offers Thomas Street as an answer, tries to lure you off track by mentioning an unrelated but specific piece of information from the passage. So choice **A** is the best answer to this question. Remember that, although choices **B** and **C** may be true desires of Mr. Kernan's friends, they are not the *best* answer to the question. Choice **A** is the best answer because religion is specifically discussed in relation to the plot.

Understanding Character

Character generalization questions appear only with the Prose Fiction passage. They ask you to reduce a lot of information about a character into a simple, digestible statement. For instance, if you have a character who hates children, kicks dogs, takes candy from babies, and steals his neighbors' mail, you could make the generalization that he is mean-spirited and cruel.

Let's take a look at a character generalization problem dealing with the sample passage:

> Mrs. Kernan would most likely agree with which of the following characterizations of her husband:
>
> **A.** He is foolish and excessive.
> **B.** He is sensible and intelligent.
> **C.** He is irreverent but generally considerate.
> **D.** He is proud of his accomplishments.

As you can see, this question is similar to the inference questions discussed above, in that it asks you to draw a conclusion from the information provided by the passage. You should note that the question doesn't ask you how *you* would characterize Mr. Kernan or how the narrator or any other character would, but how *Mrs. Kernan* would characterize him. Because this question is specific in its point of view, it helps you pinpoint the sections you must examine—the ones that give Mrs. Kernan's opinion of her husband. If you do that, you can figure out that nothing suggests choice **A** is true. Choice **B** is also incorrect according to the passage; the words "sensible" and "intelligent" are actually used to describe Mr. Cunningham. Choice **D** is not correct, although Mr. Kernan appears proud of his injury (line 31). Choice **C** is the correct answer. You can arrive at this answer through process of elimination, but you can also get to it through understanding the passage. The last paragraph reveals that Mrs. Kernan apparently thinks her husband's "tongue would not suffer by being shortened." Earlier in the passage, the narrator also describes Mr. Kernan's verbal lack of respect for Catholicism, so "irreverence" seems to describe him accurately in Mrs. Kernan's eyes. The second part of the answer, his consideration, is implied in the second paragraph, which describes Mr. Kernan's willingness to run errands for his wife.

When answering inference and character generalization questions, you should re-member that right answers are not necessarily perfect answers; they must simply be the best answer out of the four provided. For that reason, when answering these ques-tions, you should read through all the answer choices and ask yourself which one best answers the question.

Point of View

Point of view questions accompanying the Prose Fiction passage will generally ask you to describe the narrator's point of view. Questions that deal with other characters' points of view usually fall under the heading of inference or character generalization. Point of view questions are fairly rare on the Prose Fiction passage, but you may en-counter one of them on the test.

These questions tend to be pretty obvious when they're asked because they usually look like this:

The narrator's point of view is that of:

A.   a detached observer.
B.   Mr. Kernan.
C.   a biased observer.
D.   the Kernans' child.

Again, answering this question is a matter of understanding the material, not of tricks and strategies. You can eliminate choices **B** and **D** immediately if you recognize that the passage is not written in the first person. Then ask yourself whether the narrator ex-presses any biases (does he obviously prefer one character to another, for instance?). In this passage, the narrator is fairly bias-free, so the best answer to this question is **A**, a detached observer.

Cause-Effect

These questions ask you to identify either the cause or the effect of a situation. These questions are fairly rare on the Prose Fiction passage, but you should still be prepared to answer one. You will generally recognize these questions from cue words in the question, such as "resulted in" and "led to" for effect questions, and "caused by" and "because" for cause questions.

On the Prose Fiction passage, cause-effect questions will generally ask you to iden-tify how one character's actions affected another's. For example,

According to the passage, the visit paid by Mr. Kernan's friends resulted in:

A.   his unpleasant behavior toward them.
B   a completely healed tongue.
C.   his boasting of weathering two days of sickness.
D.   his politeness.

As in the example above, cause-effect questions will not make you draw inferences (only inference questions will). Cause-effect questions are interested in the facts of the passage. Both the cause (the visit paid by Mr. Kernan's friends) and the effect (one of the answer choices) should be clearly stated in the passage. You should not choose an answer choice that requires you to make an inference. After you eliminate choices **A** and **B**, which are contrary to facts stated in the third paragraph of the passage, you must choose between choices **C** and **D**. You should eliminate choice **C**, though, because it is an inference and involves guessing on your part rather than referring specifically to the text. Although the last line of the third paragraph states that Mr. Kernan appears to feel "a veteran's pride," it is never explicitly stated within the passage that this feeling arises from the visit by his friends. Because you are looking for the *best* answer choice—not the *perfect* answer choice—choice **D** is correct. The passage explicitly states that the visit causes Mr. Kernan to become "more polite" after having been cantankerous.

The Three Nonfiction Passages

The following section deals with the three nonfiction passages. First, we'll give you a sample Social Science passage (the one that directly follows Prose Fiction on the test), and then a rundown of the questions that may be asked on it. As these questions are similar to the questions asked on the other two sections, Humanities and Natural Science, we will use our sample Social Science passage as a template for the others, explaining to you exactly how to answer general question types found on all three passages. Following the Social Science section, we will discuss the specifics of the Humanities and Natural Science passages, using sample passages and questions.

The Social Science Passage

In many ways, you can think of the Social Science passage as the standard nonfiction passage on the Reading Test because it can cover all of the question types and because it represents a middle ground between the Humanities and Natural Science passages. In this section, you'll read a sample Social Science passage and learn about all the possible question types associated with Social Science:

1. Specific Detail

2. Inference

3. Main Idea and Argument

4. Cause-Effect

5. Point of View

6. Comparison

7. Vocabulary

These questions types are also found on the Humanities and Natural Science passages, so the descriptions we give of them here also apply to those passages.

The Sample Passage

The following passage is adapted from an essay on Malcolm X.

During 1963 the nation became aware of a civil rights leader making a dramatic impact on the black community. Malcolm X, the charismatic, ferociously eloquent preacher and organizer for the Nation of Islam, had been preaching his message to (usually poor) black communities since the
5   early 1950s. Malcolm X was a "black Muslim," a member of a small but crucial religious organization that proved instrumental in giving birth to the modern Black Power Movement. The Nation of Islam, led by Elijah Muhammed, believed that whites had systematically and immorally denied blacks their rights and that blacks therefore had no reason to act peacefully
10 or lovingly towards whites. Instead of supporting the philosophy of non-violence embraced by Martin Luther King, Jr., the Nation of Islam believed that whites should repay blacks for slavery and allow them to set up their own nation within America. Until that day arrived, the Nation encouraged blacks to defend themselves against white supremacy "by any means
15 necessary."

The membership and influence of the Nation of Islam grew tremendously during the late 1950s and early 1960s, in large part due to the dedication and speaking skills of Malcolm X. Like King, Malcolm X mobilized the people, leading them in rallies, protest marches, and
20 demonstrations. Though he was widely known among the black underclass and in civil rights circles, it was not until his famous "Chickens Coming Home to Roost" speech on December 1, 1963, that he truly blasted his way into the consciousness of most Americans. X gave the speech in reference to the November 22 assassination of President John F. Kennedy, and
25 described the killing as "chickens coming home to roost." The media, which had negatively portrayed the Nation of Islam in general and Malcolm X in particular, jumped on the speech immediately, claiming it as an example of Malcolm X's divisive hatred and blatant disrespect for the U.S. government. In the face of public reaction, officials within the Nation silenced X for 90
30 days. The speech not only brought Malcolm X to the forefront of the civil rights struggle but also highlighted and helped solidify a strand of civil rights activism that found inadequate the non-violent policies the movement had so far used.

Malcolm X is a highly controversial figure in black history. Many see
35 him as a spouter of hatred and divisiveness. Certainly it is true that a fair portion of X's rhetoric—his references to "white devils" and "Uncle

Tomming Negro leaders"—was angry and inflammatory, and did little to
promote the cause of integration. However, X represented an element
of black consciousness that white people refused to face: the incredible
40   rage that most black people felt after suffering so many years of oppression.

      For all of his fame, it is interesting to note that his mobilization and
participation in the civil rights movement was actually fairly slim. He
respected some civil rights leaders (King, for example), though for much of
his life he believed that the idea of integration was merely playing into the
45   hands of the white man. For the most part, Malcolm X's role in the civil
rights movement was merely to preach, to pass on the crucial message of
black rage to white America, and to become a role model for those who
began the Black Power Movement a few years later. He is vitally important
not because of what he actually did, but because of what he said and how
50   he said it.

      Malcolm X's own biography reveals that he was more nuanced and
interesting than the simple role of black rage that he was sometimes
assigned by both whites who held him up as an example of rage gone wild,
and blacks who saw him as a warrior willing to express that which most
55   blacks could not. After years of service, X eventually broke with the Nation
of Islam. Then, after a life-changing visit to Mecca in 1964, he broke with his
own previous thought and began preaching a message of cross-cultural
unity, and founded the Organization for Afro-American Unity. With his fire-
and-brimstone oratory, broad base of black community support, and knack
60   for attracting media attention, X's new path might have forged major
interracial inroads. But before he could follow this new path of more
general inclusion, X was assassinated on February 21, 1965, shot as he was
giving a speech in New York. The perpetrators have never been found,
though many presume the Nation of Islam to have been responsible. X's
65   autobiography, *The Autobiography of Malcolm X*, is an abiding document
of both his own personal journey and of his time.

The Questions

Below, we'll give you a rundown of the questions you'll likely encounter on the Social Science passage. All of the questions below pertain to the above passage on Malcolm X.

Specific Detail

Specific detail questions on the nonfiction passages are as straightforward as they are
on the fiction passage. They ask you to identify a specific detail or piece of evidence
from the passage. For example,

    According to the passage, some critics of Malcolm X censured him for being:

    A.   an "Uncle Tomming Negro leader."
    B.   an example of rage gone wild.
    C.   a warrior for African-Americans.
    D.   a civil rights leader.

If you read the section dealing with specific detail for Prose Fiction, you probably have a pretty good idea of how to answer this question. Getting the right answer is really a matter of careful reading, but you can use the question to help you eliminate answers that are clearly wrong. For instance, because the question asks you for criticisms of Malcolm X, it is probably a safe bet to eliminate choices **C** and **D**, which give positive interpretations of his career. Choosing the right answer from choices **A** and **B** is really a matter of understanding the material. If you read the passage with some care, you probably remember that Malcolm X used choice **A** as a criticism for black leaders whom he considered panderers to white supremacists. In the last paragraph of the passage, the writer notes that some white people "held him as an example of rage gone wild"—a pretty clear criticism of Malcolm X; thus **B** is the correct answer to the question.

Inference

You may remember that inference questions ask for implied information. The answers to inference questions won't be stated explicitly in the nonfiction passages; instead, you must ferret out the answer from the evidence provided by the passage. For example,

> One can reasonably infer from the passage that the Nation of Islam is widely thought responsible for Malcolm X's assassination because:
>
> **A.** X broke with the group politically and philosophically.
> **B.** X gave a controversial speech after Kennedy's assassination.
> **C.** X visited Mecca in 1964.
> **D.** X began to write an autobiography.

You should look to the last paragraph, where Malcolm X's assassination is described. Ask yourself what this paragraph focuses on. The paragraph mentions that Malcolm X broke with the Nation of Islam (choice **A**) and that he visited Mecca (choice **C**). You can safely eliminate choice **B** because his controversial "Chickens Coming Home to Roost" speech occurred well before his break with the Nation of Islam; moreover, the author explicitly states the Nation of Islam's response to the speech in line 29. Now you must choose between the remaining three answer choices: **A**, **C**, and **D**. If you can't figure out the correct answer, consider which answer choices make sense and which one best answers the question. Choice **C**, which points to Malcolm X's trip to Mecca, would probably not make sense as an answer choice, as this pilgrimage is a central element of the Islamic faith. Like choice **C**, choice **D** also does not seem to offer the proper detail. The passage offers no connection at all between Malcolm X's autobiography and his assassination. Choice **A**, meanwhile, fits the bill: Malcolm X not only split from the Nation of Islam, but also began to preach a message opposed to the group's—a message of unity and nonviolence rather than of separate nations and cultures. Choice **A** is the correct answer to the question because it best describes why the Nation of Islam would assassinate Malcolm X.

Main Idea and Argument

On the nonfiction passages, you'll encounter quite a few main idea questions. Some of the questions will deal with the passage as a whole, while others will deal with sections of the passage. In both cases, these questions will ask you to identify the main ideas or arguments presented within the passage.

Here's an example of a main idea question:

The main point made in the third paragraph (lines 34–40) is that:

A.   the "Chickens Coming Home to Roost" speech propelled Malcolm X to the forefront of the civil rights debate.

B.   Malcolm X's rhetoric promoted hatred and divisiveness.

C.   Malcolm X was an important role model for the future leaders of the Black Power Movement.

D.   although his message was controversial, Malcolm X successfully gave a voice to black people who had been oppressed for generations.

This question refers you to a specific paragraph and asks you for that paragraph's main point. For questions that direct you to a specific section, you should glance back at that section to ensure that you don't confuse it with another. If you don't glance back, you may mistake the paragraph for the one before or the one after and choose the wrong answer, such as **A** (which deals with the second paragraph) or **C** (which deals with the fourth). Also make sure that you understand the point of the whole paragraph. If you read just the first couple sentences, you may think the correct answer to this question is **B**. But the rest of the paragraph goes on to talk about Malcolm X's impact despite that controversial side of him, and ultimately the point of the paragraph is **D**. Choice **D** is the best answer because it incorporates both aspects of the paragraph: the first part of it, which discusses his controversial method; and the second part, which talks about why he was an important civil rights figure.

Many main point questions will cover the entire passage. These questions will generally be posed in one of the following three ways:

- The main idea of the passage is that:

- One of the main ideas of the passage is that:

- Which of the following best states the main point of the passage?

Here's where having read the passage carefully (but quickly) will work to your advantage. You should be able to answer general questions like these without referring back to the passage *if* you did a good job of reading the first time. Reading with an eye to answering specific questions may be an effective strategy for most questions, but you will inevitably encounter general questions like these on the Reading Test. If you choose the strategy of reading for answers, you will have to reread the passage in order to answer these questions. Ultimately, you'll waste more time than you'll save.

Another kind of main idea question asks you to identify the main *purpose* of the passage—in other words, to determine why the author wrote it. For example:

The author's purpose in writing this passage seems to be:

A.   to portray Malcolm X as the man responsible for the civil rights movement.
B.   to reveal an overlooked event in Malcolm X's life.
C.   to give a relatively balanced account of the positive and negative sides of Malcolm X's career.
D.   to expose the Nation of Islam's role in the assassination of Malcolm X.

You should be able to answer this question without referring back to the passage because it deals with the general theme and argument. When you come to a question like this, ask yourself what the author has accomplished with the passage. If you form your answer before looking at the answer choices, you're less likely to be swayed by a wrong but convincing answer choice. The author of this passage describes both negative and positive aspects of Malcolm X's career. For example, the author mentions his early rage and unwillingness to integrate, but balances that with X's crucial representation of African-Americans. Choice **C** seems the best answer to the question, but you can always double-check by eliminating the other answer choices. Choice **A** is wrong because the author states in line 42 that X's "participation in the civil rights movement was actually fairly slim." Choice **B** is also wrong; the author never mentions an overlooked event in his life. Choice **D** is wrong even though the author suggests the Nation of Islam's culpability in X's death; this suggestion is not the focus of the entire passage, and it is only briefly mentioned in the last paragraph. So you can safely select choice **C** as the best answer.

Cause-Effect

As with their Prose Fiction counterparts, cause-effect questions on the nonfiction passages will ask you to identify either the cause or the effect of a particular situation. You are more likely to see these questions on Social Science and Natural Science passages than on Humanities passages because the "science" passages often describe sequences of events.

Cue words in the question will let you know whether you must identify the cause or the effect of the relationship. Words such as "because" warn you that the question seeks the cause of an event, while words such as "resulted in," "led to," and "caused" let you know you'll need to identify the effect of a situation.

Here's an example of a nonfiction cause-effect question:

According to the passage, Malcolm X came to the forefront of the American civil rights struggle because:

A.   of his "Chickens Coming Home to Roost" speech, which generated a media frenzy.
B.   he was silenced by the Nation of Islam for 90 days.
C.   he rejected King's nonviolent message.
D.   he founded the Organization for Afro-American Unity.

As with almost all questions on the ACT Reading Test, answering this question correctly requires a careful reading of the passage. From the cue word "because," you know that the question asks you for the "cause" half of the relationship. If you're unable to answer this question without referring back to the passage, you should at least have an idea of where to look. The second paragraph deals with Malcolm X's increasing fame. There are a couple of sentences within this paragraph that clearly indicate **A** as the correct answer to this question: "it was not until his famous 'Chickens Coming Home to Roost' speech on December 1, 1963, that he truly blasted his way into the consciousness of most Americans" and "[t]he speech . . . brought Malcolm X to the forefront of the civil rights struggle."

Point of View

Point-of-view questions on the nonfiction passages differ somewhat from those on the Prose Fiction passage. As opposed to the fiction point-of-view questions, which ask you to identify the point of view of the narrator (a fictional invention), the nonfiction point-of-view questions ask you to identify how the writer (a real person) views his or her subject. As you read a passage, consider whether the writer's argument seems to support or attack the passage's subject, and pay attention to the language the writer uses. The writer's tone (is it angry? is it sympathetic?) will be a good indication of his or her feelings about the subject.

Here's an example of a point-of-view question:

The attitude of the author of the passage toward Malcolm X is apparently one of:

A.   anger.
B.   ambivalence.
C.   disapproval.
D.   respect.

The relatively objective tone of this particular Social Science passage makes this point of view question difficult—more difficult, at least, than answering a point-of-view question for a passage written by an obviously biased author. Still, you should be able to pinpoint the author's tone even here, especially with assistance from the answer choices. In this passage, the author pretty clearly does not feel negatively about Malcolm X, although she may disagree with some of his tactics, so you can eliminate choices **A** and **C**, which indicate negative sentiments. Now you are left with a positive feeling (choice **D**) and a mixed one (choice **B**). Which one more accurately describes the author's feelings for Malcolm X? While the author is fairly objective in her writing, her attitude cannot be described as mixed or ambivalent. Although she does mix praise for Malcolm X with some condemnation, her overall tone is one of respect, so the best answer is **D**.

As you can see in the example above, the answer choices for a point of view question can seem similar to one another, but there are always crucial differences. For example, words like "anger" and "disapproval" both express negative sentiments. If "anger" and "disapproval" were the two most promising answer choices for a question, you would have to know more than whether the writer approves or disapproves of the subject. You would have to identify the degree of passion in the writer's negativity. If the writer cares deeply about the subject, then "anger" may be the correct answer. If the writer is intellectually opposed to the subject, then "disapproval" may be correct.

Comparison

As the name implies, comparison questions ask you to make comparisons, usually between different viewpoints or data. Comparisons can be tricky questions to handle because you need to assimilate information on both sides of the comparison and then see how the sides compare. You'll see these types of questions more frequently on the Social Science and Natural Science passages than on the Humanities passage because the "science" passages usually contain a lot of factual information. You probably won't encounter more than a couple of these questions on the entire test.

The question will contain cue words or phrases that indicate it's a comparison question. "Compares" and "analogy" are two words that frequently appear in comparison questions.

Here's an example of a comparison question:

The author's comparison of Malcolm X to Martin Luther King Jr. focuses primarily on:

A.   their stances on integration and violence against whites.
B.   their leadership of the civil rights movement.
C.   their roles in the Nation of Islam.
D.   their influences on future black leaders.

Two key points in the passage can help you answer this question: lines 10–13 and lines 18–20. If you refer to those sections, you'll be able to select choice **A** as the best answer to the question. You can also go through the list and eliminate incorrect answers. Choice **B** is incorrect because the author explicitly states that X's role in the civil rights movement was limited. Choice **C** is incorrect because the author never connects King to the Nation of Islam (to which King did not belong). Choice **D** doesn't work because the author never discusses King's influence on future leaders.

Vocabulary

Vocabulary questions ask you to decipher the meaning of a word given its context. Usually, these words will have multiple meanings, so you must decide the function of the word in the specific context.

You will immediately recognize these questions from their formulaic phrasing. They provide you with a line number along with an italicized word or short phrase in quotation marks, and then they ask you to provide the meaning of the word in context. For example,

> As it is used in line 37, the word *inflammatory* most nearly means:
>
> A. revolutionary.
> B. flammable.
> C. violent.
> D. agitating.

To answer this particular vocabulary question (a rather difficult one), you must also know what the answer choices mean. This is where having a good vocabulary will help you on the ACT. In line 27, the author discusses how X's language was "angry and inflammatory." In the surrounding lines, you get a sense that X's speech was designed to provoke anger and disorder. Thus the correct answer to this question is **D** because "agitating" provides that sense of provocation. If you cannot figure out the answer directly, you should try to eliminate the other choices. Choice **A**, "revolutionary," is related to "inflammatory," but it is incorrect. You can think of it as a subset of inflammatory: revolutionary speech tends to be inflammatory, but inflammatory speech is not always revolutionary. "Revolutionary" contains a political connotation that "inflammatory" and "agitating" lack, so it is not as good an answer as **D**. Choice **B**, "flammable," applies to physical objects and means that something is capable of being lit on fire. While you may be tempted to choose this answer because both the tested word and the answer choice contain the root "flam," there is a crucial difference between their definitions. Choice **C**, "violent," is incorrect because it lacks the element of provocation present in "inflammatory."

The Humanities Passage

The Humanities passage will generally deal with a topic of cultural interest. You can think of it as a "softer" version of the Social Science passage, which tends to have more of an analytical and political angle. Still, the general approach to answering Social Science questions should apply to Humanities questions.

The Sample Passage

The following passage is adapted from the chapter "How I Came to Play Rip Van Winkle" in
The Autobiography of Joseph Jefferson (© 1890, 1891 by the Century Company, New York).

The hope of entering the race for dramatic fame as an individual and
single attraction never came into my head until, in 1858, I acted Asa
Trenchard in *Our American Cousin*; but as the curtain descended the first
night on that remarkably successful play, visions of large type, foreign
5 countries, and increased remuneration floated before me, and I resolved to
be a star if I could. A resolution to this effect is easily made; its
accomplishment is quite another matter.

Art has always been my sweetheart, and I have loved her for herself
alone. I had fancied that our affection was mutual, so that when I failed as
10 a star, which I certainly did, I thought she had jilted me. Not so. I wronged
her. She only reminded me that I had taken too great a liberty, and that if I
expected to win her I must press my suit with more patience. Checked, but
undaunted in the resolve, my mind dwelt upon my vision, and I still indulged
in day-dreams of the future.

15 During these delightful reveries it came up before me that in acting Asa
Trenchard I had, for the first time in my life on the stage, spoken a pathetic
speech; and though I did not look at the audience during the time I was
acting—for that is dreadful—I felt that they both laughed and cried. I had
before this often made my audience smile, but never until now had I moved
20 them to tears. This to me novel accomplishment was delightful, and in
casting about for a new character my mind was ever dwelling on
reproducing an effect where humor would be so closely allied to pathos
that smiles and tears should mingle with each other. Where could I get one?
There had been many written, and as I looked back into the dramatic
25 history of the past a long line of lovely ghosts loomed up before me,
passing as in a procession: Job Thornberry, Bob Tyke, Frank Ostland, Zekiel
Homespun, and a host of departed heroes "with martial stalk went by my
watch." Charming fellows all, but not for me, I felt I could not do them
justice. Besides, they were too human. I was looking for a myth—something
30 intangible and impossible. But he would not come. Time went on, and still
with no result.

During the summer of 1859 I arranged to board with my family at a
queer old Dutch farmhouse in Paradise Valley, at the foot of Pocono
Mountain, in Pennsylvania. A ridge of hills covered with tall
35 hemlocks surrounds the vale, and numerous trout-streams wind through
the meadows and tumble over the rocks. Stray farms are scattered through
the valley, and the few old Dutchmen and their families who till the soil were
born upon it; there and only there they have ever lived. The valley
harmonized with me and our resources. The scene was wild, the air was
40 fresh, and the board was cheap. What could the light heart and purse of a
poor actor ask for more than this?

On one of those long rainy days that always render the country so dull I
had climbed to the loft of the barn, and lying upon the hay was reading that
delightful book *The Life and Letters of Washington Irving*. I had gotten
45 well into the volume, and was much interested in it, when to my surprise I

came upon a passage which said that he had seen me at Laura Keene's
theater as Goldfinch in Holcroft's comedy of *The Road to Ruin,* and that
I reminded him of my father "in look, gesture, size, and make." Till then I
was not aware that he had ever seen me. I was comparatively obscure, and
50   to find myself remembered and written of by such a man gave me a thrill of
pleasure I can never forget. I put down the book, and lay there thinking how
proud I was, and ought to be, at the revelation of this compliment. What an
incentive to a youngster like me to go on.

And so I thought to myself, "Washington Irving, the author of *The*
55   *Sketch-Book,* in which is the quaint story of Rip Van Winkle." Rip Van
Winkle! There was to me magic in the sound of the name as I repeated it.
Why, was not this the very character I wanted? An American story by an
American author was surely just the theme suited to an American actor.

The Questions

As we stated above, your approach to questions on the Humanities passage should be essentially the same as your approach to Social Science questions. For that reason, in this section we'll skip most of the commentary on the question types and go straight to the examples.

To start with, we'll give you a rundown of the types of questions that appear most frequently on the Humanities passage, in decreasing order:

1.   Specific Detail

2.   Inference

3.   Vocabulary

4.   Main Idea

5.   Comparison

Specific Detail

Specific detail questions on the Humanities passage are exactly the same as on the rest of the test. Because you should already have a good grasp of how to answer these questions, we'll just give you some examples of questions that could accompany the passage above.

According to the passage, Washington Irving saw the author perform:

A.   Asa Trenchard in *Our American Cousin.*
B.   Goldfinch in *The Road to Ruin.*
C.   Rip Van Winkle in *The Sketch-Book.*
D.   Job Thornberry.

The author considers the following to be attractions of Paradise Valley EXCEPT:

F.   the fresh air.
G.   the untamed scenery.
H.   the long rainy days.
J.   the inexpensive board.

As you already know, the best way to answer these questions is to read the passage carefully enough the first time around that you either know the answer, or can quickly find the answer in the passage. If you made marginal notes and underlines during your preliminary reading, you will be able to refer easily to the relevant sections of the passage for these questions.

The correct answers to these questions are **B** and **H**, respectively.

Inference

By now, you should have a good idea of how to answer inference questions. An inference question on this sample Humanities passage could look like this:

It can be reasonably inferred from the passage that the character of Rip Van Winkle is:

A.　charming.
B.　very human.
C.　like Washington Irving's father.
D.　mythical.

This inference question is slightly complicated because Rip Van Winkle is mentioned in the last paragraph of the passage, but you need to refer to the third paragraph in order to answer the question. In the third paragraph, the author describes the types of characters he is unable to play and the type of character that he would like to play. The inference you must make to answer this question is that Rip Van Winkle represents an ideal character for the author and therefore must fit the description in Paragraph 3: "a myth." The correct answer to this question is **D**.

Vocabulary

The Humanities passage often contains a number of vocabulary questions, so be on the lookout. Vocabulary questions on the passage above could look like this:

As it is used in line 16, the word *pathetic* most nearly means:

A.　moving.
B.　pitiful.
C.　contemptible.
D.　weak.

As it is used in line 32, the word *board* most nearly means:

F.　a rectangular piece of wood.
G.　a group of people with managerial powers.
H.　to walk onto a ship or aircraft.
J.　the cost of lodging and meals.

These vocabulary questions deal with words that have multiple meanings. They ask you to decide which meaning best suits the context. When you see vocabulary questions like these, go to the indicated line number without even looking at the answers.

Read the relevant sentence, ignoring the tested word and coming up with a different word to fill its place. This new word will be a synonym for the tested word. If you can't come up with a word by looking at the individual sentence, read the sentences around it as well. Once you have your synonym, go back to the question and compare your synonym to the answers. When you've found a match, you have your answer. If you're at a loss for words when using this strategy, you can substitute the answer choices (as long as you know what they mean) into the sentence to see whether they make sense.

If you employ the strategy above, you should see that choices **A** and **J**, respectively, make the most sense in the sentences and thus are correct.

Main Idea

Main idea questions tend to accompany Humanities passages that are more analytical or journalistic in tone than the sample passage above. With anecdotal passages like this, it's unlikely that you'll be asked to identify the main point of the passage or of a paragraph—the anecdote itself is usually the point. If you do face a main idea question, use the same strategy that we covered under the "Social Science" passage.

Comparison

Though some Humanities passages may be accompanied by more than one comparison question, this particular passage is not very fact-heavy, so it likely would not have any comparison questions. If a comparison question did appear with this sample passage, it might look like this:

In the second paragraph of the passage, the author compares art to:

A.   a profession.
B.   a sweetheart.
C.   a star.
D.   a daydream.

The comparison in this paragraph is actually a metaphor, in which the author doesn't explicitly say that art is *like* something, but says that it *is* something that it clearly isn't. You don't need to know this literary term or any other to answer this question. The first sentence of the paragraph ("Art has always been my sweetheart") should make the answer to this comparison question pretty clear. The correct answer is **B**.

Natural Science

On the continuum of Reading Test passages, the Prose Fiction passage would be on one extreme, the Social Science and Humanities passages in the middle, and the Natural Science passage at the other extreme end. The Natural Science passage is heavy on scientific facts, argument, cause-effect logic, and details.

The Sample Passage

The following passage is adapted from an essay on Lamarckian evolutionary theory.

For many centuries, scientists and scholars did not question the origin of life on Earth. They accepted the authority of the Book of Genesis, which describes God as the creator of all life. This belief, known as creationism, was supported by observations made by scientists about the everyday

5 world. For instance, organisms seemed well adapted to their environments and ways of life, as if created specifically to fill their roles; moreover, most organisms did not seem to change in any observable manner over time.

About two centuries ago, scientists began accumulating evidence that cast doubt on the theory of creationism. As scientists began to explore

10 remote parts of the natural world, they discovered seemingly bizarre forms of life. They also discovered the fossils of animals that no longer existed. These discoveries led scientists to develop new theories about the creation of species.

Count George-Louis Leclerc de Buffon was an early pioneer of these

15 new theories, proposing that the species he and his contemporaries saw had changed over time from their original forms. Jean Baptiste Lamarck was another early pioneer. Lamarck proposed ideas involving the mechanisms of use and disuse and inheritance of acquired traits to explain how species might change over time. These theories, though in many ways

20 incorrect and incomplete, paved the way for Charles Darwin, the father of the theory of evolution.

Although he built on the work of his mentor Leclerc, Lamarck often receives credit for taking the first step toward modern evolutionary theory because he proposed a mechanism explaining how the gradual change of

25 species could occur. Lamarck elaborated on the concept of "change over time," saying that life originated in simple forms and became more complex. In his 1809 publication of *Philosophie Zoologique*, he describes the two part mechanism by which change was gradually introduced into species and passed down through generations. His theory is referred to as

30 the theory of transformation or, simply, Lamarckism.

The classic example used to explain the concept of use and disuse is the elongated neck of the giraffe. According to Lamarck's theory, a giraffe could, over a lifetime of straining to reach food on high branches, develop an elongated neck. Although he referred to "a natural tendency toward

35 perfection," Lamarck could never offer an explanation of how this development could occur, thus injuring his theory. Lamarck also used the toes of water birds as an example in support of his theory. He hypothesized that water birds developed elongated, webbed toes after years of straining their toes to swim through water.

40 These two examples attempted to demonstrate how use could change an animal's trait. Lamarck also believed that disuse could cause a trait to become reduced in an animal. The wings of penguins, he believed, are smaller than those of other birds because penguins do not fly.

The second part of Lamarck's theory involved the inheritance of

45 acquired traits. Lamarck believed that traits changed or acquired over an individual animal's lifetime could be passed down to its offspring. Giraffes

50   that had acquired long necks would have offspring with long necks rather
than the short necks their parents were born with. This type of inheritance,
sometimes called Lamarckian inheritance, has since been disproved by the
discovery of hereditary genetics.

      An extension of Lamarck's ideas of inheritance that has stood the test
of time, however, is the idea that evolutionary change takes place
gradually and constantly. Lamarck studied ancient seashells and noticed
that the older they were, the simpler they appeared. From this, he
55   concluded that species started out simple and consistently moved toward
complexity or, as he said, "closer to perfection."

The Questions

Since Natural Science passages contain so many facts, many of the questions on this passage will test whether you know these facts. These questions will come in many guises besides the standard specific detail format. For example, some questions will ask you to build on information in the passage by making you identify cause-effect relationships or comparisons. Here's a breakdown of the question types commonly asked on the Natural Science passage, in order of decreasing frequency:

1. Specific Detail
2. Inference
3. Cause-Effect
4. Comparison
5. Main Idea
6. Vocabulary
7. Point of View

Despite the scientific jargon that permeates this passage, in answering the questions you should treat the passage as you would the two other nonfiction passages. In this section, we'll give you examples of questions that could be asked on the sample passage above, so you can start getting familiar with the Natural Science section.

Specific Detail

Specific Detail, the most common question type on the ACT Reading Test, is also a biggie on the Natural Science passage. For the passage above, you could see questions like these:

The theory that describes God as the creator of all life is called:

A.   creationism.
B.   Lamarckism.
C.   the theory of transformation.
D.   the Book of Genesis.

According to the passage, the giraffe is a classic example of Lamarck's theory because of its:

F.   webbed toes.
G.   elongated neck.
H.   small wings.
J.   coloration.

According to the passage, Leclerc proposed the theory:

A.   of the mechanisms of use and disuse.
B.   of inherited traits.
C.   that giraffes developed elongated necks over time.
D.   that species changed over time from their original forms.

As we've said many times by now, the best method for answering these questions correctly is simply to refer back to the passage. If you've made marginal notes and underlines, you'll have an easier time referring back to the passage and getting the right answer.

The correct answer (choice **A**) to the first question is conveniently located in the first three lines of the passage. For the second question, look to paragraph 5, where the author discusses the example of the giraffe. The first sentence of paragraph 5 reveals choice **G** to be correct. When answering the third question, you should refer to the discussion of Leclerc. In the first mention of him (in paragraph 3), you'll discover that choice **D** is the correct answer to the question.

Inference

Inference questions on the Natural Science passage are the same as they are elsewhere on the test. For example,

It is reasonable to infer from this passage that Lamarck's most lasting work on a theory of evolution is his hypothesis that:

A.   species inherit traits acquired by their parents.
B.   the forms of animals change over time.
C.   giraffes develop long necks from straining to reach high tree branches.
D.   species evolve gradually and constantly over time into more complex forms.

The answer to this question is in the first sentence of the last paragraph: "An extension of Lamarck's ideas of inheritance that has stood the test of time, however, is the idea that evolutionary change takes place gradually and constantly." The phrase "stood the test of time" indicates that this particular aspect of Lamarck's work is still relevant today. Thus the correct answer to this question is **D**.

Cause-Effect

Cause-effect questions appear pretty frequently on Natural Science passages because of the nature of their topics. Most Natural Science passages, including the sample one above, discuss cause-effect relationships that appear in nature. For example,

According to the passage, Lamarck proposed that the changing form of animals was a result of:

A.   giraffes stretching their necks to reach high branches.
B.   a natural tendency toward perfection and the inheritance of acquired traits.
C.   organisms being created to fill specific roles.
D.   hereditary genetics.

This particular cause-effect question also tests your understanding of one of the main points of the passage, as the main point happens to be a cause-effect relationship. If you understood the passage, you should be able to identify the correct answer as **B**. Choice **A** deals specifically with Lamarck's example of giraffes, while the question calls for a general explanation for all animals. Choice **C** is the belief of creationism, and Choice **D** would not be discovered until after Lamarck's time.

Comparison

You will probably see one comparison question with the Natural Science passage. As we stated before, comparison questions usually accompany passages that contain a lot of factual information, and the Natural Science passage fits the bill.

According to the passage, the elongated neck of the giraffe is analogous to:

A.   the small wings of the penguin.
B.   the large wings of most birds.
C.   the webbed toes of water birds.
D.   the inheritance of elongated necks.

To answer this question, ask yourself what the giraffe's elongated neck can be compared to. In paragraph 5, the author names both the giraffe's neck and the water bird's toes as examples of the concept of use, so the best answer is **C**. To make sure, you can eliminate the other answers. Choice **A** deals with the concept of disuse, so it is not analogous to the giraffe's neck. Choice **B** is never discussed in the passage. Choice **D** is not an analogous situation; it is a separate aspect of Lamarck's theory.

Main Idea

Main idea questions are always pretty straightforward. The tricky part is making sure that you read carefully enough to understand the main point of the passage or of a paragraph within it. Try this example:

The main point of the passage is to:

A.   describe Lamarck's ideas on evolution and their relevance to modern theories of evolution.
B.   explain how animals change through the mechanisms of use and disuse and through the inheritance of acquired traits.
C.   discuss alternative theories to creationism.
D.   show how Lamarck built upon the work of Leclerc.

If you read the passage carefully, you should be able to eliminate choices **C** and **D**, as they are clearly not the main focus of the passage. You may get stuck trying to decide between choices **A** and **B**, but you should remember that the question asks for *the passage's* main point, and not for *Lamarck's* main point. Remembering that, you should be able to identify the correct answer, **A**.

Vocabulary

You will not see many vocabulary questions accompanying the Natural Science passage. The vocabulary questions that do appear on this passage may ask you to identify an unfamiliar scientific word from its context. You can employ the strategies described for vocabulary questions on the Humanities and Social Science passages to answer vocabulary questions here.

Point of View

Point-of-view questions are extremely rare on the Natural Science passage. If you see one, it will most likely ask you to identify the point of view of the passage's author. For example,

> With which of the following statements would the author most likely agree?
>
> **A.** Most scientists today believe in creationism.
> **B.** Leclerc, not Lamarck, should be credited with taking the first step toward modern evolutionary theory.
> **C.** Lamarck's theory that life evolves from simple to complex forms is still important today.
> **D.** Today, giraffes have long necks because early giraffes did a lot of stretching.

The author of this sample passage does not seem to hold strong views on Lamarck, but it is still possible to eliminate wrong answers here and correctly answer the question. Choices **A** and **B** are incorrect because there is little focus on them in the passage: both creationism and Leclerc are mentioned, but only briefly. Choice **C** looks like the right choice because the author states in the last paragraph that this aspect of Lamarck's theory "has stood the test of time." You can make sure that Choice **C** is correct by eliminating **D**, which Lamarck, not the author, believes.

ACT Science
Reasoning Review

The ACT Science Reasoning Test

THE ACT SCIENCE REASONING TEST is arguably the most feared Subject Test, but for the wrong reasons. Time is of the essence on the test: you are given 35 minutes to digest 7 science passages and answer 40 questions on them. But the content of the Science Reasoning test, which is what usually fills students with trepidation, shouldn't cause you any stress. The term "Science Reasoning" may sound impressive and difficult, but much of the intimidation of the test is mere bluff—big words that disguise simple concepts. In this chapter, you'll learn everything you need to know to unmask and master the ACT Science Reasoning Test.

Instructions for the Science Reasoning Test

As you've probably figured out by now, you should memorize the instructions for the Science Reasoning Test before you get to the test center. The instructions for this test are pretty straightforward, but you shouldn't even glance at them on test day because time is extremely valuable on the ACT. Read the instructions to yourself a couple times to make sure you have them memorized.

> **Instructions:** This test contains seven passages, each accompanied by several questions. You should select the answer choice that best answers each question. Within the total allotted time for the subject test, you may spend as much time as you wish on each individual passage. Calculator use is not permitted.

Science Reasoning

Don't worry about the last sentence regarding calculator use. There is absolutely no need for a calculator on this test, so it doesn't matter that you're not allowed to use one.

The Format of the Science Reasoning Test

Like the Reading Test, the two main components of the Science Reasoning Test are the passages and the questions. We'll briefly explain both below.

The Passages

The Science Reasoning Test has seven science passages:

- 3 Data Representation passages

- 3 Research Summaries passages

- 1 Conflicting Viewpoints passage

These passages appear in no particular order on the Science Reasoning Test. In the "Content" section below, we'll explain the differences between the three types of passages.

All passages on the Science Reasoning Test will contain data presented in paragraphs, tables, and/or graphs. Each passage will be preceded by a written introduction to, or explanation of, the presented data. There is no standard appearance for the passages, but they all follow the basic principle of providing graphic information in addition to written exposition. The sample passages provided later in this chapter will familiarize you with different possible passage layouts.

The Questions

Each science passage is directly followed by several questions on that passage:

- Data Representation passages are accompanied by 5 questions

- Research Summaries passages have 6 questions

- The Conflicting Viewpoints passage has 7 questions

In the "Content" segment below, you'll learn about the types of questions asked. Later in the section, you'll get an in-depth review of how to handle those questions.

The Content of the Science Reasoning Test

The "content" of the Science Reasoning Test refers to several kinds of content. First, there are the topics covered by the passages on the test. Second, there are the types of passages on the test. Third, there are the types of questions asked about the different passages. The descriptions below are meant to provide you with brief overviews of each kind of content. Later in the section, we will describe, analyze, and teach you how to handle everything you'll encounter on the Science Reasoning Test.

Passage Topics

The writers of the ACT tell you to expect content covering biology, earth/space sciences, chemistry, and physics on the Science Reasoning passages. That's good advice: the passages on the Subject Test might discuss data from any of these fields. However, in the end, the Science Reasoning Test doesn't test you on your knowledge of earth sciences or any other field; it tests you on your understanding of scientific data. Where the data comes from—whether it's taken from chemistry or biology experiments—doesn't matter. In other words, the content is not important. In this chapter, we'll teach you to ignore the confusing scientific terminology and strike at the heart of the test—the data. But if you're still dying to know about the content of the passages, we'll give you the list below.

- **Biology,** including cell biology, botany, zoology, microbiology, ecology, genetics, and evolution

- **Earth/Space Sciences,** including geology, meteorology, oceanography, astronomy, and environmental sciences

- **Chemistry,** including atomic theory, inorganic chemical reactions, chemical bonding, reaction rates, solutions, equilibriums, gas laws, electrochemistry, organic chemistry, biochemistry, and properties and states of matter

- **Physics,** including mechanics, energy, thermodynamics, electromagnetism, fluids, solids, and light waves

Passage Types

As we've already mentioned, there are three types of science passages on the Science Reasoning Test: Data Representation, Research Summaries, and Conflicting Viewpoints. You will not need to remember the names of the passages for the actual test, but being able to recognize the different passages and knowing what to expect from each will help you greatly.

Data Representation

The Science Reasoning Test contains three Data Representation passages. These passages contain one or more charts (such as tables, graphs, or illustrations). The accompanying questions test your understanding of and ability to use the information presented in these charts.

Research Summaries

There are three Research Summaries passages on the Science Reasoning Test. These passages generally present two or three related experiments and the data collected from them. You can think of Research Summaries as Data Representation placed in the context of a large experiment.

Conflicting Viewpoints

The test contains only one Conflicting Viewpoints passage. This passage presents you with two or three alternative theories on an observable phenomenon—such as cloud formation or the movement of tectonic plates—and requires that you understand the differences and similarities between the viewpoints.

The Questions

Of the 40 questions on the Science Reasoning Test, 15 will accompany Data Representation passages, 18 will follow Research Summaries, and 7 will cover the Conflicting Viewpoints passage. The four main kinds of questions you'll encounter on the Data Representation and Research Summaries passages will ask you to:

- **Read the Chart.** These questions ask you simply to identify information given on the chart, and are perhaps the most straightforward questions on the Science Reasoning Test. These questions are the equivalent of specific detail questions on the Reading Test.

- **Use the Chart.** Slightly more complicated than Read the Chart questions, these questions require that you use the information given in the chart to determine other, unstated information. For example, some of these questions might ask you to make an informed guess as to what would happen if one of the variables in an experiment changed.

- **Handle Graphs.** For these questions, you will either have to translate the information in the charts into words or translate words or numbers into a chart. Being able to manipulate and transform data in this way indicates that you understand exactly what the given information in the passage means.

- **Take the Next Step.** These questions ask you what the next step should be for research experiments. Generally, this type of question will provide you with a goal for an experiment and the current scenario. You must decide the next step that should be taken to achieve that goal. You can think of these questions as Big Picture questions that ask you to look at the research or the experiment as a whole.

The questions on the Conflicting Viewpoints section are slightly different. We've divided them into three main categories: detail, inference, and comparison.

- **Detail** questions ask you to identify specific information from the arguments presented.

- **Inference** questions ask you to draw out implied information from the arguments.

- **Comparison** questions ask you to find and analyze similarities and differences between the arguments.

As you can see, the questions on Conflicting Viewpoints resemble questions on a Reading Test passage. In our section specifically devoted to the Conflicting Viewpoints passage, we'll discuss the similarities between the Conflicting Viewpoints and Reading Test passages and how those similarities should affect your strategy.

Strategies
for the Science
Reasoning Test

IN MANY WAYS, YOU SHOULD THINK ABOUT and approach the Science Reasoning Test as you would the Reading Test. On both of these tests, the questions focus solely on the passages that precede them, so you must understand what you read in order to get the correct answers. As with the Reading Test, the best (and pretty much the only) way to get correct answers is to understand the passages. For that reason, our strategies are designed to help you with your overall comprehension of the passages—not to provide you with tricks for getting past individual questions.

Don't Be Afraid of the Scientific Jargon

The reason most people seem to be afraid of this Subject Test is actually pretty superficial: it's the language. The scientific terminology used on this test can be confusing, but it should not fill you with fear. Underneath the scary language, the Science Reasoning Test is actually quite nice. In fact, once you get past the language, the questions on this test tend to be fairly straightforward and simple to answer.

Science Reasoning

There are two ways to get past the scientific jargon. The first is simply to know that it is jargon. Once you know that the concepts tested by the Subject Test are straightforward, and merely hidden by a thin veneer of complicated terms, it becomes much easier to see through that jargon. So when you see scientific terminology that seems confusing, don't panic or get nervous. Take a deep breath and break it down. You'll get through it. The second way to defuse scientific jargon is to take practice tests. The more Science Reasoning questions you deal with, the more adept you will be at seeing through the jargon to the straightforward data beneath.

Read the Passage First

The advice that you should read the passage before looking at the questions should sound familiar. We gave you the same counsel in our chapter on the Reading Test, and it is equally applicable to the Science Reasoning Test.

Read the Passage for a General Understanding

When you read the passage for the first time, you should be reading for a general understanding of it. For Data Representation and Research Summaries passages, look at the provided charts to see what factors or variables are represented. If the passage deals with an experiment, make sure you know what the experiment tests and what the goal of the experiment is. You should not examine specific aspects of the data, such as how the value of one variable changes against another—leave that sort of analysis for when you answer specific questions.

Remember that there is very little time on this test, so you should not spend a significant amount of time reading the passages. If you labor excruciatingly over every sentence and piece of data in a passage, you will leave yourself little time to answer the questions. As we stated about the Reading Test, you should find a perfect balance between reading passages and answering questions when you take your practice tests.

Talk to Yourself and Make Notes

If you find that you're having a hard time absorbing the information in the passage, talk to yourself as you go through it. If a Research Summaries passage has three experiments, say "three experiments" to yourself, or jot it down in the margin, and then note the key differences between the experiments. For example, if each experiment tests a different variable, make sure you know what the variables are.

A few key questions you should ask yourself when reading a science passage are:

- What is being tested?

- Why is it being tested?

- What are the variables?

- What are the factors that stay the same?

If you ask yourself these questions while reading the passage and make sure you know the answers to them, you will have a leg up when answering the questions.

As you go through the passage asking these questions, jot down your answers in note form next to the relevant sections of the passage. Don't spend too much time making these notes; their main functions are to assist your comprehension of the passage and to jolt your memory when you answer the questions. If you're reading about an experiment that measures acidity, you can scribble "acidity" in the margin by the experiment. If the same experiment varies the concentration of a solution (i.e., if concentration is the variable in the experiment), you can jot down something like: "change conc." You don't have to follow these examples exactly; come up with shorthand expressions that make sense to you. Underlining sentences and circling key information (the variables, for example) will also help you comprehend and remember the passage.

Answer the Questions by Playing a Matching Game

Once you have completed your first reading of the passage and have achieved a solid understanding of what it says, you should move on to the questions. If you come across a question you don't entirely understand, try to restate the question in your own words. Once you know what information the question is looking for, refer back to the passage, using your notes as guidelines.

The most reliable method for choosing the correct answer is essentially playing a matching game. Before looking at the answers, you should try to answer the question *in your own words*. By doing this, you can avoid being influenced by incorrect but tempting answer choices. Once you've come up with your answer, look at the answers provided by the ACT writers and pick the one that best matches your answer. If your answer doesn't match up with any of the choices, you probably did something wrong. In that case, you can quickly go over the question again or move on to the next question, marking the current question so you can come back to it.

Here's a summary of the process for answering questions:

1. Read the question and, if necessary, restate it in your own words so you understand what it is asking.

2. Refer back to the passage.

3. Formulate an answer in your own words, without looking at the answer choices.

4. Match your answer to the choices provided.

Base Your Answers on the Passage

Base your answers only on the contents of the passage. In the case of the Science Reasoning Test, external knowledge has the potential to hurt you. All of the information you need to know is in the passage. You may know more about a subject than the ACT writer designing the questions. If you read something into a question that the ACT writer didn't intend, you have a good chance of getting the wrong answer.

If you use information that isn't on the test, you may be outwitting yourself.

Order of Difficulty and Answering Questions

As we've emphasized before in this book, knowing the order of difficulty will help determine your overall approach to the test. On the Science Reasoning Test, you can expect to encounter questions roughly in order of increasing difficulty within each passage; however, this order of difficulty does not always hold, and you will sometimes get an easy question at the end of a passage's section. Still, keep this order of increasing difficulty in mind as you answer the questions.

With this handy piece of knowledge, you'll know that you should be able to answer the first questions within a section fairly easily. The first questions usually deal with your comprehension of the information presented in the passage. They tend to be Read the Chart questions in Data Representation and Research Summaries passages, and Detail questions in the Conflicting Viewpoints passage. If you cannot answer these questions easily, your understanding of the passage may be fundamentally flawed. In that case, you might want to spend a little time (preferably less than a minute) reviewing the passage to make sure you understand what it means.

Passages and Questions on the Science Reasoning Test

Chapter Contents

B ELOW, WE PRESENT THREE SAMPLE
Science Reasoning passages, one for each type of
passage, in the following order: Data Representa-
tion, Research Summaries, and Conflicting Viewpoints. We also include explanations
and examples of the question types that accompany them.

Data Representation

The three Data Representation passages tend to be the most straightforward passages on the Science Reasoning Test. Each Data Representation passage begins
with a written introduction. Read this introduction for a general idea of the passage, but don't labor over it. The charts in Data Representation are the focus of the
passage's questions. Use diagrams such as the one below to clarify the often confusing
terminology in the introduction and to see graphic representations of the terminology.

The Sample Passage

If left at rest, a spring will hang at its equilibrium position. If a mass (M) is attached to that spring, the spring will grow in length by a distance known as its displacement (x). A larger mass will create a larger displacement than a small mass.

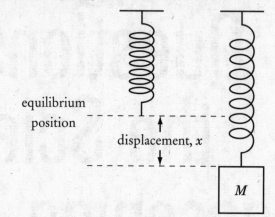

The force (F), in newtons (N), required to return the spring to its equilibrium position is the negative product of the displacement (x) and a spring constant (k), where the negative indicates the direction, not the value, of the force. The spring constant measures the elasticity of a spring: if a spring has a high k, the spring cannot be stretched easily; if a spring has a low k, it can be stretched more easily.

Various masses were attached to two springs with different spring constants, and the force was measured in each of these trials. The energy used (J) returning the spring to its equilibrium position, or Potential Energy (PE), was also measured.

Table 1

Trial	Spring Constant, k	Displacement, x (m)	Force on spring, F (N)	Potential Energy, PE (J)	Mass, M (g)
1	5	1	5	2.5	M_1
2	5	5	25	62.5	M_2
3	5	10	50	250	M_3
4	10	1	10	5	M_4
5	10	5	50	125	M_5
6	10	10	100	500	M_6

Strategy for Reading the Passage

Since the Data Representation passage is fairly straightforward, you don't necessarily need to employ specific reading strategies. But there are a couple of tips you should keep in mind when going through the passage.

We suggest that you begin by skimming the introduction to the passage. Since the introductions to passages on the Science Reasoning Test are usually full of confusing scientific terminology, you should not spend time struggling to understand everything the introduction says. Rather, use the introduction to get a general idea of what the subsequent chart illustrates. Also, consider circling key terms in the introduction to make referring back to the passage easier.

When you get to the chart (our Data Representation example has only one chart, but you will sometimes come across two), you should glance over it to make sure that you know what's being measured and that, in general, you feel comfortable finding information in the chart. Save detailed exploration of the chart for when you answer specific questions.

The Questions

Each Data Representation passage is accompanied by five questions. These questions fall into one of four categories, and we'll show you how to handle all four below. All of the following questions refer to the sample passage above.

Read the Chart

Read the Chart questions test your ability to locate and understand the information presented in the charts provided in the passage. The answers to these questions are usually explicitly stated within the charts. Here's an example of a Read the Chart question:

> Which of the following statements about displacement and the force on the spring is consistent with the data in Table 1?
>
> **A.** The force on the spring increases as displacement increases.
> **B.** The force on the spring decreases as displacement increases.
> **C.** The force on the spring does not change as displacement increases.
> **D.** The force on the spring increases then decreases as displacement increases.

Answering this question is a simple matter of reading the chart. The question explicitly tells you to look at two numbers—the displacement of the spring and the force on the spring—and identify their relationship. All of the answer choices deal with what happens when the displacement increases, so you know that your goal is to see what happens to the force on the spring. Trials 1–3 and Trials 4–6 both show displacement increasing from 1 meter to 5 meters to 10 meters. Your next step should be to check out the corresponding numbers in the Force column. In Trial 1 (a displacement of 1 meter), the force is equal to 5 newtons; in Trial 2 (a displacement of 5 meters), the force is equal to 25 newtons; in Trial 3 (a displacement of 10 meters), the force is equal to 50 newtons. These numbers seem to indicate that force increases with displacement. Now check whether the statement holds true in Trials 4–6. In Trials 4–6, the force rises from 10 newtons to 50 newtons to 100 newtons; in other words, it

Science Reasoning

increases as displacement increases. You've just successfully formulated an answer to the question ("when displacement increases, force increases"), so you can complete the last step of matching your answer with the test's. The correct answer is **A**.

Use the Chart

To answer Use the Chart questions, you must use information from the given chart or charts to decipher additional information. For instance,

> According to the information provided in the introduction and Table 1, which of the following is the largest mass?
>
> A. M_1
> B. M_3
> C. M_5
> D. M_6

The question tells you to refer to both the introduction and Table 1. In the introduction, there are two sentences that will help you solve this question. The first sentence is "A larger mass will create a larger displacement than a small mass." This sentence indicates that you should look at the amount of displacement to gauge the relative size of the masses. But if you look only at the displacement, you're probably wondering how to choose between M_3 and M_6, which both indicate a displacement of 10 meters. To solve this problem, look to the second crucial sentence in the passage, "The spring constant measures the elasticity of a spring: if a spring has a high k, the spring cannot be stretched easily; if a spring has a low k, it can be stretched more easily." This sentence points to the difference between the two springs being tested (one with $k = 5$ and the other with $k = 10$). If the spring with $k = 10$ is the tougher to stretch of the two, you can assume that it requires a heavier mass to stretch the tough spring 10 meters than it does to stretch the weaker spring 10 meters. So the heaviest mass (and the correct answer) is **D**.

Now try this Use the Chart question:

> If Trial 2 were repeated with a spring with $k = 15$, the displacement of the spring would be:
>
> A.   less than 5.
> B.   5.
> C.   greater than 5.
> D.   indeterminable from the given information.

This question resembles the last one in a key way: both questions require you understand the sentence, "The spring constant measures the elasticity of a spring; if a spring has a high k, the spring cannot be stretched easily; if a spring has a low k, it can be stretched more easily." This sentence tells you that replacing the spring in Trial 2 with a spring that's tougher to pull will result in a smaller displacement of the spring (if the mass pulling on it remains the same). When $k = 5$, Trial 2 produces a displacement of 5 meters, so with a larger k ($k = 15$) and the same mass, the displacement must be less than 5 meters. Choice **A** is correct.

Handle Graphs

These questions will generally ask you to transform the data given in the charts into graphic form. If you are unfamiliar with how to graph data and the differences between linear and exponential functions, you should review this information. Briefly, straight lines indicate linear functions, while curved lines represent exponential functions. Straight horizontal lines indicate that the variable remains constant. For example,

Which of the following graphs best represents the change in potential energy with increasing displacement for Trials 1–3 ?

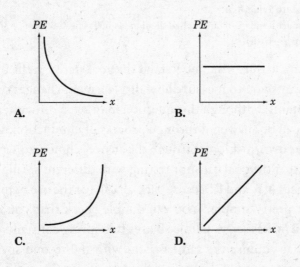

When answering such questions, you should look first at the axes of the graphs. In this question, each of the graphs represents displacement on the x-axis, or horizontal axis, while potential energy is represented on the y-axis, or vertical axis. As you move right on the x-axis and up on the y-axis, numerical values increase.

To answer this question, you should first examine the relationship between potential energy and displacement according to Table 1. From the chart, you can see that potential energy rises as displacement increases. Because you're looking for a rise in potential energy, you can eliminate choices **A** and **B**, since **A** shows potential energy decreasing with an increase in displacement, and **B** shows potential energy remaining constant. Now you've narrowed down your choices to **C** and **D**. The key difference between the graphs of these two choices is that **C** shows potential energy rising exponentially and **D** shows it rising linearly. In other words, the potential energy represented in **C** does not increase in direct proportion to displacement; instead, each incremental increase in displacement leads to an ever larger jump in potential energy. From Table 1, you can determine that **C**'s depiction of potential energy is correct because the numbers do not rise in a steady manner (as the numbers for force do).

Science Reasoning

Take the Next Step

Take the Next Step questions present you with a stated goal that can be achieved through experimentation and tests. Your object is to choose the answer that would best achieve that goal. You will not see these questions as frequently on the Data Representation passages as you will on Research Summaries; in fact, you may not see any of these questions on Data Representation passages, but you should still be prepared to answer them. Here's an example:

> What would be the best method of determining how the spring constant affects displacement?
>
> A. Reproduce Trials 1–6 but use only springs with spring constant $k = 5$.
> B. Reproduce Trials 1–3.
> C. Reproduce Trials 4–6.
> D. Reproduce Trials 1–6 but change the masses in Trials 4–6 to M_1, M_2, and M_3, respectively.

First, you should make sure you understand the goal stated in the question. This particular question wants you to measure how displacement changes when you have different spring constants. Although this question may seem difficult, it is actually fairly simple because it can be answered through process of elimination. If you don't know the answer on your own, just look through the answer choices to see which one makes sense. You know that the goal calls for testing with different spring constants, so you can eliminate choices **A**, **B**, and **C** because they all call for the use of just one spring constant. Wasn't that pretty simple? You can double check that you're right by asking yourself whether **D** makes sense. Choice **D** uses two spring constants ($k = 5$ and $k = 10$), and it proposes that you use the same masses with the second spring that you used with the first. This proposal makes a lot of sense because the only variable will be the spring constant—you won't need to take mass into account in the comparison. So **D** is the correct answer to this problem.

Research Summaries

For the three Research Summaries passages, you will have to read and understand two or three experiments and their results. The questions accompanying Research Summaries will ask you to compare data across the experiments.

The Sample Passage

Brine shrimp, also called artemia, are tiny arthropods that are often used as live food in aquariums. The shrimp begin their life cycle as metabolically inactive cysts. The cysts can remain dormant for many years if they remain dry. If these cysts come in contact with salt water, they soon rehydrate and hatch, giving rise to living embryos.

Experiment 1

Scientists placed dormant brine shrimp cysts into three different soda bottles containing salt water. The scientists maintained the water in each container at a constant temperature of 25° Celsius (77° Fahrenheit), but they kept the salt concentration (milligrams of NaCL per liter of H_2O) of each bottle at different levels. The scientists then recorded the average hatching rate for the cysts in each bottle.

	Temperature (˚C)	Salt Concentration (mg/L)	Average Time to Hatching (hours)
Bottle 1	25	0.2	20
Bottle 2	25	0.3	17
Bottle 3	25	0.4	15

Experiment 2

The scientists repeated Experiment 1, except in this experiment they kept the salt concentration constant while changing the temperature in each bottle.

	Temperature (˚C)	Salt Concentration (mg/L)	Average Time to Hatching (hours)
Bottle 1	15	0.3	33
Bottle 2	25	0.3	17
Bottle 3	35	0.3	26

Experiment 3

The scientists repeated Experiment 1, but placed all three bottles in the dark. The chart below shows the average hatching rate (in hours) for the brine shrimp in the three bottles in Experiment 1 and Experiment 3.

	Experiment 1	Experiment 3
Bottle 1	20	35
Bottle 2	17	28
Bottle 3	15	25

Strategy for Reading the Passage

Earlier, we advised you to take notes while reading the passage. Marginal notes and underlines will particularly help you in reading the Research Summaries passages, which present you with two or three sets of data each.

No matter how carefully you read, you should refer back to the passage when answering the questions. However, if you read too quickly the first time, you run the risk of misunderstanding the basic premise of a passage, and you'll waste time trying to sort out the information when you should be answering the questions.

For this particular passage, jotting down the variables in each experiment in the margins of the passage will help you recall the differences between the experiments. For instance, you might want to write "hatching time" at the top of the passage, so you'll remember that all three experiments test the effect of variables on the hatching time of brine shrimp. Next to Experiment 1, you can write something like "salt conc" to indicate that salt concentration was varied in that experiment. Next to Experiment 2, scribble "temp" to indicate that temperature was the variable. Write "light" or "light vs. dark" next to Experiment 3 to show that the experiment tested hatching time with and without light.

The Questions

Each Research Summaries passage will be followed by six questions. These questions will be similar in type to the questions on the Data Representation passages. All of the questions in this section refer to the sample Research Summaries passage above.

Read the Chart

As on the Data Representation passage, the Read the Chart questions will ask you to identify information that is explicitly stated in a chart in the passage. For example,

Based on the results from Experiment 1, one can conclude that:

A.   brine shrimp hatch less quickly as salt concentration increases.
B.   brine shrimp hatch more quickly as salt concentration increases.
C.   hatching is unaffected by salt concentration.
D.   salt concentration is dependent on temperature.

Since three of the answer choices deal with the hatching of brine shrimp, you should probably look at the column "Average Time to Hatching" and see how the numbers in it change. By reading the chart, you can see that a 0.2 salt concentration corresponds with 20 hours to hatching, a 0.3 salt concentration corresponds with 17 hours to hatching, and a 0.4 salt concentration corresponds with 15 hours to hatching; thus hatching time decreases as salt concentration increases, or brine shrimp hatch *more* quickly as salt concentration increases. Choice **B** seems to be the correct answer. Still, it's good policy to make sure that choices **C** and **D** do not work before committing to your answer. You can easily eliminate choice **C**, which states that salt concentration has no effect on hatching time, because Experiment 1 demonstrates the effect of salt concentration on hatching time. Similarly, you can eliminate choice **D** because it claims that salt concentration depends on temperature. From the chart, you can see that temperature did not vary in Experiment 1, so salt concentration, which did vary, could not have been dependent on it. You've already eliminated choice **A** by concluding that shrimp hatch more quickly as salt concentration increases, so that leaves you with the correct answer, which is **B**.

Here's another Read the Chart question:

Which of the following was studied in Experiment 3?

A.	The effect of light on the time it takes for brine shrimp to hatch.
B.	The effect of light on salt concentration.
C.	The effect of light on temperature.
D.	The effect of light on the survival rate of brine shrimp.

This question asks you about Experiment 3, and all four answer choices deal with the effect of light on an aspect of the experiment. Your job is to figure out which aspect of the experiment light affects. A quick look at your marginal notes will reveal that Experiment 3 deals with the hatching time of brine shrimp in the dark, using Experiment 1 as a control. You can either look to the chart or its written introduction to find the answer to this question. If you read the introduction, it tells you that the following chart shows the average hatching rate of brine shrimp under the altered circumstances. The chart presents you with no other information, so the experiment must be testing the effect of light on the hatching time of brine shrimp, or choice **A**.

Use the Chart

Use the Chart questions accompanying Research Summaries passages are very similar to the ones accompanying Data Representation passages. For example,

If the standard salt concentration used in Experiment 2 were changed from 0.3 mg/L to 0.4 mg/L, what would likely happen to the time it takes for the cysts to hatch?

F.	The time would increase.
G.	The time would decrease.
H.	The time would not change.
J.	The time would be reduced to zero.

Answering this question requires that you use the charts for both Experiments 1 and 2. As usual, you should see whether you can eliminate one of the answer choices right off the bat. Choice **J** seems like a prime candidate for elimination because neither experiment indicates that the brine shrimp will hatch immediately under any circumstances. To figure out the most likely hatching time, you should look at Experiment 1, which tests changes in salt concentration. The question asks you what would happen if the salt concentration were raised from 0.3 mg/L to 0.4 mg/L. Luckily for you, Experiment 1 tells you what happens to the hatching rate at 0.4 mg/L concentration and 25° temperature: the brine shrimp take 15 hours to hatch. Compare this to the 17 hours it takes for brine shrimp to hatch at 0.3 mg/L and 25°, and you can predict that hatching time will decrease with increased salt concentration. So the best answer for this question is **G**.

Here's a more difficult Use the Chart question:

Under which of the following conditions would you expect a brine shrimp cyst to hatch in the *least* amount of time?

A.   In the light, in water with 0.2 mg/L salt concentration at 25 degrees Celsius.
B.   In the dark, in water with 0.3 mg/L salt concentration at 35 degrees Celsius.
C.   In the light, in water with 0.4 mg/L salt concentration at 25 degrees Celsius.
D.   In the dark, in water with 0.2 mg/L salt concentration at 25 degrees Celsius.

This question requires that you use all three charts and a little intuition. Some of the answer choices are lifted directly from information in the charts. Choice **A**, for instance, represents Bottle 1 in Experiment 1, with a hatching time of 20 hours. Choice **C**, or Bottle 3 in Experiment 1, has a hatching time of 15 hours. Choice **D**, Bottle 1 in Experiment 3, has a hatching time of 35 hours. Choice **B** is a little trickier than the other answer choices because you must make an educated guess as to its hatching time. The choice states that the bottle is in the dark, so you should keep Experiment 3 in mind. It also states that it has a 0.3 salt concentration and 35° temperature. Since Experiment 1 keeps the temperature constant at 25°, you need to look to Experiment 2, which maintains a 0.3 salt concentration but varies the temperature among 15°, 25°, and 35°. The hatching time for Bottle 3 in Experiment 2, which has the same temperature and salt concentration as choice B, is 26 hours. Since the dark only increases the hatching time for brine shrimp, you can guess that it will take choice **B** much more than 26 hours to hatch. To keep track of all these hatching times, write down the number of hours for hatching next to each answer choice. The last step in answering the questions should be to compare these numbers and choose the smallest one. The correct answer is **C**, with a hatching time of only 15 hours.

Handle Graphs

Questions that ask you to handle graphs on the Research Summaries passage will ask you to transfer information from verbal to graphic form or the other way around. For example:

Which of the following graphs best represents the change in hatching time with increasing temperature as shown in Experiment 2?

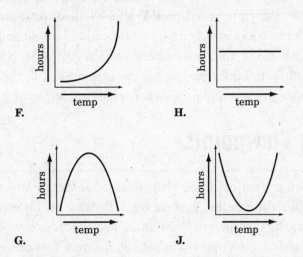

F.

H.

G.

J.

From the data given with Experiment 2, you can tell that hatching time goes from high to low to high again as temperature increases. These graphs show temperature on the x-axis, or horizontal axis, so as you move to the right along the horizontal axis, you are increasing temperature. Similarly, as you move up the y-axis, or vertical axis, which represents hatching time, you are increasing the hatching time—33 hours will be higher up on the y-axis than 17 hours. Putting all this information together, you should be able to figure out that choice **J** is correct. If you want proof, you can eliminate the other choices: **F** shows a steadily increasing hatching time; **H** shows a hatching time that doesn't change; and **G** shows a hatching time that goes from small to big to small again, the opposite of what occurs in Experiment 2. Again review the graphic representations of linear and exponential functions if you are unfamiliar with them.

Take the Next Step

These questions will be exactly like the Take the Next Step questions on the Data Representation passages. The question will provide you with a new research goal, and you must decide how to achieve it. For example,

What would be the best way to study the effects of changing pH (acidity) on the hatching time of brine shrimp cysts?

A. Putting all three bottles in the light and keeping temperature constant while changing salt concentration and pH.

B. Putting all three bottles in the dark and keeping temperature constant while changing salt concentration and pH.

C. Putting all three bottles in the light and keeping temperature and salt concentration levels constant while varying the pH in each bottle.

D. Putting all three bottles in the dark and varying temperature, salt concentration, and pH in all three bottles.

Science Reasoning

This question asks you to make pH the variable in the new experiment. Since pH is the variable in this new experiment, you want to keep the other factors as constant and as "normal" as possible. But choices A, B, and D all ask you to change other factors, such as salt concentration or temperature. These modifications would make it tough to tell whether a change in hatching time was caused by a change in pH levels or by one of the other variables, and that defeats the goal of the experiment. **C**, the only choice that keeps light, salt concentration, and temperature constant, is the correct answer.

Conflicting Viewpoints

As we briefly mentioned earlier in this chapter, the Conflicting Viewpoints passage in many ways resembles the Reading Test passages. Because of this resemblance, we advise you to divorce the Conflicting Viewpoints passage from the Science Reasoning Test in your mind and to think of it as a misplaced Reading Test passage. The new slant on this passage should affect your approach to the passage and (for most people) should make it seem less intimidating.

The Sample Passage

The theory of plate tectonics, which describes the shifting of the Earth's plates (most of which contain pieces of continents), is now widely accepted as correct. But scientists are still debating the driving mechanism behind plate tectonics; in other words, they want to know how the shifting of plates happens. Two of the most popular hypotheses for explaining this phenomenon are presented to you below.

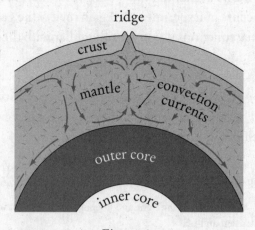

Figure 1a

Mantle Convection Theory

Proponents of this theory argue that tectonic plates are moved passively by convection currents in the Earth's mantle, which is the layer below the crust. Mantle rocks near the Earth's core become extremely hot, making them less dense than the cooler mantle rocks in the upper layers. As a result, the hot rocks rise and the (relatively) cool rocks sink, creating slow vertical convection currents within the mantle (see Figure 1a). These convection currents in turn create convection cells, pockets of circulation within the mantle. Supporters of the mantle convection theory argue that these convection cells directly cause documented seafloor spreading, which they claim is responsible for plate movement. The convection currents push up magma, forming new crust and exerting a lateral force on the plate, pushing it apart and "spreading" the seafloor (see Figure 1b). The scientists claim that this force, which ultimately results from convection currents, is the driving force behind the movement of tectonic plates.

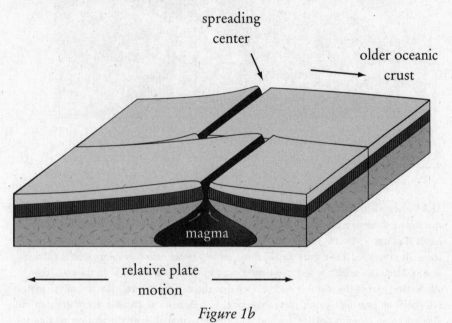

Figure 1b

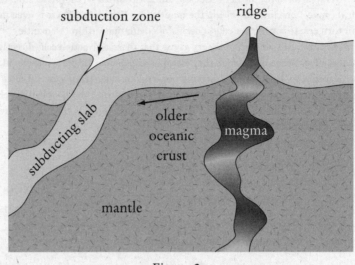

Figure 2a

Slab Pull Theory

This theory posits that gravity and the plates themselves are responsible for tectonic plate movement through a process known as subduction. Subduction zones exist at the outer edges of plates where the rock is cool and dense (as rock ages, it cools off and becomes increasingly dense) (see Figure 2a). In these zones, the old rock is so dense that it subducts, or sinks, into the mantle below it, pulled down by gravitational forces. As the slab (the subducting part of the plate) is pulled down into the mantle, it drags the rest of the plate along with it, causing tectonic plate movement (see Figure 2b). The density of the slab will affect the velocity of its subduction and thus the force it applies on the plate; a very dense slab will sink faster than a less dense slab because of gravitational pull, and it will exert a greater force on the plate attached to it. This theory explains mantle convection as a product, rather than a cause, of plate movement. The outward movement of the plate allows hot magma to bubble up from the Earth's mantle at the center ridges of the plate, forming new crust where the older crust used to be.

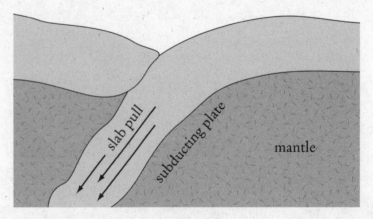

Figure 2b

Strategy for Reading the Passage

As we've already stated, your strategy here should be similar to the strategy you developed for the Reading Test passages. Because the questions accompanying this passage almost exclusively deal with the written material in the passage, it is particularly important that you have a strong grasp of what the passage says and that you can refer back to the passage efficiently. For that reason, you should underline and circle sentences and phrases that could potentially be important for answering questions. These underlines and circles will guide you through the passage when you refer back to it. Also try to get an overall sense of what each passage is arguing and the most important ways in which the two arguments differ.

The heavy use of scientific terms makes this passage difficult to digest. Mantle rocks, convection currents, subduction—what does it all mean? The figures at the end illustrate these terms, but you may still feel confused. Don't let the confusion bother you. You don't need to understand convection currents after reading this passage. Take from the passage only what it gives you: a brief explanation of the formation of convection currents and their role in the process described. As long as you understand that convection currents are related to the rise of hot rocks and the fall of cooler, denser rocks, that convection currents form convection cells, and that the two theories disagree about the cause and effect of convection currents, you're all set.

The Questions

The seven questions on the Conflicting Viewpoints passage are different from the other questions in the Science Reasoning Test. They are similar to the questions you would encounter on a Reading Test passage, but they break down into only three categories: Detail, Inference, and Comparison. As with the Reading Test questions, there aren't great strategies that can help you answer these Conflicting Viewpoints questions. There may be questions for which you can immediately eliminate one of the answer choices, but elimination will not be your standard technique for solving problems. Rather, you must develop good reading comprehension skills, since Conflicting Viewpoints is fundamentally a reading comprehension passage. All of the example questions in this section refer to the Conflicting Viewpoints passage above.

Detail

There will probably be two detail questions on the Conflicting Viewpoints passage—not as many as on the Reading Test passages, but still a significant percentage of the questions. Detail questions ask you for specific information from the passage. They address only one viewpoint at a time and usually deal with a key aspect of that viewpoint. To answer these questions, you need a fundamental grasp of what each side is arguing.

Science Reasoning

Try this detail question:

According to the Mantle Convection Theory, the heating of mantle rocks near the Earth's core directly results in:

A. the rising of the rocks to the upper mantle because they become buoyant when hot.

B. the spreading of the seafloor as magma pushes up through the crust.

C. the creation of convection cells within the mantle.

D. the subduction of cool plate edges into the less dense mantle.

A key word in this question is "directly," because it indicates that the answer should be a direct and *immediate* result of the heating of mantle rocks. While the heating of the rocks may eventually lead to more than one of the answer choices, only one answer choice directly results from it. If you run down through the choices, you will see that choice **D** discusses subduction, which is mentioned exclusively in the Slab Pull Theory; thus you can eliminate **D** because it is irrelevant to the Mantle Convection Theory. Elimination helps you on this sort of question, but, as in the case of this particular question, it might not bring you all the way to the correct answer. Now refer back to the passage and find the section on the heating of mantle rocks. Without spending much time rereading the section, recall the sequence of events (any marks you made will help you here), and then formulate an answer to the question. The correct answer to this question is **A** because the rising is the immediate result of the heating of the mantle rocks. According to the Mantle Convection Theory, choices **B** and **C** result from heated mantle rocks, but they occur later in the sequence of events.

Now try this detail question on the Slab Pull Theory:

According to the Slab Pull Theory, which of the following is NOT true?

A. Subduction zones exist far from the active central ridges of plates.

B. Tectonic plate movement results from a lateral force caused by subduction.

C. Mantle convection occurs independently of subduction.

D. Gravitational forces act on dense slab.

This question differs from the previous one because it asks you to identify the answer choice that is *false* according to the Slab Pull Theory. Because of the question's phrasing, you will not be able to come up with your own answer before matching it to the answer choices. Instead, you should make sure you understand the theory and refer back to the passage when necessary, keeping in mind that the time you spend on this step should be limited. Once you feel comfortable with the passage, run down through the answer choices and ask yourself whether you found each one in the passage. If you understood the main point of the Slab Pull Theory, choice **C** should jump out at you because it describes something occurring *independently* of subduction, while the Slab Pull Theory depends on subduction. Indeed, choice **C** is the correct answer to this question.

Inference

You will probably see two inference questions on the Conflicting Viewpoints passage. These questions ask you to make inferences (i.e., figure out implied information) based on the arguments of each viewpoint.

Sometimes inference questions will present you with a hypothetical situation and ask you how the proponents of one (and sometimes both) of the viewpoints would react to it. For instance,

> If it were discovered that slabs break off from the rest of the plates once a certain degree of force is applied, the discovery would harm:
>
> **A.**   the Mantle Convection Theory.
> **B.**   the Slab Pull Theory.
> **C.**   both theories.
> **D.**   neither theory.

This question asks you to decide what the consequences of this discovery would be. The terms used in this question will help get you started. The question discusses slabs and gravitational forces, which should immediately point you in the direction of the Slab Pull Theory. Your next step should be to consider how the new evidence affects the Slab Pull Theory. Ask yourself, "What does the theory say?" Well, the Slab Pull Theory maintains that subducting slabs exert a pull on the plates to which they're attached. If the new evidence is correct and the slabs break off from the plate when too much force is applied, the new evidence is harmful to the Slab Pull Theory, and **B** is the correct answer.

Inference questions may also ask you to identify a statement or piece of evidence that lends support to one of the viewpoints. For example,

> Scientists decide to observe the outer edges of plates. Which of the following statements about subduction zones would support the Slab Pull Theory?
>
> **A.**   Not all plates have subduction zones.
> **B.**   Slab subducts at a uniform speed in all subduction zones.
> **C.**   Slab subducts at various speeds depending on the age of the slab.
> **D.**   Where oceanic plates meet continental plates, the oceanic plates will subduct because they are more dense than continental plates.

Answering this question will require the same skills you used to answer the previous question, but here you have to figure out the consequences of four different discoveries instead of just one. Because this task is potentially time-consuming, you should first run down the answer choices to see whether you can instantly eliminate any as either absolutely incorrect or simply irrelevant to the Slab Pull Theory. Going through this particular set, you may choose to eliminate choices **A** and **D** right away. If scientists declared that choice **A** were true, they would definitely not be supporting the Slab Pull Theory, as the theory hinges on the widespread existence of subduction zones. Choice

D, you might decide, is irrelevant to the theory because the theory never mentions oceanic or continental plates. So you are left with two choices: **B** and **C**. Interestingly, they both deal with the speed at which plates subduct. Does either the Slab Pull Theory or the Mantle Convection Theory talk about speed? According to the Slab Pull Theory, "the density of the slab will affect the velocity of its subduction . . . a very dense slab will sink faster than a less dense slab." In other words, the Slab Pull Theory expects the velocity (or speed) of subduction to vary depending on the density of the slab. Choice **C** says that slabs subduct at different speeds depending on the *age* of the slab, so can it still be the correct answer? Yes, because the summary of the Slab Pull Theory also tells you that the older the rock is, the denser it will be. So choice **C** would support the Slab Pull Theory.

You may encounter other types of inference questions on the test. For instance, an inference question might ask you to identify a necessary assumption made by one of the viewpoints, but you shouldn't panic if you see a question like that. All inference questions, regardless of their phrasing, can be handled similarly. As with detail questions, getting inference questions right on this test depends almost entirely on your ability to comprehend and use the information provided in the passage.

Comparison

These questions generally account for three of the seven questions accompanying the Conflicting Viewpoints passage, so you should make sure you feel comfortable with them. They require you to compare the viewpoints in the passage in terms of specific details presented in each argument or inferences you must draw about the viewpoints.

Comparison questions frequently ask you to identify points on which the viewpoints would agree or disagree. For example,

> About which of the following points do the two theories differ?
>
> **A.** Movement of tectonic plates across the Earth's surface
> **B.** Density of hot mantle rocks
> **C.** Existence of convection currents in the Earth's mantle
> **D.** Role of mantle convection in tectonic plate movement

This question requires that you use both your ability to compare viewpoints and your ability to identify specific detail; answering it correctly involves no inference work. To start, you should read through the answer choices, eliminating anything you know is uncontroversial to the viewpoints. Choice A, for instance, is uncontroversial because both of the viewpoints acknowledge that the plates move; in fact, their goal is to explain this movement. (The theories disagree on the mechanism behind this movement, not on the movement itself.) Ideally, you should be able to get the right answer to this question without referring back to the passage, as this question deals with the fundamental difference between the two theories. If you can't answer this question on your own, you should refer back to the passage quickly, but do not waste a lot of time reading through it again. The correct answer to this problem is **D**. The Mantle Convection Theory argues that mantle convection is the driving force behind plate movement, while the Slab Pull Theory maintains that mantle convection merely results from plate movement. Choice **B** is wrong because only the Slab Pull Theory deals with the density of mantle rocks, and choice **C** is wrong because neither theory denies the existence of convection currents.

Comparison questions may also ask you to infer how one theory would address the other. For instance,

> How would supporters of the Slab Pull Theory explain the documentation of seafloor spreading cited in the Mantle Convection Theory?
>
> **A.** Seafloor spreading directly causes tectonic plate movement and slab subduction.
> **B.** Seafloor spreading does not exist.
> **C.** Seafloor spreading and slab subduction simultaneously exert moving forces on tectonic plates.
> **D.** Seafloor spreading exists, but only as a result of slab subduction.

You could call this an inference-comparison question because it asks you to figure out something that is not explicitly stated in the passage: the response of one theory to the other. The question points you to a specific issue under debate: seafloor spreading. Ask yourself whether you understand the position of the Slab Pull Theory on seafloor spreading. The passage explicitly states that Slab Pull theorists consider mantle convection and seafloor spreading to be products, not causes, of slab subduction. Which of the answer choices captures that position? **A** says that seafloor spreading directly causes slab subduction (the opposite of what the Slab Pull Theory says), so it is incorrect. **B** is also incorrect because the Slab Pull Theory does not deny that the seafloor spreads. **C** is incorrect as well because it says that both seafloor spreading and slab subduction are responsible for plate movement, whereas the Slab Pull Theory argues that only slab subduction is responsible. **D**, then, must be correct, but you should always double-check. In accordance with the Slab Pull Theory, it says that seafloor spreading is a result of slab subduction, so **D** is indeed the correct answer to the question.

You may encounter additional types of comparison questions on the actual ACT, but they will all follow the basic idea of comparing the presented arguments in terms of specific details or inferences. If you encounter a comparison question that seems unlike the examples given above, the difference is usually a matter of phrasing. A comparison question worded, "Which of the following statements about the factors that affect tectonic plate movement would be consistent with the Mantle Convection and Slab Pull theories?" really just asks you to identify specific details from both theories that agree. You shouldn't have any problem with this question if you understand how to answer the first example in this section.

If you get a Conflicting Viewpoints passage that presents three arguments, you may see other variations on the types of questions asked. For instance, a question may ask you to identify how one theory is better than the other two in a specific regard. That question would also be a detail-comparison question because it asks you about a specific aspect addressed by the three arguments. Again, you won't have a problem if you understand the examples above.

The key to avoid being intimidated by comparison questions is to remember that they are detail and inference questions that simply deal with multiple viewpoints. If you can answer detail and inference questions, you're well on your way to mastering comparison questions as well.

Practice Tests

Practice Tests Are Your Best Friends

I N THIS CRAZY WORLD OF OURS, THERE IS one thing that you can always take for granted: the ACT will stay the same. In fact, the ACT might be the most predictable test ever written. Every edition of the test covers the same topics to precisely the same degree. No matter when you take the ACT, you will see, for example, 10 questions on the English Test that cover punctuation and 14 questions on the Math Test that cover pre-algebra. In addition, the way that questions on different versions of the test address particular topics will be quite constant. A question trying your understanding of 30-60-90 triangles on one version of the ACT will be very similar to a question concerning 30-60-90 triangles on another. Obviously, the questions on one version of the ACT won't be exactly the same as the questions on another version, but they will be remarkably similar. The main difference is in the phrasing of the questions, not the skills and content that are tested.

This constancy from test to test can be of great benefit to you as you study for the ACT. To show how you can use the similarity between different versions of the ACT to your own advantage, we provide a case study.

Using the Habits of the ACT for Personal Gain

One day, an eleventh grader named Molly Bloom sits down at the desk in her room and takes a practice test for the ACT. Because it makes this case study much simpler, she takes the entire test and gets only one question wrong. Molly checks her answers and then jumps from her chair and does a little dance that would be embarrassing if anyone else were around to see her.

After her euphoria passes, she begins to wonder which question she got wrong and returns to her chair. She discovers that the question was on the Math Subject Test and dealt with triangles. Looking over the question, Molly at first thinks the test made a mistake and that she was actually right, but then she realizes that she answered the question wrong because she had thought the ratio of the sides of a 30-60-90 triangle was $1:2:\sqrt{2}$ when really it is $1:2:\sqrt{3}$. Molly doesn't know where or when she got confused about the ratio of the sides of a 30-60-90 triangle, but as she studies the question and learns how and why she got it wrong, she knows that she'll never make that mistake again.

Analyzing Molly Bloom

Molly's actions here seem inconsequential. All she did was study a question she got wrong until she understood why she got it wrong and what she should have done to get it right. But think about the implications. Molly answered the question incorrectly because she didn't understand the topic it was testing; the practice test pointed out her mistaken understanding in the most noticeable way possible: she got the question wrong. After doing her admittedly goofy little dance, Molly wasn't content simply to see what the correct answer was and to get on with her day; she wanted to see *how* and *why* she got the question wrong and what she should have done, or what she needed to know, in order to get it right. So, with a look of determination, telling herself, "I will figure out why I got this question wrong, yes I will, yes," she spent a little while studying the question, and discovered her mistaken understanding of 30-60-90 triangles. If Molly were to take that same test again, she would not get that question wrong.

"But she never will take that test again, so she's never going to see that particular question again," some poor sap who hasn't read this guide might sputter. "She wasted her time. What a dork!"

Why That Poor Sap Really Is a Poor Sap

In some sense, that poor sap is correct: Molly never will take that exact practice test again. But the poor sap is wrong to call Molly derogatory names, because, as we know, the ACT is remarkably similar from year to year, both in the topics it covers and in the way it poses questions about those topics. Therefore, when Molly taught herself about 30-60-90 triangles, she actually learned how to answer the similar questions dealing with 30-60-90 triangles that will *undoubtedly* appear on every future practice test, and on the real ACT.

In studying the results of her practice test, and in figuring out exactly why she got her one question wrong and what she should have known and done to get it right, Molly has targeted a weakness and overcome it.

Molly and You

Molly has it easy. She took a practice test and only got one question wrong. The ACT contains 215 questions, and almost no one in the country manages to get all of them right. Of course, the only reason Molly got so few questions wrong was because we wanted to use her as an easy example.

So what if you take a practice test and get a number of questions wrong on each Subject Test, and your errors span a number of different topics, from punctuation to writing style to plane geometry? You should do exactly what Molly did. Take your test and *study it*. Identify every question you got wrong, figure out why you got it wrong, and then teach yourself what you should have done to get the question right. If you can't figure out your error, find someone who can.

A wrong answer on the ACT identifies a weakness in your test taking, whether that weakness is an unfamiliarity with a particular topic or a tendency to be careless. As you study each question you got wrong, you are actually learning how to answer the very questions that will appear in similar form on the real ACT. You are discovering your exact ACT weaknesses and addressing them, and you are learning to understand not just the knowledge tested by the questions, but also the way the test writers ask their questions.

True, if you got 30 questions wrong on your first try, studying your test will take some time. But if you invest that time and study your practice test properly, you will be eliminating future mistakes. Each successive practice test you take should have fewer errors, meaning less time spent studying those errors. Also, and more importantly, you'll be pinpointing what you need to study for the real ACT, identifying and overcoming your weaknesses, and learning to answer an increasing variety of questions on the specific topics covered by the test. Taking practice tests and studying them will allow you to teach yourself how to recognize and handle whatever the ACT throws at you.

Taking a Practice Test

Through the example of Miss Molly Bloom, we've shown you why studying practice tests is an extremely powerful study tool. Now we're going to explain how you should take practice tests in order to put that tool to best use.

Controlling Your Environment

Although no one but you needs to see your practice test scores, you should do everything in your power to make the practice test feel like the real ACT. The closer your practice resembles the real thing, the more helpful it will be. When taking a practice test, follow these rules:

Take the tests timed. Don't give yourself any extra time. Be stricter with yourself than the meanest proctor you can think of. Also, don't give yourself time off for bathroom breaks. If you have to go to the bathroom, let the clock keep running; that's what'll happen on the real ACT.

Take the test in a single sitting. Training yourself to endure the full duration of the test should be part of your preparation.

Find a place to take the test that offers no distractions. Don't take the practice test in a room with lots of people walking through it. Go to a library, your bedroom, a well-lit closet, anywhere quiet.

Now, having stated the rules of practice test taking, we can relax a little bit: don't be so strict with yourself that studying and taking practice tests becomes unbearable. The most important thing is that you actually study. Do whatever you have to do in order to make your studying interesting and painless enough that you actually do it.

One way to help yourself actually take practice tests may be to take individual Subject Tests rather than the entire ACT. Yes, we just advised you to take the entire test in one sitting. And we stand by that advice. But if you don't have three free hours to throw around, that doesn't mean you shouldn't take practice tests. Since the ACT is conveniently broken up into four sections that test different subjects, you can always take a single practice Subject Test in an hour or less.

Ultimately, if you can follow all of the rules listed above to the letter, you will be better off. But, if following those rules makes studying excruciating, find little ways to bend them that won't interfere too much with your concentration.

Practice Test Strategy

You should take each practice test as if it were the real ACT. Don't be more daring than you would be on the actual test, guessing blindly even when you could first eliminate an answer. Don't carelessly speed through the test. Don't flip through this book while taking the practice exam just to sneak a peek. Follow the rules for guessing and for skipping questions that we outlined in the chapters on strategy. The more closely your attitude and strategies during the practice test reflect those you'll employ during the actual test, the more predictive the practice test will be of your strengths and weaknesses and the more fruitful your studying.

Scoring Your Practice Test

After you take your practice test, you'll no doubt want to score it and see how you did. When you score your test, don't just write down how many questions you answered correctly and tally up your score. Instead, keep a list of every question you got wrong and every question you skipped. This list will be your guide when you study your test.

Studying Your . . . No, Wait, Go Take a Break

You know how to have fun. Go do that for a while. Come back when you're refreshed.

Studying Your Practice Test

After grading your test, you should have a list of the questions you answered incorrectly or skipped. Studying your test involves going through this list and examining each question you answered incorrectly. When you look at each question, you shouldn't just look to see what the correct answer is, but also why you got the question wrong and how you could have gotten the question right. Train yourself in the process of getting the question right.

Why Did You Get the Question Wrong?

There are three reasons why you might have gotten an individual question wrong:

- **Reason 1:** You thought you knew the answer, but actually you didn't.

- **Reason 2:** You managed to eliminate some answer choices and then guessed among the remaining answers; sadly, you guessed wrong.

- **Reason 3:** You knew the answer but made a careless mistake.

You should know which of these reasons applies to every question you got wrong.

What Could You Have Done to Get the Question Right?

The reasons you got a question wrong affect how you should think about studying your practice test.

If You Got a Question Wrong for Reason 1: Lack of Knowledge

A question answered incorrectly for Reason 1 identifies a weakness in your knowledge of the material tested on the ACT. Discovering this wrong answer gives you an opportunity to target your weakness. When addressing that weakness, make sure that you don't just look at the facts.

For example, if the question you got wrong covers the formula for the area of a circle, don't just look at that formula and memorize it. Take a quick look at circles in general, since if you were confused about this one topic, you might also be unsure about others related to it. Remember, on the real ACT you will *not* see a question exactly the same as the question you got wrong. But you probably *will* see a question that covers the same topic as the practice question. For that reason, when you get a question wrong, don't just figure out the right answer to the question. Learn the broader topic of which the question tests only a piece.

If You Got a Question Wrong for Reason 2: Guessing Wrong

If you guessed wrong, review your guessing strategy. Did you guess intelligently? Could you have eliminated more answers? If yes, why didn't you? By thinking in this critical way about the decisions you made while taking the practice test, you can train yourself to make quicker, more decisive, and better decisions.

If you took a guess and chose the incorrect answer, don't let that sour you on guessing. Even as you go over the question and figure out if there was any way for you to have answered it without having to guess, remind yourself that you should always guess. It pays to engage in educated guessing where you eliminate as many wrong answers as you can— even if educated guessing doesn't always result in you getting the right answer.

If You Got a Question Wrong for Reason 3: Carelessness

If you discover you got a question wrong because you were careless, it might be tempting to say to yourself, "Oh, I made a careless error," and assure yourself you won't do that again. That is not enough. You made that careless mistake for a reason, and you should try to figure out why. Whereas getting a question wrong because you didn't know the answer constitutes a weakness in your knowledge about the test, making a careless mistake represents a weakness in your *method of taking the test.*

To overcome this weakness, you need to approach careless errors in the same critical way you would approach a lack of knowledge. Study your mistake. Reenact your thought process on the problem and see where and how your carelessness came about. Were you rushing? Did you jump at the first answer that seemed right instead of reading all the answers? Know your error and look it in the eye. If you learn precisely what your mistake was, you are much less likely to make that mistake again.

If You Left the Question Blank

Since there is no penalty for wrong answers on the ACT, you should never leave a question blank.

The Secret Weapon: Talking to Yourself

Yeah, it's embarrassing. Yeah, you might look silly. But talking to yourself is perhaps the best way to pound something into your brain. As you go through the steps of studying a question, you should talk them out. Verbalizing something to yourself makes it much harder to delude yourself into thinking that you're working if you're really not.

Practice Test 1

ACT PRACTICE TEST 1 ANSWER SHEET

TEST 1

1 Ⓐ Ⓑ Ⓒ Ⓓ	16 Ⓐ Ⓑ Ⓒ Ⓓ	31 Ⓐ Ⓑ Ⓒ Ⓓ	46 Ⓐ Ⓑ Ⓒ Ⓓ	61 Ⓐ Ⓑ Ⓒ Ⓓ
2 Ⓕ Ⓖ Ⓗ Ⓙ	17 Ⓕ Ⓖ Ⓗ Ⓙ	32 Ⓕ Ⓖ Ⓗ Ⓙ	47 Ⓕ Ⓖ Ⓗ Ⓙ	62 Ⓕ Ⓖ Ⓗ Ⓙ
3 Ⓐ Ⓑ Ⓒ Ⓓ	18 Ⓐ Ⓑ Ⓒ Ⓓ	33 Ⓐ Ⓑ Ⓒ Ⓓ	48 Ⓐ Ⓑ Ⓒ Ⓓ	63 Ⓐ Ⓑ Ⓒ Ⓓ
4 Ⓕ Ⓖ Ⓗ Ⓙ	19 Ⓕ Ⓖ Ⓗ Ⓙ	34 Ⓕ Ⓖ Ⓗ Ⓙ	49 Ⓕ Ⓖ Ⓗ Ⓙ	64 Ⓕ Ⓖ Ⓗ Ⓙ
5 Ⓐ Ⓑ Ⓒ Ⓓ	20 Ⓐ Ⓑ Ⓒ Ⓓ	35 Ⓐ Ⓑ Ⓒ Ⓓ	50 Ⓐ Ⓑ Ⓒ Ⓓ	65 Ⓐ Ⓑ Ⓒ Ⓓ
6 Ⓕ Ⓖ Ⓗ Ⓙ	21 Ⓕ Ⓖ Ⓗ Ⓙ	36 Ⓕ Ⓖ Ⓗ Ⓙ	51 Ⓕ Ⓖ Ⓗ Ⓙ	66 Ⓕ Ⓖ Ⓗ Ⓙ
7 Ⓐ Ⓑ Ⓒ Ⓓ	22 Ⓐ Ⓑ Ⓒ Ⓓ	37 Ⓐ Ⓑ Ⓒ Ⓓ	52 Ⓐ Ⓑ Ⓒ Ⓓ	67 Ⓐ Ⓑ Ⓒ Ⓓ
8 Ⓕ Ⓖ Ⓗ Ⓙ	23 Ⓕ Ⓖ Ⓗ Ⓙ	38 Ⓕ Ⓖ Ⓗ Ⓙ	53 Ⓕ Ⓖ Ⓗ Ⓙ	68 Ⓕ Ⓖ Ⓗ Ⓙ
9 Ⓐ Ⓑ Ⓒ Ⓓ	24 Ⓐ Ⓑ Ⓒ Ⓓ	39 Ⓐ Ⓑ Ⓒ Ⓓ	54 Ⓐ Ⓑ Ⓒ Ⓓ	69 Ⓐ Ⓑ Ⓒ Ⓓ
10 Ⓕ Ⓖ Ⓗ Ⓙ	25 Ⓕ Ⓖ Ⓗ Ⓙ	40 Ⓕ Ⓖ Ⓗ Ⓙ	55 Ⓕ Ⓖ Ⓗ Ⓙ	70 Ⓕ Ⓖ Ⓗ Ⓙ
11 Ⓐ Ⓑ Ⓒ Ⓓ	26 Ⓐ Ⓑ Ⓒ Ⓓ	41 Ⓐ Ⓑ Ⓒ Ⓓ	56 Ⓐ Ⓑ Ⓒ Ⓓ	71 Ⓐ Ⓑ Ⓒ Ⓓ
12 Ⓕ Ⓖ Ⓗ Ⓙ	27 Ⓕ Ⓖ Ⓗ Ⓙ	42 Ⓕ Ⓖ Ⓗ Ⓙ	57 Ⓕ Ⓖ Ⓗ Ⓙ	72 Ⓕ Ⓖ Ⓗ Ⓙ
13 Ⓐ Ⓑ Ⓒ Ⓓ	28 Ⓐ Ⓑ Ⓒ Ⓓ	43 Ⓐ Ⓑ Ⓒ Ⓓ	58 Ⓐ Ⓑ Ⓒ Ⓓ	73 Ⓐ Ⓑ Ⓒ Ⓓ
14 Ⓕ Ⓖ Ⓗ Ⓙ	29 Ⓕ Ⓖ Ⓗ Ⓙ	44 Ⓕ Ⓖ Ⓗ Ⓙ	59 Ⓕ Ⓖ Ⓗ Ⓙ	74 Ⓕ Ⓖ Ⓗ Ⓙ
15 Ⓐ Ⓑ Ⓒ Ⓓ	30 Ⓐ Ⓑ Ⓒ Ⓓ	45 Ⓐ Ⓑ Ⓒ Ⓓ	60 Ⓐ Ⓑ Ⓒ Ⓓ	75 Ⓐ Ⓑ Ⓒ Ⓓ

TEST 2

1 Ⓐ Ⓑ Ⓒ Ⓓ Ⓔ	13 Ⓐ Ⓑ Ⓒ Ⓓ Ⓔ	25 Ⓐ Ⓑ Ⓒ Ⓓ Ⓔ	37 Ⓐ Ⓑ Ⓒ Ⓓ Ⓔ	49 Ⓐ Ⓑ Ⓒ Ⓓ Ⓔ
2 Ⓕ Ⓖ Ⓗ Ⓙ Ⓚ	14 Ⓕ Ⓖ Ⓗ Ⓙ Ⓚ	26 Ⓕ Ⓖ Ⓗ Ⓙ Ⓚ	38 Ⓕ Ⓖ Ⓗ Ⓙ Ⓚ	50 Ⓕ Ⓖ Ⓗ Ⓙ Ⓚ
3 Ⓐ Ⓑ Ⓒ Ⓓ Ⓔ	15 Ⓐ Ⓑ Ⓒ Ⓓ Ⓔ	27 Ⓐ Ⓑ Ⓒ Ⓓ Ⓔ	39 Ⓐ Ⓑ Ⓒ Ⓓ Ⓔ	51 Ⓐ Ⓑ Ⓒ Ⓓ Ⓔ
4 Ⓕ Ⓖ Ⓗ Ⓙ Ⓚ	16 Ⓕ Ⓖ Ⓗ Ⓙ Ⓚ	28 Ⓕ Ⓖ Ⓗ Ⓙ Ⓚ	40 Ⓕ Ⓖ Ⓗ Ⓙ Ⓚ	52 Ⓕ Ⓖ Ⓗ Ⓙ Ⓚ
5 Ⓐ Ⓑ Ⓒ Ⓓ Ⓔ	17 Ⓐ Ⓑ Ⓒ Ⓓ Ⓔ	29 Ⓐ Ⓑ Ⓒ Ⓓ Ⓔ	41 Ⓐ Ⓑ Ⓒ Ⓓ Ⓔ	53 Ⓐ Ⓑ Ⓒ Ⓓ Ⓔ
6 Ⓕ Ⓖ Ⓗ Ⓙ Ⓚ	18 Ⓕ Ⓖ Ⓗ Ⓙ Ⓚ	30 Ⓕ Ⓖ Ⓗ Ⓙ Ⓚ	42 Ⓕ Ⓖ Ⓗ Ⓙ Ⓚ	54 Ⓕ Ⓖ Ⓗ Ⓙ Ⓚ
7 Ⓐ Ⓑ Ⓒ Ⓓ Ⓔ	19 Ⓐ Ⓑ Ⓒ Ⓓ Ⓔ	31 Ⓐ Ⓑ Ⓒ Ⓓ Ⓔ	43 Ⓐ Ⓑ Ⓒ Ⓓ Ⓔ	55 Ⓐ Ⓑ Ⓒ Ⓓ Ⓔ
8 Ⓕ Ⓖ Ⓗ Ⓙ Ⓚ	20 Ⓕ Ⓖ Ⓗ Ⓙ Ⓚ	32 Ⓕ Ⓖ Ⓗ Ⓙ Ⓚ	44 Ⓕ Ⓖ Ⓗ Ⓙ Ⓚ	56 Ⓕ Ⓖ Ⓗ Ⓙ Ⓚ
9 Ⓐ Ⓑ Ⓒ Ⓓ Ⓔ	21 Ⓐ Ⓑ Ⓒ Ⓓ Ⓔ	33 Ⓐ Ⓑ Ⓒ Ⓓ Ⓔ	45 Ⓐ Ⓑ Ⓒ Ⓓ Ⓔ	57 Ⓐ Ⓑ Ⓒ Ⓓ Ⓔ
10 Ⓕ Ⓖ Ⓗ Ⓙ Ⓚ	22 Ⓕ Ⓖ Ⓗ Ⓙ Ⓚ	34 Ⓕ Ⓖ Ⓗ Ⓙ Ⓚ	46 Ⓕ Ⓖ Ⓗ Ⓙ Ⓚ	58 Ⓕ Ⓖ Ⓗ Ⓙ Ⓚ
11 Ⓐ Ⓑ Ⓒ Ⓓ Ⓔ	23 Ⓐ Ⓑ Ⓒ Ⓓ Ⓔ	35 Ⓐ Ⓑ Ⓒ Ⓓ Ⓔ	47 Ⓐ Ⓑ Ⓒ Ⓓ Ⓔ	59 Ⓐ Ⓑ Ⓒ Ⓓ Ⓔ
12 Ⓕ Ⓖ Ⓗ Ⓙ Ⓚ	24 Ⓕ Ⓖ Ⓗ Ⓙ Ⓚ	36 Ⓕ Ⓖ Ⓗ Ⓙ Ⓚ	48 Ⓕ Ⓖ Ⓗ Ⓙ Ⓚ	60 Ⓕ Ⓖ Ⓗ Ⓙ Ⓚ

TEST 3

1 Ⓐ Ⓑ Ⓒ Ⓓ	9 Ⓐ Ⓑ Ⓒ Ⓓ	17 Ⓐ Ⓑ Ⓒ Ⓓ	25 Ⓐ Ⓑ Ⓒ Ⓓ	33 Ⓐ Ⓑ Ⓒ Ⓓ
2 Ⓕ Ⓖ Ⓗ Ⓙ	10 Ⓕ Ⓖ Ⓗ Ⓙ	18 Ⓕ Ⓖ Ⓗ Ⓙ	26 Ⓕ Ⓖ Ⓗ Ⓙ	34 Ⓕ Ⓖ Ⓗ Ⓙ
3 Ⓐ Ⓑ Ⓒ Ⓓ	11 Ⓐ Ⓑ Ⓒ Ⓓ	19 Ⓐ Ⓑ Ⓒ Ⓓ	27 Ⓐ Ⓑ Ⓒ Ⓓ	35 Ⓐ Ⓑ Ⓒ Ⓓ
4 Ⓕ Ⓖ Ⓗ Ⓙ	12 Ⓕ Ⓖ Ⓗ Ⓙ	20 Ⓕ Ⓖ Ⓗ Ⓙ	28 Ⓕ Ⓖ Ⓗ Ⓙ	36 Ⓕ Ⓖ Ⓗ Ⓙ
5 Ⓐ Ⓑ Ⓒ Ⓓ	13 Ⓐ Ⓑ Ⓒ Ⓓ	21 Ⓐ Ⓑ Ⓒ Ⓓ	29 Ⓐ Ⓑ Ⓒ Ⓓ	37 Ⓐ Ⓑ Ⓒ Ⓓ
6 Ⓕ Ⓖ Ⓗ Ⓙ	14 Ⓕ Ⓖ Ⓗ Ⓙ	22 Ⓕ Ⓖ Ⓗ Ⓙ	30 Ⓕ Ⓖ Ⓗ Ⓙ	38 Ⓕ Ⓖ Ⓗ Ⓙ
7 Ⓐ Ⓑ Ⓒ Ⓓ	15 Ⓐ Ⓑ Ⓒ Ⓓ	23 Ⓐ Ⓑ Ⓒ Ⓓ	31 Ⓐ Ⓑ Ⓒ Ⓓ	39 Ⓐ Ⓑ Ⓒ Ⓓ
8 Ⓕ Ⓖ Ⓗ Ⓙ	16 Ⓕ Ⓖ Ⓗ Ⓙ	24 Ⓕ Ⓖ Ⓗ Ⓙ	32 Ⓕ Ⓖ Ⓗ Ⓙ	40 Ⓕ Ⓖ Ⓗ Ⓙ

TEST 4

1 Ⓐ Ⓑ Ⓒ Ⓓ	9 Ⓐ Ⓑ Ⓒ Ⓓ	17 Ⓐ Ⓑ Ⓒ Ⓓ	25 Ⓐ Ⓑ Ⓒ Ⓓ	33 Ⓐ Ⓑ Ⓒ Ⓓ
2 Ⓕ Ⓖ Ⓗ Ⓙ	10 Ⓕ Ⓖ Ⓗ Ⓙ	18 Ⓕ Ⓖ Ⓗ Ⓙ	26 Ⓕ Ⓖ Ⓗ Ⓙ	34 Ⓕ Ⓖ Ⓗ Ⓙ
3 Ⓐ Ⓑ Ⓒ Ⓓ	11 Ⓐ Ⓑ Ⓒ Ⓓ	19 Ⓐ Ⓑ Ⓒ Ⓓ	27 Ⓐ Ⓑ Ⓒ Ⓓ	35 Ⓐ Ⓑ Ⓒ Ⓓ
4 Ⓕ Ⓖ Ⓗ Ⓙ	12 Ⓕ Ⓖ Ⓗ Ⓙ	20 Ⓕ Ⓖ Ⓗ Ⓙ	28 Ⓕ Ⓖ Ⓗ Ⓙ	36 Ⓕ Ⓖ Ⓗ Ⓙ
5 Ⓐ Ⓑ Ⓒ Ⓓ	13 Ⓐ Ⓑ Ⓒ Ⓓ	21 Ⓐ Ⓑ Ⓒ Ⓓ	29 Ⓐ Ⓑ Ⓒ Ⓓ	37 Ⓐ Ⓑ Ⓒ Ⓓ
6 Ⓕ Ⓖ Ⓗ Ⓙ	14 Ⓕ Ⓖ Ⓗ Ⓙ	22 Ⓕ Ⓖ Ⓗ Ⓙ	30 Ⓕ Ⓖ Ⓗ Ⓙ	38 Ⓕ Ⓖ Ⓗ Ⓙ
7 Ⓐ Ⓑ Ⓒ Ⓓ	15 Ⓐ Ⓑ Ⓒ Ⓓ	23 Ⓐ Ⓑ Ⓒ Ⓓ	31 Ⓐ Ⓑ Ⓒ Ⓓ	39 Ⓐ Ⓑ Ⓒ Ⓓ
8 Ⓕ Ⓖ Ⓗ Ⓙ	16 Ⓕ Ⓖ Ⓗ Ⓙ	24 Ⓕ Ⓖ Ⓗ Ⓙ	32 Ⓕ Ⓖ Ⓗ Ⓙ	40 Ⓕ Ⓖ Ⓗ Ⓙ

ENGLISH TEST

45 Minutes—75 Questions

DIRECTIONS: There are five passages on this subject test. You should read each passage once before answering the questions on it. In order to answer correctly, you may need to read several sentences beyond the question.

There are two question formats within the passages. In one format, you will find words and phrases that have been underlined and assigned numbers. These numbers will correspond with sets of alternative words/phrases, given in the right-hand column of the test booklet. From the sets of alternatives, choose the answer choice that works best in context, keeping in mind whether it employs standard written English, whether it gets across the idea of the

section, and whether it suits the tone and style of the passage. You will usually be offered the option "NO CHANGE," which you should choose if you think the version found in the passage is best.

In the second format, you will see boxed numbers referring to sections of the passage or to the passage as a whole. In the right-hand column, you will be asked questions about or given alternatives for the sections marked by the boxes. Choose the answer choice that best answers the question or completes the section. After choosing your answer choice, fill in the corresponding bubble on the answer sheet.

PASSAGE I

Culture Shock Treatment

[1]

[1] When my father was transferred to the Madrid

office, I thought it'd be a disaster. [2] Moving to Spain was the
    1

last thing I wanted to do. [3] Everyone told me it would be good

for me to expand my cultural horizons, of course I knew that,
                                          2

but I also knew that I was perfectly happy in the States. [4] I

talked and stormed around the house for about a month after I

found out the bad news and generally drove my parents

crazy. [3]

[2]

You probably already guessed the moral: I ended up

loving Madrid. For a while, also, I did hate it, just as I had
                          4

expected to.

[3]

When we arrived at the airport, I almost fainted from

shock. Everyone was lighting up cigarettes right there by the

1. **A.** NO CHANGE
   B. office I thought
   C. office; I thought
   D. office I thought,

2. **F.** NO CHANGE
   G. horizons of course
   H. horizons, which
   J. horizons; of course

3. Which of the following sequence of sentences makes Paragraph 1 most logical?

   A. NO CHANGE
   B. 4, 3, 2, 1
   C. 4, 1, 3, 2
   D. 2, 3, 1, 4

4. **F.** NO CHANGE
   G. but
   H. though
   J. for

GO ON TO THE NEXT PAGE.

baggage carousel! Such a thing never would have happened at

home, <u>practically</u> where smokers were pariahs.
₅

[4]

⬚6⬚ The first thing I noticed when we got off the subway

and started walking to our new apartment <u>is</u> that no one in
₇

Madrid cleans up after <u>their</u> dog. I looked around, positive that
₈

a cop was going to leap out and ticket someone for this crime,

but everyone acted like it was normal. ⬚9⬚

[5]

Over the coming weeks, I noticed more and more

differences. The older women always wore fur coats, even when

it was sixty-five degrees out. The kids at my high school had

omelets and beer for lunch, instead of sandwiches and

Coke. ⬚10⬚ People pushed you out of the way on the bus, and

no one considered it rude.

[6]

[1] But after a while, <u>they</u> seemed normal to me. [2] <u>Better</u>
₁₁

<u>than the American way.</u> [3] For a while, these differences drove
₁₂

me crazy. [4] At home I'd had to eat lunch in fifteen minutes,

and I loved it that in Madrid we got two hours to eat and play

5. **A.** NO CHANGE
B. (place after *where*)
C. (place after *smokers*)
D. (place after *were*)

6. The writer wants to begin this paragraph with a transitional sentence. Which of the following is the best choice?

F. In Manhattan, no one cleans up after pets.
G. The sight of everyone smoking in the airport threw me for a loop.
H. Matters didn't improve when we left the airport.
J. Eventually, I adjusted to the cultural differences.

7. **A.** NO CHANGE
B. was
C. are
D. has been

8. **F.** NO CHANGE
G. its
H. that
J. her

9. What tone does the writer take in the discussion of the co⬚
A. uproarious hilarity
B. amused exaggeration
C. terror
D. scolding disapproval

10. Which sentence, if added at this point, would work best in⬚ the context of this paragraph?

F. The differences were truly surprising.
G. I wondered what my principal at home would have to say about the idea of drinking beer at lunch.
H. At the movies, ushers showed you to your seat, and yo⬚ were expected to tip them.
J. After a while, I joined in.

11. **A.** NO CHANGE
B. these customs
C. these lunchtime rituals
D. the rudeness

12. **F.** NO CHANGE
G. Better, even, than the American way.
H. The American way was better.
J. They even seemed better than the American way.

GO ON TO THE NEXT PAG⬚

ound. [5] I started to like the crosswalk signs that made

irping noises, the way everyone behaved on the bus,
13

e fact that couples made out in public without giving it a

cond thought. 14

[7]

Of course, by the time my dad got transferred back to the

S. office and found out he had to switch back to working in the
15

ates, I was completely in love with Madrid.

13. **A.** NO CHANGE
    B. bus the fact
    C. bus, but the fact
    D. bus, and the fact

14. Which of the following sequences of sentences most clearly
    expresses the main idea of Paragraph 6?

    F. NO CHANGE
    G. 3, 1, 2, 4, 5
    H. 1, 2, 4, 5, 3
    J. 4, 5, 1, 2, 3

15. **A.** NO CHANGE
    B. and discovered that he had to go back to working in the
       States
    C. and he had to return to the States to work
    D. OMIT the underlined portion.

SSAGE II

John Adams: The Comeback Kid?

[1]

Interest in John Adams has been getting increasingly
16

re intense since the publication of books about him by David

Cullough and Joseph J. Ellis.

[2]

In the past, Adams has been neglected in favor of other
17

nding fathers such as Thomas Jefferson. When McCullough

gan his book on Adams, he wanted it to be about both Adams

d Jefferson, and he wondered if Jefferson would

ershadow Adams? 19 But as he wrote, he began to feel that
18

ams was actually superior to Thomas Jefferson in political

hievements and in moral fiber.

16. **F.** NO CHANGE
    G. getting more and more intense
    H. growing intenser by the minute
    J. intensifying

17. **A.** NO CHANGE
    B. is
    C. would have been
    D. were

18. **F.** NO CHANGE
    G. overshadow, Adams?
    H. overshadow Adams.
    J. overshadow Adams . . .

19. Which of the following phrases should be added at the
    beginning of the preceding sentence in order to make the
    progression of ideas more understandable?

    A. And so,
    B. Because
    C. Therefore,
    D. In fact,

GO ON TO THE NEXT PAGE.

[3]

McCullough writes that Adams was the man <u>more</u>
²⁰
responsible for the adoption of independence by the

Continental Congress. It was <u>he</u> who marshaled the requisite
²¹
number of votes to pass the measure. Adams also brokered

peace with France, <u>that</u> enabled Thomas Jefferson to complete
²²
the Louisiana Purchase.

[4]

Although less important to the nation, Adams's moral

triumphs were as resounding as his political ones. Adams

passionately loved his wife, Abigail, but in order to serve the

country, he had to spend almost all of his time away from her.

Government jobs did not pay well, and in order to make ends

meet, <u>the family farm were run by Abigail</u>. She worked in
²³
Massachusetts while her husband worked in Philadelphia. The

letters of the couple <u>is</u> a testament to the hardship they
²⁴

suffered while apart from one another. <u>There</u> sacrifice was a
²⁵
great one.

[5]

Adams was wonderfully unsentimental about his country.

He <u>objected the</u> idolization of the Founding Fathers, and never
²⁶

characterized the Revolution <u>as noble, he saw</u> it as fraught with
²⁷
disagreement, an enterprise run by ordinary people.

20. F. NO CHANGE
    G. the more
    H. most
    J. even more

21. A. NO CHANGE
    B. himself
    C. him
    D. they

22. F. NO CHANGE
    G. which
    H. who
    J. they

23. A. NO CHANGE
    B. the family farm was under the control of Abigail
    C. running the family farm was Abigail
    D. Abigail ran the family farm

24. F. NO CHANGE
    G. have
    H. are
    J. were

25. A. NO CHANGE
    B. Their
    C. They're
    D. Her

26. F. NO CHANGE
    G. objected for the
    H. objected at the
    J. objected to the

27. A. NO CHANGE
    B. as noble he saw
    C. as noble; he saw
    D. as noble, but he saw

GO ON TO THE NEXT PAGE

[6]

But John Adams's quick temper and bluntness may have
28
...de him unpopular with some people in his day, but the

...port of his deeds has made him more and more popular in

...ent years.

28. F. NO CHANGE
G. So
H. Yet
J. OMIT the underlined portion.

Questions 29 and 30 refer to the essay as a whole.

29. The writer wants to add one of the following closing sentences. Which is most appropriate, considering the essay as a whole?

A. He might have had a bad temper, but in the final analysis it does not matter.
B. Adams was the founding father perhaps most responsible for our country as we know it.
C. Adams was one of the most important founding fathers, and he seems to be becoming one of the best-loved, too.
D. He was one of the only elder statesmen capable of examining our country and our history in an objective way.

30. The writer wishes to include the following sentence in order to further clarify Adams's role:

Over the course of his career in politics, Adams made contributions that changed the course of American history.

Where should it be added?

F. At the beginning of Paragraph 2
G. At the beginning of Paragraph 3
H. At the beginning of Paragraph 4
J. At the beginning of Paragraph 5

...SSAGE III

Area 51

[1]

For believers and conspiracy theorists in alien life forms,
31

...ea 51 is a dream come true. Not only have their been
32

...merous alien sightings, and the government
33

31. A. NO CHANGE
B. (place after *for*)
C. (place after *believers*)
D. (place after *conspiracy*)

32. F. NO CHANGE
G. they're been
H. there been
J. they are being

33. A. NO CHANGE
B. since
C. yet
D. but

GO ON TO THE NEXT PAGE.

has until recently, denied the existence of the Area.
34

Area 51 which is ninety-five miles north of Las Vegas, is a piece
35

of government-owned land that includes an Air Force base.

Which is off-limits to most pilots, including military pilots
36

[2]

[1] Tourists flock to Area 51. [2] They hope to catch a

glimpse of UFOs, and they often get lucky, there have been
37

innumerable reported sightings of everything from flying

saucers to actual aliens. [3] The so-called "Cammo Dudes" is
38

one favorite tourist attraction; they are men who patrol the

Area in unmarked camouflage uniforms and white Jeeps. [4]

Many of the UFO sightings are described as strange lights in

the sky. [5] Problematically for believers in alien life, these
39

strange flashes of light can be explained: the government uses

Area 51 to test new aircraft a practice that can result in sudden
40

and seemingly inexplicable flashes of light. 41

[3]

Another difficulty for believers is that while many

tourists claim to see almost limitless and immeasurable
42

numbers of alien aircraft, many people who live near Area 51

have never seen a single alien or alien craft.

[4]

But even if those who believe in alien life forms are

disappointed, the conspiracy theorists still have something to

34. F. NO CHANGE
    G. has, until recently,
    H. has until, recently,
    J. have until recently

35. A. NO CHANGE
    B. Area 51 that
    C. Area 51, which
    D. Area 51, that

36. F. NO CHANGE
    G. The Air Force base is off-limits
    H. That is off-limits
    J. And it is off-limits

37. A. NO CHANGE
    B. lucky that there
    C. lucky; there
    D. lucky:

38. F. NO CHANGE
    G. are
    H. was
    J. were

39. A. NO CHANGE
    B. For problematically believers in alien life
    C. It is for believers, problematically, in alien life,
    D. Believers, problematically for them in alien life

40. F. NO CHANGE
    G. aircraft; a practice
    H. aircraft, a practice
    J. aircraft: a practice

41. Which of the sentences in Paragraph 2 should be
    eliminated?

    A. 1
    B. 3
    C. 4
    D. 5

42. F. NO CHANGE
    G. and, immeasurable
    H. and innumerable
    J. OMIT the underlined portion.

GO ON TO THE NEXT PAGE

ng to. The government is <u>real secretive</u> about the Air Force
43

se. They do not like to discuss it in the media, <u>but</u> they closed
44

o spots where previously the public was allowed to view

e base.

43. A. NO CHANGE
    B. real secret
    C. really secretive
    D. very secret

44. F. NO CHANGE
    G. yet
    H. and
    J. furthermore

Question 45 asks about the essay as a whole.

---

45. Does it seem that the writer of this essay believes in aliens?

    A. Yes, the writer expresses a firm belief in alien life forms.
    B. No, the writer is openly scornful of those who believe in aliens.
    C. Yes, the writer hints at a tentative belief in life on other planets.
    D. No, the writer seems not to believe in aliens.

SSAGE IV

Collegiate Therapy

[1]

[1] In recent years, college students have increasingly

gun to seek out mental health care. 46 [2] In turn, colleges

ve had to provide more mental health resources. [3] There

e several reasons for this increase in demand. [4] <u>And,</u> the
47

gma attached to therapy has lessened.

[2]

The current crop of college students <u>do</u> not think of
48

rapy as something <u>that they should feel ashamed about</u>.
49

blic awareness of the benefits and uses of therapy has been

46. Which of the following sentences should replace Sentence 1 as the topic sentence for this paragraph?

    F. NO CHANGE
    G. Therapy: it is ubiquitous.
    H. Some students are struggling in college.
    J. Certain factors can make people stressed.

47. A. NO CHANGE
    B. (Begin new paragraph) Yet,
    C. (Do NOT begin new paragraph) Therefore:
    D. (Begin new paragraph) For one thing,

48. F. NO CHANGE
    G. does
    H. have
    J. must

49. A. NO CHANGE
    B. which they must feel ashamed about
    C. shameful
    D. about which they should feel shame

GO ON TO THE NEXT PAGE.

on the raise for years, and many college students grew up
50
thinking of therapy as a normal part of normal people's lives.

[3]

But why do people seek out treatment in college, rather

than in high school or after graduation from college. Some
51
doctors explain that stresses in college can exacerbate latent

problems. Already a danger for fifteen percent of the

population, students susceptible to depression can trigger their
52

malaise by alcohol drug use and sleep deprivation.
53
[4]

Students, especially freshmen, face a new set of

worries, they have to deal with them without the support from
54
family and friends that they're used to. They must make new

friends, take responsibility for their classes and work, and

begin to think about a career. Some had to deal with the stress
55
of coming out; others must deal with being minorities in their

college setting. 56 College students face the real-world

pressures of the economy, troublesome political and world

events, and family problems.

[5]

Although colleges, and universities, has been rushing to
57   58
meet the growing need for readily accessible therapists,

demand often outpaces supply. Staff at counseling centers

---

50. F. NO CHANGE
  G. on the rise
  H. in the raise
  J. of the rise

51. A. NO CHANGE
  B. college, some
  C. college—some
  D. college? Some

52. F. NO CHANGE
  G. students' susceptibility to depression can be triggered by their malaise
  H. students, triggering their malaise, can be susceptible depression
  J. depression can be triggered in susceptible students

53. A. NO CHANGE
  B. alcohol. And drug use. And sleep deprivation.
  C. alcohol, drug use, and sleep deprivation.
  D. alcohol; drug use and sleep deprivation.

54. F. NO CHANGE
  G. worries, and they
  H. worries, or they
  J. worries, which they

55. A. NO CHANGE
  B. are having to
  C. did
  D. have to

56. Which of the following connecting words or phrases should be added at the beginning of the following sentence?

  F. Furthermore
  G. Even so
  H. Still
  J. But

57. A. NO CHANGE
  B. colleges and universities,
  C. colleges—and universities,
  D. colleges and universities

58. F. NO CHANGE
  G. it's
  H. have
  J. are

GO ON TO THE NEXT PAGE

equently have their hands full dealing with emergencies, <u>but</u>
⁵⁹
udents who have less pressing problems must oftentimes

ait for several weeks before they can get an appointment.

59. A. NO CHANGE
  B. which means that
  C. yet
  D. because

60. The writer wishes to add this sentence in order to conclude a paragraph:

> At many colleges and universities, plans and studies are underway to deal with this staff shortage.

Which paragraph would it most appropriately conclude?

  F. Paragraph 1
  G. Paragraph 2
  H. Paragraph 4
  J. Paragraph 5

ASSAGE V

The Grass Is Always Greener

[1]

I used to long for the warmth and sun of California, but

ter moving to Southern California from Buffalo, New York, I

issed the seasons more than I ever thought I would. In a place

here it's sunny all the time, I longed for <u>winter, spring</u>
⁶¹
ummer and fall.

[2]

When I lived in Buffalo, <u>I was unhappy and I love to surf</u>
⁶²
d of course I couldn't do it in Buffalo. I dreamed of beaches, a

ar-round tan, and good Mexican food—all things I couldn't get

Buffalo. I wanted to <u>move to California so bad.</u>
⁶³

[3]

[1] When I got there, <u>it wasn't what I'd</u> expected at all.
⁶⁴
Finally, I got a job and moved to Orange County. [3] After

out four months of perfect weather, all I wanted was to see

e leaves change color. [4] To my surprise, I missed the

61. A. NO CHANGE
  B. winter; spring; summer; fall
  C. winter, spring, summer, and fall
  D. winter spring summer and fall

62. F. NO CHANGE
  G. I was unhappy, I love to surf
  H. I love to surf, so I was unhappy
  J. I was unhappy because I love to surf,

63. A. NO CHANGE
  B. move to California so badly
  C. so bad to move to California
  D. move, so bad, to California

64. F. NO CHANGE
  G. it hadn't been like I'd
  H. it didn't seem to be what I was
  J. nothing was as I'm

GO ON TO THE NEXT PAGE.

seasons. [65]

[4]

I went to the beach, I didn't go surfing, I sat on the sand
_____
66

and wrote in my journal about how much I missed New York. I

missed the fall: picking apples, going for long drives to look at

the foliage, and crisp, cold Halloween nights. It didn't feel like
_____
67

Christmas without all of the things that go with Christmas, the
_____
68

traditions like decorating the tree, building snowmen, and

sitting by a real fire after a day of sledding. And when spring

came it didn't bring with it the usual feelings of relief and

renewal. It had felt like spring for months and months, so the

beginning of spring technical didn't make any difference.
_____
69

[5]

I'd always thought the aphorism "The grass is always

greener on the other side of the fence" was a stupid one. [70]

When I was in Buffalo, I wanted to be in California, and when I
_____
71

was in California, I wanted to be in Buffalo. I couldn't seem to

please me.
_____
72

---

65. Which of the following sequences of sentences makes Paragraph 3 flow most logically?

  A. NO CHANGE
  B. 1, 3, 2, 4
  C. 4, 2, 1, 3
  D. 2, 1, 4, 3

66. F. NO CHANGE
  G. When I went to the beach
  H. I was going to the beach
  J. Because I went to the beach

67. A. NO CHANGE
  B. crisp cold Halloween nights
  C. enjoying crisp, cold Halloween nights
  D. the nights of Halloween, crisp and cold

68. F. NO CHANGE
  G. the various accoutrements of Christmas,
  H. all of those wonderful things that accompany Christmas,
  J. OMIT the underlined portion

69. A. NO CHANGE
  B. (Place after *the*)
  C. (Place after *didn't*)
  D. (Place after *so*)

70. Which of the following sentences, added here, would make sense of the relationship between the first sentences of the paragraph?

  F. In general, I find that aphorisms have little bearing on my life.
  G. My California experience only convinced me further that the saying is an empty one.
  H. However, once I'd moved to California, that saying suddenly made sense.
  J. In this case, the cliché "you can't go home again" seemed applicable.

71. A. NO CHANGE
  B. since
  C. however
  D. not

72. F. NO CHANGE
  G. anyone
  H. my self
  J. myself

GO ON TO THE NEXT PAGE

[6]

Eventually, I <u>have found</u> a <u>solution, that makes me</u> very
          73   74
ppy. I moved to Cape Cod, where I can surf in the summer

d still enjoy the changing of the seasons and

uriate in the ever-volatile temperament of the weather. [75]

73. A. NO CHANGE
   B. found
   C. was finding
   D. had found

74. F. NO CHANGE
   G. solution, and it made
   H. solution that makes
   J. solution, it makes

75. If the writer changed the words "the changing of the seasons and luxuriate in the ever-volatile temperament of the weather" to read "the changing of the seasons," what would be the effect?

   A. The simplified version would be more in keeping with the tone of the rest of the essay.
   B. The grandeur needed at the end of an essay would be lost.
   C. The over-simplification would result in vagueness.
   D. The reader's contract to trust the writer would be broken.

END OF TEST 1
STOP! DO NOT TURN THE PAGE UNTIL TOLD TO DO SO.

MATH TEST

60 Minutes—60 Questions

DIRECTIONS: After solving each problem, pick the correct answer from the five given and fill in the corresponding oval on your answer sheet. Solve as many problems as you can in the time allowed. Do not worry over problems that take too much time; skip them if necessary and return to them if you have time.

Calculator use is permitted on the test. Calculators can be used for any problem on the test, though calculators may be more harm than help for some questions.

Note: unless otherwise stated on the test, you shou assume that:

1. Figures accompanying questions are *not* drawn to sca

2. Geometric figures exist in a plane.

3. When given in a question, "line" refers to a straight line.

4. When given in a question, "average" refers to the arithmetic mean.

---

1. In a population of monkeys in a zoo, 8 monkeys have gray fur while the rest have black fur. If the 8 grey monkeys make up exactly 25% of the monkey population, how large is the population of monkeys?

   A. 10
   B. 12
   C. 16
   D. 32
   E. 48

DO YOUR FIGURING HERE.

2. Point C is the midpoint of line segment $\overline{AB}$. If line segment $\overline{AB}$ measures 10 yards, then what is the length of line segment $\overline{CB}$ in yards?

   F. $2\frac{1}{2}$

   G. 4

   H. 5

   J. $7\frac{1}{2}$

   K. 10

3. What is the sixth term in the arithmetic sequence $-2, 4, -8, 16, \ldots$?

   A. −32
   B. −8
   C. 0
   D. 24
   E. 64

What is the value of x in the proportion $\frac{4}{10} = \frac{6}{x}$?

F. $\frac{2}{5}$

G. $\frac{2}{3}$

H. $\frac{1}{2}$

J. 15

K. 24

DO YOUR FIGURING HERE.

In the figure below, points A, B, and C all lie on the same line. What is the measure of $\angle EBD$?

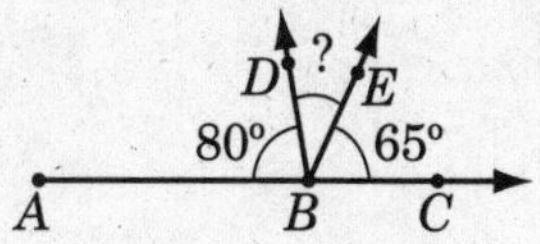

A. 10°
B. 35°
C. 55°
D. 105°
E. 215°

Train X travels 75 miles in $1\frac{1}{2}$ hours. Train Y travels 80 miles in 2 hours. What is the difference, in miles per hour, between the average speeds of train X and train Y?

F. 5
G. 10
H. 40
J. 50
K. 90

If $x = -3$, then $9 - 3(x - 1) = ?$

A. −3
B. 3
C. 15
D. 21
E. 24

$|4| \times |-2| = ?$

F. −8
G. −6
H. −2
J. 2
K. 8

Angela bought a pair of jeans that were on sale for 30% off. If the jeans originally cost $32.50, how much did they cost when Angela bought them?

A. $9.75
B. $14.00
C. $19.50
D. $22.75
E. $24.50

GO ON TO THE NEXT PAGE.

10. $(-3x^4)^2 = ?$

   F. $-9x^8$
   G. $-9x^6$
   H. $-3x^6$
   J. $9x^6$
   K. $9x^8$

DO YOUR FIGURING HERE.

11. If $59 - x = 118$, then what is the value of x?

   A. -177
   B. -59
   C. 2
   D. 59
   E. 177

12. David is 7 years older than Wallace. 15 years ago, Wallace was x years old. How old is David now?

   F. $x - 8$
   G. $x + 7$
   H. $x + 8$
   J. $x + 15$
   K. $x + 22$

13. Three corners of a rectangle graphed in the standard (x,y) coordinate plane are $(1,4)$, $(1,-2)$, and $(-2,-2)$. What point is the fourth corner of the rectangle?

   A. $(2,4)$
   B. $(2,-4)$
   C. $(-2,4)$
   D. $(-2,-4)$
   E. $(4,4)$

14. What is the factored form of $3x^2y - 6xy^2$?

   F. $3xy(x - 2y)$
   G. $3x^2y^2(x - 2y)$
   H. $xy(2x - 2y)$
   J. $2(3x^2y^2)$
   K. $-3(x^2y^2)$

15. The perimeter of a square is 4 meters. If the length of the sides of the square are increased so that the area of the square doubles in size, what would be the new perimeter of the square?

   A. $\sqrt{2}$
   B. 2
   C. $2\sqrt{2}$
   D. $4\sqrt{2}$
   E. 8

GO ON TO THE NEXT PAGE

DO YOUR FIGURING HERE.

6. In the standard (x,y) coordinate plane, a line parallel to $y = \frac{1}{2}x + 3$ must have a slope equal to?

F. -3

G. $-\frac{1}{2}$

H. $\frac{1}{2}$

J. 2

K. 3

7. Which of the following is a factor of $x^2 - 2x - 8$?

A. $(x-1)$
B. $(x-2)$
C. $(x-3)$
D. $(x-4)$
E. $(x-5)$

8. If the hypotenuse of a right triangle measures 10 meters and the shortest leg of the triangle is 6 meters, what is the measurement, in meters, of the longer leg?

F. 4
G. 6
H. 8
J. $\sqrt{136}$
K. 16

9. For the prom, Helena bought a new dress and new shoes. The dress originally cost \$295, but was on sale for 20% off. The shoes were also on sale, at 30% of their original price of \$150. How much did Helena pay for the dress and shoes?

A. \$164
B. \$281
C. \$346
D. \$391
E. \$445

10. What is the sum of the polynomials $xy^2 - 3xy$ and $4xy - 3x^2y$?

F. $xy^2 + 4xy$
G. $xy^2 + 4xy - 6x^2y$
H. $xy^2 + xy - 3x^2y$
J. $xy - 2x^2y$
K. $-3xy + 5xy^2$

11. If $3x - y = 7$ and $x + y = 5$, then what is the value of x?

A. -6
B. 0
C. 2
D. 3
E. 6

GO ON TO THE NEXT PAGE.

22. 1 yard = 36 inches. If a wood plank measures 255 inches, what is its length in yards, to the nearest tenth of a yard?

   F. 7.1
   G. 21.9
   H. 71.0
   J. 91.8
   K. 219.0

23. What is the perimeter, in centimeters, of the figure below?

   A. 84 cm

   B. 38 cm

   C. 52 cm

   D. 104 cm

   E. 76 cm

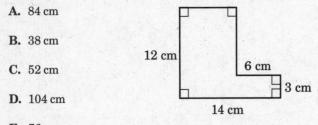

24. A store orders merchandise with the understanding that it will make a profit of $1.5p(n - u)$, where p is the wholesale price at which the store buys the items, n is the number of items the store purchases, and u is the number of items the store is unable to sell. If the store buys 50 toaster ovens at $15 an oven, and is unable to sell 12 of the ovens, what is the store's profit?

   F. $225
   G. $570
   H. $630
   J. $855
   K. $1250

25. In the figure below, $ABCD$ and $EFGH$ are both squares. If a side of $ABCD$ measures $3\sqrt{2}$ inches, then what is the area of the shaded region?

   A. $6\sqrt{4}$

   B. 9

   C. 12

   D. 18

   E. 27

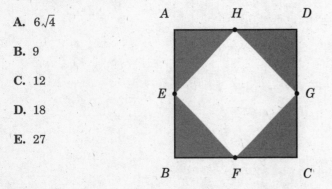

26. The number line graph below best fits which inequality?

   F. $-10 < 2x + 4 < -2$
   G. $-10 < 2x - 4 < -2$
   H. $-10 < 2x - 2 < -2$
   J. $-5 < 2x - 2 < -1$
   K. $-10 < 2x < -2$

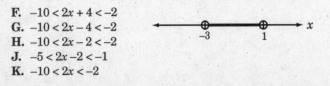

GO ON TO THE NEXT PAGE

. If $\log_x 81 = 2$, then $x = ?$

A. $\log 4$

B. $\dfrac{\log 81}{2}$

C. 3

D. 9

E. 81^2

. Two sides of a triangle are 6 inches and $3\frac{2}{3}$ inches in length. All of the following measurements, in inches, can be the length of the third side EXCEPT

F. 2
G. 3
H. 5
J. 8
K. 9

. What is the least prime factor shared by the numbers 24 and 36?

A. 2
B. 3
C. 4
D. 6
E. 8

. A triangle has sides measuring 3, 4, and 5 inches. What is the area of the triangle, in square inches?

F. 4
G. 6
H. 7
J. 12
K. 30

. A bag contains red, blue, and green marbles in the ratio of 6:5:4. If there are 12 green marbles in the bag, how many total marbles are there in the bag?

A. 15
B. 23
C. 30
D. 45
E. 120

. Triangle ABC has a hypotenuse of length $2\sqrt{2}$. What is the area of isosceles right triangle DEF if its hypotenuse is twice as long as the hypotenuse of $\triangle ABC$?

F. 2
G. 4
H. 8
J. 16
K. $\sqrt{32}$

33. $(x-3)(x+5) = ?$

    A. -15
    B. $x^2 - 15$
    C. $x^2 + 2x - 15$
    D. $2x^2 - 2x - 15$
    E. $15x - 15$

34. If the sine of $\angle A$ in a right triangle is $\frac{4}{5}$, and the tangent of $\angle A$ is $\frac{4}{3}$, then $\cos A = ?$

    F. $\frac{12}{5}$

    G. $\frac{5}{3}$

    H. $\frac{4}{3}$

    J. $\frac{4}{7}$

    K. $\frac{3}{5}$

35. Which number is closest to the value indicated by point A?

    A. 2.1950
    B. 2.1804
    C. 2.1750
    D. 2.1725
    E. 2.1150

36. Over four seasons, a baseball team averages 87 wins per season. After five seasons, the team's average is 83 wins per season. How many wins did the team have in its fifth season?

    F. 67
    G. 72
    H. 75
    J. 83
    K. 90

37. In the figure below, line segment $\overline{CD}$ bisects base $\overline{AB}$ of equilateral triangle ABC. What is the measure of angle $\angle ACD$?

    A. 15°

    B. 30°

    C. 60°

    D. 90°

    E. 120°

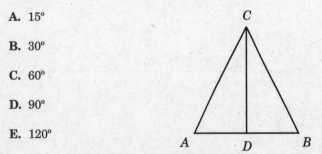

GO ON TO THE NEXT PAGE

8. If $f(x) = \dfrac{x^3 + 4x}{2x^2}$, what is the value of $f(-2)$?

   F. -2

   G. $-\dfrac{1}{2}$

   H. $\dfrac{1}{2}$

   J. 1

   K. 2

DO YOUR FIGURING HERE.

9. In the figure below, lines a and b are parallel and lines c and d are parallel. If $\triangle JHK$ is a right triangle, as shown, then what is the measure of $\angle x$?

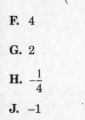

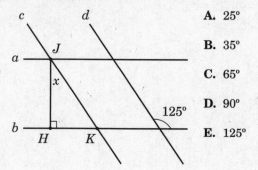

   A. $25°$

   B. $35°$

   C. $65°$

   D. $90°$

   E. $125°$

10. What is the slope of the line that passes through the origin and point $\left(-2, \dfrac{1}{2}\right)$?

   F. 4

   G. 2

   H. $-\dfrac{1}{4}$

   J. -1

   K. -4

11. When x is multiplied by three and increased by 2, the result is less than 11 but greater than -1. Which of the following graphs is the solution set for x?

   A.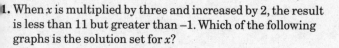

   B.

   C.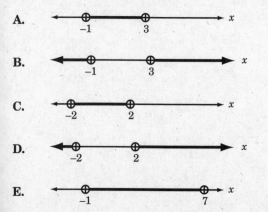

   D.

   E.

GO ON TO THE NEXT PAGE.

42. What must be the value of a, if the graph of the following system of equations is a single line in the standard (x,y) coordinate plane?

$$6x + 3y = 2a$$
$$2x + y = 6$$

F. 2
G. 6
H. 9
J. 12
K. 18

43. What is the tangent of $\angle B$ in right triangle $\triangle ABC$ below?

A. 1

B. $\frac{6}{5}$

C. $\frac{5}{4}$

D. $\frac{4}{3}$

E. $\frac{3}{5}$

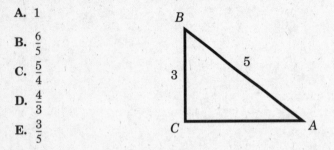

44. The following system of equations has an infinite number of solutions.

$$4x - 6y = 8$$
$$x + my = 2$$

What is the value of m?

F. -6

G. $-\frac{3}{2}$

H. 0

J. $\frac{3}{2}$

K. 6

45. In the figure below, points D and E lie on the sides of $\triangle ABC$ so that line segment $\overline{DE}$ is parallel to segment $\overline{AC}$. $\overline{BD}$ is 6 cm long, and $\overline{BA}$ is 10 cm long. If $\overline{DE}$ is 9 cm, then what is the area of $\triangle ABC$ in square centimeters?

A. 27

B. 54

C. 75

D. 135

E. 150

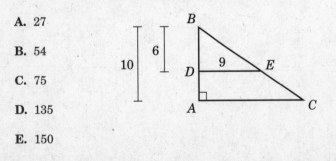

GO ON TO THE NEXT PAGE

DO YOUR FIGURING HERE.

46. The x-coordinates of a line plotted in the standard (x,y) coordinate plane are always twice as large as the y-coordinates. What is the slope of the line?

F. $\dfrac{1}{2}$

G. 1

H. 2

J. $\dfrac{5}{2}$

K. 4

47. A ship rests at anchor some distance from a straight shoreline on which two lighthouses stand. The angle between the ship and the two lighthouses is 63°, and the distance between the lighthouses is 12 miles, as seen below. What is the distance from Lighthouse 2 to the ship?

A. 5

B. 13

C. $12 \sin 63°$

D. $\dfrac{12}{\sin 63°}$

E. $\dfrac{12}{\cos 63°}$

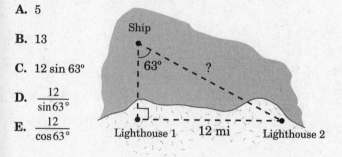

48. As the police force lines up to get its picture taken, the officers discover that when they organize themselves in rows of 3, the last row is 2 people short. When they arrange themselves in rows of 4, the last row is again 2 people short. When they line up in rows of 5, the last row is once again 2 people short. What is the smallest possible number of police officers on the force?

F. 8
G. 10
H. 28
J. 58
K. 118

49. If $f(x) = x^2 - 2x$ and $g(x) = \dfrac{(x-4)^2}{9}$, what is the value of $f(g(-2))$?

A. 0

B. $\dfrac{16}{9}$

C. 4

D. 8

E. 24

GO ON TO THE NEXT PAGE.

DO YOUR FIGURING HERE.

50. A rectangular box has a length of 4 inches, a width of 5 inches, and a height of 6 inches. What is the surface area of the box, in square inches?

    F. 15
    G. 120
    H. 136
    J. 148
    K. 160

51. What is the area, in square inches, of a circle whose circumference is 4π inches?

    A. π
    B. 2π
    C. 3π
    D. 4π
    E. 5π

52. At what value of x does the graph formed by the equation $y = x^3 - 27$ intersect with the x-axis?

    F. -27
    G. 3
    H. 0
    J. 9
    K. 27

53. If the quadratic equation $x^2 - ax + 9 = 0$ has only one possible solution for x, then what is the value of a?

    A. -2
    B. 0
    C. 2
    D. 4
    E. 6

54. In which of the following equations does y vary directly with the square of x and inversely with the square root of z?

    F. $y = x^2 \sqrt{z}$

    G. $y = \dfrac{x^2}{\sqrt{z}}$

    H. $x = y^2 \sqrt{z}$

    J. $x = \dfrac{y^2}{\sqrt{z}}$

    K. $z = \dfrac{y^2}{x^3}$

55. If $ac = \dfrac{1}{b}$, then which of the following is true?

    A. $ab = \dfrac{1}{c}$

    B. $ab = c$

    C. $ac = b$

    D. $abc = 0$

    E. $c = \dfrac{a}{b}$

GO ON TO THE NEXT PAGE

6. The sides of a square are $x + 2$ units long. If a smaller square whose sides are length x is removed from the larger square, what is the expression of the remaining area of the larger square?

F. $x^2 + 4x + 4$
G. $2x^2 + 4x + 4$
H. $4x + 4 - x^2$
J. $x + 2$
K. $4(x + 1)$

7. What is the smallest possible absolute value of x (in radians) where $y = 2 \sin x$ reaches a maximum?

A. 0

B. $\dfrac{\pi}{4}$

C. $\dfrac{\pi}{2}$

D. π

E. 2π

8. Point A (–1,–2) is the endpoint of a line segment in the standard (x,y) coordinate plane, and point C (3,–4) is the midpoint of the line segment. What is the second endpoint of the line segment?

F. (1,–3)
G. (3,–1)
H. (4,3)
J. (7,–6)
K. (7,–8)

9. In two tosses of a fair six-sided die, what is the probability of rolling either a 2 or a 3 each time? (In a fair die, each of the 6 outcomes is equally likely.)

A. $\dfrac{1}{27}$

B. $\dfrac{1}{9}$

C. $\dfrac{1}{3}$

D. $\dfrac{2}{3}$

E. $\dfrac{7}{9}$

10. What must the value of x be if the expression $(225 - x)$ is the degree measure of an obtuse angle?

F. $45 < x < 135$
G. $0 < x < 90$
H. $0 < x < 135$
J. $90 < x < 360$
K. $235 < x < 360$

DO YOUR FIGURING HERE.

END OF TEST 2
STOP! DO NOT TURN THE PAGE UNTIL TOLD TO DO SO.
DO NOT RETURN TO THE PREVIOUS TEST.

READING TEST

35 Minutes—40 Questions

DIRECTIONS: On this test, you will have 35 minutes to read four passages and answer 40 questions (ten questions on each passage). Each set of ten questions appears directly after the relevant passage. You should select the answer choice that best answers the question. There is no time limit for work on the individual passages, so you can move freely between the passages and refer to each as often as you'd like.

Passage I

PROSE FICTION: This passage is adapted from Virginia Woolf's *The Voyage Out* (1915).

Uncomfortable as the night, with its rocking movement, and salt smells, may have been, and in one case undoubtedly was, for Mr. Pepper had insufficient clothes upon his bed, the breakfast next morning wore a kind of beauty. The
5   voyage had begun, and had begun happily with a soft blue sky, and a calm sea. The sense of untapped resources, things to say as yet unsaid, made the hour significant, so that in future years the entire journey perhaps would be represented by this one scene, with the sound of sirens,
10 hooting in the river the night before, somehow mixing in.

The table was cheerful with apples and bread and eggs. Helen handed Willoughby the butter, and as she did so cast her eye on him and reflected, "And she married you, and she was happy, I suppose." She went off on a familiar train
15 of thought, leading on to all kinds of well-known reflections, from the old wonder, why Theresa had married Willoughby?

"Of course, one sees all that," she thought, meaning that one sees that he is big and burly, and has a great booming
20 voice, and a fist and a will of his own; "but—" here she slipped into a fine analysis of him which is best represented by one word, "sentimental," by which she meant that he was never simple and honest about his feelings. For example, he seldom spoke of the dead, but kept anniversa-
25 ries with singular pomp. She suspected him of nameless atrocities with regard to his daughter, as indeed she had always suspected him of bullying his wife. Naturally she fell to comparing her own fortunes with the fortunes of her friend, for Willoughby's wife had been perhaps the one
30 woman Helen called friend, and this comparison often made the staple of their talk. Ridley was a scholar, and Willoughby was a man of business. Ridley was bringing out the third volume of Pindar when Willoughby was launching his first ship. They built a new factory the very year the
35 commentary on Aristotle—was it?—appeared at the University Press. "And Rachel," she looked at her, meaning, no doubt, to decide the argument, which was otherwise too evenly balanced, by declaring that Rachel was not comparable to her own children. "She really might be six years
40 old," was all she said, however, this judgment referring to the smooth unmarked outline of the girl's face, and not co[n]demning her otherwise, for if Rachel were ever to thin[k] feel, laugh, or express herself, instead of dropping mi[lk] from a height as though to see what kind of drops it mad[e]
45 she might be interesting though never exactly pretty. Sh[e] was like her mother, as the image in a pool on a still su[m]mer's day is like the vivid flushed face that hangs over it.

Meanwhile Helen herself was under examinatio[n] though not from either of her victims. Mr. Pepper consi[d]
50 ered her; and his meditations, carried on while he cut h[is] toast into bars and neatly buttered them, took him throu[gh] a considerable stretch of autobiography. One of his pen[e]trating glances assured him that he was right last night [in] judging that Helen was beautiful. Blandly he passed h[er]
55 the jam. She was talking nonsense, but not worse nonsen[se] than people usually do talk at breakfast, the cerebral c[ir]culation, as he knew to his cost, being apt to give trouble [at] that hour. He went on saying "No" to her, on principle, [for] he never yielded to a woman on account of her sex. A[nd]
60 here, dropping his eyes to his plate, he became autobi[o]graphical. He had not married himself for the sufficie[nt] reason that he had never met a woman who command[ed] his respect. Condemned to pass the susceptible years [of] youth in a railway station in Bombay, he had seen only m[il]
65 itary women, official women; and his ideal was a woma[n] who could read Greek, if not Persian, was irreproachab[le] fair in the face, and able to understand the small things [he] let fall while undressing. As it was he had contracted ha[b]its of which he was not in the least ashamed. Certain o[f]
70 minutes every day went to learning things by heart; [he] never took a ticket without noting the number; he devot[ed] January to Petronius, February to Catullus, March to t[he] Etruscan vases perhaps; anyhow he had done good work [in] India, and there was nothing to regret in his life except t[he]
75 fundamental defects which no wise man regrets, when t[he] present is still his. So concluding he looked up sudden[ly] and smiled. Rachel caught his eye.

"And now you've chewed something thirty-seven time[s] suppose?" she thought, but said politely aloud, "Are yo[ur] legs troubling you to-day, Mr. Pepper?"

1. According to the passage, Mr. Pepper's interests include all of the following EXCEPT:

   A. Petronius.
   B. Pindar.
   C. Catullus.
   D. Etruscan vases.

2. Helen would most likely agree with the characterization of Willoughby as:

   F. inscrutable.
   G. honest and simple.
   H. emotional.
   J. unkind.

3. Given the way he is presented in the passage, Mr. Pepper can best be described as:

   A. uncritical.
   B. hard-working.
   C. inflexible.
   D. selfless.

4. Helen compares Ridley to Willoughby in all of the following respects EXCEPT:

   F. their careers.
   G. their children.
   H. landmarks in their careers.
   J. their physical appearance.

5. As described in the first paragraph, the discomfort during the night results from:

   A. insufficient bedclothes.
   B. the rocking movement of the ship.
   C. sound of sirens hooting in the river.
   D. the rough sea.

6. One can infer that Ridley is:

   F. Rachel's father.
   G. Theresa's husband.
   H. Helen's son.
   J. Helen's husband.

7. The passage suggests Mr. Pepper's attitude towards women is that:

   A. few deserve his respect.
   B. they are beautiful.
   C. they talk nonsense.
   D. several read Greek and a few Persian.

8. The analogy made in lines 45–47 suggests that:

   F. Rachel resembles her mother in appearance but perhaps lacks her mother's vitality and substance.
   G. Rachel's face is exactly like her mother's.
   H. Rachel resembles her mother in some lights but not all.
   J. Compared to her animated mother, Rachel is merely a pale reflection without substance.

9. One can infer from lines 76–78 that:

   A. Rachel pretends to be interested in the state of Mr. Pepper's legs although she is really interested only in his peculiar chewing habits.
   B. Rachel has inherited the trait from her father of not saying what she means.
   C. Mr. Pepper has chronic leg problems that he deals with by thoroughly chewing his food.
   D. Rachel secretly finds Mr. Pepper ridiculous, but she is polite when speaking to him.

10. In the passage, the narrator represents the viewpoints of:

    I. Helen.
    II. Mr. Pepper.
    III. Rachel.
    IV. Willoughby.

    F. I only
    G. I and II only
    H. I, II, and III
    J. I, II, and IV

GO ON TO THE NEXT PAGE.

Passage II

SOCIAL SCIENCE: This passage is adapted from Doris Stevens's *Jailed for Freedom* (1920).

"Where are the people?" This was Woodrow Wilson's first question as he arrived at the Union Station in Washington the day before his first inauguration to the Presidency in March, 1913.

5   "On the Avenue watching the suffragists parade," came the answer.

The suffrage issue was brought to his attention from then on until his final surrender. It lay entirely with him as to how long women would be obliged to remind him of this
10 issue before he decided to take a hand.

"The people" were on the Avenue watching the suffragists parade. The informant was quite right. It seemed to those of us who attempted to march for our idea that day that the whole world was there—packed closely on Penn-
15 sylvania Avenue.

The purpose of the procession was to dramatize in numbers the fact that women wanted to vote. What politicians had not been able to get through their minds we would give them through their eyes—often a powerful substitute. Our
20 first task seemed simple: to show that thousands of women wanted immediate action on their long delayed enfranchisement. This we did.

The Administration, without intending it, played into the hands of the women from this moment. The women had
25 been given a permit to march. Inadequate police protection allowed roughs to attack them and all but break up the pageant. The fact of ten thousand women marching with banners and bands for this idea was startling enough to wake up the government and the country, but not so star-
30 tling as ten thousand women man-handled by irresponsible crowds because of police indifference.

An investigation was demanded and a perfunctory one held. The police administration was exonerated, but when the storm of protest had subsided the Chief of Police was
35 quietly retired to private life.

A few days later the first deputation of suffragists ever to appear before a President in order to enlist his support waited upon President Wilson. Alice Paul led the deputation. The President received the deputation in the White
40 House Offices. When the women entered they found five chairs arranged in a row with one chair in front, like a classroom. All confessed to being frightened when the President came in and took his seat at the head of the class. The President said he had no opinion on the subject of
45 woman suffrage; that he had never given it any thought; and that above all it was his task to see that Congress

concentrated on the currency revision and the tar[iff] reform. It is recorded that the President was somewh[at] taken aback when Miss Paul addressed him during th[e]
50 course of the interview with this query, "But Mr. Presiden[t] do you not understand that the Administration has n[o] right to legislate for currency, tariff, and any other refor[m] without first getting the consent of women to the[se] reforms?"

55 "Get the consent of women?" It was evident that th[is] course had not heretofore occurred to him.

"This subject will receive my most careful consider[-] ation," was President Wilson's first suffrage promise.

He was given time to "consider" and a second deputati[on]
60 went to him, and still a third, asking him to include th[e] suffrage amendment in his message to the new Congre[ss] assembling the following month.

He flatly said there would be no time to consider su[f-] frage for women. But the "unreasonable" women kept rig[ht]
65 on insisting that the liberty of half the American peop[le] was paramount to tariff and currency. President Wilso[n's] first session of Congress came together April 7th, 191[3.] The opening day was marked by the suffragists' secon[d] mass demonstration. This time women delegates repr[e-]
70 senting every one of the 435 Congressional Districts in t[he] country bore petitions from the constituencies showi[ng] that the people "back home" wanted the amendme[nt] passed. The delegates marched on Congress. The same d[ay] the amendment which bears the name of Susan [B.]
75 Anthony, who drafted it in 1875, was reintroduced in[to] both houses of Congress.

The month of May saw monster demonstration[s] throughout the country, with the direct result that in Ju[ne] the Senate Committee on Suffrage made the first favorab[le]
80 report made by that committee in twenty-one year[s,] thereby placing it on the Senate calendar for action.

Not relaxing the pressure for a day we organized th[e] third great demonstration on the last of July when a pe[ti-] tion signed by hundreds of thousands of citizens w[as]
85 brought to the Senate asking that body to pass the nation[al] suffrage amendment. Women from all parts of the count[ry] mobilized in the countryside of Maryland. The delegati[on] motored in gaily decorated automobiles to Washington a[nd] went to the Senate, where the entire day was given over [to]
90 suffrage discussion.

Twenty-two senators spoke in favor of the amendme[nt.] Three spoke against it. For the first time in twenty-s[ix] years suffrage was actually debated in Congress. That d[ay] was historic.

GO ON TO THE NEXT PAG[E]

One of the main purposes of the passage is to:

A. expose Woodrow Wilson's opposition to women's suffrage.
B. describe how the amendment for women's suffrage was passed in Congress.
C. demonstrate the unjust treatment of suffragists by the government.
D. show how the persistence of the suffragists brought the suffrage debate to government.

The author's point of view is that of:

F. a feminist historian.
G. an opponent of women's suffrage.
H. a participant in the events described.
J. a leader of the deputation that met with the President.

The implication of the police chief's retirement in lines 33–35 is that:

A. he man-handled some of the parading suffragists.
B. he was ultimately responsible for the lack of protection at the parade.
C. the government publicly laid the blame on his shoulders.
D. he opposed the exoneration of the police force.

The author most likely uses the comparison of the suffragists' meeting with the President to a classroom in order to suggest that:

F. the President planned to teach the suffragists.
G. the President sought to intimidate the suffragists through a show of force.
H. the White House staff thought the suffragists were schoolchildren.
J. the President and his staff treated the suffragists in a condescending manner.

According to the passage, President Wilson's initial response to the deputation of suffragists was one of:

A. sympathetic concern.
B. intellectual consideration.
C. naïve bewilderment.
D. disinterested disdain.

16. In the sixth paragraph (lines 23–31) the author implies that the administration "played into the hands of the women" by:

F. giving the women a permit to march.
G. demanding an investigation after the parade.
H. unintentionally generating publicity for the suffragists.
J. considering the suffragists' demands.

17. According to the passage, violence directed against the parading suffragists resulted from:

A. a lack of proper policing of the event.
B. the crowd's resentment of the suffragists.
C. the police's effort to agitate the crowd.
D. the suffragists' use of inflammatory language.

18. The author states that the May demonstrations directly led to:

F. the reintroduction of the Susan B. Anthony amendment in Congress.
G. a favorable report made by the Senate Committee on suffrage.
H. a day of discussion about suffrage in the Senate.
J. twenty-two senators speaking in support of suffrage.

19. One can reasonably infer that the author believes tariff reform and currency revision are:

A. as important as suffrage for women.
B. obstructions to the liberty of half the American people.
C. empty and unfair without women's votes on the issues.
D. equally important issues to men and women.

20. The author's tone when discussing the "'unreasonable' women" in lines 64–66 can best be described as:

F. sarcastic.
G. contemptuous.
H. objective.
J. insincere.

GO ON TO THE NEXT PAGE.

Passage III

HUMANITIES: This passage is adapted from Henry James's "The Art of Fiction."

The only reason for the existence of a novel is that it does compete with life. When it ceases to compete as the canvas of the painter competes, it will have arrived at a very strange pass. It is not expected of the picture that it will
5 make itself humble in order to be forgiven; and the analogy between the art of the painter and the art of the novelist is complete. Their inspiration is the same, their process (allowing for the different quality of the vehicle) is the same, their success is the same. They may learn from each
10 other, they may explain and sustain each other. Their cause is the same, and the honor of one is the honor of another.

As the picture is reality, so the novel is history. That is the only general description (which does it justice) that we may give the novel. But history also is allowed to compete
15 with life; it is not, any more than painting, expected to apologize. The subject-matter of fiction is stored up likewise in documents and records, and if it will not give itself away, it must speak with assurance, with the tone of the historian.

20 Certain accomplished novelists have a habit of giving themselves away which must often bring tears to the eyes of people who take their fiction seriously. I was lately struck, in reading over many pages of Anthony Trollope, with his want of discretion in this particular. In a digres-
25 sion, he concedes to the reader that he and his trusting friend are only "making believe." He admits that the events he narrates have not really happened, and that he can give his narrative any turn the reader may like best.

Such a betrayal of a sacred office seems to me a terrible
30 crime; it is what I mean by the attitude of apology. It implies that the novelist is less occupied in looking for the truth than the historian. To represent and illustrate the past, the actions of men, is the task of either writer. The only difference that I can see is, in proportion as he suc-
35 ceeds, to the honor of the novelist, consisting as it does in his having more difficulty in collecting his evidence, which is so far from being purely literary. It seems to me to give him a great character.

It is of all this evidently that Mr. Besant is full when he
40 insists upon the fact that fiction is one of the fine arts, deserving in its turn of all the honors and emoluments that have hitherto been reserved for the successful professions of music, poetry, painting, architecture. It is excellent that he should have struck this note, for his doing so indicates
45 that his proposition may be to many people a novelty. I suspect that in addition to the people to whom it has never occurred that a novel ought to be artistic, there are a great many others who, if this principle were urged upon them, would be filled with an indefinable mistrust.

50 "Art" is supposed, in certain circles, to have som vaguely injurious effect upon those who make it an impo tant consideration. It is assumed to be opposed to moralit to amusement, to instruction. Literature should be eith instructive or amusing, and there is in many minds a
55 impression that these artistic preoccupations contribute neither end, interfere indeed with both.

That, I think, represents the manner in which the late thought of many people who read novels as an exercise skipping would explain itself if it were to become artic
60 late. They would argue that a novel ought to be "good," b they would interpret this term in a fashion of their ow which would vary considerably from one critic to anoth One would say that being good means representing virt ous and aspiring characters, placed in prominent po
65 tions; another would say that it depends for a "hap ending" on a distribution at the last of prizes, pension husbands, wives, babies, millions, appended paragrap and cheerful remarks.

Another still would say that it means being full of in
70 dent and movement, so that we shall wish to jump ahea to see who was the mysterious stranger, and if the stol will was ever found, and shall not be distracted from th pleasure by any tiresome analysis or "description." B they would all agree that the "artistic" idea would sp
75 some of their fun.

The "ending" of a novel is, for many persons, like that o good dinner, a course of dessert and ices, and the artist in f tion is regarded as a sort of meddlesome doctor who forbi agreeable aftertastes. It matters little that, as a work of a
80 the novel should really be as little or as much concerned supply happy endings as if it were a work of mechanics; t association of ideas, however incongruous, might easily too much for it if an eloquent voice were not sometim raised to call attention to the fact that it is at once as fr
85 and as serious a branch of literature as any other.

GO ON TO THE NEXT PAGE

. In the passage, the author compares the novel to:

A. painting.
B. history and painting.
C. music, poetry, painting, and architecture.
D. making believe.

. The author states that the worth of the novel is that it:

F. competes with life.
G. competes with painting to capture life.
H. gives an accurate historical perspective.
J. belongs to the fine arts.

. The attitude of apology, mentioned in line 30, most likely refers to:

A. the novelist's apparent lack of concern for historical truth.
B. the writings of Anthony Trollope.
C. the novelist's attempt to please the reader.
D. the admission in a novel that the described events are made-up.

. One can reasonably infer from the passage that the novelist takes his evidence from:

F. his imagination.
G. documents and records only.
H. history and the actions of men.
J. the reader's preference.

. According to the passage, Mr. Besant believes that:

A. literature should be recognized as a fine art.
B. there are many people who do not consider the novel an artistic form.
C. his ideas are new to many people.
D. many people mistrust art.

. The view of art described in lines 50–53 can best be described as:

F. admiring.
G. indifferent.
H. academic.
J. wary.

27. The main purpose of the next-to-last paragraph (lines 69–75) is to:

A. present a view of literature as mere amusement.
B. defend the artistic merit of literature.
C. illustrate the thinking of people who skip through novels.
D. describe different ways of reading novels.

28. The author's tone in lines 57–75 suggests that he:

F. disagrees with the views described in these paragraphs.
G. agrees with the views described in these paragraphs.
H. is indifferent to the views detailed in these paragraphs.
J. finds the views described in these paragraphs convincing without entirely agreeing with them.

29. In the passage the author makes all of the following analogies EXCEPT comparing:

A. happy endings of novels to dessert.
B. the literary artist to a meddlesome doctor.
C. art to mechanics.
D. the novelist to the painter.

30. Which of the following best states the main point of the passage?

F. The novel must finally be recognized by both novelists and readers as a form of artistic expression.
G. When crafting their novels, novelists should use painters and historians as their models.
H. A work of art is created in the same manner as a work of mechanics.
J. People who skip through novels do not regard fiction as artistic expression.

GO ON TO THE NEXT PAGE.

Passage IV

NATURAL SCIENCE: This passage is adapted from Stacey Dworkin's "Signing."

Some animal activities have become ritualized over the course of evolution so that they now serve a communicative function. Protective reflexes, for example, such as narrow-
5 ing the eyes and flattening the ears, prepare an animal in danger to protect sense organs. These movements also may indicate fear or anger to other animals. Intention move-ments such as these are incomplete behavior patterns that provide information about the activity a particular animal is about to perform. A bird will generally crouch, raise its
10 tail, and pull back its head before it takes flight. If a bird takes flight without first performing these movements, it acts as an alarm signal, and the whole flock will suddenly take flight.

Ritualized behaviors allow for the evolution of a signal
15 by increasing conspicuousness, stereotypy, and separation from its original function. An example of such increasing exaggeration can be found in bower birds. Males decorate their nest with blue objects. They will steal any blue object, including pieces of paper, plastic, and glass. This behavior
20 began as nest building and has evolved to attract females.

The process of ritualization first involves the receiver noticing the correlation between the signal and the actions of the sender. The sender then ritualizes his signal to receive the optimal ideal response from the receiver and the
25 receiver modifies his response to optimally benefit himself. As an example, a dog who is preparing to bite retracts his lips into the familiar growl snarl. This particular behavior began so that the dog does not bite his own lips as he bites. However at some point in evolutionary history, the receiver
30 noticed that the snarling dog presented a danger to him. The signaling dog now notices the receiver often backs down before the fight even begins, and continues retracting his lips as a way to ward off the receiver. However, this ritu-alization can have a "dog who cried wolf" result, where the
35 receiver will become so accustomed to the snarling without attack that he will no longer retreat.

Signals of conflict, such as that of predator to prey, involve a signaler who intends to manipulate the receiver. The receiver then interprets the signal as a warning sign
40 and evolves resistance. The result is a co-evolutionary arms race, which can lead to increasingly exaggerated signals.

According to Zahavi's handicap principle, in order to be honest, a signal must be costly to the signaler. Thus only the most fit individuals can afford to brandish an honest
45 signal. For females looking for a mate, such a declaration of fitness will identify a particular male as a quality choice.

For this reason, some signals, such as peacock's tail become extremely exaggerated: males are trying to declar their fitness, since only the toughest males can survive wi
50 such a costly, conspicuous tail. Another example is t black bib of dominant male Harris sparrows. Only dor nant males have this black bib. An experiment in whi males were given a black bib by means of a magic mark showed that that male was attacked by other sparrows. T
55 male with an artificial black bib could not survive t attack; only the fittest males could have the black bib dominance and not lose fights by challengers.

There is currently a great deal of debate about the val ity of the handicap principle, and there is some eviden
60 that the principle does not always hold true. However, general, costly signals such as peacock tails can serve other purpose than as honest indicators of fitness.

Cooperation, on the other hand, involves a mutual int est of the signaler and receiver. In terms of cooperation, t
65 signaler and receiver both want to be able to communica while remaining as little noticed as possible by potent predators. Such inconspicuous signaling offers a distin selective advantage. Evolution therefore results in "co spiratorial whispers," where both signaler and receiv
70 evolve to make the signal as inconspicuous as possi while still reaching its receiver without alerting un tended receivers.

. The main idea of the first paragraph (lines 1–13) is that:

A. signals develop as animals ritualize their behavior.
B. animals use their reflexive movements to communicate with other animals.
C. animals' reflexes and movements can often assume a communicative function.
D. animals respond physically to danger.

. The passage states that the first step of ritualization involves the:

F. sender's ritualization of his signal to receive an optimal response.
G. recognition by the receiver of a relationship between the sender's actions and the signal.
H. modification of the receiver's response for optimal benefit.
J. increased conspicuousness of the sender's activity.

. The author states that a "dog who cried wolf" situation results when:

A. a signal becomes so familiar that it fails to affect the receiver.
B. a signal is used to create an impression of strength and viciousness.
C. an animal assumes the appearance of a stronger animal.
D. an animal uses a signal indiscriminately.

. According to the passage, the male bower bird attracts a female mate by:

F. building a nest decorated with blue objects.
G. stealing blue objects.
H. demonstrating fitness.
J. raising its tail before flight.

. In the passage, the author uses all of the following animals as examples EXCEPT:

A. dogs.
B. cats.
C. peacocks.
D. sparrows.

36. The primary conclusion of the experiment described in lines 52–57 is that:

F. altering the physical appearance of male Harris sparrows could also alter their fitness.
G. male Harris sparrows given false black bibs were instantly attacked by sparrows with real black bibs.
H. male Harris sparrows with black bibs are constantly faced with challenges to their fitness.
J. the black bib on a male Harris sparrow is a sign of dominance and fitness.

37. The passage suggests that the main difference between signals of conflict and cooperation is that:

A. signals of conflict are less conspicuous than signals of cooperation.
B. only signals of conflict involve two-way communication.
C. signals of cooperation develop from mutual interest and benefit.
D. signals of cooperation attempt to manipulate receivers.

38. The main purpose of the passage is to:

F. argue that signals primarily function as indicators of fitness.
G. explain how signals of conflict operate.
H. show that animals use a complicated system of signals to attract mates.
J. describe how communication can occur through animal behavior and appearance.

39. The author would most likely agree that Zahavi's handicap principle:

A. is fundamentally unsound.
B. needs to be replaced by a new principle that takes into account derivations from Zahavi's principle.
C. is questionable but points to a general truth.
D. accurately explains which signals are honest.

40. According to the passage, all of the following are characteristics of honest signaling except:

F. it can attract the attention of unwanted receivers, such as predators.
G. it is constant over time and does not change.
H. it eventually leads to extremely exaggerated and impractical signals.
J. after a while, some signals fail to work.

END OF TEST 3
STOP! DO NOT TURN THE PAGE UNTIL TOLD TO DO SO.
DO NOT RETURN TO A PREVIOUS TEST.

SCIENCE REASONING TEST

35 Minutes—40 Questions

DIRECTIONS: This test contains seven passages, each accompanied by several questions. You should select the answer choice that best answers each question. Within the total allotted time for the subject test, you may spend as much time as you wish on each individual passage. Calculator use is not permitted.

Passage I

An atomic nucleus consists of protons and, typically, neutrons, which have roughly the same mass as protons. (An electron has so little mass as to be negligible in these calculations.) A proton is said to have a charge of +1, and an electron a charge of −1. When combined in an atom, the charges of electrons and protons cancel out (the charge of an atom with 26 protons and 28 electrons, for instance, would be −2). The *atomic number* of an element is determined by the number of protons in its nucleus. When an atom loses protons, its atomic number changes. Each element has a unique atomic number. While the atomic number of an element does not change, the number of neutrons in the nucleus can vary. Atoms of the same element but with different numbers of neutrons are referred to as different isotopes of the same element. Isotopes are identified by their *atomic weight*, which is the sum of their protons and neutrons: lead-214, for example, has an atomic weight of 214.

A radioactive element is one that is naturally unstable and decays by radiation. Among the types of radiation possible for radioactive elements are alpha, beta, and gamma radiation. In alpha radiation, a particle containing two protons and two neutrons leaves the decaying atom. Beta radiation consists of high-speed electrons. During beta decay a neutron in the atom splits into a proton, which stays in the nucleus, and an electron, which is emitted. Gamma rays are high-energy electromagnetic waves. An atom that decays by any of these three forms of radiation is called an *emitter* of that type of radiation. Different isotopes often have different radioactive properties. The *half-life* of a radioactive isotope determines its rate of decay—during one half-life period, approximately 50% of the atoms in a given sample of the isotope will decay according to the radioactive properties of that isotope. The half-life for a given isotope does not change.

Table 1 shows the atomic number, atomic weight, radioactive qualities, and half-life for several elements. (The atomic weight for a given isotope is the number following the name of the element.) Note that nearly all naturally radioactive elements emit gamma radiation, so this is not listed in the "Radiation" column.

Table 1			
Name	Atomic number	Radiation	Half-life
uranium-238	92	Alpha	4,470,000,000 years
uranium-234	92	Alpha	245,500 years
protactinum-234	91	Beta	6.7 hours
thorium-234	90	Beta	24.1 days
thorium-230	90	Alpha	75,400 years
radium-226	88	Alpha	1600 years
radon-222	86	Alpha	3.8 days
polonium-218	84	Alpha	3.1 minutes
bismuth-214	83	Beta	19.9 minutes
bismuth-210	83	Beta	5.0 days
lead-214	82	Beta	26.8 minutes
lead-206	82	None	—

Figure 1 shows a visual representation of the half-life curve.

Figure 1

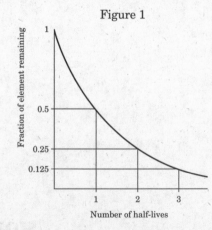

Number of half-lives

GO ON TO THE NEXT PAGE

According to the table, thorium is:

A. an alpha emitter.
B. a beta emitter.
C. not radioactive.
D. an alpha and beta emitter.

Which of the following graphs best represents the relationship between atomic number and length of half-life?

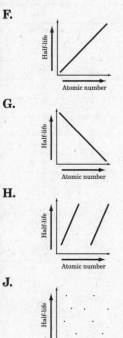

F.

G.

H.

J.

3. An atom begins as a uranium-234 isotope, and undergoes four stages of radioactive decay, as indicated in the table per element. After four stages of decay, what element does it become?

A. Thorium
B. Uranium
C. Polonium
D. Bismuth

4. Given a 10 gram sample of thorium-234, how many days will it take for 7.5 grams to decay?

F. 3.8 days
G. 48.2 days
H. 24.1 days
J. 5.0 days

5. If an isotope with a relatively short half-life is found in abundance somewhere in nature, which of the following would most likely be true?

A. A natural process exists by which the isotope is created.
B. The half-life for the portion of isotope found is longer than other known samples of that isotope.
C. The isotope is emitting unusually high levels of gamma radiation.
D. It is physically distant from other isotopes of the same atomic number.

Passage II

Baseball players use a bat to hit a thrown ball. Generally, hitters want to use a bat that will hit a ball as far as possible. Since the start of the sport, bat manufacturers have experimented with different shapes, designs, and types of wood in order to produce optimal bats. One important principle of bat design is the "sweet spot"—a location on the barrel of the bat that produces the greatest distance for a hit ball. (Batters often note that a ball hit on the sweet spot will produce almost no resistance at all, whereas a ball hit on another part of the bat can produce jarring, painful vibrations.) The sweet spot is roughly halfway between the endpoint of the barrel and the point where the barrel narrows to the handle (in Figure 1, the narrow handle is on the right and the barrel is on the left).

Figure 1

The force that a batter applies to a bat when he or she swings can be roughly modeled by the following equations:

$$F = ma$$

$$a = \frac{v}{t}$$

F is the total force applied to the bat by the hitter, m is the mass (equivalent in this case to weight) of the bat, a is the rotational acceleration of the bat, v is the velocity of the middle of the bat, and t is the time of the swing. Assuming a batter is swinging as hard as possible, the amount of force exerted is constant from swing to swing.

Table 1 shows tests done with a machine to test several b models at constant swing velocities. Note that maple is harder wood than ash.

Table 1			
Wood Type	Length (inches)	Weight (ounces)	Travel distance (fee
Ash	34	28	406
Ash	34	30	412
Ash	34	32	418
Ash	36	30	412
Ash	36	32	418
Maple	34	28	414
Maple	34	30	428
Maple	34	32	440
Maple	36	30	428
Maple	36	32	440

When a ball hits the sweet spot, it will travel:

F. a greater distance than if it hits any other part of the bat.
G. a shorter distance than if it hits any other part of the bat.
H. the same distance as if it hits any other part of the bat.
J. no distance at all.

Which of the following illustrates the relationship between velocity of the bat and the distance a hit ball will travel?

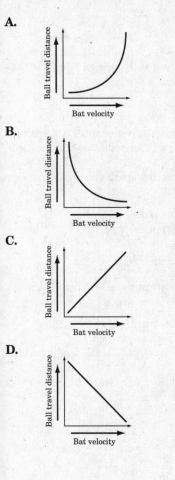

A.

B.

C.

D.

8. Which of the following statements is true, according to the data in the passage and Table 1?

F. The weight of a bat has more effect than the length of the bat on the distance a ball will travel.
G. A bat swung with greater speed than another will not make a ball travel farther, assuming all other factors are constant.
H. A 36-inch bat is generally better than a 34-inch bat.
J. A shorter maple bat is more effective than a longer maple bat.

9. Which of the following would most likely not make a ball travel farther?

A. Using a metal bat, which is harder than either wood
B. The batter adopting a "tighter" batting swing, meaning the arc of the bat through the swing will be smaller
C. Using a bat made from a heavier type of wood than either ash or maple
D. The batter lifting weights to increase arm strength and bat velocity

10. Based on the passage, which of the following historical baseball developments would be expected to result in baseballs being hit farther?

F. Batters using tar pine to get a better grip on the bat handle
G. Baseballs wound tighter (made harder)
H. New baseball parks made smaller than old ones
J. Batters using gloves to reduce the sting on the hands from a badly-hit ball

11. In the 1950s, professional baseball players began using bats that had thinner handles, although the barrel ends of the bats stayed about the same width. (In fact, the bat in Figure 1 is one of these "modern" bats.) What might the advantage be of such a bat?

A. The newer bat would have greater durability.
B. The newer bat could be swung faster.
C. The newer bat would have a larger sweet spot.
D. The newer bat would be longer.

GO ON TO THE NEXT PAGE.

Passage III

A forced vibration is a term used to describe a system consisting of a driving force and a receiving object, typically called a resonator. Generally, a resonator has one natural vibratory frequency called the resonant frequency. As the driving force approaches the resonant frequency, the maximum amplitude, or displacement, of the resonator increases. The following equation governs resonant frequencies of springs:

$$f_r = \sqrt{\frac{s}{2\pi m}}$$

f_r is the resonant frequency, s is the stiffness of the spring, and m is the mass of the spring. Each spring also has a characteristic impedance, which is defined as stiffness divided by mass.

Figure 1 shows the resonator amplitude resulting from a single driving force operating at different frequencies on a spring.

Figure 1

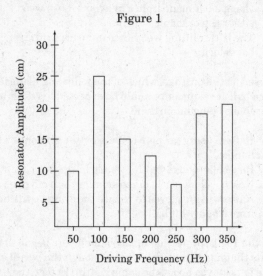

Table 1 lists resonance information for three separate springs, each with their own mass, M_1, M_2, and M_3.

Table 1			
Spring mass (g)	Spring stiffness (g/s²)	Driving force frequency (Hz)	Resonator amplitude (cm)
M_1	10	50	28
M_1	10	100	9
M_1	10	150	17
M_2	20	50	23
M_2	20	100	30
M_2	20	150	21
M_3	40	50	14
M_3	40	100	15
M_3	40	150	17

12. Judging from Figure 1, which of the following is the most likely resonant frequency of the spring?

F. 90 Hz
G. 160 Hz
H. 240 Hz
J. 330 Hz

13. If the stiffness of the spring increases while the mass remains constant, the resonant frequency will:

A. increase.
B. decrease.
C. remain constant.
D. turn unpredictable.

14. If the resonant frequency of both springs 1 and 2 in the table is 75 Hz, then spring 2:

F. is heavier than spring 1.
G. is lighter than spring 1.
H. has a higher characteristic impedance than spring 1.
J. has a lower characteristic impedance than spring 1.

15. If M_2 and M_3 are the same, it would appear that resonator amplitude:

A. decreases as mass increases.
B. increases as mass increases.
C. decreases as stiffness increases.
D. increases as stiffness increases.

16. If another spring had a stiffness of 100 g/s² and a mass equal to M_1, M_2, or M_3, then we would expect:

F. its mass to be greater than M_3.
G. its characteristic impedance to vary.
H. a driving force frequency of 150 Hz to produce a low resonator amplitude.
J. its resonator amplitude to vary very little with a change in driving force frequency.

Scientists and doctors have proposed many theories for why e human body begins to break down as it approaches old age. ree of the most common theories are oxidation reaction, sub-timal hormone levels, and cross-linkage.

xidation Reaction

Oxygen combustion occurs during many biological pro-sses, and often results in by-products called free oxygen radi-ls. This *singlet oxygen* molecule has only one electron, sulting in a strong electronegative charge that creates a high gree of instability. The molecule generally reacts quickly th any nearby molecules, resulting in the destruction or cor-ption of cellular parts, including DNA. Free radicals other an singlet oxygen molecules can also be ingested through od, inhaled through air pollutants, or caused by electromag-tic radiation such as x-rays. The cellular damage from free dicals is cumulative; over time, the build-up of damage comes too great for a cell to continue to function normally.

ub-optimal Hormone Levels

The human body relies on a variety of hormones for normal eration. As the body ages, production declines for various ands of hormones such as progesterone, melatonin, andros-nedione, testosterone, estrogen, and human growth hormone GH). HGH is linked with the general growth and upkeep of lls and organs. Melatonin regulates sleep (a decrease in elatonin levels is associated with difficulty in sleeping) and ay help prevent cancer. Testosterone, estrogen, and progest-one together regulate sex drive, bone structure, muscle owth, and mental sharpness. While a slowdown of thyroid rmone production does not always occur, it can cause heart sease. In addition, as the body ages, the production of several rmones, including insulin and cortisol, increases. As insulin vels increase, blood sugar levels respond proportionally. Cor-sol is believed to induce stress.

Cross-linkage

Collagen is a protein that plays a major role in the connec-tive tissues of the body. These tissues fill numerous roles, including cushioning and supporting the body. (Cartilage, bone, and tendons are all types of connective tissue.) Col-lagen can exist in several forms, some soluble, others insolu-ble. The cross-linkage theory states that during aging, protein mechanisms called cross-linkages convert soluble collagen into insoluble collagen. This, in turn, reduces cell elasticity and permeability. The theory holds that cross-link-age reduces passage of nutrients and waste across cell boundaries, and also decreases diffusion of necessary nutri-ents to cells far removed from blood capillaries. Cross-link-ing agents are prevalent in many types of foods, as well as in environmental factors such as UV rays in sunlight and high-energy electromagnetic radiation.

17. Which of the following do the cross-linkage and oxidation reaction theories agree does NOT cause aging?

    A. Certain protein mechanisms that produce insoluble collagen
    B. Molecular instability in cells
    C. Increased cell elasticity
    D. Detrimental chemical reactions in connective tissues

18. If DNA corruption causes cancer, as many scientists believe, which of the theories can help explain cancer as well as aging?

    F. Oxidation reaction
    G. Sub-optimal hormone levels
    H. Cross-linkage
    J. None of the theories can adequately explain the cause of cancer.

19. Elastin is a protein in the skin that can become less effective or even harmful due to excess solar radiation. A likely agent of elastin's decay is:

    A. Low levels of insulin
    B. Cross-linkage agents
    C. Connective tissues
    D. High stress levels

20. Scientists in a medical laboratory find that mice kept in an iron-covered environment age at slightly slower rate than mice that are not. Which of the following explanations, if true, would support both the oxidation reaction theory and the cross-linkage theory?

    F. Iron helps deflect electromagnetic radiation.
    G. Iron particles in the air enter the mice as anti-oxidants.
    H. Iron particles in the bloodstream tend to make proteins soluble.
    J. Iron particles aid in the production of HGH.

21. Which of the following is an argument in favor of oxidation reaction over sub-optimal hormone levels to explain the overall cause of aging?

    A. Free radicals can exert cellular damage on glands.
    B. Children with unusually low levels of HGH seem to age faster.
    C. As life expectancy in many countries has increased, so has pollution.
    D. Obesity often leads to premature cellular stress and damage.

22. A pharmaceutical company develops a drug that enhances the ability of cells to rebuild structures that have sustained long-term damage. According to which theory would this drug be the most effective at slowing the aging process?

    F. Oxidation reaction
    G. Sub-optimal hormone levels
    H. Cross-linkage
    J. None of the theories would predict this drug to help against aging.

23. Doctors at a certain hospital begin to notice that a number of older patients had tissues damaged by excess blood sugar content. According to the sub-optimal hormone levels theory, which of the following is the most likely explanation?

    A. The thyroid gland has become over-active.
    B. Insulin production has increased.
    C. Progesterone levels have dropped.
    D. Melatonin levels have risen to higher-than-normal levels.

Passage V

Thin-layer chromatography (TLC) is a technique used to determine the various components of compounds. The TLC process consists of the following steps:

A slide is coated with a silica gel adsorbent, leaving some empty space near the top for handling, and a groove is cut near the top of the slide with a sharp object.

The slide is then *spotted*—this involves dropping a small sample (usually between 1 and 5 ml) of the compound near the bottom of the slide.

The slide is heated and dried, and developed by placing the bottom of the slide in an eluent (solvent), letting the eluent be absorbed to the notch at the top of the slide. On its way, the eluent will force the parts of the compound upwards along the slide.

A nonpolar eluent will force nonpolar elements up the slide, whereas a polar eluent will force both polar and nonpolar elements up the slide. The distance traveled by each substance is unique, which means that in a successful TLC process the elements of a compound will end up at different points on the slide.

Table 1 shows the polarity of several substances (polarity is measured in debye, where 1 debye is 3.33×10^{-30} coulomb meters).

Table 1	
Compound	Polarity (debye)
HF	1.82
HCl	1.08
HBr	0.82
HI	0.44
Paraffin	0.0
P-dichlorobenzene	0.0
Ether	0.0

The TLC process was run on three different slides, each holding a different compound. The results are shown in Figures 1–4.

Figure 1

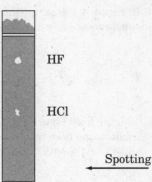

HF

HCl

Spotting →

Eluent Polarity: 3.4

Figure 2

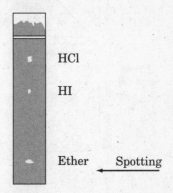

HCl

HI

Ether Spotting →

Eluent Polarity: 5.6

Figure 3

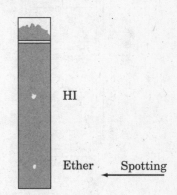

HI

Ether Spotting →

Eluent Polarity: 8.2

Figure 4

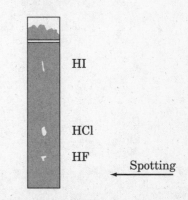

HI

HCl

HF

Spotting →

Eluent Polarity: 0.0

GO ON TO THE NEXT PAGE.

24. In Figure 4, the compound consists of how many different substances?

F. 1
G. 2
H. 3
J. 4

25. Judging from Figure 4, which graph best represents the relationship between distance traveled on slide and substance polarity (for a nonpolar eluent)?

A.

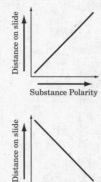

B.

C.

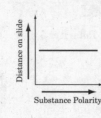

D.

26. A TLC process is successfully implemented, but the samp moves up the slide and does not separate. The sample is most likely:

F. polar.
G. nonpolar.
H. a single element.
J. a compound.

27. Based on the data in the passage, if the same compound was spotted in Figure 2 and Figure 3, why would HCl not appear on Figure 3?

A. It appears at the same spot as HI, and thus cannot be seen.
B. The high polarity of the eluent has pushed HCl off the top of the adsorbent.
C. The high polarity of the eluent caused the HCl to be sucked directly to the bottom of the slide.
D. The high polarity of the eluent caused the HCl to evaporate.

28. Two substances that are believed to be identical are teste on separate TLC plates using the same polar eluent. The results show that the two substances have traveled simila but slightly different distances to approximately the midd of the slide. The most likely explanation is:

F. The substances have very different polarities.
G. There was a small but significant amount of human error resulting in a difference at spotting.
H. The slides were not coated with absorbent.
J. Accidentally, the eluent used on one slide was polar while the other was nonpolar.

29. *Cospotting* is the term for spotting one slide with two samples of the unknown next to each other, and then spotting another agent on top of one of the first two spots. What might be a problem with cospotting?

A. If the spots are too close, they might blend together.
B. The eluent would absorb only one of the spots.
C. Too much silica gel would hinder both spots from separating.
D. The second substance added might be polar.

ssage VI

The liquid phase of any substance consists of molecules
ving with varying amounts of kinetic energy. Additionally,
ch substance has a distinct, invariant molecular force that
lls molecules of that liquid together. When a molecule's
netic energy exceeds the bonding forces in the liquid, it
capes from the liquid's surface and exists in gaseous form. If
t in a closed container, these molecules will exert pressure
the container. This pressure is called *vapor pressure*. Also,
te that any liquid will boil (turn completely to gas) when the
por pressure reaches 760 mm Hg.

ble 1 shows the vapor pressures of different liquids at differ-
t temperatures. Vapor pressure is measured in mm Hg.

		Table 1		
mperature	Water	Ethyl alcohol	Benzene	Carbon tetrachloride
−15°C	1.62	4.55	11.23	13.57
0°C	4.58	12.17	27.51	33.34
15°C	12.72	32.22	57.97	71.08
30°C	31.83	78.76	118.16	142.56
45°C	71.91	174.04	225.31	263.42
60°C	149.38	352.69	389.52	450.93
75°C	289.09	666.13	642.89	720.18

gure 1 shows vapor pressure versus temperature for the
me liquids.

Figure 1

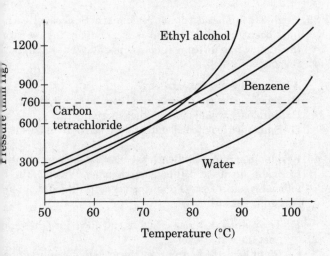

. Which liquid's vapor pressure increases least as its
temperature increases from 0 to 60°C?

F. Water
G. Ethyl alcohol
H. Benzene
J. Carbon tetrachloride

31. Which of the following best illustrates the relationship
between molecular bond strength and vapor pressure?

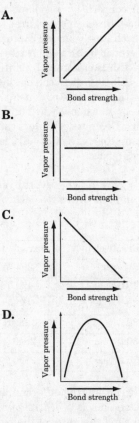

32. Compared to benzene, the molecular bonds in water are:

F. stronger.
G. weaker.
H. about the same.
J. impossible to compare.

33. Which liquid will boil at the lowest temperature?

A. Water
B. Benzene
C. Carbon tetrachloride
D. Ethyl alcohol

34. Which experiment would best help to determine whether
the force of attraction between molecules varies as a
substance changes phase?

F. Measuring the vapor pressure of a frozen mixture of the
four substances in the chart
G. Freezing ice to extremely low temperatures (below
−50°C) and measuring vapor pressure
H. Comparing the vapor pressures of ice, liquid benzene,
and gaseous ethyl alcohol
J. Comparing the vapor pressures of ice and water at its
melting point, and comparing the vapor pressures of
solid and liquid benzene at its melting point

GO ON TO THE NEXT PAGE.

Passage VII

Water erosion is an important concern for residents near coastlines. The residents of Suncoast Beach, a resort area supported by tourists who visit the beach each year, are concerned because the beach is slowly being eroded by an inlet. An inlet is a channel that separates islands. Inlets can grow by natural erosion of land, or by strong storms. Their growth can be slowed by unusual geological formations, the presence of dense plant growth beneath the water surface, or occasionally by buildings and other man-made developments. Dealing with inlets can be difficult, because simple-seeming solutions can often have long-term ecological and even geological impact.

Scientists monitored the inlet's growth over several years, taking note of the size of the inlet and rate of growth each year:

Table 1		
Year of measurement	Growth rate of inlet	Size of inlet
1987	90 ft/year	205 ft
1989	140 ft/year	420 ft
1991	210 ft/year	740 ft
1993	480 ft/year	1280 ft
1995	330 ft/year	2040 ft
1997	370 ft/year	2690 ft

Residents of Suncoast Beach are considering different plans to deal with the inlet's growth. One plan is *beach renourishment*—building up with imported sand the parts of the beach that are consumed by the growing inlet. Typical beach sand consists of ground-up rocks together with organic remnants of sea creatures such as mollusks. Here are the estimated costs for such a plan:

Table 2	
Length of beach to renourish	Estimated cost
100 feet	$900,000
400 feet	$2,250,000
800 feet	$3,900,000

The other plan is to dredge the inlet so that it migrates away from the beach entirely. This would cost an estimated $26 million, but would stop the inlet's destruction of Suncoast Beach entirely. An alternate plan, by far the cheapest, is to use an extremely large number of sandbags far below the water level of the inlet to stop its growth, but these would have to be replaced every 5 years due to decay of the bags.

35. According to the erosion rates measured by the scientists the overall rate of erosion of Suncoast Beach from 1987 to 1997:

A. stayed about the same.
B. slowed down.
C. sped up.
D. impossible to determine.

36. What might be a possible reason for the high rate of erosi in 1993?

F. A lot of tourists
G. A large hurricane
H. Many boats traveling close to the beach
J. New buildings being built along the beach

37. What is the most likely estimate for the erosion rate measured in 1985?

A. 410 ft/year
B. 60 ft/year
C. 330 ft/year
D. 150 ft/year

38. Assuming the erosion continues as the chart indicates fo 15 more years, which plan to save the beach would cost t least over that time?

F. Rebuild 100 feet of beach in spring and 100 ft in fall, every year
G. Rebuild 400 feet of beach every year
H. Rebuild 800 feet of beach every two years
J. Dredge the inlet

39. Unable to finance dredging, residents of Suncoast Beach have been largely opposed to using sandbags to take care the inlet, while favoring renourishment. What might be a reason?

A. Sandbags are too expensive.
B. Sandbags need to be replaced regularly.
C. Sandbags would damage the environment.
D. Sandbags look too visually unattractive to tourists.

40. Residents of Suncoast Beach are also considering plantin trees and shrubs at points along the inlet. Which of the following side effects of planting vegetation would not he stave off erosion?

F. The plants grow roots that extend down into the sand past the water level.
G. Plant life would encourage the growth of populations organisms like clams and mussels.
H. Plants would create shade along various portions of t beach, reducing the temperature of the sand.
J. In the fertile soil of Suncoast Beach, plants reproduce quickly.

END OF TEST

STOP! DO NOT RETURN TO ANY OTHER TES

Practice Test 1
Explanations

Answers to ACT Practice Test 1

Question Number	Answer	Right	Wrong	Question Number	Answer	Right	Wrong
	English Test				English Test		
1.	A			57.	D		
2.	J			58.	H		
3.	A			59.	B		
4.	H			60.	J		
5.	D			61.	C		
6.	H			62.	J		
7.	B			63.	B		
8.	J			64.	F		
9.	B			65.	D		
10.	H			66.	G		
11.	B			67.	C		
12.	J			68.	J		
13.	D			69.	B		
14.	G			70.	H		
15.	D			71.	A		
16.	J			72.	J		
17.	A			73.	B		
18.	H			74.	H		
19.	D			75.	A		
20.	H				Math Test		
21.	A						
22.	G			1.	D		
23.	D			2.	H		
24.	H			3.	E		
25.	B			4.	J		
26.	J			5.	B		
27.	C			6.	G		
28.	J			7.	D		
29.	C			8.	K		
30.	G			9.	D		
31.	C			10.	K		
32.	H			11.	B		
33.	D			12.	K		
34.	G			13.	C		
35.	C			14.	F		
36.	G			15.	D		
37.	C			16.	H		
38.	G			17.	D		
39.	A			18.	H		
40.	H			19.	B		
41.	B			20.	H		
42.	J			21.	D		
43.	C			22.	F		
44.	H			23.	C		
45.	D			24.	J		
46.	F			25.	B		
47.	D			26.	G		
48.	G			27.	D		
49.	C			28.	F		
50.	G			29.	A		
51.	D			30.	G		
52.	J			31.	D		
53.	C			32.	H		
54.	G			33.	C		
55.	D			34.	K		
56.	F						

Question Number	Answer	Right	Wrong	Question Number	Answer	Right	Wrong—
Math Test				**Reading Test**			
35.	D			28.	F		
36.	F			29.	C		
37.	B			30.	F		
38.	F			31.	C		
39.	B			32.	G		
40.	H			33.	A		
41.	A			34.	F		
42.	H			35.	B		
43.	D			36.	J		
44.	G			37.	C		
45.	C			38.	J		
46.	F			39.	C		
47.	D			40.	G		
48.	J						
49.	D			**Science Reasoning Test**			
50.	J			1.	D		
51.	D			2.	J		
52.	G			3.	C		
53.	E			4.	G		
54.	G			5.	A		
55.	A			6.	F		
56.	K			7.	C		
57.	C			8.	F		
58.	J			9.	B		
59.	B			10.	G		
60.	F			11.	B		
Reading Test				12.	F		
				13.	A		
1.	B			14.	F		
2.	F			15.	C		
3.	C			16.	J		
4.	J			17.	C		
5.	B			18.	F		
6.	J			19.	B		
7.	A			20.	F		
8.	F			21.	A		
9.	D			22.	F		
10.	H			23.	B		
11.	D			24.	H		
12.	H			25.	B		
13.	B			26.	H		
14.	J			27.	B		
15.	D			28.	G		
16.	H			29.	A		
17.	A			30.	F		
18.	G			31.	C		
19.	C			32.	F		
20.	F			33.	C		
21.	B			34.	J		
22.	F			35.	C		
23.	D			36.	G		
24.	H			37.	B		
25.	A			38.	J		
26.	J			39.	C		
27.	C			40.	H		

Calculating Your ACT Score

Calculating your score on the ACT practice tests in this book is a three-step process.

1. Calculate your raw score for each section.

2. Use the conversion table (on the following page) to find your scaled score for each subject test.

3. Average your subject test scaled scores to find your composite score.

Calculating Subject Test Raw Scores

Your raw score on a subject test is equal to the number of questions you answered correctly on that test. The subject test answer keys on the preceding pages will help you to figure out your raw scores.

_____ _____ _____ _____

English Raw Score   Reading Raw Score   Math Raw Score   Science Reasoning Raw Score

Calculating Subject Test Scaled Scores

The conversion table on the following page allows you to look up your raw score for each subject test and see the corresponding scaled score.

_____ _____ _____ _____

English Scaled Score   Reading Scaled Score   Math Scaled Score   Science Reasoning Scaled Score

Calculating the Composite Score

Your composite ACT score, the one that really matters, is the average of your scaled scores on the four subject tests. Add up your scaled scores and divide that sum by four.

_____

Composite Score

ACT Raw–Scaled Score Conversion Chart

Scaled Score	English Raw Score	Math Raw Score	Reading Raw Score	Science Reasoning Raw Score
36	75	60	40	40
35	74	59	39	39
34	73	58	38	38
33	72	57	37	37
32	71	55–56	36	–
31	69–70	53–54	35	36
30	67–68	51–52	34	35
29	65–66	50	33	34
28	63–64	48–49	32	33
27	61–62	45–47	31	32
26	59–60	43–44	29–30	31
25	56–58	41–42	28	29–30
24	53–55	39–40	27	27–28
23	51–52	37–38	26	26
22	49–50	35–36	25	25
21	46–48	33–34	24	24
20	44–45	31–32	22–23	22–23
19	42–43	29–30	20–21	21
18	39–41	26–28	19	19–20
17	37–38	23–25	18	17–18
16	34–36	20–22	17	16
15	32–33	17–19	16	15
14	29–31	14–16	15	14
13	27–28	12–13	14	13
12	24–26	9–11	13	12
11	22–23	8	12	10–11
10	19–21	7	10–11	8–9
9	16–18	6	8–9	7
8	14–15	5	7	6
7	11–13	4	6	5
6	8–10	–	5	4
5	6–7	3	4	3
4	4–5	2	–	2
3	3	–	3	–
2	2	1	2	1
1	1	–	1	–
0	0	0	0	0

English Test

Passage I

1. **A**   No error

2. **J**   *Comma Splices*
Adding a semicolon is a common solution when you have a run-on sentence. You can have two independent clauses side by side if you have a semicolon separating them. **G** does not solve the run-on problem. **H** uses the word *which* between clauses, and *which* is logically flawed in this context.

3. **A**   No error

4. **H**   *Connecting and Transitional Words*
Though makes the sentence logical. **G** makes logical sense, but is grammatically incorrect.

5. **D**   *Sentence Reorganization*
Moving *practically* after *were* makes the meaning of the sentence correct: smokers were almost pariahs.

6. **H**   *Transitions and Topic Sentences*
The correct answer refers back to the previous paragraph with the phrase *matters didn't improve*, and introduces the next paragraph with the phrase *when we left the airport*. **F** is illogical. The writer is trying to contrast Madrid to what she's used to, not suggest that the States and Madrid are similar. **G** is exclusively about the previous paragraph. **J** is too forward-looking; it would fit more naturally in the sixth paragraph.

7. **B**   *Verb Tenses*
This sentence should use the past tense, as does the rest of the paragraph.

8. **J**   *Subject-Verb Agreement*
No one is singular, and must be matched with a singular pronoun like *her*. *Its* doesn't work because we're talking about people, not objects. *That* doesn't work because we're not talking about one specific dog.

9. **B**   *Identifying Tone*

The writer is exaggerating when she says she thinks a cop is going to *leap out*. She is also amused. The language of **A** is too extreme; the writer does not find the situation uproarious, just mildly amusing. **C** and **D** go in the wrong direction. The author is not scared or disapproving; she is a curious tourist observing cultural differences.

10. **H**   *Additional Detail and Evidence*

The box is surrounded by two sentences that give examples of Madrileños' behavior, so the additional sentence should provide another example of Madrileños' behavior.

11. **B**   *Vague Words*

The correct answer replaces *they* with the more specific phrase *these customs*.

12. **J**   *Sentence Fragments*

The correct answer uses the verb *seemed* to make the sentence complete.

13. **D**   *Connecting and Transitional Words*

In a list of items, the final item should be preceded by a comma and a connecting word, not just a comma.

14. **G**   *Paragraph Reorganization*

The correct answer makes the sentences follow chronological order: first the writer didn't like it, then she did, and finally, it seemed better than America.

15. **D**   *Redundancy*

Because the sentence includes the phrase *transferred back to the U.S.*, the underlined phrase is redundant.

Passage II

16. **J**   *Redundancy*

The correct answer connotes the same meaning as the underlined phrase, and in half the space.

17. **A**   No error

The sentence already in the passage is the best choice.

18. **H**   *Periods, Question Marks, and Exclamation Points*

Even though it mentions a question, this sentence should end in a period, not a question mark, because the sentence itself is declarative: *he wondered*.

19. D *Transitions and Topic Sentences*

Adding *in fact* smoothes the transition from the first to the second sentence.

20. H *Misplaced Modifiers*

You can't say Adams was *more* responsible, because the sentence doesn't say he was more responsible than someone else. Therefore, grammatically speaking, he must be the *most* responsible.

21. A No error

22. G *Word Choice*

When you have a non-essential clause, as you do here, use *which*, not *that*.

23. D *Subject-Verb Agreement*

The best answer fixes the subject-verb disagreement and eliminates the passive voice.

24. H *Subject-Verb Agreement*

The subject is *letters*, which is plural, so the plural verb is correct. **G**'s *have* is non-idiomatic usage, and **J**'s *were* is past tense, which is incorrect, because the letters are a testament currently.

25. B *Possessives*

The writer is talking about a sacrifice made by the couple, so the phrase should be *their sacrifice*.

26. J *Idioms*

English idiom dictates that we *object to* things, not *object* them, *object for* them, or *object at* them.

27. C *Run-on Sentences*

The correct answer fixes the run-on by inserting a semicolon between the two independent clauses. **B** is a run-on. **D** solves the problem by adding a connecting word, but that connecting word is illogical.

28. J *Redundancy*

The only *but* we need is the second one, which comes after the comma. The writer is trying to contrast the second idea to the first, so the first *but* is inappropriate.

29. C *Big Picture Purpose*

Only answer **C** refers to the essay as a whole. **A** and **B** are too specific.

30. G *Additional Detail and Evidence*

Both this sentence and the third paragraph are about Adams's contributions to politics.

Passage III

31. C *Misplaced Modifiers*

The original sentence makes it sound as if the believers and theorists are in the shape of alien life forms. By moving the underlined phrase, it becomes clear that we're talking about people who believe in alien life forms.

32. H *Word Choice*

There is what's needed, since we're talking about a physical location.

33. D *Connecting and Transitional Words*

Typically, a sentence that starts *not only* goes like this: *Not only ___, but ___* . The use of *and*, *since*, or *yet* to begin that second clause is idiomatically incorrect.

34. G *Commas*

The comma provided by **G** is needed for clarity.

35. C *Commas*

Again, you need an additional comma for the sake of clarity. Also, in this context, the word *which* should be preceded by a comma.

36. G *Sentence Fragments*

The sentence given by **G**, unlike the original sentence, has a subject: the Air Force base. **H** and **J** are both sentence fragments.

37. C *Run-on Sentences*

The correct answer fixes the problem by placing a semicolon between the two halves of the sentence.

38. G *Subject-Verb Agreement*

We're talking about plural "*Cammo Dudes*," so the verb must be plural. Therefore, the plural *are* is correct. *Was* is singular and the wrong tense, and *were* is the wrong tense.

39. A No error

40. H *Commas*

The added comma increases clarity. **G** and **J** use overly strong marks of punctuation. We don't need a full stop here, just a pause.

41. B *Paragraph Reorganization*

The third sentence in this paragraph is unnecessary. The rest of the sentence is about tourists seeing alien phenomena, and the Cammo Dudes aren't aliens, they're humans.

42. J *Redundancy*

Because the word *limitless* is already there, *immeasurable* is redundant.

43. C *Adverbs and Adjectives*

Real secretive is okay in speech, but not in writing. The adverb *really* is required to describe the adjective *secretive*.

44. H *Connecting and Transitional Words*

The last sentence discusses two secretive things. Since the two things are similar, they should be joined by *and*, not *but*, which implies a contrast.

45. D *Analysis*

The writer takes an amused, removed tone and discusses the tourists who believe in aliens with a little bit of humor. This implies that he does not believe in aliens. **B** is too strongly worded. The writer is not scornful.

Passage IV

46. F *Transitions and Topic Sentences*

There is nothing wrong with the existing topic sentence.

47. D *Paragraph Reorganization*

The second paragraph is entirely about the reasons college students are seeking therapy. The last sentence of the first paragraph is also a reason why college students seek therapy, so it belongs in the second paragraph. Changing the *and* to *for one thing* alerts the reader that a list of reasons will follow.

48. G *Subject-Verb Agreement*

The subject is *crop*, which is singular, so the verb should be *does*, which is also singular.

49. C *Redundancy*

Shameful means the same thing as the underlined phrase and is much more concise.

50. G *Idioms*

The correct expression is *on the rise*.

51. **D**   *Periods, Question Marks, and Exclamation Points*
The sentence is asking a question, so it should end in a question mark.

52. **J**   *Misplaced Modifiers*
The original sentence makes it sound like students are a danger. **J** solves the problem by making it clear that depression is the danger.

53. **C**   *Commas*
The sentence contains a list, and only **C** separates the items in the list with two commas.

54. **G**   *Run-on Sentences*
Simply adding the conjunction *and* fixes the problem.

55. **D**   *Verb Tenses*
Since the rest of the paragraph is in the present tense, this sentence should be too.

56. **F**   *Connecting and Transitional Words*
Furthermore alerts the reader that elaboration or more examples will follow, which is the case. The other answer choices suggest that a contradiction or contrast follows, which is not the case.

57. **D**   *Commas*
Both commas should be omitted.

58. **H**   *Subject-Verb Agreement*
Colleges and universities is a compound plural subject, so the plural verb form *have* is correct.

59. **B**   *Connecting and Transitional Words*
This sentence is talking about a cause and effect—the overloaded staff causes the wait. **B** is the only answer choice that makes this causal relationship clear.

60. **J**   *Additional Detail and Evidence*
Only the fifth paragraph discusses staff shortages.

Passage V

61. **C**   *Commas*
Commas are needed to separate the seasons' names, since the names are in a list.

62. **J**   *Connecting and Transitional Words*

In the original sentence, the word *and* does not express the right relationship between the fact that the writer was unhappy and the fact that he loved to surf. The writer was unhappy *because* he loved to surf and could not do it.

63. **B**   *Adverbs and Adjectives*

It's common, in speech, to say *I wanted it so bad*, but in formal writing, the phrase should be *I wanted it so badly*. The adverb *badly* is needed, because the writer is describing the verb *to want*.

64. **F**   No error

65. **D**   *Paragraph Reorganization*

The sentence order suggested by **D** puts the writer's actions in chronological order: he moves, he finds it's not what he expected, he misses the seasons, he longs for the changing leaves.

66. **G**   *Connecting and Transitional Words*

The word added by **G** makes it clear that the surfing and writing took place when the writer was at the beach.

67. **C**   *Parallelism*

Because the first two items in the list begin with gerunds (*picking* and *going*), the third item must also begin with a gerund (*enjoying*).

68. **J**   *Redundancy*

The word *traditions* means exactly the same thing as the wordy phrase *all of the things that go with Christmas*, so the underlined phrase should be omitted.

69. **B**   *Misplaced Modifiers*

The writer is saying that the official beginning of spring was anticlimactic, so the correct phrase is *the technical beginning of spring*.

70. **H**   *Additional Detail and Evidence*

H spells out the writer's implication that by moving to California, he learned the meaning of the saying "the grass is always greener."

71. **A**   No error

72. **J**   *Pronoun Cases*

Since an object is needed, *myself*, not the pronoun *me*, is correct here.

73. B   *Verb Tenses*

This essay takes place in the past, so the past tense verb *found* is correct.

74. H   *Commas, Word Choice*

The quick rule about choosing between *which* and *that*, which are often used incorrectly in place of one another, is that if you have a comma, that comma should be followed by *which*. If there is no comma, use *that*. In this sentence, no comma is required, so *that* is correct.

75. A   *Identifying Tone*

The original phrasing breaks with the tone of the rest of the essay, which is casual.

Math Test

1. D   *Pre-Algebra: Percents*

This question tests your basic understanding of percentages. There are 8 gray monkeys, they make up 25% of the population, and the whole population (by definition) contains 100% of the monkeys. The question, therefore, is asking for ratios: $\frac{8}{x} = \frac{25}{100}$, where x is the total number of monkeys. This means that the answer is 8×4, so **D** is the answer.

2. H   *Plane Geometry: Lines and Angles*

To answer this question, you just need to know the basic definition of midpoint—it's the point halfway along a line segment. Therefore, line segments $\overline{AC}$ and $\overline{CB}$ are each half the length of $\overline{AB}$. Since $\overline{AB}$ is 10 yards, $\overline{CB}$ is 5 yards and **H** is the answer.

3. E   *Pre-Algebra: Series*

There's no set way to find out what this series might be. The best bet is to look at it for a little while, then start with the first number and see if there's one operation you can do over and over again that keeps giving you the right numbers in the series, and then do it one more time to get the answer. For this series, you can see that the sign of the number shifts, which may mean that each number is being multiplied by a negative number (if you keep multiplying something by a negative number, the sign of the result will keep switching back and forth). This seems to be right, since each number is increasing in absolute value. In fact, it turns out that in this series, each number is the previous number multiplied by –2. Doing this to 16 gives you –32 (the fifth number in the series), and doing it once more gives you 64, which is answer **E**.

4. J *Pre-Algebra: Ratios*

To solve this question, all you need to do is cross-multiply the terms and solve for x. Cross-multiplication gives you $4x = 60$, and solving for x reveals that it equals 15. Therefore, **J** is the right answer.

5. B *Plane Geometry: Lines and Angles*

To answer this question, you only need to know one thing: a straight line is equivalent to a 180° angle, and therefore any angles that combine to make a straight line must add up to 180°. Knowing this, you can find out that $\angle EBD = 180° - 80° - 65° = 35°$. Therefore, **B** is correct.

6. G *Pre-Algebra: Numbers*

The main point to this question is figuring out the speed of each train. Train Y is pretty easy—80 miles in 2 hours means 40 miles per hour (you divide the total distance by the time). Train X is not so easy, so you need to convert the numbers to something you can handle more easily. If train X travels 75 miles in 1½ hours, then it would naturally travel twice as far in twice the time: 150 miles in 3 hours. You can divide these numbers to find out that train X is traveling at 50 miles per hour (if you have a calculator, you could simply divide 75 by 1.5 to get the same answer). The question asks for the difference in speed, so the answer is **G**.

7. D *Algebra: Substitution*

Since the question lets you know the value of x, you can just plug that value into the second equation. Doing this gives you $9 - 3(-3 - 1)$, which simplifies to $9 + 12$. This means that **D** is the right answer.

8. K *Pre-Algebra: Absolute Value*

This question tests the most basic understanding of absolute value. To answer the question correctly you just need to know that $|-2| = 2$, and then carry out the indicated operations: $|4| \times |-2| = 4 \times 2 = 8$, so the answer is **K**.

9. D *Pre-Algebra: Percents*

This question asks you to make just one calculation: what is 70% of $32.50? (If the jeans are 30% off, then they cost 70% of the original price.) With a calculator, it's easy to work out $.70 \times \$32.50 = \$22.75$, which makes **D** the answer.

10. **K**   *Pre-Algebra: Exponents*

This question is testing your ability to distribute an exponent across the different variables and constants it affects. Since the exponent 2 is outside the main parentheses, it applies to each of the terms inside the parentheses. First, it operates on the constant -3, which evaluates to 9 (-3×-3). It then applies to the variable term x^4. Here, you need to remember that when an exponent is raised to another exponent, they are multiplied. These two steps result in the correct answer, **K**.

11. **B**   *Algebra: Linear Equations*

This question asks you to isolate x on one side of the equal sign. Probably the easiest way to do this is first to add x to both sides of the equation, which gives you $59 = 118 + x$. Subtracting 118 from each side gives you $-59 = x$, so **B** is the right answer.

12. **K**   *Algebra: Expressions*

This question is short, but maybe a little tricky. Formulating the answer involves two steps: calculating Wallace's current age, and then calculating David's age. If Wallace was x years old 15 years ago, then he's $x + 15$ years old now. And if David is 7 years older than Wallace, he must be $x + 15 + 7$, or $x + 22$, years old. Therefore, **K** is the right answer.

13. **C**   *Coordinate Geometry: Coordinate Plane*

The best way to answer this question is probably just to draw a rough set of axes and quickly plot all four points. This allows you to see that the missing point should be in the upper left-hand quadrant. It turns out that only one of the answer choices fits this description, so **C** is the answer. If you want to find the point more explicitly, you can try to find the "match" for each coordinate that doesn't have a pair. For instance, there are two points with the x-coordinate 1, but only one with the x-coordinate -2. This means the other coordinate must have a -2 x-coordinate. The same reasoning will reveal that the y-coordinate for the missing point is 4.

14. **F**   *Algebra: Simplification*

When factoring, you need to look at the different terms and find numbers, along with variables, that are common to the different terms and can be divided out. Looking at the numerical coefficients, we can see that 3 is a factor of both numbers. Moreover, each term has an x variable raised to at least a power of one, and a y variable raised to the power of one. Taking out these three things gives you $3xy(x - 2y)$, so **F** is the right answer.

15. **D**   *Plane Geometry: Polygons*

This question might seem a little imposing, but if you know how to go about answering it, it isn't hard. If the perimeter of a square is 4 meters, that means each side must be 1 meter (since the square has four sides and they are all equal). The area of a square is simply the square of a side, so the area of this square is 1 square meter. If the area of the square doubles, it would be 2 square meters, and the length of a side would be the square root of that, $\sqrt{2}$ meters. The perimeter is equal to four times the length of a side, so the new perimeter is $4\sqrt{2}$ and **D** is the right answer.

16. **H**   *Coordinate Geometry: Slope*

If two lines are parallel, their slopes are by definition equal. The standard equation for a line is $y = mx + b$, where m is the slope. For the given line, $m = \frac{1}{2}$, so a new line must also have a slope of $\frac{1}{2}$. This means **H** is the right answer.

17. **D**   *Intermediate Algebra: Quadratics*

This question is an example of the straight-ahead factoring you will probably see on the ACT exam. To factor the equation, look at the factors of the last term (−8). Ignoring the negative sign, they are 1, 2, 4, and 8. How can you combine any pair of these factors by addition or subtraction to get −2 (the middle term's coefficient)? 2 and 4 are the best candidates (they multiply to form 8, and 4 less 2 is 2). This means you have the two binomials of the factored equation, except for the correct signs: $(x\ ?\ 2)(x\ ?\ 4)$. One of the signs has to be negative, and the other positive (to get −8). Since the middle term is negative, this means the larger factor gets the negative sign (if you add a positive and negative number when the negative number has a greater absolute value, the result will be a negative number). Now you have the solution: $(x + 2)(x - 4)$. This means **D** is the right answer.

18. **H**   *Plane Geometry: Triangles*

For a right triangle, the hypotenuse equals the square root of the sum of the squares of the other two sides, or, put into equation form, $A = \sqrt{B^2 + C^2}$, where A is the hypotenuse and B and C are the smaller sides. Plugging in the information known, you get $10 = \sqrt{B^2 + 6^2}$. Simplifying and squaring both sides results in $100 = B^2 + 36$, and solving for B gives you $B = \sqrt{64} = 8$. This means **H** is the answer.

19. **B**   *Pre-Algebra: Percents*

This question is not hard, but has several parts—you must calculate the price for the dress and the shoes separately. The price of the dress has dropped 20%, which means it costs 80% of its original price, or $236. The shoes, however, cost only 30% of their original price, which is $45 ($150 × 0.3). In total, this is $281, so **B** is the right answer.

20. **H**   *Algebra: Simplification*

This question asks you to add two polynomials, so the first thing to do is to find which terms in each polynomial have the same variables raised to identical exponents. Here, there are two of them: $-3xy$ and $4xy$, which, when added, result in xy. Putting the terms together yields $xy^2 + xy - 3x^2y$, so **H** is the answer.

21. **D**   *Intermediate Algebra: Systems of Equations*

Finding the solution for one variable and then plugging that value into the other equation is probably the simplest way to solve this problem. The second equation seems a little simpler to work with, so solving for y gives you $y = 5 - x$. This can be plugged into the first equation to give you $3x - (5 - x) = 7$, which in turn simplifies to $4x - 5 = 7$. A few steps of addition and division give you $x = 3$, so **D** is the right answer.

22. **F**   *Pre-Algebra: Ratios*

This question is perhaps deceptively simple; all you need to do is divide 255 by 36. This is because you want to find out how many times a yard (36 inches) goes into the total length. Doing this calculation (a calculator is helpful) reveals that the plank is roughly 7.1 yards long, so **F** is the right answer.

23. **C**   *Plane Geometry: Polygons*

To sum up all the sides of the figure, you need to calculate the length of the top side and the longer vertical side on the right. Since the figure has all right angles, the total length on the top and right sides have to match the total on the bottom and the left, respectively. Since the left-hand side is 12 cm tall, the right side has to be a total of 12 cm; since the bottom left part is 3 cm, the taller part has to be 9 cm. On the top, the top portion plus 6 cm must equal 14 cm, so it's 8 cm long ($8 + 6 = 14$). Adding up all the sides, in a clockwise direction, gives you $12 + 8 + 9 + 6 + 3 + 14 = 52$, so **C** is the correct answer.

24. **J**   *Algebra: Substitution*

This question might seem imposing because of its length, but it's not bad. If you take the numbers scattered in the different parts of the question and plug them into the equation, you get $1.5(15)(50 - 12)$. Multiplying these numbers out gives you 855, so **J** is the right answer.

25. **B**   *Plane Geometry: Polygons*

A good way to find the shaded area is simply to calculate the area of the four triangles in the corners of the outside square. Since H is the midpoint of $\overline{AD}$, $\overline{AH} = (3\sqrt{2})/2$, and $\overline{AE}$ is the same length. Since the area of a triangle is one-half base times height, the area of $\triangle AEH$ is $\frac{1}{2}(3\sqrt{2}/2)^2$, which is $\frac{1}{2}(9 \times 2)/4$, and simplifies to $\frac{9}{4}$. Since there are four of these triangles, the shaded area is four times this amount, or 9. Therefore, **B** is the right answer.

26. **G**   *Coordinate Geometry: Number Lines and Inequalities*

The graph shows that x ranges from greater than –3 to less than 1. Putting this into an inequality gives you $-3 < x < 1$. Unfortunately, this isn't one of the answers. This means you'll have to simplify each of the answer choices to see which one is equivalent to the correct answer. For **F**, simplification gives you first $-14 < 2x < -6$, and then $-7 < x < -3$, which is incorrect. Simplifying **G** results in $-6 < 2x < 2$, and then $-3 < x < 1$, so it is the right choice.

27. **D**   *Intermediate Algebra: Logarithms*

The first step in almost any logarithm question is to convert the logarithm into a more typical equation. $\log_x 81 = 2$ is equivalent to $x^2 = 81$. You can take the square root of each side to get the answer: $x = 9$ (answer **D**).

28. **F**   *Plane Geometry: Triangles*

This question is unusual in that answering depends more on your intuitive understanding of triangles than numerical calculations. Essentially, you need to look at all the answer choices and find the one that couldn't possibly be the length of the third side. What would make a length impossible? Well, it would have to be a length that was either longer than the other two sides combined or shorter than one existing side minus the other one (in both of these cases, there would be no way to connect the two smaller sides to the longest one, so the triangle wouldn't be "closed," and therefore would not be a real triangle). It turns out that answer **F** is the right one, since it's too short (2 plus $3\frac{2}{3}$ is less than 6, and there would be no way to construct a real triangle using these side lengths). All the other answers are possible values, so they're incorrect.

29. **A**   *Pre-Algebra: Multiples*

To answer this question, you need to know the definition of prime factor: any factor of the number (that is, a number that evenly divides into the original number) that is prime (can only be divided by itself and 1). The prime factors of 24 are: 2 and 3 (because $2^3 \times 3 = 24$). The prime factors of 36 are: 2 and 3 ($2^2 \times 3^2 = 36$). Therefore, the least prime factor shared by 24 and 36 is 2, and **A** is the answer.

30. **G**   *Plane Geometry: Triangles*

This question might be frustrating, because (in a sense) you either know it or you don't. 3, 4, and 5 form one of the "Pythagorean triples," meaning that a triangle with these lengths is a right triangle. (If you don't know this, and you see a question very much like this one, it's pretty safe to assume that the triangle is a right triangle, since finding the area of a triangle without a right angle can be extremely tricky.) The formula for the area of a triangle is $A = \frac{1}{2}bh$, where b is the base length and h is the height. The two shorter sides of the triangle form the base and the height (it doesn't matter which is which), so you can plug in the values provided to get the answer: $A = \frac{1}{2}(3)(4) = \frac{1}{2}(12) = 6$. Therefore, **G** is the answer.

31. **D**   *Pre-Algebra: Ratios*

This problem might be confusing since it's not clear how to use the information in the question to form an equation. You know, however, that there are 12 green marbles, and the ration of red to blue to green is 6 : 5 : 4. This means that each number in the ratio should be multiplied to 3 to find the number of marbles of that color. (You can also break the question down a bit: if you know that the ratio of blue to green is 5 : 4 and there are 12 green, you can solve an equation like $\frac{5}{4} = \frac{x}{12}$, where x is the number of blue marbles. The same approach works to find the number of red marbles.) Using either technique, you can calculate that there are 18 red marbles, 15 blue marbles, and 12 green marbles. Adding these up gives you 45, so **D** is the right answer.

32. **H**   *Intermediate Algebra: Triangles*

As stated in the question, the hypotenuse of ΔDEF is twice as big as $2\sqrt{2}$. $2 \times 2\sqrt{2}$ is $4\sqrt{2}$. Since it's a right triangle, you can use the Pythagorean theorem to find the lengths of its legs, and since it's isosceles, those lengths will be identical.

$$
\begin{aligned}
(4\sqrt{2})^2 &= x^2 + x^2 \\
16 \times 2 &= 2x^2 \\
32 &= 2x^2 \\
16 &= x^2 \\
4 &= x
\end{aligned}
$$

You can plug the value of the legs of *DEF* right into the area equation for triangles.

$$A = \frac{1}{2}bh$$
$$A = \frac{1}{2}(4)(4)$$
$$A = 8$$

H is the right answer.

33. **C** *Algebra: Binomials*

This question just tests your basic ability to expand a binomial. The only trick is to keep track of which terms you've multiplied together, which is why it's useful to always use the same order, like FOIL. Following this order gives you $x^2 + 5x - 3x - 15$, which simplifies to $x^2 + 2x - 15$. This means that **C** is the right answer.

34. **K** *Trigonometry: SOHCAHTOA*

Remember SOHCAHTOA. In this case, it will let you determine all the side lengths of the triangle, which will allow you to get the answer. If the sine of $\angle A$ is ⁴⁄₅, then the opposite leg is of length 4 and the hypotenuse is of length 5. Since the tangent is ⁴⁄₃, the adjacent leg must be 3 (we already know that the opposite leg is 4). Now, you've got all three sides of the triangle, so you can figure out what the cosine of $\angle A$ is: the adjacent leg over the hypotenuse. This is ³⁄₅, so **K** is the right answer.

35. **D** *Coordinate Geometry: Number Lines and Inequalities*

The first step to solve this problem is to figure out how many intervals there are marked between 2.17 and 2.18. Counting, you can see that there are ten, which means that each mark indicates an increase of 0.001. Since point *A* is about halfway between the second and third marks (counting marks after the first one) suggests that the value is around 2.1725 (translating between this number and the graph, the "2" represents the second mark, and the "5" indicates halfway to the third mark). This matches choice **D**, so it is the answer.

36. **F** *Pre-Algebra: Mean*

Here you are tested on your knowledge of the mean and your ability to translate a word problem into a solvable equation. We know that the team won an average of 87 games the first four seasons, an unknown number the fifth season, and an average of 83 wins over all five years. This means that the number of wins over all five years, averaged, is 83. We can write this as $(87 \times 4 + x)/5 = 83$, where x is the number of wins in the fifth season. Multiplying both sides of the equation by 5 and multiplying 87 by 4 gives you $348 + x = 415$. This lets you find the answer, **F**.

37. B *Plane Geometry: Triangles*

There's no good way to "figure out" this question; you simply need to know that when you bisect a side of an equilateral triangle, you bisect the opposite angle. (This is also true when a line segment bisects the base of an isosceles triangle.) Also, you need to know what the measurement of each angle of an equilateral triangle is, although you can figure this out (since each angle is the same, you can formulate the equation $x + x + x = 180°$, and solving for x gives you $x = 60°$). Since bisecting an angle gives you two angles half the size of the original, $\angle ACD$ measures 30°, answer **B**.

38. F *Intermediate Algebra: Functions*

Questions on functions like this one aren't really any different from typical substitutions. Here, you should just replace all the x variables with -2 and calculate the answer. By substitution:

$$\frac{(-2^3 + 4(-2))}{2(-2)^2} = \frac{-16}{8} = -2$$

Therefore, **F** is the right answer.

39. B *Plane Geometry: Lines and Angles*

There are lots of different ways to solve this problem, so the following is only one of several approaches. Since the angle indicated between lines d and b is 125°, the corresponding angle between lines c and b must also be 125°. Since any angles that add up to a straight line must add up to 180°, this means that $180° = \angle JKH + 125°$, and $\angle JKH = 55°$. The angles inside a triangle must also add up to 180°, so $180° = 90° + 55° + \angle x$, and $x = 35°$. This means **B** is the answer.

40. H *Coordinate Geometry: Slope*

The definition of slope, loosely worded, is how much a line changes in the y-coordinate as it changes along the x-coordinate. Therefore, you can think of slope as "change in y divided by change in x." With the two points in the question, you can calculate this: $(y_2 - y_1)/(x_2 - x_1) = (0 - \frac{1}{2})/(0 - (-2)) = (-\frac{1}{2})/2 = -\frac{1}{4}$. Therefore, **H** is the right answer.

41. A *Coordinate Geometry: Number Lines and Inequalities*

The first part of this problem is to translate the words in the question into an inequality. "x multiplied by three and increased by 2" can be written as $3x + 2$, and the rest of the information can be formulated as $-1 < 3x + 2 < 11$. If you solve for x, you get first $-3 < 3x < 9$, and then $-1 < x < 3$. Looking for a graph where valid values are greater than -1 but less than 3, you can see that choice **A** matches, so it's the correct choice.

42. **H**   *Intermediate Algebra: Systems of Equations*

If the two equations form one line, it means that they are the same equation (one can be reduced to the other by some series of arithmetic operations). Looking at the first two terms of each equation, it becomes apparent that the first equation is identical to the second, except that each term is multiplied by 3. In order for this to be true of the last term (and thus making the two equations equivalent), $2a$ must be equal to 6 multiplied by 3. Putting this into an equation gives you $2a = 6 \times 3$. Solving for a, you get $a = 9$, so the answer is **H**.

43. **D**   *Trigonometry: SOHCAHTOA*

You may well recognize the triangle in the diagram as a 3-4-5 right triangle, but in case you don't, you can use the Pythagorean Theorem ($\overline{BA} = \sqrt{(\overline{BC})^2 + (\overline{CA})^2}$) to figure out the length of the side opposite $\angle B$. $5 = \sqrt{3^2 + (\overline{CA})^2}$, which after squaring both sides and simplifying gives you $(\overline{CA})^2 = 25 - 9$. Solving for $\overline{CA}$ reveals that it does indeed equal 4. SOHCAHTOA reminds us that the tangent of an angle is equal to the opposite side over the adjacent side, so the answer is $4/3$ (choice **D**).

44. **G**   *Intermediate Algebra: Systems of Equations*

To solve this question, you need to find the value of m that makes the two equations equivalent (if they are equivalent, then the system really only has one equation and two variables, which leads to an infinite number of solutions). If you look at the first term in each equation, the first equation's term is a multiple of 4 of the second equation's. This is true also of the last term in each equation ($8 = 2 \times 4$). This means that m has to be one-fourth of -6. $-6 \div 4 = {}^{-3}/_2$, so **G** is the right answer.

45. **C**   *Plane Geometry: Triangles*

Answering this question correctly hinges on you knowing that triangles $\triangle DEB$ and $\triangle ABC$ are similar. This is because line segments $\overline{DE}$ and $\overline{AC}$ are parallel, resulting in all the corresponding angles in both triangles being equal (for instance, $\angle BDE$ is equal to angle $\angle BAC$). To find the area of $\triangle ABC$, you need to know the length of line segment $\overline{AC}$, since the area for a triangle is A = ½bh, where b is the base ($\overline{AC}$) and h is the height ($\overline{BA}$ = 10). Since all the corresponding sides in the two triangles have the same ratio of sizes, you can set up a ratio to find the length of $\overline{AC}$: $6/10 = 9/\text{AC}$. Cross-multiplication gives you $6\overline{AC} = 90$, which reduces to $\overline{AC} = 15$. Now you know enough to calculate the area of $\triangle ABC$:

$$A = \frac{1}{2}(15)(10)$$
$$= \frac{1}{2}(150)$$
$$= 75$$

Therefore, **C** is correct.

46. **F**   *Coordinate Geometry: Slope*

The most straightforward way to answer this question is to figure out two points and get the slope from there. If the x-coordinates are always twice as large as the y-coordinates, two valid points are $(2,1)$ and $(4,2)$. The slope is just the change in the y-dimension divided by the change in the x-dimension, so the slope is equal to $(y_2 - y_1)/(x_2 - x_1) = (2 - 1)/(4 - 2) = ½$. Thus, the correct answer is **F**.

47. **D**   *Trigonometry: Solving Right Triangles*

If you know SOHCAHTOA, you can figure out that since you want to deal with the side opposite the 63° angle and the hypotenuse of the ship/lighthouse triangle, you want to use the sine function. The sine of 63° is equal to the distance between the lighthouses (12 mi) divided by the distance from the ship to Lighthouse 2 (the hypotneuse). Put into equation form, this looks like $\sin 63° = {}^{12}/_d$, where d is the distance. Solving for d involves multiplying both side by d and then dividing both sides by $\sin 63°$, and the result is $d = 12/(\sin 63°)$. Therefore, choice **D** is correct.

48. **J**   *Pre-Algebra: Multiples*

This question is actually very tricky, and to solve it quickly you must work backward. (There are ways of solving this without going backwards from the possible answers, but they are actually rather complicated and well beyond the scope of the ACT exam.) First, you need to translate the information in the question to mathematical statements that can help you solve the problem. Let x be the number of police officers. The question states that if they are lined up in rows of 3, the last row will be 2 officers short. The key to solving this question lies in realizing that this is equivalent to saying that a division of x by 3 gives a remainder of 1. That is, if x is divided by 3, the number that results from that operation is irrelevant (it's the number of rows of officers). The remainder is 1 (the extra police officer; the row is short 2 people so it must only contain 1 person). This logic applies to the two other statements, which means that x divided by 4 leaves a remainder of 2, and x divided by 5 leaves a remainder of 3. Now, you need to check which of the answers presented matches these criteria. (It may be helpful to review the tips to check for divisibility of numbers given in the math review chapter.) 8 divided by 3 leaves 2, so it's out. 10 divided by 5 leaves 0, so it's out. 28 divided by 4 leaves 0, so it's out. 58 matches all the criteria, so **J** is correct. 118 fits the criteria, but it's larger than 58, and therefore incorrect.

49. **D**   *Intermediate Algebra: Functions*

This question might look complicated, but it's just a series of fairly simple steps. Whenever you're asked to calculate the function of another function, you should always calculate the innermost one first. $g(-2)$ is $((-2-4)^2)/9$, which is $^{36}/_9$, which simplifies to 4. The second part of the question is to calculate $f(4)$, since $g(-2) = 4$. $f(4) = 4^2 - 2(4)$, which multiplied out is $16 - 8$, which simplifies to 8. This means **D** is the right answer.

50. **J**   *Plane Geometry: Three Dimensions*

This question is pretty straightforward, but you have to be careful to figure out surface area rather than volume, which is the easier calculation. It might help to draw a diagram of the box in order to keep track of the sides. There are six in total, and each side is the same size as the opposite side (the top is the same size as the bottom, for instance). If you calculate each of the three unique sides, total them, and then multiply that number by two (to account for the fact that each unique side has an opposite side) you'll get the answer. The size of the top is the length times the width, $4 \times 5 = 20$, the size of the front is the width times the height, $5 \times 6 = 30$, and the size of one of the sides is the length times the height, $4 \times 6 = 24$. 20 plus 30 plus 24 is 74, and if you multiply this by 2 you get 148. Therefore, **J** is the right answer.

51. **D**   *Plane Geometry: Circles*

For this question you need to remember the formula for area of a circle, $A = \pi r^2$, and the formula for circumference, $C = 2\pi r$. Since you know the circumference, you can use the second equation to solve for the radius: $4\pi = 2\pi r$, which can be molded into $r = 2$. Using this value in the first equation, you get $A = \pi(2)^2$, which simplifies to $A = 4\pi$. Therefore **D** is the answer.

52. **G**   *Coordinate Geometry: Graphing Equations*

The graph crosses the x-axis at any point where the y-coordinate is zero. Plugging in the answer choices to the expression $x^3 - 27$, you see that only $3^3 - 27 = 0$. Therefore **G** is the answer.

53. **E**   *Intermediate Algebra: Quadratics*

This question is tricky, because the wording assumes that you're comfortable factoring quadratic equations. In essence, if a quadratic equation has only one possible solution, that means that its two factors are identical. The factors of 9 are 1, 3, and 9, but only 3 multiplies by itself to form 9 (since 3 is the square root of 9). Since the last term of the equation is positive, and the middle term is negative (for the moment, we won't worry about the first answer choice, which would make the middle term positive), it means that each factor is negative. Now you can actually factor the equation, despite not knowing the coefficient of the middle term: $(x - 3)(x - 3) = 0$. This fits what the question has told us: there is only one solution (3), and the last term (if you multiply the factored form out) is 9. If you now multiply out these two terms you'll get the original equation, and you'll find out what y equals: $x^2 - 6x + 9 = 0$. This means that $a = 6$, and **E** is the right answer. It might seem like we somehow got more information out of the equation than was originally there – how could we learn what a is if we have one equation with two variables? The key is that the question provides you with one piece of information that allows the deduction of the value of a: The equation has only one possible solution. This tells you how to factor the equation and then work backwards to find out the middle coefficient. This question is hard because it might not be obvious to first factor and then multiply out again.

54. **G**   *Intermediate Algebra: Relationships*

This question asks you to look at a variable in two relationships. The correct answer is one where, if y increases, the square of x (x^2) increases and the square root of z ($\sqrt{z}$) decreases. **F** is incorrect, because if y increases, $\sqrt{z}$ decreases (in all cases, if you look at the relationship between two variables, you should keep any other variables in the equation constant). **G** is correct, because when y increases, so does x^2, and if y increases $\sqrt{z}$ must decrease. **H** is incorrect, because y does not vary directly with x^2 (it varies with $\sqrt{x}$). **J** is incorrect, because x varies with y^2, instead of the other way around. **K** is incorrect, because y does not vary with x^2.

55. **A**   *Algebra: Linear Equations*

This question is potentially time consuming, since it involves checking (potentially) several answers. Therefore, you need to quickly pick a mini-strategy: do you want to compare the expression in the question as-is, or modify it a bit? It might be easier to multiply through by b to get $abc = 1$, which is simpler to deal with (but you don't have to). Looking at the answers, you can simplify **A** by multiplying through by c, giving you $abc = 1$. Success! If you want to make sure, you can check the other answers too. **B** is incorrect, since dividing by c gives you ${}^{ab}\!/_{c} = 1$. **C** is incorrect, because dividing by b gives you ${}^{ac}\!/_{b} = 1$. **D** is wrong, since there's nothing you can multiply 0 with to get anything other than 0. **E** is incorrect, because dividing through by c gives you ${}^{a}\!/_{bc} = 1$.

56. **K**   *Algebra: Binomials*

This question is tricky, in part because it tests both your ability to multiply binomials and your knowledge of squares. The question assumes you know that the area of a square is equal to the square of the lengths of one of the square's sides. Given this knowledge, you know that the larger square has an area of $(x + 2)^2$, while the smaller square has an area of x^2. To find the area of the first square you need to multiply the binomial $x + 2$ by itself, using FOIL:

$$(x + 2)(x + 2) = x^2 + 4x + 4$$

This is the expression for the area of the large square, which is *not* what the question asks for. But this expression *does* appear among the answer choices **F** in an attempt to trick you into thinking you've done all the work when in fact you haven't. The question asks you to calculate the area of the large square minus the area of the smaller square. So you need to subtract x^2 from the expression we just calculated:

$$x^2 + 4x + 4 - x^2 = 4x + 4$$

Now that's the expression we're looking for. But it isn't among the answer choices! Here's the final trick of the question: the correct answer is another form of $4x + 4$: $4(x + 1)$.

57. **C**   *Trigonometry: Trigonometric Graphs*

The position along the x-axis where the graph reaches its maximum is not affected by the coefficient in front of the sine function—that number merely controls how high the maximum reaches (in this case, values of y will be twice as high as that of an ordinary sine graph). An ordinary sine graph reaches its first maximum at $\pi/2$, so that's the answer here (choice **C**). If you have a graphing calculator, you can find this out easily enough, but it's good to memorize the maximums and minimums of the three basic trig graphs (sine, cosine, and tangent).

58. **J**   *Coordinate Geometry: Distance and Midpoints*

Remember that the midpoint of a line segment is just the average of the x- and y-coordinates. This means that you can work backwards to get the other endpoint. For the x-coordinate, for instance, you know that 3 is the average of –1 and the other endpoint's x-coordinate. To put that into equation form, $3 = \frac{-1 + a}{2}$ (where a is the unknown x-coordinate). Simplification gives you $6 = -1 + a$, and solving for a results in $a = 7$. Following the same procedure for the y-coordinate, you get $-4 = \frac{-2 + b}{2}$. Solving for b, gives you $b = -6$. The coordinates, therefore, are (7, –6), and **J** is the right answer.

59. B   *Pre-Algebra: Probability*

This question tests you on basic probability. First, you need to determine what the odds are of getting 2 or 3 on a single roll. Since there are six possible outcomes, 2 and 3 represent two of those outcomes—that is, there is a one third chance to roll a 2 or 3 any one time. The odds of getting one of these two numbers on two separate rolls is $\frac{1}{3} \times \frac{1}{3} = \frac{1}{9}$. (You multiply them together because you want the odds of an event happening twice—you want the odds for rolling a 2 or 3 the first time and the second time.) Therefore, **B** is the answer.

60. F   *Algebra: Inequalities*

This question is a little confusing because the variable given (x) is not the same as the angle whose possible range is given. You also need to know that an obtuse angle measures between 90° and 180°. So, putting the information in the question into an inequality gives you $90 < 225 - x < 180$. This is not one of the answers, however, so you need to modify it a bit. To isolate x, you can subtract 225 from all three terms: $-135 < -x < -45$. However, when you multiply each term in an extended inequality by a negative number, not only do the signs change, but the order of the terms gets reversed. This gives you $45 < x < 135$. (To see how, you can break down the original inequality to $90 < 225 - x$ and $225 - x < 180$.) This means that **F** is the right answer.

Reading Test

Passage I

1. B   *Specific Details and Facts*

According to the passage, Helen's husband Ridley, not Mr. Pepper, studies Pindar.

2. F   *Character*

The best answer to this question is **F** because Helen has a relatively difficult time figuring out Willoughby's character in this passage. According to the passage, she has long wondered what attracted her friend to this man, and she considers his physical appearance as well as his behavior regarding his wife's death. You can arrive at this answer through elimination: **G** is incorrect because Helen thinks the opposite; **H** is incorrect—emotional should not be confused with the sentimental take on Willoughby; and **J** is incorrect because it is never implied in the passage—although Helen suspects that Willoughby is a bully.

3.   **C**   *Character*

For a question that asks for the best answer, you should always read through all the answer choices because there may be more than one true answer—but there is only one correct answer. Mr. Pepper hardly seems uncritical in the passage; he reveals himself to be the exact opposite, in fact, so you can cross off answer **A**. You can perhaps describe him as hard working, given his diligence in studying ancient civilizations. But the next answer seems to work much better: Mr. Pepper seems inflexible—in his opinions about women and his ideal woman, even in his daily routine. By ruling out **D** for lack of evidence to support it, you arrive at **C**.

4.   **J**   *Comparisons and Analogies*

This is really a specific-information question masquerading as comparison. Helen compares the men in all respects but appearance; although she does comment on Willoughby's looks, she draws no comparison to Ridley.

5.   **B**   *Specific Information*

This is another specific-information question in disguise—this time as cause-effect. Answer **A** can be eliminated because only Mr. Pepper lacked sufficient bedclothes. Sirens blew during the night, but they were not described as a source of discomfort, so answer **C** is wrong. There is no evidence for answer **D** so that too is wrong.

6.   **J**   *Drawing Inferences*

Ridley's relationship to the other characters is never explicitly stated within the passage, but this is a fairly easy inference question. Since Helen attempts to compare her husband to her friend's husband, Willoughby, and since the comparison she makes is between Ridley and Willoughby, it follows that Ridley is Helen's husband.

7.   **A**   *Drawing Inferences*

You can eliminate answer **B** because there is no suggestion that he finds all women beautiful. Answer **C** is wrong because Mr. Pepper thinks in the passage that people (not specifically women) talk nonsense at breakfast. Answer **D** is also wrong; it seems, in fact, that Mr. Pepper has a difficult time finding women who read Greek or Persian. Thus answer **A** can be arrived at through elimination.

8.   **F**   *Comparisons and Analogies*

Consider the analogy before looking at the answer choices. Rachel is like the reflection on still water of a vivid face. The stillness of the water suggests that the mirror image is clear and exact, but does that mean Rachel is exactly like her mother? The analogy points to a difference in form rather than superficial appearance. The vivid face has life and flesh. The reflection on the pond has no real form; it can be broken with a light touch. Of the given answer choices, answer **F** best provides this interpretation of the analogy. Answer **G** makes the mistake of saying the women are exactly alike; answer **H** is nowhere suggested by the analogy; and answer **J**, although providing one part of the answer, misses out on the aspect of their physical resemblance. So answer **F** is correct.

9. **D**   *Drawing Inferences*

In the lines referred to, Rachel mentally addresses Mr. Pepper with a fairly snide remark, making fun of his chewing habits, while outwardly being polite and inquiring about his leg. Answer **A** is wrong because Rachel is not actually interested in his chewing. There is no evidence to support answer **B** or answer **C**. So the correct answer is answer **D**.

10. **H**   *Point of View*

The narrator passes through the perspectives of several characters in this passage—this technique is called free indirect discourse, but you don't need to know that. In this passage, we see the viewpoints of Helen, Mr. Pepper, and, briefly at the end, Rachel. So the correct answer to this question is answer **H**.

Passage II

11. **D**   *Main Idea*

The passage is basically a chronology of events beginning with a march held the day before President Wilson's inauguration and ending on the day when women's suffrage was first debated in Congress. Because the passage never deals with the actual granting of suffrage, you can eliminate answer **B** as incorrect. Although the author doesn't seem overly fond of Wilson, her main purpose is not to "expose" him in any way, so answer **A** can also be eliminated. Similarly, although the author doesn't seem to condone the treatment of suffragists, in this passage she doesn't seek to prove any arguments about the unjustness of their treatment, so choice **C** can be eliminated. The correct answer to this question is answer **D** because the passage primarily shows how persistent demonstrations ultimately brought the suffrage movement to Congress.

12. **H**   *Point of View*

The author clearly supports the suffragists' cause, so you can quickly eliminate answer **G**. You can also eliminate answer **F** because there is little implication that the author is a historian. It is clear from the passage that the author lived during the events she described and, in fact, participated in them. She uses "we" several times. Both answers **H** and **J** place the author in the events described, but you must figure out the extent of her involvement. She never suggests that she led the deputation that met with the President. The point of view of that paragraph is of one who had the events described to her, so the correct answer to this question is answer **H**: the author participated in the events, but she did not participate in the deputation.

13. **B**   *Drawing Inferences*

The author states that although the police force was exonerated of guilt in the man-handling of the suffragists, the police chief quietly left office after the investigation. His retirement suggests his culpability in this case—whether it was directly his fault or not.

14. **J**   *Comparisons and Analogies*

Answers **F** and **H** are incorrect; there is no suggestion of teaching or schoolchildren in the passage—the classroom is used only as a means of comparison. Answer **G** seems possible, although the arrangement of the furniture is not exactly a show of force. The better answer to this question is answer **J** because it demonstrates the point of the furniture arrangement: to demean the suffragists.

15. **D**   *Specific Details and Facts*

If you read the section on the first deputation, you can rule out answer **A** because Wilson is definitely not portrayed as sympathetic or concerned in the passage. Make sure not to mistake the tone of the section. When the author describes how Wilson promised to consider the issue, she puts "consider" in quotation marks to indicate that it's a false word: he never intended to consider the issue, but he wanted to get the women off his back. When he asks the question "Get the consent of women?" he is not showing naïve bewilderment; he's indicating how preposterous the suggestion seems to him. The best way to describe Wilson's response is with answer **D** because Wilson seems neither interested in nor respectful of the suffragists.

16. **H**   *Drawing Inferences*

In the first sentence of that paragraph, the author states that the administration played into the women's hands "without intending it." That phrase should instantly alert you to answer **H** as a probable answer to this question because it uses the word "unintentionally." You can also use the phrase "without intending it" to eliminate answers **F** and **G**. Both of those represent actions intentionally made by the government in fairness to the suffragists. Answer **J** is never implied in the passage.

17. **A**   *Cause-Effect*

This is a pretty simple cause-effect question. The answer to it can be found at the end of the sixth paragraph, where the author writes that women were man-handled by the crowd because of police indifference.

18. **G** *Cause-Effect*

This is another simple cause-effect question, and it requires that you do some careful reading in order to get the correct answer. While all of the answer choices give events that occurred after periods of protesting, only the May demonstrations, according to the passage, resulted in the writing of a favorable report by the Senate Committee on Suffrage.

19. **C** *Point of View*

In general, the author's views seem to be in line with the views she attributes to the suffrage leaders in the passage. The author describes how Alice Paul tells a surprised Wilson that the government has no right to legislate for any reform without women's consent to the reforms. It is safe to assume that the author feels the same way as Paul, whom she portrays favorably in the passage.

20. **F** *Identifying Tone*

The author places the word "unreasonable" in quotation marks to indicate that it is a quotation, an adjective that people other than herself would use to describe these women. Since she does incorporate it into her writing without comment (other than the quotation marks), its use can best be described as sarcastic. Essentially, she writes "unreasonable" while meaning something else; in fact, she most likely considers these women to be anything but unreasonable. The best answer to this question is answer **F** because it comes the closest to capturing the author's intention of saying one thing while meaning another. While answer **J** offers "insincere" to describe her, that answer suggests a different motive in writing "unreasonable": deceit. The use of "unreasonable" in the passage is supposed to draw even greater attention to the author's belief that the women were quite reasonable; there is no deceit intended.

Passage III

21. **B** *Comparisons and Analogies*

You can immediately eliminate answer **D** if you remember that the author complains in the third paragraph about the comparison of the novel to making believe. Answer **C** is wrong because the author does not make that comparison; rather, Mr. Besant makes it. In choosing between the remaining answers, remember to pick the best possible answer to the question. While the author certainly does compare the novel to painting throughout the passage, he also compares it to history.

22. **F** *Specific Details and Facts*

The answer to this question is in the first sentence of the passage. There the author states that "the only reason for the existence of a novel is that it does compete with life."

23. **D** *Drawing Inferences*

The attitude of apology refers to the desire to make fiction "humble" by making clear the fictional aspect of the novel—to the extent that the novelist diminishes the authority of his writing.

24. **H** *Drawing Inferences*

The author states that the task of fiction is to represent and illustrate the past, so it is a fair inference that the novelist mines history in researching the novel. Answer **H** is correct because it gives a more general answer than answer **G**—historical evidence can be found in sources other than documents and records.

25. **A** *Specific Details and Facts*

This question asks for specific information. While all of the answer choices are mentioned in the fourth paragraph of the passage, the correct answer, **A**, is given in the first sentence of that paragraph. The rest of the answer choices are all suggested by the author of the passage, not by Mr. Besant, later in the paragraph.

26. **J** *Specific Details and Facts*

You can answer this question by reading the sentences immediately preceding the lines referred to. There the author states that the notion of an artistic novel would fill certain people with mistrust.

27. **C** *Main Idea*

The next-to-last paragraph attempts to articulate the arguments and thoughts of "people who read novels as an exercise in skipping." Answer **A** is incorrect because the author himself does not propose this view, although he does present the thinking behind it. While the author ultimately wants to defend the art of the novel, that defense is not the focus of this paragraph, so answer **B** is wrong. Answer **D** may sound possible, but it is a vague and unspecific answer. The author discusses a specific approach to reading the novel in this paragraph—the approach that says novels are mere amusement or instruction, insubstantial enough to justify skipping.

28. **F** *Identifying Tone*

The author does not agree with people who skip through novels. The use of quotation marks to accent certain words heightens the tone of contempt for those kinds of readers. You can also answer this question just by knowing that the views described in this paragraph are opposed to the arguments the author makes throughout the passage.

29. C   *Comparisons and Analogies*

Close reading of the passage will help you answer this question. Answer **D** is obviously wrong because the analogy of novelist to painter is dealt with thoroughly in the passage. The remaining answer choices can be found in the last part of the passage. A close reading of the last paragraph will show that answer **C** is the right answer to this question because it is not an analogy made in the passage—although both art and mechanics are mentioned in the same sentence.

30. F   *Main Idea*

Answers **G** and **H** are not points made in the passage, although they incorporate words and phrases used in the passage. Answer **J** is a point made in the passage, but it is primarily made in the second-to-last paragraph. Thus answer **F** is correct; it sums up the author's argument throughout the passage.

Passage IV

31. C   *Main Idea*

The paragraph deals with the way that physical movements can communicate messages to other animals—whether these messages are intended or not. Although ritualization is mentioned in the first sentence of this paragraph, the paragraph itself does not focus on the link between ritualized behavior and intended signals, so answer **A** is not the correct answer to this question. Similarly, answer **B** is incorrect since it suggests that the paragraph deals with intended signals or intended forms of communication. While the paragraph does give examples of how some animals (birds) will respond to moments of danger, that response is not the main focus of the paragraph—it is only an illustrative example—so answer **D** is also wrong. The correct answer is answer **C** because it points to the communicative function of physical movement.

32. G   *Specific Details and Facts*

You can find the answer to this question at the beginning of the third paragraph. There the author states that the "process of ritualization first involves the receiver noticing the correlation between the signal and the actions of the sender."

33. A   *Cause-Effect*

The story goes that a boy cried wolf so many times that when a wolf finally appeared no one believed his calls. You don't need to know this tale in order to answer the question, but it can help you eliminate answers **B** and **C** without referring back to the passage. The comparison between the dog and the boy gets a little confusing when you're choosing between answers **A** and **D**. In the story, the boy cries wolf rather indiscriminately—when there was no real danger. But in the passage, the "dog who cried wolf" situation arises because the dog uses his snarl to warn off attackers so often that attackers learn to ignore the signal.

34. **F** *Specific Details and Facts*

The bower bird is discussed in the second paragraph, where the author describes how the male birds will steal blue objects to decorate their nests and how this decoration attracts females. The correct answer to this question is answer **F** because it is the decoration of the nest, not the stealing of blue objects, that ultimately attracts mates.

35. **B** *Specific Details and Facts*

The author uses dogs as an example in the third paragraph, and she uses peacocks and sparrows in the sixth paragraph. She never mentions cats.

36. **J** *Specific Details and Facts*

It is possible to arrive at several conclusions from the black bib experiment, but only one is relevant to the point the author makes in the paragraph. Which of the answer choices seems the most relevant to the author's argument? To start, you can eliminate answer **F** because, according to the experiment, it is incorrect. Answer **G** does not represent a conclusion the author is trying to draw from the experiment; she never touches the idea that sparrows with false bibs are targeted by those with real bibs. Answer **H** is wrong because the experiment (as the author describes it) doesn't deal with the frequency of challenges made against black-bib sparrows. The correct answer to this question is answer **J** because the author uses the experiment to show that exaggerated signals are usually adopted by only the fittest of a species.

37. **C** *Drawing Inferences*

In the fourth and fifth paragraphs, the author describes how signals of conflict involve the sender's manipulation of unsuspecting receivers, while in the last paragraph she discusses how signals of cooperation involve the mutual cooperation of senders and receivers.

38. **J** *Main Idea*

Answer **F** is incorrect because the author begins to discuss the relationship between signals and fitness only toward the end of the passage, and answer **G** is incorrect because signals of conflict are described only in the fourth paragraph. Answer **H** provides a pretty limited answer to this question; the passage often discusses how animals attract mates, but these discussions are usually evidence used to support the main idea of the passage: that animal behavior and appearance serve a communicative purpose.

39. C *Point of View*

In the second-to-last paragraph, the author mentions debate over the handicap principle but says that the principle seems to support general observations about honest signals. Given that, you can rule out answers **A** and **B**. You should also rule out answer **D** because the author never implies that the principle is accurate, but she does imply that the principle points to a general truth about animal signals.

40. G *Drawing Inferences*

All of the answer choices given are characteristics of honest signaling except answer choice **G**. Paragraph 5 explains the evolution of extremely exaggerated signals, and the author devotes considerable space explaining why some signals fail to work. The last paragraph of the passage explains how cooperation can limit the attraction and attention of unwanted receivers, which is a danger and thus characteristic of signaling.

Science Reasoning Test

Passage I

1. D *Read the Chart*

Thorium-234 is a beta emitter, and thorium-230 is an alpha emitter. This means that the element thorium can be either an alpha or a beta emitter, depending on the isotope. **A** and **B** are incorrect, because they are incomplete. **C** is incorrect, since both isotopes are radioactive. **D** is correct, since it states that thorium can be both an alpha and a beta emitter.

2. J *Handle Graphs*

The graph shows no clear correlation between atomic number and length of half-life. That is, when atomic number increases, the effect on half-life is unpredictable. **F** is incorrect, since is shows half-life increasing along with atomic number. **G** is incorrect because it shows half-life decreasing as atomic number increases. **H** is incorrect because it shows half-life increasing, then returning to a low value and increasing again when atomic number increases. **J** is correct, because it shows that increasing atomic number has an unpredictable effect on the length of half-life.

3. C *Use the Chart*

For this question, you need to follow the chart and remember the definitions of the different types of radiation. Uranium-234 undergoes alpha decay, which means it loses two protons and two neutrons. (Its atomic number goes from 92 to 90 and its weight goes from 234 to 230.) It thus becomes thorium-230. This element, in turn, undergoes alpha radiation to become radium-226. This isotope decays into radon-222, which in the fourth step becomes polonium-218. Therefore, polonium is correct and **C** is the right answer. **A**, **B**, and **D** are incorrect since the atom does not turn into any of these elements after four steps of decay.

4. **G**   *Use the Chart*

To answer this question, it helps to look at Figure 1. We want to find out how long it takes ¾ of the sample to decay, which means that ¼ will remain. This corresponds to two half-lives' worth of decay. **F** is incorrect, since it is the half-life for a different isotope (radon-222). **G** is correct, because it corresponds to two half-lives of thorium-234. **H** is incorrect, because it is only one half-life. **J** is incorrect because 5.0 days is the half-life of another isotope (bismuth-210).

5. **A**   *Take the Next Step*

If a large sample of an isotope with a short half-life is found, it suggests that it was either recently created, or that there was an exponentially massive amount of the isotope there for a long time. **A** is correct, since it explains how that isotope might come to exist. **B** is incorrect, since the half-life for a given isotope always remains constant. **C** is incorrect, because gamma radiation would not explain why the isotope is there in the first place (and gamma radiation for an isotope does not vary either). **D** is incorrect, because it would not explain why a lot of the radioactive isotope was found.

Passage II

6. **F**   *Detail*

The passage implies that the sweet spot is the area of the bat where the maximum energy is transferred from bat to ball, making the flight of the ball as long as possible. Thus, **F** is correct, and **G**, **H**, and **J** are incorrect.

7. **C**   *Handle Graphs*

In the first equation, you can substitute v/t for a in order to get a better idea of how velocity affects the force exerted by the bat. Making this substitution gives $F = mv/t$. This new equation means that as bat velocity increases, the force increases in a linear manner, as does the distance the ball travels. **A** is incorrect, because it shows distance increasing exponentially as velocity increases. **D** is incorrect because it shows distance decreasing as velocity increases. **C** is correct, because it shows distance increasing linearly along with velocity. **B**, like **D**, is incorrect because it shows distance decreasing as velocity increases.

8. **F**   *Use the Chart*

Here, you need to look carefully at all the answers to see which one is consistent with the passage. **F** is correct, since the chart shows that for the same wood and same weight, the length of the bat has no effect on distance, while for the same wood and same length, the weight of the bat will affect distance. **G** is incorrect, because the equation shows that a bat swung with greater velocity will have greater force to impart to the ball, driving it farther. **H** is incorrect, because the passage shows no difference between the lengths traveled by balls hit by bats of different lengths. **J** is incorrect, because the table shows that maple bats of two different lengths do equally well, if other conditions are identical.

9. **B**   *Use the Chart*

A is incorrect, because metal is harder than wood, so a metal bat would presumably hit a ball farther. **B** is correct, because there is nothing in the passage that suggests that a smaller swing would lead to greater power. **C** is incorrect, since in Table 1 the heavier bats are more effective. **D** is incorrect, since greater arm strength would presumably enable the batter to exert more force on the bat.

10. **G**   *Take the Next Step*

Here you need to find the answer that, together with the information in the passage, would lead to baseballs traveling farther. **F** is incorrect, because there is no mention of grip in the passage (nor is it measured in any equations). **G** is correct, because the passage states that maple is harder than ash. The maple bats make the ball travel farther, which suggests that a harder ball might travel farther than a softer one. **H** is incorrect—it might result in more home runs, but it has no effect on the distance hit balls travel. **J** is incorrect because there is no mention of hands in the passage and they are not accounted for in the data.

11. **B**   *Take the Next Step*

Recall the force equation: $F = ma$. Assuming that the force exerted by the batter on the bat (the value on the left) remains constant, and the mass of the bat decreases (due to the thinner handle), the acceleration (a) will increase, resulting in greater bat velocity. This, in turn, makes the ball travel farther. **A** is incorrect, because there is no reason to think that a thinner bat would be more durable (it turns out that modern bats are a lot more likely to break). **B** is correct, since newer bats could be swung faster. **C** is incorrect, because the barrel size remains the same, so there is nothing that suggests the sweet spot would become larger (in fact, it gets smaller). **D** is incorrect, because making the handle thinner is unrelated to the length of the bat.

Passage III

12. F   *Read the Chart*

The passage states that the overall amplitude of a resonator reaches its peak when the frequency of the driving force is equal to the resonant frequency. Thus, the tallest line on the figure suggests the closest frequency to the resonant frequency. **F** is correct, since 90 Hz is close to the tallest bar in the figure. **G**, **H**, and **J** are incorrect, since they are closer to shorter bars.

13. A   *Read the Chart*

For this question, you need to look at the equation given by the passage. Because the resonant frequency is a function of the square root of the stiffness divided by the mass, the frequency will increase when the stiffness increases. **A** is correct, since it accurately states that frequency will increase along with stiffness. **B** is incorrect, since stiffness increasing will increase frequency. **C** is incorrect because the frequency cannot stay constant if stiffness increases while mass remains constant. **D** is incorrect because the equation accurately details what will happen to the frequency when the stiffness increases.

14. F   *Use the Chart*

Here, you need to look both at the equation and at the table of data. If spring 1 and spring 2 have the same resonant frequencies, then for each spring the stiffness divided by the mass has to be equal. **F** is correct, because spring 2 needs a greater mass to compensate for its greater stiffness ($M_2/20 = M_1/10$). **G** is incorrect since spring 2 needs to be heavier. **H** and **J** are incorrect, since if both springs have the same resonant frequency they must have the same characteristic impedance.

15. C   *Use the Chart*

Since M_2 and M_3 are the same, you need to look at the bottom two-thirds of the table. **A** and **B** are incorrect, since mass is not increasing for the relevant data. **C** is correct because spring 3 has a higher stiffness than spring 2, but appears to have an overall lower resonator amplitude. **D** is incorrect, because resonator amplitude seems to decrease, not increase, when stiffness increases.

16. J   *Take the Next Step*

In this case, each answer needs to be looked at to answer the question. **F** is incorrect, because mass and stiffness are unrelated—we cannot predict the mass of the new spring given its stiffness. **G** is incorrect because characteristic impedance is a function of mass (whatever it may be) and stiffness, neither of which vary. **H** is incorrect, since we cannot predict what the resonator amplitude will be for this new stiffness. **J** is correct, because for each mass in the table, a higher stiffness leads to less variance among amplitude values. This suggests that a very stiff spring would not vary very much in its resonator amplitude.

Passage IV

17. C   *Detail*

In this case, you need to see which of the four answers is not listed as a cause of aging in the first and the last theories listed in the passage. **A** is incorrect, because the cross-linkage theory states that one of the reasons for aging is the protein mechanisms that convert soluble collagen to insoluble collagen. **B** is incorrect, because the oxidation reaction theory states that free radicals are unstable molecules that are attracted to other molecules and lead to cellular damage. **C** is correct because neither of the two theories holds that increased cell elasticity causes aging. The cross-linkage theory actually states that a reduction in cell elasticity contributes to aging, while the oxidation reaction theory is silent on the matter. **D** is incorrect, because the cross-linkage theory states that connective tissue is where collagen becomes insoluble.

18. F   *Inference*

Here, you need to see which theory could account for DNA corruption. **F** is correct, because the passage states that free radicals can disrupt DNA molecules, which in turn can lead to cancer. **G** is incorrect, because none of the hormones listed have an effect on DNA. **H** is incorrect, because the cross-linkage that makes collagen insoluble is not said to have an effect on DNA. **J** is incorrect, because one of the theories (oxidation reaction) does offer an explanation as to the cause of cancer.

19. B   *Inference*

Two details in the question are especially important: the facts that elastin is a protein, and that it can be damaged by the radiation in sunlight. This suggests a process similar to the cross-linkage of collagen. **A** is incorrect, because an excess of insulin leads to increased blood sugar, but does not necessarily affect proteins. **B** is correct, because cross-linkage agents are said to be responsible for the conversion of soluble collagen to harmful insoluble collagen, and can be found in sunlight. **C** is incorrect since connective tissues themselves have no effect on elastin. **D** is incorrect because high stress levels are an effect of excess levels of cortisol, which is unrelated to elastin.

20. **F**   *Comparison*

Each answer needs to be examined to see whether it is in accordance with both the oxidation reaction theory and the cross-linkage theory. **F** is correct, because both theories state that electromagnetic radiation can be the cause of aging (free radicals in the oxidation reaction and cross-linkage agents in the cross-linkage theory). **G** is incorrect, because only the oxidation reaction theory states that free radicals cause aging. **H** is incorrect because increased protein solubility would support only the cross-linkage theory. **J** is incorrect, because neither of the two theories states that HGH (human growth hormone) slows the aging process.

21. **A**   *Comparison*

Here, you need to find the answer that best promotes the oxidation reaction theory over the sub-optimal hormone levels theory. **A** is correct, because the sub-optimal hormone levels theory states that hormone production declines during aging, but does not directly describe why the glands that produce the hormones decay. The oxidation reaction theory suggests a way in which this might occur. **B** is incorrect, because it is in favor of the hormone levels theory. **C** is incorrect, because it is an argument against the oxidation reaction theory (pollution causes free radicals, which contribute to aging in the oxidation reaction theory). **D** is incorrect, because neither theory explicitly mentions obesity as a cause of aging.

22. **F**   *Comparison*

The answer to this question is the theory in which general cellular damage is the most direct cause of aging. **F** is correct, because in the oxidation reaction theory cellular damage occurs cumulatively, which leads to aging when cells can no longer rebuild themselves. **G** is incorrect, because the primary cause of aging in the sub-optimal hormone levels theory is incorrect glandular production of hormones, and it is less clear that faster cellular rebuilding would have as great an effect against aging. **H** is incorrect, because the cross-linkage theory states that the conversion of collagen, a protein, into insoluble form is the cause of aging, so increased cellular rebuilding would not be as effective against aging. **J** is incorrect, because the oxidation reaction theory predicts this drug would be extremely helpful against aging.

23. B *Detail*

The hormone level theory states that insulin level increases lead to blood sugar increases. **A** is incorrect, because an under-productive thyroid can lead to heart disease, so an over-productive thyroid is unlikely to lead to high blood sugar levels. **B** is correct, because insulin is mentioned as being related to blood sugar levels. **C** is incorrect, because progesterone helps regulate muscle growth and bone maintenance, among other things, but does not have a direct effect on blood sugar. **D** is incorrect, because melatonin regulates sleep, not blood sugar.

Passage V

24. H *Read the Chart*

From the passage, we know that a successful TLC process separates unique substances out of a compound. In Figure 4, there are 3 spots left after the procedure. Thus, **H** is correct because there are three different substances. **F, G,** and **J** are incorrect, since there cannot be 1, 2, or 4 substances on the slide.

25. B *Handle Graphs*

Looking at Figure 4, the slide shows that for a non-polar eluent, substances with higher polarity do not travel as far as the substances with lower polarity. **A** is incorrect, because it shows distance increasing with polarity. **B** is correct, because it shows distance decreasing as polarity increases. **C** is incorrect, since it shows distance remaining constant as polarity increases. **D** is incorrect, since it shows distance increasing, then decreasing, as polarity increases.

26. H *Use the Chart*

One of the key results to a TLC procedure is to separate a compound into its individual elements. If it is done correctly, we expect a sample to separate. The only reason a compound will not separate is if there's nothing to separate. In other words, a substance won't separate if it is all made up of the same element. **F** and **G** are incorrect, because we are not told the polarity of the compound or the eluent, so we cannot infer that the polarity was the cause of a sample's lack of separation. **H** is correct—if the sample were pure we would expect it not to separate. **J** is incorrect because if the sample were a compound, we would expect it to separate after a successful TLC procedure.

27. **B**   *Use the Chart*

From the various figures, it becomes apparent that a higher-polarity eluent will push a polar substance further towards the top of the slide. **A** is incorrect, since we know that two different substances (with different polarities) will travel different distances on the slide. **B** is correct, since it is the explanation most consistent with the data in the passage. **C** is incorrect, because there is nothing that suggests a substance can travel downwards along the slide while the eluent is being absorbed upwards. **D** is incorrect, because the passage does not mention evaporation being related to polarity.

28. **G**   *Take the Next Step*

There could be lots of explanations for differences among separate TLC procedures, so you need to look at all the answers. **F** is incorrect, since it is highly unlikely for the two compounds to have different polarities, since they are using the same polar eluent (we would expect them to travel distances very different from each other). **G** is correct, since the passage states that the spotting is done by hand and uses slightly imprecise measurements. This could account for slight variations across different slides, even when all other factors remain constant. **H** is incorrect, since without adsorbent the TLC process would not work (it is the reason the eluent moves up the slide). **J** is incorrect, because using eluents of different polarities would create very different results, and the question states that both plates used the same polar eluent.

29. **A**   *Take the Next Step*

For this question, you need to compare the information in the passage with the drawings of the slides. **A** is correct, because when the spots are dropped onto the slide, they might bleed into each other and confuse the findings. **B** is incorrect, because the eluent would work equally well on both spots on a well-prepared slide. **C** is incorrect because silica gel is simply the adsorbent used to prepare the slide, and would not hinder the spots. **D** is incorrect, because the polarity of the second substance would not necessarily affect the results of the TLC process.

Passage VI

30. **F**   *Read the Chart*

For this question, you need only look at Table 1 (since Figure 1 doesn't begin until 50°). **F** is correct, since the vapor pressure of water increases 144.8 mm Hg, while the vapor pressures of the other liquids increase by more than 300 mm Hg.

31. **C**   *Handle Graphs*

Here, it's key to realize that when molecular bond strength increases, it becomes less likely for a molecule to have the amount of kinetic energy necessary to overcome these bonds. So, as bond strength increases, vapor pressure decreases, since vapor pressure is a measure of the relative number of molecules with sufficient kinetic energy to become vaporous. **A** is incorrect, since it shows vapor pressure increasing with bond strength. **B** is incorrect because it shows vapor pressure being unaffected by bond strength. **C** is correct since it shows vapor pressure decreasing as bond strength increases. **D** is incorrect because it shows vapor pressure increasing, then decreasing as bond strength increases.

32. **F**   *Use the Chart*

The stronger the molecular bonds, the less likely it is that an individual molecule will have sufficient kinetic energy to break free and become vapor. **F** is correct, because water has a lower vapor pressure than benzene at comparable temperatures, which means its bonds are stronger. **G** is incorrect, since water would have a higher vapor pressure than benzene if its bonds were weaker. **H** is incorrect, since water and benzene do not have the same vapor pressures. **J** is incorrect, since the data in the table allows you to determine the relative strength of the bonds.

33. **C**   *Use the Chart*

Remember that any liquid will boil when its vapor pressure reaches 760 mm Hg. To find the answer, you need to look at Figure 1 and find the line that crosses 760 mm Hg the farthest to the left (at the lowest temperature). **A**, **B**, and **D** are incorrect, since they are farther to the right than carbon tetrachloride. **C** is correct, because the line for carbon tetrachloride crosses the 760 mm Hg line farthest to the left.

34. **J**   *Take the Next Step*

You need to look for the experiment that will most closely look at the effect of phase change on vapor pressure for individual substances. **F** is incorrect, because measuring the vapor pressure of a frozen mixture would not be very useful in gaining information about individual substances. **G** is incorrect, because we are interested in phase changes, and ice at various temperatures is still in the same phase. **H** is incorrect because it involves comparisons of different phases, but for different substances (comparing ice to liquid benzene, for instance, says nothing about the effects of phase changes on water's vapor pressure). **J** is correct, because it isolates the experiment for phase changes of an individual substance rather than for temperature, and does this for two different substances separately.

Passage VII

35. C *Read the Chart*

The numbers in the middle column of the first table show that not only is the inlet growing, but that the rate of its growth is increasing. **C** is correct, since it states that erosion is speeding up, whereas **A**, **B**, and **D** claim otherwise.

36. G *Read the Chart*

In the passage, it states that one cause of inlet growth is strong storms, like hurricanes. **F** is incorrect, since the passage does not correlate tourist visits directly with erosion. **G** is correct, since a hurricane is a feasible reason for the inlet to grow. **H** is incorrect because the passage does not mention boat traffic as a factor in erosion. **J** is incorrect, because the passage states that buildings often help slow the growth of inlets.

37. B *Use the Chart*

Looking at the first table, you can see that the growth rate has been increasing since 1987, which means it was most likely less than that in 1985. **B** is correct, since it is the only estimate that's lower than 90 ft/year. **A**, **C** and **D** are all much higher.

38. J *Use the Chart*

Assuming the inlet grows at a steady rate of 400 ft/year (and the data suggests it may grow a lot faster than that), in 15 years it will have grown to a total length of almost 9,000 ft. However, in order to answer the question you just have to calculate how much money each solution costs. **F** is incorrect, because it would end up costing almost $2 million a year for 15 years. **G** is incorrect since it would cost more than $2 million each year. **H** is incorrect because it would cost almost $2 million a year on average. **J** is correct, because it would cost $26 million, which is cheaper than the other solutions.

39. C *Take the Next Step*

The passage states that sandbags are cheap and efficient, but that they decay. **A** is incorrect, since the passage states sandbags are the cheapest solution. **B** is incorrect, because even though sandbags do need to be replaced regularly, renourishment involves even more frequent work. **C** is correct, since using sandbags would mean a tremendous amount of decaying bags in the vicinity of the beach. **D** is incorrect, since sandbags are placed below the water level, and are thus not visible to tourists.

40. **H** *Take the Next Step*

For this question, you need to refer back to the passage. **F** is incorrect, because the passage states that plants help prevent erosion if they are below water level. **G** is incorrect, because the passage also states that sand consists of particles of sea creatures. If plants bring more creatures, the creatures themselves contribute to the sand and help stop erosion. **H** is correct, because the temperature of the sand is not mentioned in the passage as having an effect on erosion. **J** is incorrect, because rapid plant growth will simply increase the overall level of plant life, and the passage states that "dense" plant life is good for preventing erosion.

Practice Test 2

ACT PRACTICE TEST 2 ANSWER SHEET

TEST 1

1 Ⓐ Ⓑ Ⓒ Ⓓ	16 Ⓐ Ⓑ Ⓒ Ⓓ	31 Ⓐ Ⓑ Ⓒ Ⓓ	46 Ⓐ Ⓑ Ⓒ Ⓓ	61 Ⓐ Ⓑ Ⓒ Ⓓ
2 Ⓕ Ⓖ Ⓗ Ⓙ	17 Ⓕ Ⓖ Ⓗ Ⓙ	32 Ⓕ Ⓖ Ⓗ Ⓙ	47 Ⓕ Ⓖ Ⓗ Ⓙ	62 Ⓕ Ⓖ Ⓗ Ⓙ
3 Ⓐ Ⓑ Ⓒ Ⓓ	18 Ⓐ Ⓑ Ⓒ Ⓓ	33 Ⓐ Ⓑ Ⓒ Ⓓ	48 Ⓐ Ⓑ Ⓒ Ⓓ	63 Ⓐ Ⓑ Ⓒ Ⓓ
4 Ⓕ Ⓖ Ⓗ Ⓙ	19 Ⓕ Ⓖ Ⓗ Ⓙ	34 Ⓕ Ⓖ Ⓗ Ⓙ	49 Ⓕ Ⓖ Ⓗ Ⓙ	64 Ⓕ Ⓖ Ⓗ Ⓙ
5 Ⓐ Ⓑ Ⓒ Ⓓ	20 Ⓐ Ⓑ Ⓒ Ⓓ	35 Ⓐ Ⓑ Ⓒ Ⓓ	50 Ⓐ Ⓑ Ⓒ Ⓓ	65 Ⓐ Ⓑ Ⓒ Ⓓ
6 Ⓕ Ⓖ Ⓗ Ⓙ	21 Ⓕ Ⓖ Ⓗ Ⓙ	36 Ⓕ Ⓖ Ⓗ Ⓙ	51 Ⓕ Ⓖ Ⓗ Ⓙ	66 Ⓕ Ⓖ Ⓗ Ⓙ
7 Ⓐ Ⓑ Ⓒ Ⓓ	22 Ⓐ Ⓑ Ⓒ Ⓓ	37 Ⓐ Ⓑ Ⓒ Ⓓ	52 Ⓐ Ⓑ Ⓒ Ⓓ	67 Ⓐ Ⓑ Ⓒ Ⓓ
8 Ⓕ Ⓖ Ⓗ Ⓙ	23 Ⓕ Ⓖ Ⓗ Ⓙ	38 Ⓕ Ⓖ Ⓗ Ⓙ	53 Ⓕ Ⓖ Ⓗ Ⓙ	68 Ⓕ Ⓖ Ⓗ Ⓙ
9 Ⓐ Ⓑ Ⓒ Ⓓ	24 Ⓐ Ⓑ Ⓒ Ⓓ	39 Ⓐ Ⓑ Ⓒ Ⓓ	54 Ⓐ Ⓑ Ⓒ Ⓓ	69 Ⓐ Ⓑ Ⓒ Ⓓ
10 Ⓕ Ⓖ Ⓗ Ⓙ	25 Ⓕ Ⓖ Ⓗ Ⓙ	40 Ⓕ Ⓖ Ⓗ Ⓙ	55 Ⓕ Ⓖ Ⓗ Ⓙ	70 Ⓕ Ⓖ Ⓗ Ⓙ
11 Ⓐ Ⓑ Ⓒ Ⓓ	26 Ⓐ Ⓑ Ⓒ Ⓓ	41 Ⓐ Ⓑ Ⓒ Ⓓ	56 Ⓐ Ⓑ Ⓒ Ⓓ	71 Ⓐ Ⓑ Ⓒ Ⓓ
12 Ⓕ Ⓖ Ⓗ Ⓙ	27 Ⓕ Ⓖ Ⓗ Ⓙ	42 Ⓕ Ⓖ Ⓗ Ⓙ	57 Ⓕ Ⓖ Ⓗ Ⓙ	72 Ⓕ Ⓖ Ⓗ Ⓙ
13 Ⓐ Ⓑ Ⓒ Ⓓ	28 Ⓐ Ⓑ Ⓒ Ⓓ	43 Ⓐ Ⓑ Ⓒ Ⓓ	58 Ⓐ Ⓑ Ⓒ Ⓓ	73 Ⓐ Ⓑ Ⓒ Ⓓ
14 Ⓕ Ⓖ Ⓗ Ⓙ	29 Ⓕ Ⓖ Ⓗ Ⓙ	44 Ⓕ Ⓖ Ⓗ Ⓙ	59 Ⓕ Ⓖ Ⓗ Ⓙ	74 Ⓕ Ⓖ Ⓗ Ⓙ
15 Ⓐ Ⓑ Ⓒ Ⓓ	30 Ⓐ Ⓑ Ⓒ Ⓓ	45 Ⓐ Ⓑ Ⓒ Ⓓ	60 Ⓐ Ⓑ Ⓒ Ⓓ	75 Ⓐ Ⓑ Ⓒ Ⓓ

TEST 2

1 Ⓐ Ⓑ Ⓒ Ⓓ Ⓔ	13 Ⓐ Ⓑ Ⓒ Ⓓ Ⓔ	25 Ⓐ Ⓑ Ⓒ Ⓓ Ⓔ	37 Ⓐ Ⓑ Ⓒ Ⓓ Ⓔ	49 Ⓐ Ⓑ Ⓒ Ⓓ Ⓔ
2 Ⓕ Ⓖ Ⓗ Ⓙ Ⓚ	14 Ⓕ Ⓖ Ⓗ Ⓙ Ⓚ	26 Ⓕ Ⓖ Ⓗ Ⓙ Ⓚ	38 Ⓕ Ⓖ Ⓗ Ⓙ Ⓚ	50 Ⓕ Ⓖ Ⓗ Ⓙ Ⓚ
3 Ⓐ Ⓑ Ⓒ Ⓓ Ⓔ	15 Ⓐ Ⓑ Ⓒ Ⓓ Ⓔ	27 Ⓐ Ⓑ Ⓒ Ⓓ Ⓔ	39 Ⓐ Ⓑ Ⓒ Ⓓ Ⓔ	51 Ⓐ Ⓑ Ⓒ Ⓓ Ⓔ
4 Ⓕ Ⓖ Ⓗ Ⓙ Ⓚ	16 Ⓕ Ⓖ Ⓗ Ⓙ Ⓚ	28 Ⓕ Ⓖ Ⓗ Ⓙ Ⓚ	40 Ⓕ Ⓖ Ⓗ Ⓙ Ⓚ	52 Ⓕ Ⓖ Ⓗ Ⓙ Ⓚ
5 Ⓐ Ⓑ Ⓒ Ⓓ Ⓔ	17 Ⓐ Ⓑ Ⓒ Ⓓ Ⓔ	29 Ⓐ Ⓑ Ⓒ Ⓓ Ⓔ	41 Ⓐ Ⓑ Ⓒ Ⓓ Ⓔ	53 Ⓐ Ⓑ Ⓒ Ⓓ Ⓔ
6 Ⓕ Ⓖ Ⓗ Ⓙ Ⓚ	18 Ⓕ Ⓖ Ⓗ Ⓙ Ⓚ	30 Ⓕ Ⓖ Ⓗ Ⓙ Ⓚ	42 Ⓕ Ⓖ Ⓗ Ⓙ Ⓚ	54 Ⓕ Ⓖ Ⓗ Ⓙ Ⓚ
7 Ⓐ Ⓑ Ⓒ Ⓓ Ⓔ	19 Ⓐ Ⓑ Ⓒ Ⓓ Ⓔ	31 Ⓐ Ⓑ Ⓒ Ⓓ Ⓔ	43 Ⓐ Ⓑ Ⓒ Ⓓ Ⓔ	55 Ⓐ Ⓑ Ⓒ Ⓓ Ⓔ
8 Ⓕ Ⓖ Ⓗ Ⓙ Ⓚ	20 Ⓕ Ⓖ Ⓗ Ⓙ Ⓚ	32 Ⓕ Ⓖ Ⓗ Ⓙ Ⓚ	44 Ⓕ Ⓖ Ⓗ Ⓙ Ⓚ	56 Ⓕ Ⓖ Ⓗ Ⓙ Ⓚ
9 Ⓐ Ⓑ Ⓒ Ⓓ Ⓔ	21 Ⓐ Ⓑ Ⓒ Ⓓ Ⓔ	33 Ⓐ Ⓑ Ⓒ Ⓓ Ⓔ	45 Ⓐ Ⓑ Ⓒ Ⓓ Ⓔ	57 Ⓐ Ⓑ Ⓒ Ⓓ Ⓔ
10 Ⓕ Ⓖ Ⓗ Ⓙ Ⓚ	22 Ⓕ Ⓖ Ⓗ Ⓙ Ⓚ	34 Ⓕ Ⓖ Ⓗ Ⓙ Ⓚ	46 Ⓕ Ⓖ Ⓗ Ⓙ Ⓚ	58 Ⓕ Ⓖ Ⓗ Ⓙ Ⓚ
11 Ⓐ Ⓑ Ⓒ Ⓓ Ⓔ	23 Ⓐ Ⓑ Ⓒ Ⓓ Ⓔ	35 Ⓐ Ⓑ Ⓒ Ⓓ Ⓔ	47 Ⓐ Ⓑ Ⓒ Ⓓ Ⓔ	59 Ⓐ Ⓑ Ⓒ Ⓓ Ⓔ
12 Ⓕ Ⓖ Ⓗ Ⓙ Ⓚ	24 Ⓕ Ⓖ Ⓗ Ⓙ Ⓚ	36 Ⓕ Ⓖ Ⓗ Ⓙ Ⓚ	48 Ⓕ Ⓖ Ⓗ Ⓙ Ⓚ	60 Ⓕ Ⓖ Ⓗ Ⓙ Ⓚ

TEST 3

1 Ⓐ Ⓑ Ⓒ Ⓓ	9 Ⓐ Ⓑ Ⓒ Ⓓ	17 Ⓐ Ⓑ Ⓒ Ⓓ	25 Ⓐ Ⓑ Ⓒ Ⓓ	33 Ⓐ Ⓑ Ⓒ Ⓓ
2 Ⓕ Ⓖ Ⓗ Ⓙ	10 Ⓕ Ⓖ Ⓗ Ⓙ	18 Ⓕ Ⓖ Ⓗ Ⓙ	26 Ⓕ Ⓖ Ⓗ Ⓙ	34 Ⓕ Ⓖ Ⓗ Ⓙ
3 Ⓐ Ⓑ Ⓒ Ⓓ	11 Ⓐ Ⓑ Ⓒ Ⓓ	19 Ⓐ Ⓑ Ⓒ Ⓓ	27 Ⓐ Ⓑ Ⓒ Ⓓ	35 Ⓐ Ⓑ Ⓒ Ⓓ
4 Ⓕ Ⓖ Ⓗ Ⓙ	12 Ⓕ Ⓖ Ⓗ Ⓙ	20 Ⓕ Ⓖ Ⓗ Ⓙ	28 Ⓕ Ⓖ Ⓗ Ⓙ	36 Ⓕ Ⓖ Ⓗ Ⓙ
5 Ⓐ Ⓑ Ⓒ Ⓓ	13 Ⓐ Ⓑ Ⓒ Ⓓ	21 Ⓐ Ⓑ Ⓒ Ⓓ	29 Ⓐ Ⓑ Ⓒ Ⓓ	37 Ⓐ Ⓑ Ⓒ Ⓓ
6 Ⓕ Ⓖ Ⓗ Ⓙ	14 Ⓕ Ⓖ Ⓗ Ⓙ	22 Ⓕ Ⓖ Ⓗ Ⓙ	30 Ⓕ Ⓖ Ⓗ Ⓙ	38 Ⓕ Ⓖ Ⓗ Ⓙ
7 Ⓐ Ⓑ Ⓒ Ⓓ	15 Ⓐ Ⓑ Ⓒ Ⓓ	23 Ⓐ Ⓑ Ⓒ Ⓓ	31 Ⓐ Ⓑ Ⓒ Ⓓ	39 Ⓐ Ⓑ Ⓒ Ⓓ
8 Ⓕ Ⓖ Ⓗ Ⓙ	16 Ⓕ Ⓖ Ⓗ Ⓙ	24 Ⓕ Ⓖ Ⓗ Ⓙ	32 Ⓕ Ⓖ Ⓗ Ⓙ	40 Ⓕ Ⓖ Ⓗ Ⓙ

TEST 4

1 Ⓐ Ⓑ Ⓒ Ⓓ	9 Ⓐ Ⓑ Ⓒ Ⓓ	17 Ⓐ Ⓑ Ⓒ Ⓓ	25 Ⓐ Ⓑ Ⓒ Ⓓ	33 Ⓐ Ⓑ Ⓒ Ⓓ
2 Ⓕ Ⓖ Ⓗ Ⓙ	10 Ⓕ Ⓖ Ⓗ Ⓙ	18 Ⓕ Ⓖ Ⓗ Ⓙ	26 Ⓕ Ⓖ Ⓗ Ⓙ	34 Ⓕ Ⓖ Ⓗ Ⓙ
3 Ⓐ Ⓑ Ⓒ Ⓓ	11 Ⓐ Ⓑ Ⓒ Ⓓ	19 Ⓐ Ⓑ Ⓒ Ⓓ	27 Ⓐ Ⓑ Ⓒ Ⓓ	35 Ⓐ Ⓑ Ⓒ Ⓓ
4 Ⓕ Ⓖ Ⓗ Ⓙ	12 Ⓕ Ⓖ Ⓗ Ⓙ	20 Ⓕ Ⓖ Ⓗ Ⓙ	28 Ⓕ Ⓖ Ⓗ Ⓙ	36 Ⓕ Ⓖ Ⓗ Ⓙ
5 Ⓐ Ⓑ Ⓒ Ⓓ	13 Ⓐ Ⓑ Ⓒ Ⓓ	21 Ⓐ Ⓑ Ⓒ Ⓓ	29 Ⓐ Ⓑ Ⓒ Ⓓ	37 Ⓐ Ⓑ Ⓒ Ⓓ
6 Ⓕ Ⓖ Ⓗ Ⓙ	14 Ⓕ Ⓖ Ⓗ Ⓙ	22 Ⓕ Ⓖ Ⓗ Ⓙ	30 Ⓕ Ⓖ Ⓗ Ⓙ	38 Ⓕ Ⓖ Ⓗ Ⓙ
7 Ⓐ Ⓑ Ⓒ Ⓓ	15 Ⓐ Ⓑ Ⓒ Ⓓ	23 Ⓐ Ⓑ Ⓒ Ⓓ	31 Ⓐ Ⓑ Ⓒ Ⓓ	39 Ⓐ Ⓑ Ⓒ Ⓓ
8 Ⓕ Ⓖ Ⓗ Ⓙ	16 Ⓕ Ⓖ Ⓗ Ⓙ	24 Ⓕ Ⓖ Ⓗ Ⓙ	32 Ⓕ Ⓖ Ⓗ Ⓙ	40 Ⓕ Ⓖ Ⓗ Ⓙ

ENGLISH TEST

45 Minutes—75 Questions

DIRECTIONS: There are five passages on this subject test. You should read each passage once before answering the questions on it. In order to answer correctly, you may need to read several sentences beyond the question.

There are two question formats within the passages. In one format, you will find words and phrases that have been underlined and assigned numbers. These numbers will correspond with sets of alternative words/phrases, given in the right-hand column of the test booklet. From the sets of alternatives, choose the answer choice that works best in context, keeping in mind whether it employs standard written English, whether it gets across the idea of the section, and whether it suits the tone and style of the passage. You will usually be offered the option "NO CHANGE," which you should choose if you think the version found in the passage is best.

In the second format, you will see boxed numbers referring to sections of the passage or to the passage as a whole. In the right-hand column, you will be asked questions about or given alternatives for the sections marked by the boxes. Choose the answer choice that best answers the question or completes the section. After choosing your answer choice, fill in the corresponding bubble on the answer sheet.

PASSAGE I

Growing up with the Beatles

[1]

Last week, I walked by the living room and looked in to see my five-year-old cousin. As he lied on the rug, working on a coloring book, he sang along to the Beatles' "I Want to Hold Your Hand."

[2]

There are several reasons why children love the Beatles' early work, and those reasons are: the melodies are sweet and catchy, the lyrics are pleasant and easily memorized, and the artistry is exciting. I can remember that at a very young age, when I was just a child, I listened to "Do You Want to Know a Secret" over and over. I wasn't old enough to be able to explain why I loved the music, but I knew I loved it.

[3]

[4] Plenty of groups from the 1960s appeal to children

1. **A.** NO CHANGE
B. was lying
C. lay
D. did lie

2. **F.** NO CHANGE
G. work, some of the reasons:
H. work:
J. work, because:

3. **A.** NO CHANGE
B. as a child
C. when I was a child
D. OMIT the underlined portion.

4. The writer wants to add a topic sentence here. Which of the following is best?

F. Oldies are nice, but they don't age well.
G. The Beatles are quite different than other groups.
H. In contrast to other groups, the Beatles changed so much that as children grow up, Beatles music grows up with them.
J. While you listen to certain albums when you're little, your taste changes as you grow up.

GO ON TO THE NEXT PAGE.

with their zippy melodies and fun <u>lyrics, in</u> almost all cases,
5

when the children grow up, they grow out of the sweet but

dated music. Most groups that <u>makes</u> child-appropriate music
6

never mature and make more complex music. <u>Not the Beatles.</u>
7

<u>Though</u> the Beatles changed and developed so much over the
8

course of their musical existence, their music matures along

with their listeners. You can enjoy "Please Please Me" when

you're five, "A Hard Day's Night" when you're ten, and

"Revolver" when you're fifteen.

[4]

Some Beatles albums can only be fully appreciated by

adults. Representing a giant musical leap forward, <u>Eastern</u>

<u>mysticism and psychedelic themes influenced *Sgt. Pepper's*</u>
9

Lonely Hearts Club Band. And *The White Album*, with <u>it's</u>
10

political and social commentary, finds musical inspiration in

everything from traditional pop to reggae. The music on the

Beatles' later albums is challenging, inventive, and, <u>most of all;</u>
11

<u>exhilarating</u>.

[5]

[1] I almost envied my young cousin as I watched him

color and sing. [12] [2] In a few years, when he broke up with his

---

5. **A.** NO CHANGE
   B. lyrics, but in
   C. lyrics; in
   D. lyrics in

6. **F.** NO CHANGE
   G. made
   H. did make
   J. make

7. **A.** NO CHANGE
   B. The Beatles? No.
   C. The Beatles are different.
   D. With the Beatles, no.

8. **F.** NO CHANGE
   G. And
   H. While
   J. Because

9. **A.** NO CHANGE
   B. psychedelic themes and Eastern mysticism had an
     influence on *Sgt. Pepper's Lonely Hearts Club Band*
   C. *Sgt. Pepper's Lonely Hearts Club Band* was influence
     by Eastern mysticism and psychedelic themes
   D. influence was had by Eastern mysticism and
     psychedelic themes on *Sgt. Pepper's Lonely Hearts Cl
     Band*

10. **F.** NO CHANGE
    G. it is
    H. its
    J. its'

11. **A.** NO CHANGE
    B. most of all, exhilarating
    C. most of all exhilarating
    D. exhilarating for the most part

12. What is the author's tone in the preceding sentence?

    F. angry
    G. miserable
    H. cynical
    J. wistful

GO ON TO THE NEXT PAG

t girlfriend, he would listen to "Yesterday." and pity himself
13

l feel sorry for himself; when feeling political, he

uld listen to "Come Together"; when rueful and

ical, he would listen to "I'm So Tired." [3] As he'd grow up,

Beatles would grow up with him.
14

13. A. NO CHANGE
  B. pity he and
  C. take pity on himself
  D. OMIT the underlined portion.

14. F. NO CHANGE
  G. will grow up
  H. have grown up
  J. did grow up

15. The writer wants to add this sentence to the final
paragraph:

  He had a lifetime of Beatles music to look forward to.

Where in the paragraph should he place it?

  A. Nowhere. The sentence doesn't fit this paragraph.
  B. After Sentence 1
  C. Before Sentence 3
  D. After Sentence 3

SSAGE II

The Salem Witch Trials

[1]

In 1692, in the town of Salem in the state of Massachusetts,
16

William Griggs examined two girls who had fallen ill.
17

diagnosis; the girls were bewitched. This diagnosis set off a
18

ies of events that would ultimately, in the final diagnosis,
19

ult in the deaths of thirty-seven people.

[2]

The events that took place in Salem that year are known

the Salem witch trials. In 1692, British law, which governed

16. F. NO CHANGE
  G. the Massachusetts town of Salem
  H. Salem, Massachusetts
  J. Salem, a town in Massachusetts

17. A. NO CHANGE
  B. fallen badly
  C. fallen into bad health
  D. gotten ill

18. F. NO CHANGE
  G. diagnosis, the
  H. diagnosis: the
  J. diagnosis the

19. A. NO CHANGE
  B. finally, in the ultimate diagnosis, result
  C. ultimately in the final diagnosis, result
  D. ultimately result

GO ON TO THE NEXT PAGE.

Massachusetts, <u>held that, people</u> who consorted with the devil
20

had committed a crime against the <u>government—a crime</u>
21

punishable by death. When sick girls began calling out names

of townspeople who were supposedly tormenting them, the

accused citizens were jailed, tried, and, if convicted, <u>hung</u>.
22

[3]

A court was formed to try cases. This court convicted

people based on no evidence <u>other</u> than what the "victim"
23

believed. When the court <u>pronounced them with vigor, handing</u>
24

<u>out guilty verdicts</u>, it revealed not the accused people's guilt,

but the town's thirst for blood. Over the course of only three

days, fourteen women and five men were put to death by

hanging. [25] One man was pressed to death for refusing to

testify. Seventeen people died in jail. The governor, William

Pitts, came and <u>breaks</u> up the court. [27] Why did this frenzy of
26

capital punishment occur? Why did the girls accuse people of

20. F. NO CHANGE
   G. held that people
   H. held, that people
   J. held that people,

21. A. NO CHANGE
   B. government; a crime
   C. government, a crime
   D. government a crime

22. F. NO CHANGE
   G. were hung
   H. hanging
   J. hanged

23. A. NO CHANGE
   B. (place after *based*)
   C. (place after *than*)
   D. (place after *the*)

24. F. NO CHANGE
   G. vigorously pronounced them, handing out guilty verdicts,
   H. handing out guilty verdicts, pronouncing them with vigor,
   J. pronounced, handing out guilty verdicts, with vigor,

25. In the preceding sentence, what does the word *only* emphasize?

   A. That the trials were not that serious, since they lasted for a short time
   B. That in a surprisingly short time, many people were put to death
   C. That not many people were executed
   D. That corporal punishment took the form of hangings

26. F. NO CHANGE
   G. break
   H. had broken
   J. broke

27. In the preceding sentence, which of the following phrases should be added before *the governor* in order to clarify meaning?

   A. At last
   B. It happened that
   C. Thank goodness
   D. Just in time

tchcraft in the first place? 28 Several factors had made

lem society punitive, fearful, and judgmental. Salem was on

e edge of an uncharted wilderness; personal vendettas

isted; there were rivalries with nearby towns; a smallpox

idemic had recently occurred; people strongly believed in the

vil. As for what motivated the girls, everything from

olescent hysteria to poison-induced hallucinations has been

amed. But for all the theories floated, nothing has

tisfactorily explained either the girls' behavior or the town's

action. 29

28. The writer wants to add a sentence here in order to make the transition from questions to explanations less abrupt. Which of the following sentences should be added?

F. Why did the town seemingly go mad?
G. The factors causing such a panic are almost unimaginable.
H. In truth, no one has an explanation.
J. Many theories exist to explain the harshness of the town and the hysteria of the girls.

29. The last paragraph of this essay is very long, and should be broken into two paragraphs. Where is the most natural place to begin a new paragraph?

A. With the sentence that begins *One man was pressed . . .*
B. With the sentence that begins *Why did this frenzy . . .*
C. With the sentence that beings *Why did the girls . . .*
D. With the sentence that begins *But for all the theories . . .*

30. Which of the following, as a concluding sentence, would best support the author's ideas?

F. NO CHANGE
G. I feel confident that one day, a perfect theory will be found to explain the occurrence of the witch trials.
H. It is impossible that any further progress be made in understanding the witch trials.
J. Governor William Pitts is key to any real understanding of the witch trials.

SSAGE III

Henry Ford

[1]

No wonder the contraption broke down. It was created

m a bicycle seat, a tiny engine, and rickety wheels.

lookers said it looked like nothing so much like a baby
                                        31

rriage. It made its way down the streets of Detroit in the year

96 attracting the attention of people on the street. There
   32

re plenty of onlookers watching as the rickety vehicle

lapsed.

31. A. NO CHANGE
B. so much as
C. as much as
D. like much as

32. F. NO CHANGE
G. 1896 to attract
H. 1896, attracting
J. attracting, in 1896,

GO ON TO THE NEXT PAGE.

[2]

The rickety vehicle was called the Quadricycle, and the

inventor was Henry Ford who was then 28 years old. If Ford
33

was to have any success in the automotive industry, he will
34

have to recover from this inauspicious beginning. Recover he

did. A mere five years later. He raced an improved version of his
35

car against the world's fastest car. Eight thousand people were

on hand to watch Ford's car win the race.

[3]

36 Automobiles had been owned exclusively by the rich,

therefore Henry Ford changed that. He was able to make cars
37

that were not particularly costly as a result of his famous
38

innovation the assembly line. Not only did the assembly line
39

make cars more affordable, it revolutionized the entire
40

manufacturing process.

[4]

Sure, there are plenty of unsavory things about Henry

33. A. NO CHANGE
  B. Ford, who
  C. Ford whom
  D. Ford that

34. F. NO CHANGE
  G. he did require
  H. having to
  J. he would have to

35. A. NO CHANGE
  B. later, racing
  C. later, he
  D. late. He

36. The writer wants to add a topic sentence at the beginning this paragraph. Which of the following would be most appropriate?

  F. Most automobiles were owned by rich people.
  G. Ford not only made faster cars, he made affordable ca
  H. Ford came up with the assembly line, an innovation that had an industry-wide effect.
  J. Despite his success, Ford was not without his flaws.

37. A. NO CHANGE
  B. so
  C. yet
  D. and

38. F. NO CHANGE
  G. cars, which were not very costly
  H. inexpensive cars
  J. cars, and not particularly expensive ones,

39. A. NO CHANGE
  B. innovation: the
  C. innovation that was the
  D. innovation of the

40. F. NO CHANGE
  G. they revolutionized
  H. it revolutionaried
  J. the revolution of

GO ON TO THE NEXT PAG

rd. [41] He was close friends with Jewish <u>men, and</u> he wrote
₄₂
onymous articles in his newspaper expressing anti-Semitic
wpoints. He was often accused of treating his workers like
chines. Whatever Henry Ford's personal and professional
rtcomings, he indisputably shaped the automotive and
nufacturing worlds.

[5]

Ford also changed the way factory workers were treated.
instituted the idea of the time <u>clock, workers</u> had to punch
₄₃

when they arrived at work, <u>left for and returned from lunch,</u>
₄₄
departed for the day. He asked them to work hard and
exemplary personal lives. He paid them well for their
uble.

41. Which of the following is the best revision of the preceding sentence?

  A. Yeah, there are lots of unsavory things about Henry Ford.
  B. Indeed, plenty of unsavory factoids about Henry Ford exist.
  C. There are several unsavory facts about Henry Ford.
  D. Unsavory facts about Henry Ford, yes, they exist.

42. F. NO CHANGE
  G. men, so
  H. men, therefore
  J. men, yet

43. A. NO CHANGE
  B. clock workers
  C. clock the workers
  D. clock; workers

44. F. NO CHANGE
  G. left for and from lunch
  H. left for lunch and returned from it
  J. left and returned for lunch

Question 45 refers to the essay as a whole.

45. Which of the following paragraph sequences would make this essay most readable?

  A. 1, 2, 3, 5, 4
  B. 2, 1, 3, 4, 5
  C. 3, 2, 1, 5, 4
  D. 5, 4, 1, 3, 2

SSAGE IV

Abstract Expressionism and Pop Art

[1]

[1] Abstract expressionism began in New York City in the
40s. [2] Expressionism is parodied in films by showing artists
domly flinging paint at a <u>canvas, it was actually</u> a
₄₆
vement with well-defined guidelines. [3] The artists of the
vement painted on very large <u>canvases, they</u> refused to favor
₄₇

46. F. NO CHANGE
  G. canvas, since it was actually
  H. canvas, yet it was actually
  J. canvas, and it was actually

47. A. NO CHANGE
  B. canvases they
  C. canvas, they
  D. canvases; they

GO ON TO THE NEXT PAGE.

the center of the canvas instead of <u>it's</u> sides; they capitalized on
48

accidents that happened during the painting process, instead

of painting over them; they tried to make paintings that <u>is</u>
49

expressions of emotion. [4] Abstract expressionism influenced

many movements that followed it, especially <u>from</u> its new way
50

of using color and paint. [5] Around that time, the painter

Arshile Gorky began the movement. 51

[2]

[1] Pollock worked by splattering, dripping, and

throwing paint onto the canvas. [2] Jackson Pollock was

<u>expressionist</u> another influential abstract artist. [3] It was his
52

work that brought abstract expressionism to the attention of

the public. 53

[3]

The abstract expressionist movement is sometimes

known as action painting, or the New York school. 54

[4]

<u>Pop art, began</u> as a reaction against abstract
55

expressionism. In the eyes of practitioners of pop art, abstract

expressionism took itself far too seriously. Pop art was playful

and tongue-in-cheek. 56 Pop artists aimed to find an artistic

48. F. NO CHANGE
  G. it is
  H. its
  J. its'

49. A. NO CHANGE
  B. was
  C. has
  D. were

50. F. NO CHANGE
  G. because of
  H. since
  J. in spite of

51. In order to improve the flow of Paragraph 1, where would
  Sentence 5 be best placed?

  A. Where it is
  B. After Sentence 1
  C. After Sentence 2
  D. After Sentence 3

52. F. NO CHANGE
  G. (Place after *another*)
  H. (Place after *influential*)
  J. (Place after *abstract*)

53. Which of these sentence sequences makes the second
  paragraph most logical?

  A. NO CHANGE
  B. 3, 1, 2
  C. 3, 2, 1
  D. 2, 3,1

54. Where would the preceding sentence best be placed?

  F. In Paragraph 1
  G. In Paragraph 2
  H. Where it is
  J. In Paragraph 4

55. A. NO CHANGE
  B. Pop art: began
  C. Pop art began
  D. Pop art, it began

56. To make the transition between sentences more clear,
  which of the following phrases should be added at the
  beginning of the sentence "Pop art was playful and tongu
  in-cheek?"

  F. In contrast,
  G. Similarly,
  H. Yet
  J. On that front,

GO ON TO THE NEXT PAG

...ace <u>how</u> the artist and the citizen could meet. <u>To this end,</u>
57   58

...ey used images from comic strips and household products.

57. A. NO CHANGE
    B. in
    C. which
    D. where

58. F. NO CHANGE
    G. Thus
    H. On this end
    J. To the end

...ae of the <u>famouser</u> images from pop art is <u>where the</u> can of
59   60

...mpbell's tomato soup. Such images blurred the line between

...gh and low art.

59. A. NO CHANGE
    B. famousest
    C. most famous
    D. most famousest

60. F. NO CHANGE
    G. where that
    H. just the
    J. simply a

...SSAGE V

I Was a Teenage Barista

[1]

Barista. 61 It sounded so glamorous on the hand-lettered

...tice outside the coffee shop. I certainly was <u>a person with</u>
                                               62

<u>tle experience or cynicism</u>. Little did I know that working at

...ciano's Coffee during the <u>month's</u> of summer would be
                            63

...rdest, even compared to my previous job flipping burgers. 65
64

61. Why does the author use a fragment as her first sentence?

    A. It is a grammatical error.
    B. To mimic the experience of reading the word "barista"
       on the notice
    C. To impress the reader with her knowledge of foreign
       languages
    D. To minimize her own intelligence

62. F. NO CHANGE
    G. a person lacking in experience and cynicism
    H. naïve
    J. without innocence

63. A. NO CHANGE
    B. months
    C. months'
    D. month

64. F. NO CHANGE
    G. harder
    H. quite hardest
    J. hard

65. Which of the following exclamations, if any, should be added
    at the end of the first paragraph?

    A. NO CHANGE
    B. Golly, it was awful!
    C. Heavens, but I hated it!
    D. Wow, I had no idea what I was in for!

[2]

It turned out that *barista* was just a fancy word to

...scribe the guy standing behind the counter making lattes

GO ON TO THE NEXT PAGE.

and <u>ringing in</u> people's purchases. Before I could even start
66

being a <u>barista however I</u> had to go through a month-long
67

training course. I watched thousands of videos on the various

kinds of <u>coffee, I read</u> hundreds of books on foaming milk, and
68

listened to millions of lectures from my fastidious boss on

cleaning the espresso machine. 69

[3]

I hated working at the fast-food place because I

always smelled like French fries, but Luciano's was even worse.

I could never get the coffee grinds out from under my

fingernails, <u>but</u> people always thought I had dirt under my
70

nails.

[4]

Although now I'm glad that I know so much about coffee, I

don't think the trade-off was worth it. I <u>should've</u> borrowed a
71

book on coffee from the library and saved my fingernails and

my good nature.

[5]

I preferred the customers in the fast-food place to

Luciano's customers. The people ordering fast food were

friendly and polite, but the people ordering tall lattes with a

shot of chocolate syrup <u>are</u> rude. They didn't tip well, and they
72

left their empty cups and used napkins all over the <u>store, it was</u>

<u>quite</u> unpleasant.
73

66. F. NO CHANGE
   G. ring in
   H. ringing on
   J. ringing up

67. A. NO CHANGE
   B. barista; I
   C. barista, I
   D. barista: I

68. F. NO CHANGE
   G. coffee, read
   H. coffee I read
   J. coffee, and I read

69. How do the words *thousands*, *hundreds*, and *millions* function in the preceding sentence?

   A. They connote the writer's uncontrollable rage.
   B. They humorously understate the situation.
   C. They show, by exaggeration, the author's frustration.
   D. They demonstrate, gradually, that the writer has an unrealistic grasp of the job requirements.

70. F. NO CHANGE
   G. yet
   H. since
   J. and

71. A. NO CHANGE
   B. shouldv'e
   C. shouldn't have
   D. should of

72. F. NO CHANGE
   G. were
   H. is
   J. had been

73. A. NO CHANGE
   B. store it was quite
   C. store; it was quite
   D. store so it was quite

GO ON TO THE NEXT PAG

[6]

After a while, all that snobbery started to make me

ⁿobby. Whenever someone asked for "expresso" instead of

ⁿspresso," I rolled my eyes. If a customer wanted <u>their</u> coffee
74

ⁿcaf, <u>of disgust</u> I heaved a sigh. I had turned into a bona fide
75

ⁿffee snob, and it was time for me to leave.

74. F. NO CHANGE
　　G. its
　　H. his
　　J. there

75. A. NO CHANGE
　　B. (place after *wanted*)
　　C. (place after *heaved*)
　　D. (place after *sigh*)

END OF TEST 1
STOP! DO NOT TURN THE PAGE UNTIL TOLD TO DO SO.

MATH TEST

60 Minutes—60 Questions

DIRECTIONS: After solving each problem, pick the correct answer from the five given and fill in the corresponding oval on your answer sheet. Solve as many problems as you can in the time allowed. Do not worry over problems that take too much time; skip them if necessary and return to them if you have time.

Calculator use is permitted on the test. Calculators can be used for any problem on the test, though calculators may be more harm than help for some questions.

Note: unless otherwise stated on the test, you shou assume that:

1. Figures accompanying questions are *not* drawn to sca

2. Geometric figures exist in a plane.

3. When given in a question, "line" refers to a straight line.

4. When given in a question, "average" refers to the arithmetic mean.

---

1. What is the value of x in the proportion $\frac{8}{6} = \frac{x}{9}$?

   A. $\frac{1}{3}$

   B. $\frac{3}{4}$

   C. $\frac{1}{2}$

   D. 11

   E. 12

2. A professor asked the students in his class to rate the guest lecturer. The lecturer received a rating of Excellent from 7 of the students, while 14 students rated the lecturer as Average, and 4 believed the lecturer was Poor. What percent of the students thought the lecturer was Excellent?

   F. 7%
   G. 16%
   H. 28%
   J. 50%
   K. 56%

3. Five students received an average score of 82 on a test. When the score of a sixth student is included with the first five, the average score jumps to an 84. What was the sixth student's score?

   A. 84
   B. 87
   C. 90
   D. 94
   E. 98

DO YOUR FIGURING HERE.

GO ON TO THE NEXT PAG

A 50 meter long log is cut into 8 pieces of equal length, with some of the log left over. (The leftover piece is shorter than the 8 equal pieces.) How many meters long is the leftover piece of log?

F. 2
G. 3
H. 4
J. 5
K. 6

DO YOUR FIGURING HERE.

If $\dfrac{x+28}{7} = 8,$ then what is the value of x?

A. 84
B. 56
C. 52
D. 28
E. 2

What is the area of a square with perimeter $4x - 12$?

F. $4x - 12$
G. $2x - 6$
H. $x - 3$
J. $x^2 - 6x - 9$
K. $x^2 - 6x + 9$

What is the perimeter, in centimeters, of the figure below?

A. 54

B. 76

C. 80

D. 92

E. 280

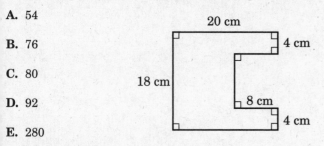

What is the simplified form of $6b - 3a - 2b$?

F. $3(2b - a - 2)$
G. $38b - 3a$
H. $(3 - 2b)(a + b)$
J. $4b - 3a$
K. $3a(6 - 2)$

In the right triangle below, how long is side $\overline{AB}$?

A. $\sqrt{13}$

B. $\sqrt{75}$

C. $\sqrt{85}$

D. 26

E. 42

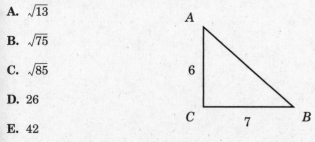

GO ON TO THE NEXT PAGE.

10. $-|5| + |-5| = ?$

   F. −10
   G. −5
   H. 0
   J. 5
   K. −8

DO YOUR FIGURING HERE.

11. Jimmy put his savings of $2,700 in the bank. His account will gain 3% interest over the course of the next year. How much money will he have in his account when the year is over?

   A. $2,703
   B. $2,781
   C. $2,810
   D. $3,000
   E. $3,510

12. Which of the following pairs of numbers have a greatest common factor of 3 and a least common multiple of 27?

   F. 3 and 6
   G. 3 and 9
   H. 6 and 9
   J. 3 and 27
   K. 9 and 27

13. If $x = 4$ and $y = -1$, then $(x + y)^2 - 2x - 2y = ?$

   A. −15
   B. 1
   C. 3
   D. 11
   E. 27

14. What is the area, in square inches, of the parallelogram *ABCD* pictured below?

   F. $30\sqrt{3}$

   G. 34

   H. $36\sqrt{3}$

   J. $48\sqrt{3}$

   K. 60

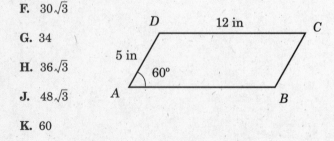

15. Which of the following is a factor of $x^2 + 3x - 10$?

   A. $(x + 1)$
   B. $(x + 2)$
   C. $(x + 3)$
   D. $(x + 4)$
   E. $(x + 5)$

GO ON TO THE NEXT PAGE

At an ice-skating rink, skates used to be rented at a rate of $5 per hour. Now the skates are rented for $7 per hour. What is the percent increase from the former price to the present price?

F. 4%

G. 20%

H. 25%

J. 40%

K. 50%

DO YOUR FIGURING HERE.

What is the slope of a line parallel to the line $2x - 4y = 8$?

A. -2

B. -1

C. $\frac{1}{2}$

D. 2

E. 4

Which of these graphs shows the equation $y = x^3 - 2$?

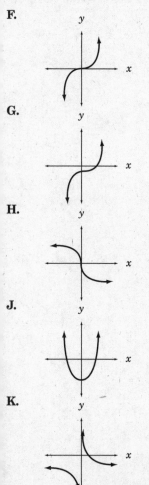

F.

G.

H.

J.

K.

GO ON TO THE NEXT PAGE.

19. What is the sum of the polynomials $2xy^2 + 4xy$ and $x^2y^2 - 3xy^2$?

A. $4xy + x^2y^2$
B. $4xy + x^2y^2 - 5xy^2$
C. $4xy + x^2y^2 - xy^2$
D. $3xy - xy^2$
E. $3xy - x^2y^2$

20. Four companies donated an average of \$135,000 to the Red Cross. If a fifth company donated \$170,000 to the Red Cross, what is the average donation for the 5 companies?

F. \$135,500
G. \$142,000
H. \$152,500
J. \$163,000
K. \$169,500

21. Which expression is equivalent to $\dfrac{2x+4}{8x}$?

A. $\dfrac{2+x}{4x}$

B. $\dfrac{x+4}{4x}$

C. $\dfrac{1}{4}$

D. $\dfrac{1}{2}$

E. 1

22. A right triangle has sides of length 2, $2\sqrt{3}$, and 4. What is the cosine of the smallest angle in the triangle?

F. 2

G. $\dfrac{4}{\sqrt{3}}$

H. $\dfrac{\sqrt{3}}{2}$

J. $\dfrac{1}{2}$

K. $\dfrac{1}{4}$

23. Sarah has n marbles. Margaret has seven more marbles than Sarah does, while Emma has two marbles fewer than Margaret has. How many marbles do the three girls have together?

A. $n+5$
B. $n+7$
C. $2n+5$
D. $3n+5$
E. $3(n+4)$

GO ON TO THE NEXT PAGE

4. If the quadratic equation $x^2 - 8x + z = 0$ has only one possible solution for x, then what is the value of z?

F. 64
G. 16
H. 8
J. 4
K. 2

DO YOUR FIGURING HERE.

5. The lengths of the sides of a triangle are 4, 4, and $4\sqrt{2}$. What is the measure of the angle between the two shortest sides?

A. 30°
B. 45°
C. 60°
D. 90°
E. 135°

6. $(2a^3)^2 + (-a^2)^3 = ?$

F. a^6
G. $3a^5$
H. $3a^6$
J. $5a^5$
K. $5a^6$

7. There are 12 inches in a foot. If a 2.5-foot hero sandwich costs $7.50, how much does the hero cost per inch? (Note: round price to the nearest cent.)

A. $0.25
B. $0.63
C. $3.00
D. $5.50
E. $18.75

8. If $2x - 2y = 4$ and $2x + y = 13$, then what is the value of x?

F. −9

G. −3

H. 3

J. 5

K. $\dfrac{11}{2}$

9. Which of the following is the graph of the solution set of $x + 1 > -2$?

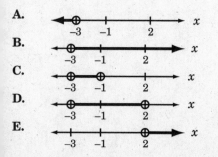

A.
B.
C.
D.
E.

GO ON TO THE NEXT PAGE.

DO YOUR FIGURING HERE.

30. In which of the following equations does y vary inversely with x?

F. $y = x^2$

G. $y = \dfrac{2x}{3}$

H. $y = \dfrac{2}{x}$

J. $x = y^2$

K. $x = \dfrac{3y}{2}$

31. Points $J\,(-2,4)$ and $K\,(6,2)$ are the endpoints of line segment $\overline{JK}$ in the standard (x,y) coordinate plane. What is the midpoint of the line segment?

A. $(-2,2)$
B. $(6,4)$
C. $(4,6)$
D. $(2,3)$
E. $(3,2)$

32. In the standard (x,y) coordinate plane, the lines $y = 3x - 1$ and $y = mx + 1$ are parallel. What is the value of m?

F. -3

G. $-\dfrac{1}{3}$

H. $-\dfrac{1}{3}$

J. 1

K. 3

33. The number line graph below best fits which inequality?

A. $x = -3$
B. $x > -4$
C. $x < -4$
D. $-4 < x < -2$
E. $-4 > x$ or $x > -2$

34. At Joe's Pizza, it costs \$3.50 to buy x sodas, and \$4.40 to buy y slices of plain pizza. How much does it cost in dollars to buy 4 sodas and 3 slices of plain pizza?

F. $3\left(\dfrac{y}{3.50}\right) + 4\left(\dfrac{x}{4.40}\right)$

G. $3\left(\dfrac{3.50}{y}\right) + 4\left(\dfrac{4.40}{x}\right)$

H. $4\left(\dfrac{x}{3.50}\right) + 3\left(\dfrac{y}{4.40}\right)$

J. $4\left(\dfrac{3.50}{x}\right) + 3\left(\dfrac{4.40}{y}\right)$

K. $\dfrac{3.50}{x+4} + \dfrac{4.40}{y+3}$

GO ON TO THE NEXT PAGE

5. If $3x + y = 7$ and $2x - 2y = 10$, then what is the value of x?

A. -2
B. 0
C. 3
D. 7
E. 17

DO YOUR FIGURING HERE.

6. In a right triangle, if the sine of $\angle B$ is $\dfrac{5}{13}$, then what is the cosine of $\angle B$?

F. $\dfrac{13}{5}$

G. 1

H. $\dfrac{12}{13}$

J. $\dfrac{4}{13}$

K. $\dfrac{4}{5}$

7. If $a - b = 2$ and $a + b = 8$, then $(a - b)^2 = ?$

A. -2
B. 2
C. 4
D. 16
E. 64

8. If $x = y + 1$, then $x^2 - 2(y + 1)^2 = ?$

F. $-3x^2$
G. $-x^2 + 2x^4$
H. $-x^2$
J. $x^2 - 4x^4$
K. $3x^2$

9. A car insurance company reimburses claimants according to the formula $p \times \dfrac{1}{1.25n}$, where p is the original price of the car and n is the number of years that the claimant has owned the car. How much would a claimant receive as reimbursement for a car that originally cost \$8,000 and that the claimant owned for 5 years?

A. \$50,000
B. \$10,000
C. \$6,400
D. \$2,000
E. \$1,280

GO ON TO THE NEXT PAGE.

DO YOUR FIGURING HERE.

40. If the measure of the perimeter of right triangle *A* is denoted by *x*, then the perimeter of right triangle *B* is 2*x*. If the two triangles are similar, and the lengths of the two legs of right triangle *A* are 5 cm and 12 cm, what is the measure of the hypotenuse of triangle *B*, in centimeters?

    F. 10
    G. 13
    H. 24
    J. 26
    K. 34

41. A square has sides of length *x* inches. If the width of the square is increased by 2 inches, and the length is increased by 1 inch, what is the difference between the area of the new rectangle and the area of the old square?

    A. x^2
    B. $x + 2$
    C. $3x + 2$
    D. $x^2 + 2$
    E. $x^2 + 3x + 2$

42. If the radius of the circle in the figure below is 4 inches, and the base of the triangle passes through the center of the circle, what is the area of the shaded region, in square inches?

    F. π
    G. 4π
    H. $4^2(\pi - 1)$
    J. 16π
    K. $16\pi - 1$

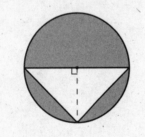

43. The circumference of a particular circle is π feet. What is the radius of the circle, measured in feet?

    A. $\dfrac{1}{3}$

    B. $\dfrac{1}{2}$

    C. 1

    D. $1\dfrac{1}{2}$

    E. 2

44. A family has a rectangular yard with a width of 8 feet and a length of 20 feet. If the family increases the width of the yard by 2 feet, how much additional space will they gain, in square feet?

    F. 4
    G. 20
    H. 40
    J. 100
    K. 200

GO ON TO THE NEXT PAGE

5. What is the solution of the equation $3x^2 - x - 2 = 0$, where $x > 0$?

A. $\dfrac{1}{3}$

B. $\dfrac{2}{3}$

C. $\dfrac{3}{2}$

D. 1

E. 2

DO YOUR FIGURING HERE.

6. What is the area, in square centimeters, of the figure below?

F. 24

G. 54

H. 108

J. 132

K. 180

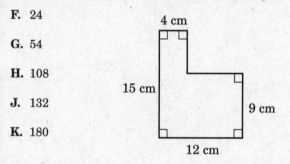

7. If $\log_x 16 = 4$, then $x = ?$

A. $\log 4$

B. $\dfrac{\log 16}{4}$

C. 2

D. 4

E. 16^4

8. If $X = \begin{bmatrix} -1 & 3 \\ 4 & -2 \end{bmatrix}$ and $Y = \begin{bmatrix} 1 & -3 \\ 4 & -2 \end{bmatrix}$ then $X - Y = ?$

F. $\begin{bmatrix} 0 & 0 \\ 0 & 0 \end{bmatrix}$

G. $\begin{bmatrix} -2 & 6 \\ 0 & 0 \end{bmatrix}$

H. $\begin{bmatrix} -2 & 0 \\ -8 & -4 \end{bmatrix}$

J. $\begin{bmatrix} -2 & -6 \\ -8 & 0 \end{bmatrix}$

K. $\begin{bmatrix} -2 & -6 \\ -8 & -4 \end{bmatrix}$

GO ON TO THE NEXT PAGE.

DO YOUR FIGURING HERE.

49. If the area of a square is greater than 4 square units and smaller than 81 square units, then which of the following inequalities expresses the possible range of values for a side of the square, where x signifies the measure of the side of the square in units?

  A. $2 < x$
  B. $4 < x$
  C. $2 < x < 9$
  D. $2 < x < 81$
  E. $4 < x < 81$

50. What is the sine of $\angle A$ in right triangle ABC?

  F. $\dfrac{1}{10}$

  G. $\dfrac{3}{10}$

  H. $\dfrac{1}{\sqrt{10}}$

  J. $\dfrac{3}{\sqrt{10}}$

  K. $\dfrac{1}{3}$

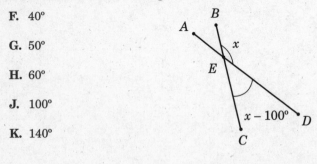

51. What is the amplitude of the graph of $y - 1 = 2 \sin x$?

  A. $\dfrac{1}{2}$

  B. 1

  C. 2

  D. 3

  E. 4

52. Line segments $\overline{AD}$ and $\overline{BC}$ intersect at point E. What is the measure of $\angle CED$ in degrees?

  F. 40°

  G. 50°

  H. 60°

  J. 100°

  K. 140°

GO ON TO THE NEXT PAGE

. In the figure below, $\overline{BD}$ is an altitude of equilateral triangle ABC. How many inches long is $\overline{BC}$?

A. 3

B. $2\sqrt{3}$

C. $3\sqrt{3}$

D. $6\sqrt{3}$

E. 6

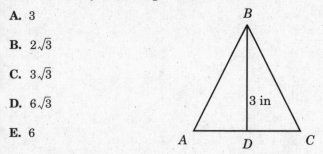

DO YOUR FIGURING HERE.

. Two cars leave the same location at the same time and travel along the same route to the same destination, which is 120 miles away. If car A arrived at the destination in 3 hours, and car B arrived 2 hours after car A, what was the average difference in speed, measured in miles per hour, of car A and car B?

F. 40
G. 24
H. 16
J. 10
K. 2

. A rectangular box has the dimensions shown in the figure below. What is the length of line segment $\overline{AB}$?

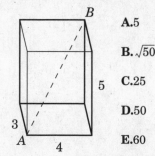

A. 5

B. $\sqrt{50}$

C. 25

D. 50

E. 60

. Ten students on a class trip walk into a store and are about to buy 10 individual cans of soda for $1 a can, but notice that six-packs of soda are on sale for $5.40. If the 10 students get 2 other friends to join in and buy 2 six-packs, and they all divide the price equally, how much will each of the original 10 students save?

F. $.05
G. $.10
H. $.50
J. $1.20
K. $4.60

GO ON TO THE NEXT PAGE.

57. Which of the following equations could produce the ellipse pictured in the (x,y) coordinate plane?

A. $\dfrac{(x-4)^2}{4} + \dfrac{(y-2)^2}{9} = 1$

B. $\dfrac{(x-4)^2}{2} + \dfrac{(y-2)^2}{3} = 1$

C. $\dfrac{(x-2)^2}{9} + \dfrac{(y-4)^2}{4} = 1$

D. $\dfrac{(x-2)^2}{3} + \dfrac{(y-2)^2}{2} = 1$

E. $\dfrac{(x-9)^2}{2} + \dfrac{(y-4)^2}{3} = 1$

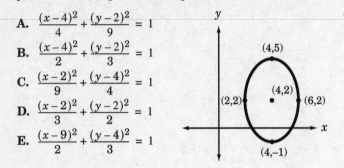

58. How many times does the graph of

$$y = \left(\frac{x+2}{4}\right)\left(\frac{x-4}{2}\right)(x+3)$$

intersect the y-axis?

F. 0
G. 1
H. 2
J. 3
K. 4

59. In the standard (x, y) coordinate plane, how many times do the graphs of the equations $y = x^2$ and $y = x^3$ intersect?

A. 0
B. 1
C. 2
D. 3
E. an infinite number of times

60. In three tosses of a fair coin, what is the probability of getting at least 2 heads? (A fair coin is equally likely to come up heads or tails.)

F. $\dfrac{1}{8}$

G. $\dfrac{3}{8}$

H. $\dfrac{1}{2}$

J. $\dfrac{5}{8}$

K. $\dfrac{7}{8}$

END OF TEST

STOP! DO NOT TURN THE PAGE UNTIL TOLD TO DO S

DO NOT RETURN TO THE PREVIOUS TES

READING TEST

35 Minutes—40 Questions

DIRECTIONS: On this test, you will have 35 minutes to read four passages and answer 40 questions (ten questions on each passage). Each set of ten questions appears directly after the relevant passage. You should select the answer choice that best answers the question. There is no time limit for work on the individual passages, so you can move freely between the passages and refer to each as often as you'd like.

Passage I

PROSE FICTION: This passage is adapted from E. M. Forster's *A Room With A View* (1908).

"The Signora had no business to do it," said Miss Bartlett, "no business at all. She promised us south rooms with a view close together, instead of which here are north rooms, looking into a courtyard, and a long way apart. Oh, Lucy!"

"And a Cockney, besides!" said Lucy, who had been further saddened by the Signora's unexpected accent. "It might be London." She looked at the two rows of English people who were sitting at the table; at the row of white bottles of water and red bottles of wine that ran between the English people; at the portraits of the late Queen and the late Poet Laureate that hung behind the English people, heavily framed; at the notice of the English church (Rev. Cuthbert Eager, M. A. Oxon.), that was the only other decoration of the wall. "Charlotte, don't you feel, too, that we might be in London? I can hardly believe that all kinds of other things are just outside. I suppose it is one's being so tired."

"This meat has surely been used for soup," said Miss Bartlett, laying down her fork.

"I want so to see the Arno. The rooms the Signora promised us in her letter would have looked over the Arno. The Signora had no business to do it at all. Oh, it is a shame!"

"Any nook does for me," Miss Bartlett continued; "but it does seem hard that you shouldn't have a view."

Lucy felt that she had been selfish. "Charlotte, you mustn't spoil me: of course, you must look over the Arno, too. I meant that. The first vacant room in the front—"

"You must have it," said Miss Bartlett, part of whose traveling expenses were paid by Lucy's mother—a piece of generosity to which she made many a tactful allusion.

"No, no. You must have it."

"I insist on it. Your mother would never forgive me, Lucy."

"She would never forgive me."

The ladies' voices grew animated, and—if the sad truth be owned—a little peevish. They were tired, and under the guise of unselfishness they wrangled. Some of their neighbors interchanged glances, and one of them—one of the ill-bred people whom one does meet abroad—leant forward over the table and actually intruded into their argument. He said:

"I have a view, I have a view."

Miss Bartlett was startled. Generally at a pension people looked them over for a day or two before speaking, and often did not find out that they would "do" till they had gone. She knew that the intruder was ill-bred, even before she glanced at him. He was an old man, of heavy build, with a fair, shaven face and large eyes. There was something childish in those eyes, though it was not the childishness of senility. What exactly it was Miss Bartlett did not stop to consider, for her glance passed on to his clothes. These did not attract her. He was probably trying to become acquainted with them before they got into the swim. So she assumed a dazed expression when he spoke to her, and then said: "A view? Oh, a view! How delightful a view is!"

"This is my son," said the old man; "his name's George. He has a view too."

"Ah," said Miss Bartlett, repressing Lucy, who was about to speak.

"What I mean," he continued, "is that you can have our rooms, and we'll have yours. We'll change."

The better class of tourist was shocked at this, and sympathized with the new-comers. Miss Bartlett, in reply, opened her mouth as little as possible, and said:

"Thank you very much indeed; that is out of the question."

"Why?" said the old man, with both fists on the table.

"Because it is quite out of the question, thank you."

"You see, we don't like to take—" began Lucy.

Her cousin again repressed her.

"But why?" he persisted. "Women like looking at a view; men don't." And he thumped with his fists like a naughty child, and turned to his son, saying, "George, persuade them!"

"It's so obvious they should have the rooms," said the

GO ON TO THE NEXT PAGE.

son. "There's nothing else to say."

Lucy saw that they were in for what is known as "quite a
80 scene," and she had an odd feeling that whenever these ill-
bred tourists spoke the contest widened and deepened till
it dealt, not with rooms and views, but with—well, with
something quite different, whose existence she had not
realized before. Now the old man attacked Miss Bartlett
85 almost violently: Why should she not change? What possible objection had she? They would clear out in half an hour.

Miss Bartlett, though skilled in the delicacies of conversation, was powerless in the presence of brutality. It was
impossible to snub any one so gross. Her face reddened
90 with displeasure.

1. Lucy's main impression of the pension is that:

A. it resembles a lodging house in London.
B. it gives the feeling of being in London.
C. many English people stay there.
D. its proprietor is probably English.

2. Lucy's chief complaint at the pension arises from:

F. dining with the English guests, who remind her of
   home.
G. being served poor quality meat.
H. seeing the Arno from her room.
J. not having a south-facing room with a view.

3. The old man at the pension proposes that Miss Bartlett and
   Lucy:

A. exchange rooms with him and his son.
B. go out for a swim with him.
C. not argue in front of strangers.
D. see the Arno from his son's room.

4. One can infer from the passage that Lucy and Miss Bartlett
   are:

F. sisters.
G. strangers meeting at the pension.
H. traveling companions.
J. old school friends.

5. In the passage, Miss Bartlett's behavior toward Lucy can
   described as:

A. motherly concern for Lucy's happiness.
B. stern and uncompromising.
C. unselfish and full of gratitude towards Lucy's mother.
D. a mixture of deference and control.

6. In lines 29–35, Lucy and Miss Bartlett disagree over:

F. who should take the first available room with a view.
G. whether to accept the old man's offer.
H. Lucy's selfishness.
J. what Lucy's mother would do.

7. One can reasonably infer from the passage that Miss
   Bartlett refuses the old man's offer because:

A. of a mixture of pride and snobbery.
B. she dislikes his appearance.
C. she considers the offer inappropriate.
D. she thinks Lucy's mother would disapprove if she
   accepted.

8. The passage suggests that Miss Bartlett first finds the ol
   man ill-bred primarily because:

F. he initiates a conversation with female strangers.
G. of the childish look in his eyes.
H. he interrupts her conversation with Lucy.
J. he wears unattractive clothing.

9. Miss Bartlett would most likely agree with the
   characterization of the old man as:

A. immature.
B. rude and offensive.
C. impetuous but generous.
D. manipulative.

10. Lines 85–86 represent the point of view of:

F. George.
G. Miss Bartlett.
H. the old man.
J. the narrator.

GO ON TO THE NEXT PAG

SOCIAL SCIENCE: This passage is adapted from Oscar Wilde's *The Soul of Man under Socialism* (1891).

While under the present system a very large number of people can lead lives of a certain amount of freedom and expression and happiness, under a system of economic tyranny, nobody would be able to have any such freedom at all. It is to be regretted that a portion of our community should be practically in slavery, but to propose to solve the problem by enslaving the entire community is childish. Every man must be left quite free to choose his own work. No form of compulsion must be exercised over him. If there is, his work will not be good for him, will not be good in itself, and will not be good for others.

I hardly think that any Socialist, nowadays, would seriously propose that an inspector should call every morning at each house to see that each citizen rose up and did manual labor for eight hours. But I confess that many of the socialistic views that I have come across seem to me to be tainted with ideas of authority, if not of actual compulsion. Of course, authority and compulsion are out of the question. All association must be quite voluntary. It is only in voluntary associations that man is fine.

But it may be asked how Individualism, which is now more or less dependent on the existence of private property for its development, will benefit by the abolition of such private property. The answer is very simple. It is true that, under existing conditions, a few men who have had private means of their own, such as Byron, Shelley, Browning, Victor Hugo, Baudelaire, and others, have been able to realize their personality more or less completely. Not one of these men ever did a single day's work for hire. They were relieved from poverty. They had an immense advantage. The question is whether it would be for the good of Individualism that such an advantage should be taken away. Let us suppose that it is taken away. What happens then to Individualism? How will it benefit?

It will benefit in this way. Under the new conditions Individualism will be far freer, far finer, and far more intensified than it is now. I am not talking of the great imaginatively-realized Individualism of such poets as I have mentioned, but of the great actual Individualism latent and potential in mankind generally. For the recognition of private property has really harmed Individualism, and obscured it, by confusing a man with what he possesses. It has made gain not growth its aim. So that man thought that the important thing was to have, and did not know that the important thing is to be. The true perfection of man lies, not in what man has, but in what man is.

Private property has crushed true Individualism, and set up an Individualism that is false. It has debarred one part of the community from being individual by starving them. It has debarred the other part of the community from being individual by putting them on the wrong road, and encumbering them. Indeed, so completely has man's personality been absorbed by his possessions that the English law has always treated offenses against a man's property with far more severity than offenses against his person, and property is still the test of complete citizenship.

The industry necessary for the making of money is also very demoralizing. In a community like ours, where property confers immense distinction, social position, honor, respect, titles, and other pleasant things of the kind, man, being naturally ambitious, makes it his aim to accumulate this property, and goes on wearily and tediously accumulating it long after he has got far more than he wants, or can use, or enjoy, or perhaps even know of. Man will kill himself by overwork in order to secure property, and really, considering the enormous advantages that property brings, one is hardly surprised.

One's regret is that society should be constructed on such a basis that man has been forced into a groove in which he cannot freely develop what is wonderful, and fascinating, and delightful in him—in which, in fact, he misses the true pleasure and joy of living. He is also, under existing conditions, very insecure. An enormously wealthy merchant may be— often is—at every moment of his life at the mercy of things that are not under his control. If the wind blows an extra point or so, or the weather suddenly changes, or some trivial thing happens, his ship may go down, his speculations may go wrong, and he finds himself a poor man, with his social position quite gone. Now, nothing should be able to harm a man except himself. What a man really has is what is in him. What is outside of him should be a matter of no importance.

With the abolition of private property, then, we shall have true, beautiful, healthy Individualism. Nobody will waste his life in accumulating things, and the symbols for things. One will live. To live is the rarest thing in the world. Most people exist, that is all.

11. The author states that under a system of economic tyranny:

   A. a portion of the community would practically be in slavery.
   B. many people would live with a certain degree of freedom and expression.
   C. every man would choose his work.
   D. no one would have freedom.

12. One can reasonably infer from the passage that the author primarily values:

   F. the right to choose.
   G. the right to work.
   H. the equal treatment of people under all circumstances.
   J. the treatment of all people as criminals.

GO ON TO THE NEXT PAGE.

13. The author uses the examples in lines 26–27 to:

  A. show how wealth helps a few men attain Individualism under the present system.
  B. set an example for individuals under an ideal socialist state.
  C. argue that only with wealth can a person attain individualism under the present system.
  D. demonstrate the products of a socialist state.

14. According to the passage, private property results in:

  F. the establishment of English property law.
  G. the confusion of the man with his property.
  H. the goal of growth, not gain.
  J. the stifling of all forms of Individualism.

15. In lines 72–73 the author states that the man who acquires private property is insecure. This is because:

  A. he is constantly threatened by external, uncontrollable events.
  B. his social position can change at any time.
  C. he feels no joy of living.
  D. in order to acquire more property, he may have to kill himself.

16. One of the main arguments of the passage is that:

  F. Byron, Shelley, and Browning are known for what they possessed, not for what they created.
  G. Individualism under socialism will not be as great as Individualism under private property, but it will be more widespread.
  H. Byron, Shelley, and Browning attained the greatest form of Individualism.
  J. the abolition of private property is necessary for the attainment of universal Individualism.

17. The author of the passage would most likely agree with the definition of true, healthy Individualism as:

  A. a strong, charismatic personality.
  B. the pleasure and joy of living for the people one loves.
  C. the realization of one's personality, free from external influence.
  D. the expression of one's personality through art.

18. As it is used in line 17, the word "compulsion" most nearly means:

  F. requirement.
  G. force.
  H. absolute rule.
  J. threat.

19. According to the passage, English law:

  A. protects property and person equally.
  B. ignores infractions against property.
  C. was developed to protect property.
  D. values property more than the person.

20. One can reasonably infer from the passage that the author:

  F. supports socialism unconditionally.
  G. supports the socialist emphasis on abolishing property but opposes socialist authoritarianism.
  H. supports socialism on the condition that it provide work for all men.
  J. opposes socialism in all forms.

GO ON TO THE NEXT PAGE

ssage III

HUMANITIES: This passage is adapted from Arnold Bennett's *Literary Taste* (1909).

Style cannot be distinguished from matter. When a writer conceives an idea he conceives it in a form of words. That form of words constitutes his style, and it is absolutely governed by the idea. The idea can only exist in words, and it can only exist in one form of words. You cannot say exactly the same thing in two different ways. Slightly alter the expression, and you slightly alter the idea. Surely it is obvious that the expression cannot be altered without altering the thing expressed!

A writer, having conceived and expressed an idea, may, and probably will, "polish it up." But what does he polish up? To say that he polishes up his style is merely to say that he is polishing up his idea, that he has discovered faults or imperfections in his idea, and is perfecting it. An idea exists in proportion as it is expressed; it exists when it is expressed, and not before. It expresses itself. A clear idea is expressed clearly, and a vague idea vaguely. You need but take your own case and your own speech.

For just as science is the development of common sense, so is literature the development of common daily speech. The difference between science and common sense is simply one of degree; similarly with speech and literature. Well, when you "know what you think," you succeed in saying what you think, in making yourself understood. When you "don't know what to think," your expressive tongue halts. And note how in daily life the characteristics of your style follow your mood; how tender it is when you are tender, how violent when you are violent. You have said to yourself in moments of emotion: "If only I could write—," etc. You were wrong. You ought to have said: "If only I could think—on this high plane."

When you have thought clearly you have never had any difficulty in saying what you thought, though you may occasionally have had some difficulty in keeping it to yourself. And when you cannot express yourself, depend upon it that you have nothing precise to express, and that what incommodes you is not the desire to express, but the vain desire to think more clearly. All this just to illustrate how style and matter are coexistent, and inseparable, and alike.

You cannot have good matter with bad style. Examine the point more closely. A man wishes to convey a fine idea to you. He employs a form of words. That form of words is his style. Having read, you say: "Yes, this idea is fine." The writer has therefore achieved his end. But in what imaginable circumstances can you say: "Yes, this idea is fine, but the style is not fine"? The sole medium of communication between you and the author has been the form of words. The fine idea has reached you. How? In the words, by the words. Hence the fineness must be in the words. You may say, superiorly: "He has expressed himself clumsily, but I can *see* what he means." By what light? By something in

the words, in the style. That something is fine. Moreover, if the style is clumsy, are you sure that you can see what he means? You cannot be quite sure. And at any rate, you cannot see distinctly. The "matter" is what actually reaches you, and it must necessarily be affected by the style.

Still further to comprehend what style is, let me ask you to think of a writer's style exactly as you would think of the gestures and manners of an acquaintance. You know the man whose demeanor is "always calm," but whose passions are strong. How do you know that his passions are strong? Because he "gives them away" by some small, but important, part of his demeanor, such as the twitching of a lip or the whitening of the knuckles caused by clenching the hand. In other words, his demeanor, fundamentally, is not calm. You know the man who is always "smoothly polite and agreeable," but who affects you unpleasantly. Why does he affect you unpleasantly? Because he is tedious, and therefore disagreeable, and because his politeness is not real politeness. You know the man who is awkward, shy, clumsy, but who, nevertheless, impresses you with a sense of dignity and force. Why? Because mingled with that awkwardness and so forth is dignity. In every instance the demeanor, while perhaps seeming to be contrary to the character, is really in accord with it. The demeanor never contradicts the character. It is one part of the character that contradicts another part of the character. For, after all, the blunt man is blunt, and the awkward man is awkward, and these characteristics are defects. The demeanor merely expresses them.

GO ON TO THE NEXT PAGE.

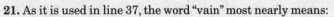

21. As it is used in line 37, the word "vain" most nearly means:

   A. egotistical.
   B. proud.
   C. futile.
   D. pretty.

22. The author uses all of the following comparisons in the passage EXCEPT:

   F. science and literature.
   G. speech and common sense.
   H. literary style and human demeanor.
   J. style and content.

23. According to the passage, by slightly altering the style of a piece of writing, one:

   A. alters the ideas of the piece.
   B. improves the tone of the piece.
   C. polishes the writing.
   D. does not change the content or ideas.

24. The author states that a person's gestures:

   F. have little to do with his true personality.
   G. reveal his true personality.
   H. sometimes contradict his public behavior.
   J. are always extravagant.

25. One of the main points of the passage is that:

   A. it is impossible to divorce style from subject matter.
   B. people who cannot write cannot think.
   C. calm men often have raging passions.
   D. demeanor never contradicts character.

26. The "you" addressed by the narrator is most likely:

   F. a friend of the author's.
   G. someone who has written to the author for help.
   H. the author's child.
   J. the general reader of the essay.

27. The narrator's tone can best be described as:

   A. hectoring.
   B. condescending.
   C. lecturing.
   D. respectful.

28. The author would most likely agree with the statement that:

   F. a book's cover is indistinguishable from its contents.
   G. surface reveals substance.
   H. an artist's technique is integral to the meaning of the work.
   J. a girl's loveliness reflects the loveliness of her soul.

29. The main purpose of the last paragraph is to:

   A. introduce the author's argument about a person's demeanor.
   B. expose the defects of various people.
   C. bring the passage to its logical conclusion.
   D. support the author's argument by expanding upon an analogy.

30. As it is used in lines 36–37, the word "incommodes" most nearly means:

   F. causes difficulty.
   G. disables.
   H. beguiles.
   J. worries.

GO ON TO THE NEXT PAG

ssage IV

NATURAL SCIENCE: This passage is adapted from Mary Maish's *Theories of Addiction.*

There are many different kinds of addictions, from drugs to interpersonal relationships. Although these diverse addictions vary in many ways, there are common threads that bind them together. There are several theories that model addiction: genetic theories, exposure theories (both biological and conditioning), and adaptation theories.

The genetic theory of addiction, known as addictive inheritance, attempts to separate the genetic and environmental factors of addictive behavior. Studies have been done to control for environmental components to determine if genetics plays the main role. Most studies looking at alcoholism have determined that children born from alcoholic parents who are adopted into non-alcoholic families have a three- to fourfold increase in the rate of alcoholism over the rest of the population. Indeed, children born and raised by alcoholic parents have an even greater rate of alcoholism. This data suggests that there is some genetic predisposition to alcoholic addiction. Though a genetic component seems likely, exactly how genes might code for alcoholism has not been determined.

The biological exposure model is based on the belief that the introduction of a substance into the body on a regular basis will inevitably lead to addiction. Underlying the model is an assumption that the introduction of a narcotic into the body causes metabolic adjustments requiring continued and increasing dosages of the drug in order to avoid withdrawal. Although changes in cell metabolism have been demonstrated, as of yet they have not been linked with addiction. Some experts theorize that, if used on a regular basis, drugs that mimic endorphins (naturally occurring pain killers) will reduce the body's natural endorphin production and bring about a reliance on the external chemical agent for ordinary pain relief.

Endorphin-related explanations have been associated with other kinds of addiction. It has been suggested that food and alcohol can also affect endorphin levels. This could explain the craving, or the continued psychological need, for these non-narcotic substances. The argument is even stronger for those individuals addicted to running and exercise. The "runner's high" that is commonly experienced by well-conditioned athletes is likely a result of endorphin production.

Nicotine has also been implicated in stimulating endorphin receptors as a basis for addiction. One view is that cigarette smokers are physically dependent on nicotine. They continue to smoke in order to maintain habitual levels of cellular nicotine in order to avoid withdrawal. Still controversial, the exposure theory, and its implication that endorphins play a role in addiction, continues to be favored by some investigators and is a focus of much research.

55　The basis of conditioning theories is that addiction is the cumulative result of the reinforcement of drug administration. The substance acts as a powerful reinforcer and gains control over the user's behavior. In contrast to the biological models of the exposure theories, these conditioning models suggest that anyone can be

60　driven to exhibit addictive behavior given the necessary reinforcements, regardless of their biology. Two conditioning models, the opponent-process model of motivation and the classical conditioning model, both define addiction as a behavior that is refined because of the pleasure associated with its reinforcement.

65　There are two proposals that account for the relentless pursuit of drugs, according to the exposure models. The first (the biological theory) is that the drug provides an inherent, biological reward to prevent the pain of withdrawal. The second (the conditioning theory) is that

70　the experiences brought on by the drugs bring on inordinate pleasure or euphoria. These mechanisms can act independently or synergistically. In both cases, though, the primary motivation is the reinforcement of the behavior by some tremendous reward, one that is other-

75　wise perceived to be unattainable.

Studies by Chein questioned the notion that addiction is a consequence of rewarded behavior. He noted that when normal subjects were given narcotics, although they found the experience pleasurable, they did not

80　become compulsive drug users. His work states that drugs are not inherently rewarding as one of the above proposals suggested. Furthermore, he found that a percentage of addicts actually found the initial drug experience unpleasant, but became addicted anyway. Despite

85　these concerns, the conditioning model is well supported and emphasizes once again that addictive behavior is complex and difficult to place into a single model.

The adaptation theories include the psychological, environmental and social factors that influence addic-

90　tion. Advocates of these theories have analyzed how expectations and beliefs about what a drug will do for the user influence the rewards and behaviors associated with its use. They recognize that any number of factors, including internal and external cues, as well as subjec-

95　tive emotional experiences, will contribute to addictive potential. They support the view that addiction involves cognitive and emotional regulation to which past conditioning contributes.

31. The passage states that all of the following kinds of addictions can be explained by looking at endorphin levels EXCEPT:

A. alcohol.
B. interpersonal relationships.
C. food.
D. nicotine.

GO ON TO THE NEXT PAGE.

32. According to the biological exposure model, drug addiction occurs because:

   F. drugs bring pleasure and euphoria to users.
   G. drug use rewards the user with heightened physical performance.
   H. users develop a psychological need for certain drugs.
   J. users need to consume the drugs to avoid the pain of withdrawal.

33. According to the passage, a "runner's high" probably results from:

   A. a genetic predisposition for exercise.
   B. the pleasurable feeling of exercising.
   C. endorphin production stimulated by running.
   D. social rewards for those who stay in shape.

34. Chein's studies suggest problems with the:

   F. biological exposure theory.
   G. conditioning exposure theory.
   H. addictive inheritance theory.
   J. adaptation theory.

35. The adaptation theory argues that addiction can be influenced by:

   I.   psychological factors.
   II. social factors.
   III. inherited factors.

   A. I only
   B. III only
   C. I and II only
   D. I and III only

36. The passage suggests that the biological and conditioning models of exposure differ chiefly over the role of:

   F. a person's biology in the development of addiction.
   G. reinforced drug use in the development of addiction.
   H. types of addiction in determining biological and conditioned factors.
   J. a user's initial response to an addictive substance in maintaining the addiction.

37. One can reasonably infer from the passage that the biological and conditioning models are grouped together under the exposure theory because they both agree that:

   A. addictions are sustained by pleasurable responses.
   B. the introduction of a narcotic into the body results in metabolic adjustments.
   C. drug use reduces the body's natural endorphin production.
   D. the reinforcement of addiction is fueled by the rewards of drug use.

38. In line 10 "to control for" most nearly means:

   F. to direct.
   G. to authorize.
   H. to monitor.
   J. to regulate.

39. The alcoholism studies described in lines 11–17 suggest that:

   A. environmental factors do not affect addiction, while genetic predisposition is a likely component of addiction.
   B. both environmental factors and genetic predisposition seem likely components of addiction.
   C. genetic predisposition does not affect addiction, while environmental factors are a likely component of addiction.
   D. neither environmental factors nor genetic predisposition plays a role in addiction.

40. One can reasonably infer that the models of addiction described in this passage are:

   F. opposed to each other and mutually exclusive.
   G. representative of a debate between biologists and psychologists.
   H. alternatives to one another, but not necessarily exclusive.
   J. equally well-supported components of a general theory of addiction.

END OF TEST

STOP! DO NOT TURN THE PAGE UNTIL TOLD TO DO S

DO NOT RETURN TO A PREVIOUS TES

SCIENCE REASONING TEST

35 Minutes—40 Questions

DIRECTIONS: This test contains seven passages, each accompanied by several questions. You should select the answer choice that best answers each question. Within the total allotted time for the subject test, you may spend as much time as you wish on each individual passage. Calculator use is not permitted.

Passage I

The electrons of an atom travel around the atom's nucleus [in] orbitals of varying distance and energy. *Valence electrons* [occ]upy the furthermost orbitals. These electrons are not held [as] tightly to the nucleus and play a key role in the formation [of] chemical bonds between atoms, such as occur when atoms [com]bine to form molecules. In certain molecules containing [at]oms called *hydrides*, valence electrons of different atoms [com]bine in a way that leaves no free electrons in the mole[cu]le. Thus, hydride molecules have no "extra" electrons with [wh]ich to interact with other molecules. The attractive forces [be]tween these molecules are weak forces called van der [Wa]als forces. Increases in the total number of electrons will [re]sult in larger van der Waals forces. All hydrides experience [va]n der Waals forces.

Because of their highly electronegative molecular composi[tio]n and physical shape, in addition to van der Waals forces cer[tai]n hydrides can form bonds of great strength with hydrogen [at]oms. These bonds are called *hydrogen bonds*. Hydrogen [bo]nds are roughly 10 times stronger than van der Waals forces. [Wa]ter (H_2O) is an important example of a molecule that exhib[its] hydrogen bonding. The hydrogen bonds in different mole[cu]les have varying strengths based on the proximity of [ele]ctronegative atoms to hydrogen; the closer the atoms, the [mo]re powerful the bond.

Hydrogen bonding and van der Waals forces play an impor[tan]t role in melting and boiling points of substances; the stron[ge]r the forces of attraction in a molecule, the more energy [(hi]gher temperature) needed to melt or boil that molecule. Fig[ur]e 1 shows the boiling points of several hydrides. The row [nu]mber on the bottom refers to the row number on the periodic [tab]le. Only row 2 hydrides on the graph can form hydrogen [bo]nds. Molecules connected by a line have the same number of [hy]drogen atoms.

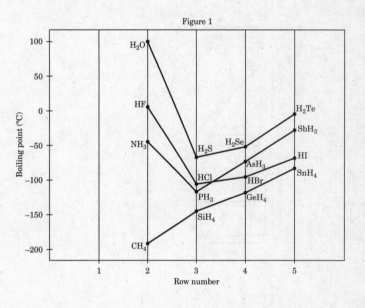

Figure 1

GO ON TO THE NEXT PAGE.

1. H_2Se has a higher boiling point than SiH_4 due to:

   A. hydrogen bonding.
   B. van der Waals forces.
   C. temperature increases.
   D. hydrogen atoms.

2. What graph best illustrates the relationship between temperature and hydrogen bond strength?

   F.

   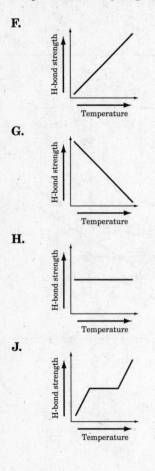

   G.

   H.

   J.

3. Both diethyl ether $(CH_3CH_2)_2O$ and propanol $CH_3(CH_2)_2O$ exhibit hydrogen bonding. What might explain propanol' much higher boiling point?

   A. Propanol molecules have smaller van der Waals force than diethyl ether.
   B. Propanol molecules have greater van der Waals force
   C. Propanol molecules have larger valence orbitals.
   D. Propanol molecules have a different arrangement of highly electronegative atoms.

4. CH_4 molecules are attracted to each other mainly throug

   F. hydrogen bonds.
   G. van der Waals forces.
   H. kinetic energy.
   J. the melting of hydrides.

5. Which of the following hypotheses about hydrides is supported by the information in the passage and the data Figure 1?

   A. Hydrogen bonds are more powerful among row 5 elements than they are among row 4 elements.
   B. The total number of electrons in a molecule increases the row number of a molecule increases.
   C. Molecules with the same number of hydrogen atoms have equally strong van der Waals forces.
   D. Hydrogen bonds and van der Waals forces can sometimes counteract each other.

A comet is a relatively small astrological body that
nsists mostly of ice and dust. When heated by a star, it
pically leaves a visible trail of particles behind, called a tail.
mets often follow highly elliptical orbits. Figures 1–4 show
e paths of four different comets (all paths are seen from the
me perspective in space).

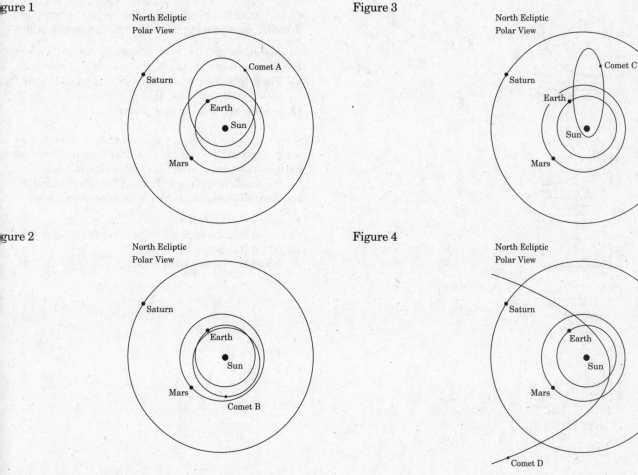

gure 1

Figure 3

gure 2

Figure 4

Comets, like planets, have fixed orbits. Also, like planets,
mets hold to their orbits due to the gravitational force of the
n. The narrower the path of a comet, the more elliptical the
bit is said to be. The eccentricity of an orbit measures how
iptical it is. Eccentricity for an orbit is measured as the dis-
nce from the center of the orbit to one of the foci (the two foci
e the central points of any ellipse), divided by half the dis-
nce of the orbit's longest axis. (Eccentricity can vary from 0 to
a high eccentricity means a skinny ellipse, and a low eccen-
city reflects a rounder, more circular shape.) A comet's period
the time it takes the comet to complete one complete path
ound its orbit—comets whose periods are less than 200 years
e said to be periodic. A comet's perihelion distance measures
distance to the sun at the closest point in its orbit. Comets
pically form at the same time as the planets in a solar system,
t can vary greatly in age.

Table 1				
	Period (years)	Eccentricity	Perihelion (AU)	Comet diameter (meters)
Comet A	6	0.23	0.4423	11
Comet B	52	0.06	0.9242	47
Comet C	266	0.73	0.2685	750
Comet D	2302	0.48	0.7201	1400

The AU (Astronomical Unit) is defined as the distance between the Earth and the Sun.

GO ON TO THE NEXT PAGE.

6. Halley's comet has an orbital period of 76 years. It is:

   F. periodic.
   G. non-periodic.
   H. sometimes periodic and sometimes non-periodic.
   J. neither periodic nor non-periodic.

7. Which graph best illustrates the relationship between period and comet diameter among the data in Table 1?

   A.

   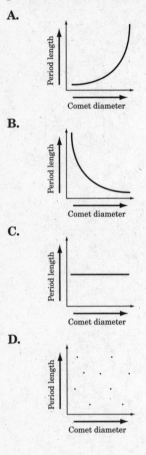

   B.

   C.

   D.

8. According to the data in the passage, Figures 1–4, and Table 1, which of the following is correct?

   F. Eccentricity varies inversely with period length.
   G. Comet C gets roughly twice as hot as comet A.
   H. Period is unrelated to orbit size.
   J. Eccentricity is proportional to comet speed.

9. To an observer standing on Earth, the stellar paths of comets appear markedly different from those of planets (this is true even of comets with nearly circular orbits). Which of the following can best explain why this occurs?

   A. The orbits of comets can change significantly over time.
   B. The speed of comets gradually decreases over time.
   C. The orbits of comets don't lie in the same plane as the solar system and the Milky Way galaxy.
   D. Comets are smaller than planets.

10. A comet's tail is formed by nuclear reactions of various compounds as the comet approaches the sun. The elements in these reactions are lost in space as the tail extends behind the comet. If comet B is judged to have a much smaller tail than comet C, we might conclude that:

    F. comet B is older than comet C.
    G. comet B has a more elliptical orbit than comet C.
    H. comet B is larger than comet C.
    J. comet B is slower than comet C.

ssage III

Scientists have long speculated on how the universe began, d have developed numerous theories on the subject. The two st common explanations are the big bang theory and the ady state theory.

e Big Bang Theory

The big bang theory states that the universe began instantaously about 15 billion years ago, in a tiny point of infinite nsity. Although almost nothing is known for certain about e chaotic first fraction of a second, it is believed that this inil point was the result of a quantum fluctuation of matter. All atter and energy were created at once during this explosion. first, there was only ionized plasma (another phase of matr beyond solid, liquid, and gas), but this soon cooled and sepated into radiation and more ordinary matter (mostly drogen and helium). Eventually, discrepancies in the distrition of matter caused some atoms to clump together and m stars and galaxies. Since then, the universe has continued expand, which means that today all galaxies are drifting farer and farther away from each other. Additionally, the further vay a galaxy is, the faster it appears to be moving. The law of lativity predicts that for any observer at any point in the unirse, it will appear as though the big bang occurred at preely the location the observer occupies. One strong point in vor of the big bang theory is cosmic background radiation: ter 100,000 years, matter started to form into atoms, and the maining radiation could not interact with mostly empty ace. Thus, the big bang theory predicts large amounts of sidual radiation drifting through space. This prediction has rned out to be the case, as radiation increases the temperare of space to about 3K (three degrees above absolute zero).

e Steady State Theory

The steady state theory holds that the laws of physics are e same today as they have always been, and that the universe s always existed. Additionally, the universe is expanding, but t through galaxies receding; rather, more space is continuly being created between galaxies. The matter in the universe s not created at one point, but is instead created continually. this way, the creation of new matter balances out the reducn in density caused by the universe's expansion. New matter created from an as yet unknown energy source that has a gative amount of energy, so that the more matter is created, e less energy is in the source. The opposing phenomena of pansion of matter and the continual creation of matter therere exist in a "steady state." Support for the steady state they comes partly from quantum mechanics, in which athematical calculations suggest that electromagnetic waves metimes travel backwards in time, but can only do so when ey are mathematically symmetrical to other waves traveling rwards in time.

GO ON TO THE NEXT PAGE.

11. Quasars are believed to be extremely distant nuclei of galaxies that are moving farther away. They support which theory?

    A. The big bang theory
    B. The steady state theory
    C. Both theories
    D. Neither theory

12. In 1996, the Hubble Telescope managed to get images of many galaxies billions of light years away. If all of these galaxies looked to be about the same age as our galaxy right now, it would support:

    F. the big bang theory.
    G. the steady state theory.
    H. both theories.
    J. neither theory.

13. According to the big bang theory, at the very start of the universe the plasma was almost, but not quite, perfectly smoothly distributed. This slight discrepancy in distribution eventually led to:

    A. the formation of stars and galaxies.
    B. the expansion of the universe.
    C. background radiation.
    D. radiation waves travelling backwards in time.

14. About which of the following points do the theories differ?

    F. The unequal distribution of matter in the galaxy
    G. The continual expansion of the universe
    H. The continual creation of matter
    J. The existence of physical matter traveling backwards in time

15. Both theories agree that:

    A. the universe is a result of quantum fluctuation.
    B. the universe, as we know it, has always existed.
    C. matter in the universe is not completely evenly distributed.
    D. cosmic radiation is a cause of the universe's expansio

16. For the steady state theory to be true, it requires:

    F. the universe to be relatively new.
    G. a large amount of residual radiation in space.
    H. galaxies to be moving faster than scientists currently believe.
    J. other universes or forces to exist that are as yet undetected.

17. One of the fundamental laws of physics is the First Law Thermodynamics, which states that matter and energy may never be created or destroyed. How might a support of the big bang theory reconcile the theory with this law?

    A. Matter and energy were both plasma at the start of t big bang.
    B. At the start of the big bang, other physical laws may have applied.
    C. Matter was not distributed evenly as the universe expanded.
    D. Matter was caused by background radiation.

GO ON TO THE NEXT PAG

Passage IV

Frisbees work on several important scientific principles. One of these is angular momentum—when a frisbee spins, it resists changes in its direction and the speed at which it spins. Another is the aerodynamic principle of lift. According to the Bernoulli principle, when the air below the frisbee moves faster than the air above the frisbee, the pressure below the frisbee becomes greater than the pressure above, and the air below the frisbee pushes up on the bottom half of the frisbee, creating lift.

Frisbee - Top View

Frisbee - Side View

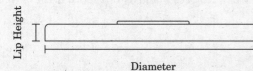

Diameter

The flight distance of twelve frisbees was measured. Each frisbee was thrown with the same amount of initial forward force and angular momentum, and all were launched at the same angle. The frisbees all had the same diameter, but varied in their mass (equivalent to their weight) and in the size of the lip that extends down around the circumference of the frisbee.

Table 1			
Frisbee mass (in grams)	Lip height (in centimeters)	Length of flight (in meters)	Maximum height of flight (in meters)
140	1	25	5
140	1.5	28	6
140	2	30	8
140	2.5	27	9
150	1	23	4
150	1.5	25	7
150	2	26	9
150	2.5	25	10
160	1	20	3
160	1.5	23	5
160	2	22	8
160	2.5	21	11

18. The data in Table 1 allows for analysis of the effects of what characteristic(s) on frisbee flight length?

    F. frisbee mass
    G. lip height
    H. frisbee mass and lip height
    J. maximum flight height

19. According to the table, the flight length of a frisbee can be increased by:

    A. increasing the angle at which the frisbee is thrown.
    B. reducing the lip height.
    C. increasing the lip height.
    D. decreasing the mass of the frisbee.

20. Which of the following graphs best represents the relationship between lip height and flight distance?

    F.

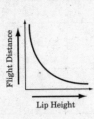

    G.

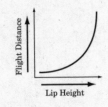

    H.

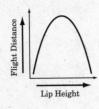

    J.

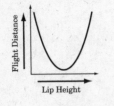

21. According to the data presented in the table, which of the following is the best suggestion to increase the height of a frisbee's flights?

    A. Make the frisbees larger in diameter
    B. Increase lip height of each frisbee
    C. Spin the frisbees at a greater rate of rotation
    D. Make the frisbees heavier

22. What would be the best way to determine the relationship between a frisbee's mass and the maximum height of its flight?

    F. Test with one frisbee, and vary the angle at which the frisbee is thrown
    G. Test with three frisbees of different masses, but with identical lip heights
    H. Test with three frisbees of different masses, but with different lip heights
    J. Test with three frisbees of identical masses, but with different diameters

23. A new company wants to design frisbees with holes in the middle for easier throwing and catching. Suppose three of these new frisbees, weighing 140 grams, 150 grams, and 160 grams respectively, are subjected to precisely the same tests as the frisbees in the experiment above. What would be the most accurate prediction for their flight?

    A. The new frisbees would not fly as high as the old ones.
    B. The new frisbees would fly higher than the old ones.
    C. The new frisbees would not fly as far as the old ones.
    D. The new frisbees would fly farther than the old ones.

ssage V

Lasers are devices that produce highly focused and precise ams of electromagnetic radiation (usually, this radiation is in e form of visible light). Laser is actually an acronym that nds for Light Amplification by Stimulated Emission of Radi- on. The general principle of the laser is based on a property electrons, which are a part of atoms. Each atom has a cleus, consisting of protons and neutrons. Electrons orbit the cleus. Electrons usually inhabit a constant energy level, but n be stimulated to enter high-energy, "excited" states. When ey return to their normal levels, each electron will emit a oton (an electromagnetic particle). One way to induce excited ctrons to their ordinary levels is to pass other photons by em. If the incident photon is of a particular frequency, an ectron will drop to ordinary levels and emit a photon of the me frequency and direction as the original photon.

One type of laser is the ruby laser. It consists of a cylindrical by rod, whose volume is proportional to the diameter of the l times the length. The rod is completely reflective at one end d partly reflective at the other, emitting end. An electric coil ines around the length of the rod. The coil is used to flash ctromagnetic energy at the rod, which causes emission of otons by electrons. The photons in the rod that end up travel- g along the rod lengthwise bounce back and forth on the lective ends, until the increasing intensity of the energy uses a burst of photons at the partly reflective end. The sultant beam of electromagnetic energy is extremely focused, ich means that it can travel a long distance without the size the burst increasing or its strength fading.

One laser manufacturer wants to test the output of lasers th ruby rods of varying dimensions. In addition, the company nts to vary the amount of reflectivity at the end of the rod ere the photon burst is emitted. Table 1 shows data from rious tests. (Note that ruby lasers are rarely built with diam- ers greater than about an inch, due to the expense and diffi- ty of constructing a larger ruby rod.) Figure 1 shows formation on one particular ruby rod as it is stimulated by an ectric coil.

Table 1			
Rod diameter (inches)	Rod length (inches)	End reflectivity	Burst power (Joules)
.5	3	.25	.24
.5	3	.50	.47
.5	3	.75	.36
.4	5	.25	.46
.4	5	.50	.83
.4	5	.75	.75
.8	4	.25	.77
.8	4	.50	1.02
.8	4	.75	.84

Figure 1

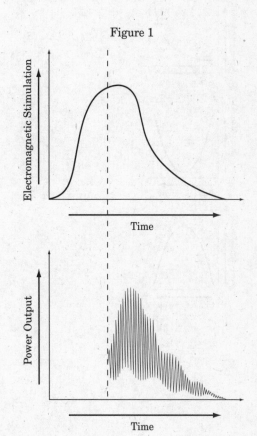

24. According to the passage, the electrons in the crystal are caused to emit photons by:

    F. other photons.
    G. electrons.
    H. protons.
    J. neutrons.

25. Which of the following best represents the relationship between the reflectivity of the emitting end of the rod and power output?

    A.

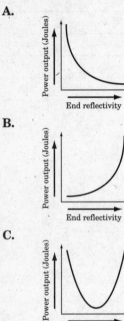

    B.

    C.

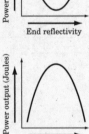

    D.

26. What is the significance of the vertical line in Figure 1?

    F. It shows the maximum power output of the laser.
    G. It shows how long an individual laser burst lasts.
    H. It shows the point where photon excitement is sufficie for a burst.
    J. It shows the maximum amount of electromagnetic stimulation that can be applied to the rod.

27. Which of the following will always lead to an increase in power output?

    A. Decreasing the length of the rod
    B. Increasing the density of the rod
    C. Increasing the volume of the rod
    D. Increasing the reflectivity of the emitting end of the r

28. What might happen to the photons in the ruby that aren' traveling in the direction of the rod?

    F. They increase the reflectivity of the emitting end.
    G. They detract from the total burst output energy.
    H. They get converted into electrons.
    J. They escape along the sides of the rod.

29. For which of the following purposes might lasers be the most useful (assuming that the emitted light is of a frequency and type safe for all types of life forms)?

    A. Signal communications between space satellites
    B. Large spotlights at music concerts
    C. Emergency flashlights
    D. Car headlights

GO ON TO THE NEXT PAG

Passage VI

Luminescence, also called chemiluminescence, is the emission of light without heating. Luminescence occurs when an atom drops from one energy level to another and emits energy in the process. A certain chemical company makes phosphorescent solutions that are used in glowing objects, such as light sticks. The company uses a chemical reaction between a hydrogen peroxide solution, a mixture of a phenyl oxalate ester, and a fluorescent dye to produce the light. When combined, the peroxide oxidizes the ester, which results in an unstable peroxyacid ester. This new ester eventually decomposes into carbon dioxide, and this breakdown releases energy into the dye. The company used various concentrations of solutions, and measured the light output. The time listed refers to the total time for the reaction, that is, how long the solution glowed.

Table 1: Wavelengths of visible light

Color	Wavelength (nanometers)
Red	710
Yellow	635
Green	550
Blue	470
Violet	405

Table 2

Experiment 1

Percent ester/ dye solution #1	Percent hydrogen peroxide solution	Temperature (°C)	Time of reaction (minutes)	Light wavelength (nanometers)
40	60	15	75	715
40	60	20	65	710
40	60	25	58	705
40	60	30	53	700
70	30	15	38	650
70	30	20	30	630
70	30	25	25	610
70	30	30	22	590

Table 3

Experiment 2

A different, newer phenyl oxalate ester was used in testing.

Percent ester/ dye solution #2	Percent hydrogen peroxide solution	Temperature (°C)	Time of reaction (minutes)	Light wavelength (nanometers)
40	60	15	105	500
40	60	20	100	490
40	60	25	97	480
40	60	30	95	470
70	30	15	38	440
70	30	20	34	430
70	30	25	32	420
70	30	30	31	410

GO ON TO THE NEXT PAGE.

30. Which combination and proportion of solutions should be used to make a yellow light stick?

   F. 40% ester/dye solution #1 and 60% hydrogen peroxide solution

   G. 70% ester/dye solution #1 and 30% hydrogen peroxide solution

   H. 40% ester/dye solution #2 and 60% hydrogen peroxide solution

   J. 70% ester/dye solution #2 and 30% hydrogen peroxide solution

31. Which graph best represents the relationship between temperature and reaction time in the tables?

A.

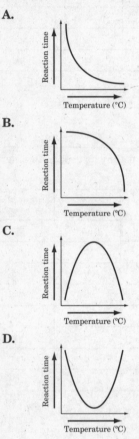

B.

C.

D.

32. Judging by the data in the passage, which of the following statements is correct?

   F. Light color is independent of ester/dye solution concentration.

   G. Increasing the percentage of hydrogen peroxide solution will always cause the reaction time to increase.

   H. Reducing the percentage of hydrogen peroxide solution makes the emitted light more blue.

   J. The effectiveness of hydrogen peroxide in the reaction above is more temperature-dependent than either ester/dye solution.

33. Compared to esther/dye solution #1, ester/dye solution #2

   A. is less susceptible to temperature changes.

   B. is less visible when reacting with hydrogen peroxide solution.

   C. reacts for a longer time.

   D. emits more non-visible light when reacting with hydrogen peroxide solution.

34. If someone has a light stick filled with the chemicals in Table 2 and starts the reaction, the best way to lengthen the reaction time is to put the stick

   F. in a dark closet.

   G. under a bright light.

   H. in a cold cooler or icebox.

   J. in an oven on low heat.

35. What would be the best way to measure the relationship between concentration of the hydrogen peroxide solution and overall reaction time?

   A. Run three tests, each with different concentrations of hydrogen peroxide, and each at a different temperature but with the same ester/dye solution

   B. Run three tests, each with the same concentration of hydrogen peroxide and at the same temperature, but with different ester/dye solutions

   C. Run three tests, each with different concentrations of hydrogen peroxide, but at the same temperature and with the same ester/dye solution

   D. Run three tests, each with the same concentration of hydrogen peroxide, but with different temperatures and ester/dye solutions for each test

A phase diagram shows the temperatures and pressures at ich a substance changes from solid to liquid (melting), liquid ·apor (boiling), and solid to vapor (sublimating). Whenever a ·stance undergoes a phase change from a solid to liquid or ·m a liquid to a vapor, heat is added while the temperature of · substance remains constant. After a phase change is com- ·te, the substance will increase in temperature until the next ·se change. The triple point is defined as the temperature ·l pressure at which the vapor, liquid, and solid phases of a ·stance coincide. Figure 1 is the phase diagram for water and ·ws the triple point:

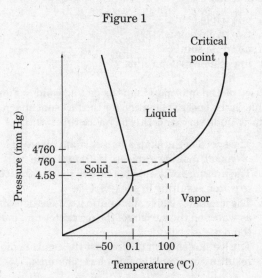

Figure 1

·Note that 760 mm Hg represents one Atmosphere of pres- ·e, which is equivalent to normal air pressure at sea level. At ·s pressure, solid ice converts to liquid water at 0°C and liquid ·ter converts to water vapor at 100°C. Also important is the ·itical point" for a substance. Beyond this temperature, the ·stance cannot exist as a liquid, regardless of pressure.

Figure 2 shows the triple point for carbon dioxide.

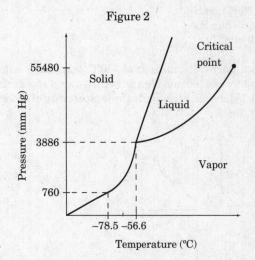

Figure 2

Figure 3 shows helium, which has two separate liquid phases, depending on whether individual atoms bond together or not.

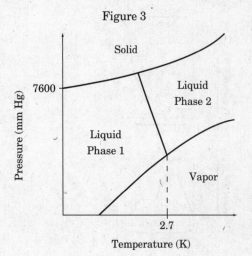

Figure 3

36. The highest pressure at which carbon dioxide will sublimate is:

   F. 55480 mm Hg.
   G. 3886 mm Hg.
   H. 760 mm Hg.
   J. 0 mm Hg.

37. A container of ice, initially at –50°C, is kept at constant pressure of 4760 mm Hg and heated over a steady flame. Which diagram represents the temperature of the water over time?

   A.

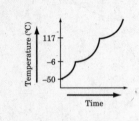

   B.

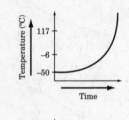

   C.

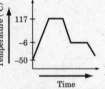

   D.

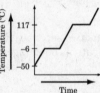

38. When pressure increases, a substance naturally wants to return to a more dense phase. According to Figures 1, 2, and 3, which of the following statements are correct?

   F. Carbon dioxide in solid form is less dense than in liquid form.
   G. Liquid phase 2 of helium is more dense than its solid form.
   H. Liquid phase 1 of helium is more dense than its solid form.
   J. Water in solid form is less dense than in liquid form.

39. According to the definitions in the passage and Figure 3, helium has:

   A. one triple point.
   B. two triple points.
   C. no triple points.
   D. impossible to determine.

40. Based on the information in the passage and in Figure 1, what is the best explanation for the fact that sharp ice skates glide very smoothly on an ice rink?

   F. The speed of the skates causes small pieces of ice to break off, making a smooth path in the ice.
   G. The pressure of the skates causes some of the ice to melt to water, resulting in slick, wet ice.
   H. The ice skates cause sublimation, which then condenses as water on the surface of the ice skates and makes them wet.
   J. The ice skates push the ice past the critical point, resulting in unpredictable phase changes.

Practice Test 2
Explanations

Answers to ACT Practice Test 2

Question Number	Answer	Right	Wrong	Question Number	Answer	Right	Wrong
	English Test				**English Test**		
1.	C			57.	D		
2.	H			58.	F		
3.	D			59.	C		
4.	H			60.	J		
5.	B			61.	B		
6.	J			62.	H		
7.	C			63.	B		
8.	J			64.	J		
9.	C			65.	A		
10.	H			66.	J		
11.	B			67.	C		
12.	J			68.	G		
13.	D			69.	C		
14.	F			70.	J		
15.	B			71.	A		
16.	H			72.	G		
17.	A			73.	C		
18.	H			74.	H		
19.	D			75.	D		
20.	G				**Math Test**		
21.	A						
22.	J			1.	E		
23.	A			2.	H		
24.	H			3.	D		
25.	B			4.	F		
26.	J			5.	D		
27.	A			6.	K		
28.	J			7.	D		
29.	B			8.	J		
30.	F			9.	C		
31.	B			10.	H		
32.	H			11.	B		
33.	B			12.	J		
34.	J			13.	C		
35.	C			14.	F		
36.	G			15.	E		
37.	D			16.	J		
38.	H			17.	C		
39.	B			18.	G		
40.	F			19.	C		
41.	C			20.	G		
42.	J			21.	A		
43.	D			22.	H		
44.	F			23.	E		
45.	A			24.	G		
46.	H			25.	D		
47.	D			26.	H		
48.	H			27.	A		
49.	D			28.	J		
50.	G			29.	B		
51.	B			30.	H		
52.	J			31.	D		
53.	D			32.	K		
54.	F			33.	E		
55.	C			34.	J		
56.	F						

Question Number	Answer	Right	Wrong	Question Number	Answer	Right	Wrong
Math Test				**Reading Test**			
35.	C			28.	H		
36.	H			29.	D		
37.	C			30.	F		
38.	H			31.	B		
39.	E			32.	J		
40.	J			33.	C		
41.	C			34.	G		
42.	H			35.	C		
43.	B			36.	F		
44.	H			37.	D		
45.	D			38.	J		
46.	J			39.	B		
47.	C			40.	H		
48.	G			**Science Reasoning Test**			
49.	C						
50.	H			1.	B		
51.	C			2.	H		
52.	F			3.	D		
53.	B			4.	G		
54.	H			5.	B		
55.	B			6.	F		
56.	G			7.	A		
57.	A			8.	H		
58.	G			9.	C		
59.	C			10.	F		
60.	H			11.	C		
Reading Test				12.	F		
				13.	A		
1.	B			14.	H		
2.	J			15.	C		
3.	A			16.	J		
4.	H			17.	B		
5.	D			18.	H		
6.	F			19.	D		
7.	C			20.	H		
8.	F			21.	B		
9.	B			22.	G		
10.	H			23.	A		
11.	D			24.	F		
12.	F			25.	D		
13.	A			26.	H		
14.	G			27.	C		
15.	A			28.	J		
16.	J			29.	A		
17.	C			30.	G		
18.	G			31.	A		
19.	D			32.	J		
20.	G			33.	A		
21.	C			34.	H		
22.	J			35.	C		
23.	A			36.	G		
24.	G			37.	B		
25.	A			38.	J		
26.	J			39.	C		
27.	C			40.	G		

Calculating Your ACT Score

Calculating your score on the ACT practice tests in this book is a three-step process.

1. Calculate your raw score for each section.

2. Use the conversion table (on the following page) to find your scaled score for each subject test.

3. Average your subject test scaled scores to find your composite score.

Calculating Subject Test Raw Scores

Your raw score on a subject test is equal to the number of questions you answered correctly on that test. The subject test answer keys on the preceding pages will help you to figure out your raw scores.

_____   _____   _____   _____

English Raw Score   Reading Raw Score   Math Raw Score   Science Reasoning Raw Score

Calculating Subject Test Scaled Scores

The conversion table on the following page allows you to look up your raw score for each subject test and see the corresponding scaled score.

_____   _____   _____   _____

English Scaled Score   Reading Scaled Score   Math Scaled Score   Science Reasoning Scaled Score

Calculating the Composite Score

Your composite ACT score, the one that really matters, is the average of your scaled scores on the four subject tests. Add up your scaled scores and divide that sum by four.

_____

Composite Score

ACT Raw-Scaled Score Conversion Chart

Scaled Score	English Raw Score	Math Raw Score	Reading Raw Score	Science Reasoning Raw Score
36	75	60	40	40
35	74	59	39	39
34	73	58	38	38
33	72	57	37	37
32	71	55–56	36	–
31	69–70	53–54	35	36
30	67–68	51–52	34	35
29	65–66	50	33	34
28	63–64	48–49	32	33
27	61–62	45–47	31	32
26	59–60	43–44	29–30	31
25	56–58	41–42	28	29–30
24	53–55	39–40	27	27–28
23	51–52	37–38	26	26
22	49–50	35–36	25	25
21	46–48	33–34	24	24
20	44–45	31–32	22–23	22–23
19	42–43	29–30	20–21	21
18	39–41	26–28	19	19–20
17	37–38	23–25	18	17–18
16	34–36	20–22	17	16
15	32–33	17–19	16	15
14	29–31	14–16	15	14
13	27–28	12–13	14	13
12	24–26	9–11	13	12
11	22–23	8	12	10–11
10	19–21	7	10–11	8–9
9	16–18	6	8–9	7
8	14–15	5	7	6
7	11–13	4	6	5
6	8–10	–	5	4
5	6–7	3	4	3
4	4–5	2	–	2
3	3	–	3	–
2	2	1	2	1
1	1	–	1	–
0	0	0	0	0

English Test

Passage I

1. **C** *Verb Tenses*
The past tense of *he lies* is *he lay*.

2. **H** *Redundancy*
The colon already suggests that you're about to list reasons, which makes redundant the phrase *and those reasons are*.

3. **D** *Redundancy*
Because the phrase *at a very young age* is already there, the phrase *when I was just a child* is redundant.

4. **H** *Transitions and Topic Sentences*
The sentence proposed by **H** sums up the main idea of the third paragraph. **F** contradicts the argument this writer is making, which is that Beatles music *does* age well. **G** and **J** are too vague. They're not terrible, but they're not as good as **H**.

5. **B** *Run-on Sentences*
Both **B** and **C** correct the run on, but only **B** adds the connecting word "but," which makes the most sense in the context of the opposition set up by the sentence. **D** is a run-on.

6. **J** *Subject-Verb Agreement*
Groups is plural, so the plural verb form *make* is correct. *Made* and *did make* are in the wrong tense.

7. **C** *Sentence Fragments*
The presence of verbs is crucial to complete sentences, and **C** has one: *are*. Neither of the other answer choices has a verb.

8. **J** *Connecting and Transitional Words*
This sentence is explaining a cause-and-effect relationship: *because* the Beatles changed, their music is appealing.

9. **C** *Misplaced Modifiers*
The original sentence makes it sound as if Eastern mysticism represented a musical leap. What the writer wants to say is that the album was a musical leap. **B** implies that psychedelic themes represented a musical leap; **D** implies that influence was a musical leap.

10. **H**   *Apostrophes*

To refer to commentary belonging to the album, the possessive *its* is needed. In **G**, *it is* is the expanded version of the incorrect *it's* in the original sentence. The apostrophe in *its'* is incorrect, since *its* is the possessive form of *it*.

11. **B**   *Semicolons*

To separate a modifying phrase ("most of all") from the word it modifies ("exhilarating"), you would use a comma, not a semicolon.

12. **J**   *Identifying Tone*

The author is wistful here, remembering his own childhood and watching his cousin.

13. **D**   *Redundancy*

You don't need both *pity himself* and *feel sorry* for himself, since they mean the same thing; one of the phrases will do. Since *pity himself* is the underlined phrase, that's the one that goes.

14. **F**   No error

15. **B**   *Additional Detail and Evidence*

Adding this after the first sentence clarifies why the writer envies his cousin. Adding it before or after Sentence 3 is redundant.

Passage II

16. **H**   *Redundancy*

There is no need to use the phrases *in the town of* and *in the state of*. They are awkward and superfluous.

17. **A**   No error

18. **H**   *Colons*

The colon, in its succinct way, stands in for the words *was that*. The original semicolon would leave a sentence fragment. **G** and **J** are run-ons.

19. **D**   *Redundancy*

Either *ultimately* or *in the final diagnosis* is sufficient, since they mean the same thing.

20. **G**   *Commas*

The comma is unnecessary.

21. **A**   No error

22. **J**   *Verb Tenses*

When you're talking about hanging a person (as opposed to a painting, for example) the correct past tense is *hanged*.

23. **A**   No error

24. **H**   *Misplaced Modifiers*

In context, the original sentence makes it sound as if the court pronounces victims with vigor. You know from context that what it actually did was pronounce guilty verdicts with vigor, as **H** suggests.

25. **B**   *Identifying Tone*

The word *only* precedes the phrase *three days*, which suggests that the author is emphasizing the brevity of the trials in comparison to the large number of people who died.

26. **J**   *Verb Tenses*

The sentence is in the past tense, so the verb must be as well.

27. **A**   *Additional Detail and Evidence*

At last indicates that Pitts showed up after the damage had been done. *It happened that* is too folksy; *thank goodness* is too casual; and *just in time* is just incorrect, since Pitts came too late to save the many who died.

28. **J**   *Transitions and Topic Sentences*

You're asked to find a good transitional sentence, and **J** does the job by referring back to the previous questions, which had to do with the town and the girls' hysteria, and by looking forward to the next part of the paragraph, which is about theories. **F** is just another question. **G** and **H** are false: there are imaginable factors and various explanations, which the writer proceeds to list.

29. **B**   *Paragraph Reorganization*

It's best to begin a new paragraph after the summary of the historical facts and before the list of questions.

30. **F**   No error

Passage III

31. B *Idioms*

For no particular reason, the rules of idiom state that the correct expression is *nothing so much as*.

32. H *Commas*

The comma makes reading this sentence easier. It separates the time of the event from the reaction of the onlookers. The phrase that begins "attracting" modifies the word *it* and functions as an appositive. Appositives are set off from the rest of the sentence by commas.

33. B *Commas*

This is exactly the same problem encountered in the previous question. The added comma separates the two ideas: Henry Ford was the inventor, and Henry Ford was twenty-eight. The phrase beginning "who" is an appositive, or a descriptive phrase referring to Henry Ford.

34. J *Verb Tenses*

Since Ford recovered in the past, the expression should be "he would have to." *He will have to* suggests that Ford will recover sometime in the future.

35. C *Sentence Fragments*

The comma makes the sentence fragment a dependent clause in a complete sentence.

36. G *Topic Sentences*

Since this paragraph is about the fast, affordable cars Ford made, **G** is best. **F** merely repeats the existing first sentence of the paragraph. **H** is too specific to work as a topic sentence, since it deals with only one small part of the paragraph. **J** would be appropriate not in the third paragraph, but in the fourth.

37. D *Connecting and Transitional Words*

And makes the most sense.

38. H *Redundancy*

Inexpensive means the same thing as *cars that were not particularly costly*, but it is more succinct and therefore better than the original version.

39. B *Colons*

The colon is used to prepare the reader for a list, a question, or, in this case, an explanation.

40. **F** No error

41. **C** *Identifying Tone*

The original sentence is too informal. **C** is more formal and is grammatically correct. **A**, like the original version, is too casual. **B** uses the slangy and imprecise word *factoids*. **D**'s tone is fine, but its syntax is awkward.

42. **J** *Connecting and Transitional Words*

J suggests the contradiction between Ford's friendships and his article-writing. Both **G** and **H** incorrectly imply that because Ford had Jewish friends, he wrote anti-Semitic articles.

43. **D** *Semicolons*

Semicolons are a good way to separate two closely related clauses when both could also stand as independent sentences.

44. **F** No error

45. **A** *Passage Reorganization*

The fourth and fifth paragraphs should be switched. The fifth paragraph should follow the third paragraph, since both paragraphs discuss how Ford changed the industry. The fourth paragraph, which mentions Ford's flaws, should not come between the two related paragraphs. Also, the end of the fourth paragraph makes a better concluding sentence than the end of the fifth paragraph.

Passage IV

46. **H** *Run-on Sentences*

The word *yet* correctly suggests that people's ideas about abstract expressionism are wrong.

47. **D** *Run-on Sentences*

The correct answer solves the run-on by changing the comma to a semicolon. This change allows the two independent clauses to exist side by side.

48. **H** *Apostrophes*

The passage is talking about the sides belonging to the painting, so the word used should be the possessive *its*.

49. **D**   *Subject-Verb Agreement, Verb Tenses*

Only **D** both matches the plural verb *were* with the plural noun *paintings,* and puts the verb in the past tense. **B** and **C** are singular verbs.

50. **G**   *Idioms*

There's no grammar rule to explain it, but *from* is wrong in this context. *Because of* sounds much more formal and correct. *Since* is also idiomatically incorrect. *In spite of* expresses precisely the opposite of the intended meaning.

51. **B**   *Paragraph Reorganization*

The tip-off that this sentence should go after the second sentence is the phrase *around that time*. The only other mention of time is in the first sentence, with *1940s*. Since *that time* must refer to something, the two sentences should go together.

52. **J**   *Sentence Reorganization*

The passage is talking about Pollock, the abstract expressionist. The word *expressionist* should follow the word *abstract*.

53. **D**   *Paragraph Reorganization*

The order proposed by **D** goes in increasing order of specificity: who Pollock was, who he was in the movement, how he worked.

54. **F**   *Passage Reorganization*

This is a general sentence describing the art movement, so it should go in the first paragraph, which is a general description of the movement.

55. **C**   *Commas*

The correct answer eliminates the superfluous comma.

56. **F**   *Additional Detail and Evidence*

Answer **F** fits the context, telling the reader that what's coming will contrast with what's just been said.

57. **D**   *Idioms*

In English, the expression is "a place where __ and __ could meet." It's got to be *where*.

58. **F**   No error

59. **C**   *Comparative and Superlative Modifiers*

C is the only answer choice comprised of two words that are in the English language. *Famouser* and *famousest* are not actual words.

60. **J**   *Idioms*

The original phrasing is commonly heard in spoken English, but it is incorrect in formal writing.

Passage V

61. **B**   *Analysis*

The author does not write the single word *barista* in error, but as an interesting way of starting the essay. The word by itself is meant to replicate the writer's original experience of seeing the sign.

62. **H**   *Redundancy*

Naïve expresses the exact meaning of the underlined phrase, and in half the space.

63. **B**   *Apostrophes*

We're talking about plural *months*. *Month's*, with its possessive apostrophe *s*, suggests something belonging to a *month*, so the apostrophe must be removed.

64. **J**   *Comparative and Superlative Modifiers*

Because the writer hasn't yet mentioned a second job for comparison, she must use *hard*. The superlative *hardest* can only be used when comparing three or more items.

65. **A**   *No Error*

All of the exclamations are inappropriate. Each of the three exclamations listed is too informal and breathless to work with the rest of the essay.

66. **J**   *Idioms*

Because of customs of the English language, we use the phrase *ringing up* to describe the process of tallying purchases.

67. **C**   *Commas*

The additional comma makes the sentence more readable.

68. **G**   *Parallel Structure*

The structure of the sentence is " I watched … , read … , and listened."

69. **C**   *Identifying Tone*

The writer does not actually believe she was exposed to *millions* of lectures; she is exaggerating to stress her own frustration.

70. **J** *Connecting and Transitional Words*

The word *but* is illogical in this sentence.

71. **A** *No error*

72. **G** *Verb Tenses*

Since the essay is written entirely in the past tense, this sentence should be no exception. **G** is the only choice that uses the past tense verb *were*.

73. **C** *Run-on Sentences*

C makes the sentence complete by inserting a semicolon between the two independent clauses.

74. **H** *Pronoun-Antecedent Agreement*

The passage is talking about one customer, so the pronoun used to refer to that customer must be singular.

75. **D** *Sentence Reorganization*

The phrase *a sigh of disgust* is correct.

Math Test

1. **E** *Pre-Algebra: Ratios*

This question is fairly straightforward—all you need to do is cross-multiply the terms and solve for x. Cross multiplication gives you $6x = 72$, and dividing both sides by six gives you $x = 12$. Therefore, **E** is the right answer.

2. **H** *Pre-Algebra: Percents*

This question tests basic definitions of percentages. To find the percentage of the students who gave an "Excellent" rating, you need to know the total number of students. This is 7 (Excellent) plus 14 (Average) plus 4 (Poor), which is 25. The percentage, then, is just 7 divided by 25 (a calculator might be useful for this calculation). Therefore, **H** is the right answer.

3. **D** *Pre-Algebra: Mean*

This question indirectly tests you on your knowledge of the mean. The difficult part of the question is translating the words into an equation that can be solved (once this is done, the question is fairly easy). Given the information presented, you know all six scores average to 84. We don't know any of the individual test scores, but we do know that the first five scores averaged to 82. Put another way, the first five scores (which, taken together) are known, and added to the sixth score (which we don't know) all average to 84. This can be written as $(82 \times 5 + x)/6 = 84$, where x is the unknown test score. Multiplying both sides of the equation by 6 and multiplying 82 with 5 results in $410 + x = 504$. This, in turn, gives you the answer, **D**.

4. **F**   *Pre-algebra: Numbers*

Conceivably, there could be many different lengths that would answer this question correctly, so you have to look at the different options presented in the answers. The key is that the answer, multiplied by 8, is less than 50, and also that the difference between 50 and the multiplied number is less than the length of the piece. 2×8 is 16, and the leftover piece (34 meters) is longer than the length of the pieces. 3×8 is 24, and the leftover piece is too long. 4×8 is 32, and the leftover piece is too long. 5×8 is 40, and the leftover piece is too long. 6×8 is 48, and the leftover piece is 2 meters, which answers the question. Therefore, **F** is the answer.

5. **D**   *Algebra: Linear Equations*

To solve for a variable, you want to get it alone on one side of the equal sign. Here, you first need to eliminate the fraction, which you can do by multiplying both sides by the denominator (7). This gives you $x + 28 = 56$. Subtracting 28 from both sides yields $x = 28$, so **D** is the answer.

6. **K**   *Plane Geometry: Polygons*

You should know that the area of a square is the length of a side, well, squared. So you need to know the length of a side, which is equal to one-fourth of the perimeter (since a square has four equal sides). Dividing the length of the perimeter by four can be done a couple of ways; the easiest is just to divide each of the two terms by four. This leaves the length of a side as $x - 3$. The square of this value can be written as $(x - 3)^2$, and if you use FOIL to multiply it out you get $x^2 - 6x + 9$. This means **K** is the answer.

7. **D**   *Plane Geometry: Polygons*

To answer this question, you need only add up the different values in the picture and do one small calculation. The only distance you don't know is the middle part on the right side, but the entire right side has to equal 18 cm, since the angles joining all the sides are right angles. If you call the unknown part x, then you can formulate $18 = 4 + 4 + x$, and solving for x gives you $x = 10$. Now you can add all the sides together: $18 + 20 + 20 + 4 + 4 + 10 + 8 + 8 = 92$. This means **D** is the right answer.

8. **J**   *Algebra: Simplification*

This question tests your basic ability to simplify an expression. Combining like terms, you get $4b - 3a$, and if you look at the answers, you'll see that **J** matches.

9. **C**   *Plane Geometry: Triangles*

Solving this question involves nothing more than the Pythagorean theorem. The Theorem is $c = \sqrt{a^2 + b^2}$, where c is the hypotenuse ($\overline{AB}$ in the diagram) and a and b are the two shorter sides. Plugging the information from the diagram into the theorem gives you $\overline{AB} = \sqrt{6^2 + 7^2} = \sqrt{36 + 49} = \sqrt{85}$. **C** is the right answer.

10. **H**   *Pre-Algebra: Absolute Value*

This question tests your knowledge of not only the meaning of the absolute value operator, but also the order in which this operator gets evaluated when other operators are involved (in this case, the other operator is the minus sign, –). $-|5|$ means to take the value of $|5|$ (which is 5) and negate it. $|-5|$, however, evaluates to 5 since it asks you to evaluate the absolute value of –5. Thus, the question asks for the sum of –5 and 5, which is 0. Thus, the right answer is **H**.

11. **B**   *Pre-Algebra: Percents*

Here, you need to know how to calculate percentage increases in a number. You can do this in two ways: find 3% of $2,700 and add it to the total, or simply multiply $2,700 by 1.03 (which is like calculating 103% of $2,700, which is the same thing). Either way, the answer is $2,781, answer **B**.

12. **J**   *Pre-Algebra: Multiples*

Answering this question depends on just knowing the definitions of greatest common factor (GCF) and least common multiple (LCM). You need to look at each answer pair and see if it fits the question. 3 and 6 have GCF 3, but their LCM is 6. 3 and 9 have GCF 3, but their LCM is 9. 6 and 9 have a GCF of 3, but their LCM is 18. 3 and 27 have GCF 3 and an LCM of 27 (therefore **J** is right). 9 and 27 have GCF 9 and LCM 27.

13. **C**   *Algebra: Substitution*

Even though this question involves two variables, it is a straightforward substitution: wherever you see x and y in the long equation, you should replace them by 4 and –1, respectively. Doing this gives you $(4 + (-1))^2 - 2(4) - 2(-1)$. If you do all these calculations, you get $9 - 8 + 2$, which is 3. This means **C** is the right answer.

14. **F**   *Plane Geometry: Polygons*

When calculating the area of a parallelogram, remember to use width (or base) times height, not width times length. In order to find out the height of this parallelogram, your best bet is to draw an imaginary line (an altitude) straight down from corner D to form a triangle on the left side. Since the new line will make a right angle with the base of the parallelogram, the new triangle is a 30-60-90 triangle (you know the inside angle by point D will be 30° since a triangle's angles have to add up to 180°, and the other two angles are known to be 60° and 90°). In a 30-60-90 triangle, the ratio of side lengths are

$2 : 1 : \sqrt{3}$, which measure the hypotenuse, the short leg, and the long leg, respectively. The diagram gives you the length of the hypotenuse, so you have to come up with the long leg of the triangle. A good way to do this is to set up a ratio. If you call the altitude x, you get $\frac{5}{x} = 2/\sqrt{3}$. Cross-multiplication yields $5\sqrt{3} = 2x$, and solving for x leaves you with $x = \frac{5}{2}\sqrt{3}$. Now you can find the area of the parallelogram: base $\times$ height $= 12 \times \frac{5}{2}\sqrt{3} = 30\sqrt{3}$. Therefore, choice **F** is correct.

15. **E**   *Intermediate Algebra: Quadratics*

To factor a quadratic equation, your best bet is usually to look at the factors of the last term, in this case 1, 2, 5, and 10. Which pair has 10 as a product and can be added or subtracted to form 3 (the middle term's coefficient)? It turns out to be 5 and 2, since $5 \times 2 = 10$ and $5 - 2 = 3$. You now have the two terms of the factoring, but need their signs. Since the middle term is positive and the last term is negative, one of the factored terms has to be negative and the other positive, and the larger factor is the positive one. All this information gives you the factored equation: $(x + 5)(x - 2)$. Given this, the right answer is **E**.

16. **J**   *Pre-Algebra: Percents*

This question might be a little trickier than it first appears (the answer is not 5 divided by 7, for instance). You need to find what percentage increase, when multiplied by 5, results in 7. You can set up a small equation to do this: $5x = 7$. Solving for x gives you $x = \frac{7}{5}$, or $x = 140\%$ This means that 5 has to be increased by 40% (since 140% is 100% of 5 plus another 40%) to get the value of 7. Therefore, **J** is the right answer.

17. **C**   *Coordinate Geometry: Slope*

To find the slope of a line, you have to get the line in the standard equation $y = mx + b$. In other words, you should solve for y. Doing that for this equation first gives you $4y = 2x - 8$, and another step of algebra results in $y = \frac{1}{2}x - 2$. Therefore, the m term (the slope) is $\frac{1}{2}$, and **C** is the right choice, because parallel lines have the same slope.

18. **G**   *Coordinate Geometry: Graphing Equations*

To answer this question, you need to know what the graph of a cubed variable looks like. Unless you have a graphing calculator, there aren't really any good ways of figuring it out (if you ever get desperate, you can always try random values for x and try to quickly sketch the graph, but it's good to go to the test knowing these graphs). Answers **F** and **G** show typical cubic graphs, but only one of them is the correct choice. Remember that the term in a polynomial without a variable determines where the graph crosses the y-axis; in this case the -2 term indicates that the function crosses the y-axis at -2. That means **G** is the right answer.

19. **C**   *Algebra: Simplification*

When adding two polynomials, you often can't do much. You can only combine terms that have the same variable(s) raised to the same power(s). In this case, the only terms that can be combined are $2xy^2$ and $-3xy^2$, which gives you $-xy^2$. Putting the terms all together gives you $4xy + x^2y^2 - xy^2$, which means that **C** is the right answer.

20. **G**   *Pre-Algebra: Mean*

This question tests your basic knowledge of average, or the mean. All you need to know is the mean for the five total donations. Even though you don't know what the individual first four donations were, this is not important—all you need to know is the number of donations and their total value. The total value is $4 \times \$135,000 + \$170,000$, which is \$710,000. Divided by 5, this gives the answer, **G**.

21. **A**   *Algebra: Simplification*

When simplifying an expression, there are a number of things you can try. Your best bet is to first try to simplify numerical coefficients. Here, all the numbers have a factor of 2, so dividing every number by 2 (or, put another way, multiplying top and bottom of the fraction by ½) gives you $^{x\,+\,2}/_{4x}$. A look at the answers reveals that this is equivalent to answer **A**.

22. **H**   *Trigonometry: SOHCAHTOA*

It might be useful to draw out this triangle to solve the question. The longest side of the right triangle is always the hypotenuse, and the smallest angle will be the one opposite the shortest leg (the angle opposite the side of length 2). According to SOHCAHTOA, the cosine of the angle is the adjacent leg over the hypotenuse, which in this case must be $2\sqrt{3}/4$. This reduces to $\sqrt{3}/2$, so **H** is correct.

23. **E**   *Algebra: Expressions*

This question is fairly tricky, largely because of the way it's worded. If you find yourself confused by the wording of a question like this, just take one sentence, or phrase, at a time. Sarah has n marbles, while Margaret has seven more than her. This can be written as $n + 7$. Emma, in turn, has two fewer than Margaret. This can be written as $n + 7 - 2$, or just $n + 5$. Now you know how many marbles all the girls have (or at least you sort of know; you don't know what n is, but that doesn't matter) so you can add them up. This gives you $3n + 12$. Typically, this is not one of the answers, which might make you think the calculations have been wrong. However, $3n + 12$ can be factored into $3(n + 4)$, which is answer **E**. There's no set method to try if an answer you think is correct doesn't appear among the choices, but factoring your answer is often a good bet.

24. **G**   *Intermediate Algebra: Quadratics*

This question might look hard or confusing, but if you know how to approach it, it isn't too difficult. The key to getting the right answer is using the fact that the equation has only one possible solution; this means that when factored, each of the two binomials is identical. Moreover, you should know that when you multiply out a factored quadratic equation, the middle term is the sum of the second term of each binomial. So, you know that −8 is the sum of two numbers, each of which is identical. This means the number has to be −4. Now, you have a factored form of the equation: $(x − 4)(x − 4)$, and can multiply it out to determine the value of z: $x^2 − 8x + 16 = 0$. z, therefore, is 16, and **G** is the answer.

25. **D**   *Plane Geometry: Triangles*

The easiest way to answer this question is to realize that the triangle is not just isosceles, but a 45-45-90 triangle, a special right triangle. You can discover this by seeing that two sides are equal, and the third is the length of one of the sides multiplied by $\sqrt{2}$. This means the answer is a right angle; answer **D**. If you don't realize that this is a special right triangle, there are ways to figure out the measure of the angle. However, this goes beyond the material covered in the ACT so we won't go over it here. If a question ever gives you the lengths of a triangle's sides and asks you for an angle, it's practically guaranteed that the triangle is one of the special right triangles.

26. **H**   *Pre-Algebra: Exponents*

This question can look imposing, but if you keep track of the proper order of operations it isn't bad. First, you will need to distribute the exponents outside the first and second set of parentheses. In the first set of parentheses, the 2 as well as the a^3 are squared, resulting in $4a^6$ (note that when one exponent is raised to another one, they are multiplied). In the second set of parentheses, cubing the $-a^2$ results in $-a^6$ (you can imagine that the − sign in front stands for a −1 that gets cubed, if that makes more sense). Adding these two terms together is possible, since in each term the variable is raised to the same exponent, and gives you **H**.

27. **A**   *Pre-Algebra: Ratios*

In order to find price per inch, you need to find the total number of inches: 2.5 feet × 12 inches per foot = 30 inches. The total sandwich price divided by 30 is $0.25, which is answer **A**.

28. **J**   *Intermediate Algebra: Systems of Equations*

Here, you should first solve for one variable and then plug in the value into the other equation. Choosing the second equation to use to solve for y gives you $y = 13 - 2x$. This can be used in the first equation to get $2x - 2(13 - 2x) = 4$. Multiplying out gives you $2x - 26 + 4x = 4$. Another step of simplification yields $6x = 30$, which means $x = 5$ and **J** is the answer.

29. **B**   *Coordinate Geometry: Number Lines and Inequalities*

To best figure out what the answer should look like, you should isolate x: $x > -3$. Looking at this form of the question, you can see that a valid value for x can be any value greater (but not equal to) –3. Only graph **B** matches this description, so it's the correct answer.

30. **H**   *Intermediate Algebra: Relationships*

If a variable varies inversely with another, then one must increase when the other decreases. For this question, you'll need to look at every answer to see if it meets this criterion. **F** is incorrect, because if x increases, so does y (although it increases faster). **G** is incorrect, because if x increases, y increases also. **H** is correct, because if x increases, the value of y decreases. **J** is incorrect, because if x increases so does y, although y increases more slowly. **K** is incorrect, because if x increases, y must increase along with it.

31. **D**   *Coordinate Geometry: Distance and Midpoints*

To find the midpoint of a line segment, you simply average the coordinates of its endpoints. The average x-coordinate is $^{-2\,+\,6}\!/_2 = {}^4\!/_2 = 2$, and the average y-coordinate is $^{4\,+\,2}\!/_2 = {}^6\!/_2 = 3$. This means the coordinates are (2, 3), and **D** is the right answer.

32. **K**   *Coordinate Geometry: Parallel and Perpendicular*

It is part of the definition of "parallel-ness" that if two lines are parallel, they have exactly the same slope. In the general equation for a line, $y = mx + b$, m is the slope. This means that the slope of the first line is 3, and the slope of the second line is 3. Therefore, **K** is the right answer.

33. **E**   *Coordinate Geometry: Number Lines and Inequalities*

Looking at the graph, you can see that valid values of x are those that are less than –4 or greater than –2. These inequalities can be expressed as $x < -4$ or $x > -2$. This means choice **E** is correct.

34. **J**   *Algebra: Expressions*

This question tests your ability to write expressions for relationships between variables and numbers. The key to answering this question is knowing how to represent the price of one soda and the price of one slice of pizza. Even though you can't know exactly what those prices are, you know, for instance, that \$3.50 buys x sodas. This means that one soda costs $3.50 \div x$ (meaning, the price of one soda goes into \$3.50 x times), or $^{3.50}\!/_x$. The same line of reasoning allows you to calculate the price of one slice of pizza: $^{4.40}\!/_y$. Now that you know what the individual prices of sodas and slices are, you can actually answer the original question: the price for 4 sodas and three slices. Four sodas is just 4 times the price of one soda, $4(^{3.50}\!/_x)$; and three slices is three times the price of one slice, $3(^{4.40}\!/_y)$. Adding them together gives you $4(^{3.50}\!/_x) + 3(^{4.40}\!/_y)$, or answer **J**.

35. **C**   *Intermediate Algebra: Systems of Equations*

The best approach here is to solve for one variable using one equation, and then solve for the other variable using the other equation. Solving first for y using the first equation, you get $y = 7 - 3x$, and plugging this into the second equation results in $2x - 2(7 - 3x) = 10$. Multiply this out, and you get $2x - 14 + 6x = 10$. Combine like terms to get $8x = 24$. Dividing, you get $x = 3$, and the right answer is **C**.

36. **H**   *Trigonometry: SOHCAHTOA*

You might recognize the dimensions of this right triangle right away: it's a 5-12-13 triangle, and comes up quite a bit on the ACT. However, you don't need to know this to answer the question. Since the triangle is a right triangle, if you know two side lengths you can use the Pythagorean theorem to find the third: $c = \sqrt{a^2 + b^2}$ Filling in the numbers from the equation (remember that according to SOHCAHTOA, 5 is the length of the leg opposite $\angle B$, and 13 is the length of the hypotenuse) gives you $13 = \sqrt{a^2 + 5^2}$. Squaring both sides and simplifying yields $a^2 = 169 - 25$, and solving for a reveals that $a = 12$. Now you have the side adjacent to $\angle B$, so you can calculate the adjacent side over the hypotenuse: $^{12}\!/_{13}$. Therefore, **H** is the answer.

37. **C**   *Intermediate Algebra: Systems of Equations*

This question consists of several different types of calculation. The first part is to solve for a and b. In the first equation, you can isolate a to get $a = b + 2$, which you can plug into the second equation to get $b + 2 + b = 8$. Solving for b, you get $b = 3$. In turn, use this value in the first equation to find a: $a - 3 = 2$, which reduces to $a = 5$. $a - b$, then, is equal to $5 - 3 = 2$, and 2^2 is 4, so **C** is the answer.

38. **H**   *Algebra: Substitution*

This question is different from many substitution questions, and therefore a little tricky. In fact, the best substitution to do is not the one that you may find the most intuitive. If you look at the answers, you'll see that all of them are expressions in terms of the variable x (when it comes to substitution questions, glancing quickly at the answers is sometimes especially useful). Since there are two equations and two variables, you could substitute one variable for the other in either equation. Looking at the second one, $y + 1$ appears as a term. Since this is the value of x, it might make sense to replace this term with x. This gives you $x^2 - 2(x)^2$, which simplifies to answer **H**. If it seems like the suggested substitution is random, well, it is. The fact that $y + 1$, the exact value of x, appears as a term in the second equation is a clue as to how to solve the problem in the easiest possible way. With some practice, you can learn how to spot clues like these to solve questions as quickly as possible.

39. **E**   *Algebra: Substitution*

Don't let any foreign terms in this question confuse you—it's actually pretty simple. The problem gives you one equation with two variables, and values for those two variables to plug in. Substituting the original price and the number of years into the original equation, you get $\$8000 \times 1/(1.25(5))$, or $\$8000/6.25$. The final calculation (a calculator is useful) results in $\$1280$, which means **E** is correct.

40. **J**   *Plane Geometry: Triangles*

Answering this question requires several steps, and a familiarity with properties of similar triangles. If the perimeter of ΔB is twice that of ΔA, that means each of the sides of B are twice as long as those of A. This, in turn, means that the two shorter sides of ΔB are 10 cm and 24 cm. To find the hypotenuse of B, you need to use the Pythagorean Theorem (it might seem tempting to try to use the perimeter somehow, but it isn't possible to find the hypotenuse using anything except the Pythagorean Theorem in this case). The theorem is $c = \sqrt{a^2 + b^2}$ where c is the hypotenuse and a and b are the two smaller sides. You know a and b, so you can plug in those values (ignoring units for simplicity): $c = \sqrt{10^2 + 24^2} = \sqrt{100 + 576} = \sqrt{676} = 26$. Therefore, **J** is the right answer.

41. **C**   *Plane Geometry: Polygons*

If the square has a side length of x, then its area must be x^2. If the new rectangle has length $x + 1$, and width $x + 2$, then its area is $(x + 1)(x + 2)$. Using FOIL, you get $x^2 + 3x + 2$. The difference in area is the new area minus the old one, which can be written as $x^2 + 3x + 2 - x^2$ and simplifies to $3x + 2$. Therefore, **C** is correct.

42. **H**   *Plane Geometry: Circles*

A glance at the diagram might make this question seem tough, but to answer it you need only know how to calculate two things: the area of a triangle and the area of a circle. The area of the triangle is $A = \frac{1}{2}bh$, where b is the base and h is the height. Since the triangle passes through the radius r of the circle, $b = 2r$ and $h = r$. The problem states that $r = 4$, so solve for the area of the triangle: $A = \frac{1}{2}(2h)(h) = \frac{1}{2}(2 \times 4)(4) = \frac{1}{2}(32) = 16$. The area of a circle is $A = \pi r^2 = \pi(4)^2 = 16\pi$. The shaded area represents the area of the circle minus the area of the triangle, which is $A' = 16\pi - 16$. However, this isn't one of the answers, so you need to do some more work. Looking at the result, you should see that it can be factored—each term in the binomial has a coefficient of **16**. Factoring gives you $16(\pi - 1)$. Again, this is not one of the answer choices. But if you look at all the answers, you can see that choice **H** is similar (don't be lured by **K**, which is not equivalent to the answer). $4^2 = 16$, which means that **H** is the right answer. The ACT will often try to trick you by presenting the right answer in a format that's not the same as you got by answering the question. If you answer a question and don't see your answer among the choices, don't panic. If you're confident you did it right, try to tweak your answer a bit using factoring or some other technique.

43. **B**   *Plane Geometry: Circles*

The formula for circumference of a circle is $C = 2\pi r$, where C is circumference and r is radius. Since $C = \pi$, you can write $\pi = 2\pi r$, and solve for r. It might look strange to see π on both sides of the equation, but remember that it's just an ordinary number. Since it's on both sides, it cancels out, and dividing each side by 2 gives you $r = \frac{1}{2}$, meaning **B** is the answer.

44. **H**   *Plane Geometry: Polygons*

To answer this question you need to know the old yard area and the new yard area. The area of a rectangle is width times length, so the old area is $8 \times 20 = 160$. The new area is $(8 + 2) \times 20 = 10 \times 20 = 200$. $200 - 160 = 40$, which means **H** is the answer.

45. **D**   *Intermediate Algebra: Quadratics*

A key to doing well on the ACT is being able to work quickly, and a big part of this is recognizing the correct approach to a problem quickly. If you're asked to solve a quadratic equation that looks like it might be hard to factor, your best bet is to use the quadratic formula. (If you try to factor, you might be tempted to get rid of the 3 by multiplying everything in the equation by ⅓, but this just leads to trouble.) You could use the quadratic formula to solve any quadratic equation, but usually it's faster to factor. But not in this case. The formula, if you remember (and you should definitely memorize it), is

$$x = \frac{-b \pm \sqrt{b^2 - 4ac}}{2a}$$

In this question, a is 3, b is −1, and c is −2. Plugging these values into the formula gives you

$$x = \frac{1 \pm \sqrt{(-1)^2 - 4(3)(-2)}}{2(3)}$$

Simplifying, you get

$$x = \frac{1 \pm \sqrt{1 + 24}}{6}$$

You could also factor this equation into $(3x + 2)(x - 1) = 0$ and solve for $x = 1$ or $x = {}^{-2}\!/_3$. Since the question asks for a positive answer, it must be 1, or choice **D**. One more step of simplification results in $x = {}^{(1 \pm 5)}\!/_6$, and since the question requests a positive answer, the answer is $x = {}^6\!/_6$, which simplifies to 1. Therefore, **D** is the answer.

46. **J**   *Plane Geometry: Polygons*

When you're asked to calculate the area of an irregular figure, it's usually best to separate it into manageable parts. In this case, the figure can be broken down into two rectangles. The only dimension that's not known yet is the height of the smaller rectangle. Since all the angles are right angles, you know that the height of the smaller rectangle, plus 9 cm, must equal the height of the entire left side, which is 15 cm. This means that the height of the little rectangle is 6 cm. The area of a rectangle is its width times its height, so the area of the small rectangle is $6 \times 4 = 24$. The area of the larger rectangle is $12 \times 9 = 108$. Adding them together, you get $24 + 108 = 132$, so **J** is the answer. You can also divide the figure into two rectangles by drawing a line of length 9 parallel to the 9 cm side. This gives you two rectangles with areas of $9 \times 8 = 72 + 15 \times 4 = 60$ or 132.

47. **C**   *Intermediate Algebra: Logarithms*

To answer this question, you need to remember how to convert a logarithmic equation into a more conventional one. $\log_x 16 = 4$ is equivalent to $x^4 = 16$. This might not be so helpful, however, but you can simplify it further (if you have a calculator that can calculate this root, you're all set, but you don't need one). You can take the square root of both sides, which leaves you with $x^2 = 4$. This is more manageable, and in fact you can do the same thing again to give you $x = 2$. Therefore, **C** is the right answer.

48. G   *Intermediate Algebra: Matrices*

Matrices can seem imposing, but adding and subtracting them isn't very hard at all. If you're subtracting one matrix from another, as this question asks you to do, all you have to do is subtract each corresponding member in the second matrix from the first. For example, the top left element of matrix Y has the value 1, and the corresponding element in matrix X has the value -1. Subtracting, $-1 - 1 = -2$, so the resultant matrix should have a -2 value at the top left. If you do this for all four elements in each matrix, you get the correct matrix:

$$\begin{bmatrix} -2 & 6 \\ 0 & 0 \end{bmatrix}$$

49. C   *Algebra: Inequalities*

For this question, you first need to translate the description of the problem into an extended inequality. If x is the length of the side of a square, then x^2 represents the area. Dropping units for simplicity's sake, we get $4 < x^2 < 81$. It's perfectly legal to do an operation to an inequality as long as you do it to all terms, so we can take the square root of everything in order to get an expression for x: $2 < x < 9$. Looking at the provided answers, we see that **C** is correct.

50. H   *Trigonometry: SOHCAHTOA*

To find the sine of $\angle A$, you first need to know the length of hypotenuse $\overline{CA}$ (according to SOHCAHTOA, the sine of an angle is the opposite leg over the hypotenuse). Since $\triangle ABC$ is a right triangle, you can use the Pythagorean theorem to get the hypotenuse: $\overline{CA} = \sqrt{(\overline{CB})^2 + (\overline{BA})^2} = \sqrt{1^2 + 3^2} = \sqrt{1 + 9} = \sqrt{10}$. The sine of $\angle A$, then, is $1/\sqrt{10}$, so choice **H** is correct.

51. C   *Trigonometry: Trigonometric Graphs*

The amplitude of a standard sine curve is 1, so you have to look how the other parts of the equation might modify that (remember that amplitude is the difference between the highest value and average value of a function). Isolating y gives you $y = 2 \sin x + 1$. The 2 in front of the sin means that the amplitude is going to be multiplied by 2, giving the graph an amplitude of 2. The $+1$ only raises the graph one unit; it does not alter the amplitude, and **C** is the right answer.

52. F   *Plane Geometry: Lines and Angles*

The right approach to this question might not be obvious. The key to finding the value of x (and then the answer to the question) is knowing that opposite angles are equal. This means that $\angle AEB = x - 100°$. Also, angles that form a straight line add up to 180°, so $\angle AEB + \angle BED = 180°$. Replacing the angles with their values, you get $x - 100° + x = 180°$. Solving for x gives you $x = 140°$. This allows you to solve the question, since $\angle CED = x - 100° = 140° - 100° = 40°$. Therefore, **F** is the right answer.

53. B   *Plane Geometry: Triangles*

This question is a little difficult—to answer it, you'll need to know several properties of triangles and do harder-than-average arithmetic. Since $\overline{BD}$ is an altitude, it forms a 90° angle with $\overline{AC}$, and $\angle ABC$ is 60° (because ΔABC is equilateral, all its angles are 60°). The three angles in a triangle must add up to 180°, so $180° = 90° + 60° + \angle DBC$. Solving for $\angle DBC$ gives you $\angle DBC = 30°$, which means ΔDBC is a 30-60-90 triangle, a special right triangle. Recall that in one of these triangles, if the hypotenuse is $2x$, the shorter leg is x and the longer leg is $x\sqrt{3}$. You know that the longer leg is length 3, but you have to use these relationships to find the length of the hypotenuse. One way to do it is to set up a proportion: call the length of $\overline{BC}$ y, and you get: $\frac{3}{y} = (x\sqrt{3})/2x$. Multiplying out, you get $6x = yx\sqrt{3}$. The x variables on each side cancel out, and solving for y results in $y = 6/\sqrt{3}$. However, this isn't one of the answers, so you have to do some formatting. You should always keep in mind that it's a good idea to get square roots (and all sorts of roots) out of the denominators of fractions, and multiplying top and bottom of the right side of the equation by $\sqrt{3}$ gives you $y = 6\sqrt{3}/3$, which reduces to $y = 2\sqrt{3}$. Therefore, **B** is the answer.

54. H   *Pre-Algebra: Numbers*

To find the difference in speed between the two cars, you need to know their individual speeds. (Remember that speed is distance divided by time.) The speed of car A is 120 miles divided by 3 hours, which is 40 miles per hour. It took car B two hours longer to arrive at the destination, so its speed is $120 \div 5 = 24$ miles per hour. The difference between these two speeds is 16 miles per hour, so **H** is the answer.

55. B   *Plane Geometry: Three Dimensions*

This question is actually pretty tricky, because it involves several steps and you need to know your geometry fairly well. The key is figuring out the triangle whose hypotenuse is the diagonal in the diagram. This triangle stands "straight up" from the bottom of the box as you look down into it. The base of the triangle you want to find is the line that runs between point A and the corner below point B (call this point C for reference). In order to find the length of this line, you need to make another, preliminary triangle. The hypotenuse is the line segment $\overline{AC}$, and the shorter sides go from point A to the point directly to the right of A (the bottom right-hand corner, call it point D) and from D to C. This is a right triangle, so you can use the Pythagorean formula to figure out the length of $\overline{AC}$: $\overline{AC} = \sqrt{4^2 + 5^2} = \sqrt{41}$. This is an inconvenient length, but leave it as is for now. Now you've got all the information you need to answer the original question, which asks for the length of $\overline{AB}$. The base of the triangle is $\overline{AC}$, which has length $\sqrt{41}$, and the height is 3, the length of $\overline{BC}$, which you can determine from the diagram. This is also a right triangle, so you can use the Pythagorean theorem again to find the length of $\overline{AB} = \sqrt{(\sqrt{41})^2 + 3^2} = \sqrt{41 + 9} = \sqrt{50}$. This means **B** is the answer. This question is fairly involved, but if you know the right approach, each of the individual calculations is fairly easy. It goes to show that practicing ACT math questions like this one can save you a lot of time on the real exam.

56. **G** — *Pre-Algebra: Mean*

The main point of this problem is to figure out what each of the ten original students pays for a can of soda. We know that 6 sodas cost $5.40, and the students are buying 12, split 12 ways. The total cost is $10.80, and divided by 12 this comes out to $.90 per person. Each of the ten original students would have spent $1.00 to buy 10 sodas, so this allows them to save $0.10, or **G**.

57. **A** — *Coordinate Geometry: Conic Sections*

To answer this question, you have to look at the diagram to "piece together" the equation for an ellipse. The generic equation for an ellipse is $(x-h)^2/a^2 + (y-k)^2/b^2 = 1$, where each of the letters has a different meaning. (h, k) is the center of the ellipse, so in this equation h should equal 4 and k should be 2. This has already narrowed down the possible answers to the first two choices! The length of the horizontal axis of the ellipse is $2a$, so a in this case should equal 2. This is because the length of the horizontal axis is the farthest right-hand point's x coordinate minus the farthest left-hand point's x coordinate ($6 - 2 = 4$). This means $2a = 4$, and $a = 2$. Remember that the equation states that the denominator of the first term is a^2, which in this case is 4, so now you know that **A** has to be the correct answer.

58. **G** — *Coordinate Geometry: Graphing Equations*

This question might seem imposing, but if you know your functions it's actually very easy. For any equation where y isn't raised to an exponent, and x is raised to only whole number exponents ($\ldots, -1, 0, 1, 2, \ldots$) the function will cross the y-axis exactly once, because a function, by definition, can't have the same x value (in this case, $x = 0$) for more than one y value. Therefore, **G** is correct.

59. C   *Coordinate Geometry: Graphing Equations*

It might seem tricky, but you can actually work through this question without graphing anything. If you consider the case where x values are negative, the graphs will never cross, because x^3 will always be negative and x^2 will always be positive. At 0, they both meet, so that's one intersection. Between 0 and 1, x^3 values will be smaller than x^2 values, but at 1 they meet again (another intersection). At values greater than 1, x^3 will always be greater than x^2. That's a total of two intersections, so **C** is correct. For a question like this, it's important to keep a few key values in mind—negative values, positive values, 0, and 1. Beyond that, equations are usually pretty well-behaved (unless they have coefficients for which you have to account).

60. H   *Pre-Algebra: Probability*

This question is more complicated than it might first appear, and the best way to tackle it on the test is to write down all the possible combinations of heads and tails you could get by tossing a coin three times. It turns out there are eight of those combinations (head—tails—tails, head—head—tails, etc.), and in four of them there are two or more heads. Therefore, the odds are ½, and **H** is the answer.

Reading Test

Passage I

1. B   *Specific Details and Facts*

The answer to this question falls in a gray area between specific information and inference. You can solve it by referring to the second paragraph, which illustrates the pension through Lucy's eyes. While any of the answers may be true, the second paragraph suggests only that Lucy thinks the pension looks as if it could be in London.

2. J   *Specific Details and Facts*

The correct answer to this question is **J**. Don't be confused by **H**, which could be correct if it said "not seeing the Arno from her room."

3. A   *Specific Details and Facts*

As with the last question, this one asks for specific information from the passage: the old man proposes to switch rooms with Miss Bartlett and Lucy.

4.　**H**　　　　　　　　　　　　　　　　　　　*Draw Inferences*

This is an easy inference question, which you can answer through elimination, if you find it necessary. Answer **F** is wrong because the passage makes it clear that the girls have different mothers. Answer **G** is wrong because the passage states that Lucy's mother has helped pay for Miss Bartlett's trip, so it is unlikely that they are strangers. Although answer **J** may be true, it is not suggested in the passage. So answer **H** is the correct answer.

5.　**D**　　　　　　　　　　　　　　　　*Character and Character Motivation*

This question wants you to characterize Miss Bartlett, specifically in her behavior towards Lucy. From the dispute over the room, you may be tempted to answer either **A** or **C**, but by reading further in the passage you'll see that Miss Bartlett stifles Lucy's attempts to speak.

6.　**F**　　　　　　　　　　　　　　　　　　　*Specific Details and Facts*

Here's another simple specific-information question. You may find it necessary to look at the section preceding the reference lines in order to choose the correct answer: Lucy and Miss Bartlett argue over who will take the first room with a view.

7.　**C**　　　　　　　　　　　　　　　　　　　　　　*Draw Inferences*

This question requires you to do a fairly difficult bit of inferring. Look for a plausible answer, one that is suggested by the passage. You can eliminate **D** because there is no evidence of it in the passage. Similarly, **A** seems a stretch because the passage doesn't suggest that Miss Bartlett is particularly proud. From the last two choices, you can eliminate **B**; although Miss Bartlett doesn't approve of the old man's appearance, this answer is too limited to be a plausible explanation for her refusal. The correct answer is **C**: she does not think the offer is proper, and she is backed up by the shock of the "better class of tourist" when they hear of the offer.

8.　**F**　　　　　　　　　　　　　　　　　　　　　　*Draw Inferences*

This is another difficult inference question. Remember to find a plausible answer suggested by the passage. You can immediately eliminate **J** and **G** because they are not plausible answers—Miss Bartlett finds the old man ill-bred even before she looks at him and these answers require that she first see him. Choosing between the last two choices is tricky, but **H** is wrong because, while Miss Bartlett finds the interruption rude, she seems most outraged by his audacity in speaking to strangers. Thus the correct answer is **F**.

9. **B**   *Character and Character Motivation*

This question asks how Miss Bartlett regards the old man—not how you do. She's not particularly impressed by his offer in this passage; in fact, she considers it impolite, so **B** is the correct answer to this question.

10. **H**   *Point of View*

This point-of-view question is kind of tricky. You can immediately eliminate answers **F** and **G**, but that elimination leaves a difficult choice. If you think **J** is correct because there are no quotation marks, you're wrong. Answer **H** is correct because the lines referred to represent what the old man says to Miss Bartlett.

Passage II

11. **D**   *Specific Details and Facts*

The correct answer to this question is in the first paragraph of the passage. There the author states that under an economic tyranny everyone loses freedom. Knowing the definition of tyranny can help you answer this question without referring back to the passage. If you do refer back, read with caution because the other three answer choices are all mentioned in that first paragraph; **A** and **B** describe what the author calls the present condition, and **C** describes the ideal situation.

12. **F**   *Draw Inferences*

You can answer this question from the first two paragraphs of the passage. The author makes clear there that he opposes authority and compulsion. **G** does provide an alluring choice, however, because the author does seem to support work. But the right to work is subsumed by the right to choose, making **F** the better answer. Answer **H** is incorrect because the author states that he would prefer freedom for a few to enslavement for all, and **J** is incorrect because it is never suggested by the author.

13. **A**   *Specific Details and Facts*

These examples are used to describe the present state, according to the passage, so you can rule out answers **B** and **D**. Answer **C** is incorrect because the author does not argue at any time that wealth is the only means through which one can become an individual. Rather, he argues that it is a distinct advantage in realizing the individual, so **A** is correct because it is the best possible answer.

14. G *Cause-Effect*

This cause-effect question asks you to identify what arises from private property, according to the passage. The correct answer is **G**, which is stated in the fourth paragraph. While **F** may be true, it is not expressed in the passage. Answer **H** states the opposite of what appears in the passage. The passage never claims **J**—in fact, the author describes certain cases of Individualism under private property—so that answer too is wrong.

15. A *Cause-Effect*

You can figure out the correct answer to this question if you read the sentence immediately after the one referred to. There the author talks about the threat to the property owner from "things that are not under his control."

16. J *Main Idea*

You can immediately eliminate answers **F** and **H** because Byron, Shelley, and Browning do not figure in any of the main arguments of the passage. **G** is not an argument made anywhere in the passage, while the author spends nearly all his time making the case for the evils of private property.

17. C *Point of View*

In this passage, the author never states what he considers true, healthy individualism to be, so you must do a fair amount of inferring to answer this question. Answer **A** does not seem to be an adequate definition of individualism—the passage never suggests that a true individual is charismatic. Answer **B** seems like it could be correct until the part about living for other people. Living for others is distinctly opposed to the author's ideas about the individual; it is symptomatic of life under the rule of private property. Answer **C** sounds correct: the passage talks about the realization of personality and emphasizes the necessity of developing the individual free from external pressures. You can establish that this is the correct answer by eliminating **D**, which states that individualism happens through art. The author claims that Byron and Shelley achieved individualism through art, but he also says that their individualism was diminished because it existed under private property.

18. G *Words in Context*

The correct answer to this question is **G**. "Compulsion" means the act of compelling or being compelled—in other words, forcing someone to do something or being forced to do something.

19. **D** *Specific Details and Facts*

This is a simple specific-information question. When you see that it asks about English law, you should immediately refer back to the section that mentions English law in the fifth paragraph. This section states: "English law has always treated offenses against a man's property with far more severity than offenses against his person, and property is still the test of complete citizenship," which clearly indicates that the English law values property more than the person.

20. **G** *Draw Inferences*

The author suggests at several points (the second paragraph, for example) that he supports socialism in its attempt to abolish personal property but not in its desire to control the actions of men.

Passage III

21. **C** *Words in Context*

In this context, "vain" means futile—hopeless or useless.

22. **J** *Comparisons and Analogies*

This is a fairly difficult comparison question because the answer choices all seem to appear in the passage. But think closely about which of the answer choices are actually comparisons made by the author. Answer **J** is not actually a comparison made in the passage; although the author says that one is dependent on the other, he does not compare one to the other. In other words, saying that one thing is dependent on another is not the same as making a comparison between those two things.

23. **A** *Comparisons and Analogies*

This question strikes at the heart of the essay. The author's claim is that style affects content, so by changing the style, one necessarily changes the content.

24. **G** *Specific Details and Facts*

The author believes that gestures reveal the nature of the person, so the correct answer is **G**. You can eliminate the other answers quickly, if you wish: **F** states the opposite of the author's belief; **H** may tempt you if you remember the example of the polite man who seems unpleasant, but you should also recall that the author does not distinguish between unpleasant gestures and polite behavior (he claims the gestures are as public as the politeness); and answer **J** is not suggested anywhere in the passage.

Practice Test 2 Explanations

25. **A**   *Main Idea*

The opening paragraph to this passage should clue you in to the main idea. The author is pretty explicit about his argument: "style cannot be distinguished from matter." This statement is the primary argument of the passage; the other answer choices can be found in the passage, but they are relatively minor points.

26. **J**   *Draw Inferences*

There is no indication in this passage that the addressee is a specific person. The most likely addressee is an unspecified, general reader.

27. **C**   *Point of View*

The tone of the passage is not extreme in any way—the author neither snubs, admires, nor badgers the reader. The best way to describe the tone of the narrator is to call it instructive.

28. **H**   *Draw Inferences*

This question ultimately asks you to come up with an analogy for the author's argument. The correct answer to this question is **H** because the technique-substance relationship the analogy points to is the same as the relationship the author describes when he discusses style and matter.

29. **D**   *Main Idea*

In the final paragraph, the author discusses how demeanor can reveal the true personality of a man. The purpose of this discussion is to support his claim that style is indistinguishable from content by expanding on the analogy he makes between style and demeanor. Both are public manifestations of matter—the matter of writing and the matter of man.

30. **F**   *Words in Context*

The context reveals that **F** is the most sensible answer to this question. The easiest way to answer a question like this is to replace the tested words with the answer choices. You could also look to the root of this word, *com-*, and deduce that it is related to "comfort." The *in* at the word's beginning expresses the idea of "not."

Passage IV

31. **B**   *Specific Details and Facts*

This is a basic specific-information question. From the third to the fifth paragraphs, the author cites endorphin-related explanations for certain addictions, including alcohol, food, and nicotine—but not for interpersonal relationships.

Passage IV • 447

32. J *Cause-Effect*

According to the passage, the biological exposure model explains addiction as a biological need. Answer **F** represents the conditioning exposure model, which explains addiction as a result of reinforcement—not a specific biological response—so it is incorrect. Answer **G** is never suggested by the passage, so it too is incorrect. Answer **H** points to a psychological rather than biological response, so you can rule that answer out too. The correct answer to this question is **J**, as you can see from the third and seventh paragraphs.

33. C *Cause-Effect*

The author describes exercise addiction as a possible product of endorphin stimulation in the fourth paragraph of the passage. In this passage, she never discusses alternative explanations for exercise addiction.

34. G *Draw Inferences*

Chein's studies are discussed in the second-to-last paragraph of the passage. The first sentence of that paragraph states: "Studies by Chein questioned the notion that addiction is a consequence of rewarded behavior." The theory that argues for the role that behavior rewarded with pleasure plays in addiction is the conditioning exposure theory.

35. C *Specific Details and Facts*

Refer back to the last paragraph of the passage for information on the adaptation theory. You can think of the adaptation theory as covering the factors left out by the biological theory: the environmental, psychological, and social components of addiction. The main factor left out by the adaptation theory is the biological one, which includes inherited traits. The correct answer to this question is **C** because it leaves out inherited factors while including psychological and social ones.

36. F *Comparisons and Analogies*

The biological model argues that addiction arises from a biological necessity after prolonged addiction, while the conditioning model argues that addictive behavior can occur regardless of biology. The correct answer to this question is **F** because it points to the debate over the biological element of addiction.

37. D *Comparisons and Analogies*

The last question dealt with the main difference between the biological and conditioning models; this question deals with their main similarity. Why are these two models grouped together under the exposure theory? They both maintain that an addict is rewarded for the reinforcement of addiction: the biological model says that the reward is freedom from the pain of withdrawal, and the conditioning model says that the reward is pleasure or euphoria induced by the addiction.

38. **J**   *Words in Context*

In performing scientific experiments, you usually have "controlled" factors; that is, factors that you've fixed so they won't change from test to test. The purpose of these controls is to eliminate the confusion of having two changing factors and thereby help a researcher determine the true effect of the factor that he or she really wants to test. That said, "to control for" most nearly means "to regulate" in the context of experiments, so the correct answer to this question is **J**. In the described experiment, environmental conditions are "controlled" as much as possible so that differences in the experiments results can broadly be interpreted as genetic products.

39. **B**   *Draw Inferences*

The studies look at children of alcoholic parents raised in both non-alcoholic and alcoholic families and show that in both cases the rates of alcoholism in these children are higher than the rate of alcoholism in the rest of the population. The author of the passage states that these studies suggest a genetic component of alcoholism, so you can immediately eliminate answers **C** and **D** because they both state there is no genetic predisposition. To make your final choice, you should compare the rates of alcoholism between the two types of families: the children in these studies who remain in alcoholic families have a higher rate of alcoholism than those raised in non-alcoholic families. This in turn suggests a certain environmental factor.

40. **H**   *Draw Inferences*

In answering this question, you should ask what the relationship seems to be among the models described in the passage. The passage never clearly states the relationship, so you must infer it from the way the models are presented. You need to stick as close as you can to the passage when answering this question. An answer such as **G** strays too far from the material covered by the passage because there is no implication whatsoever of a debate between biologists and psychologists. Now ask yourself: are the models mutually exclusive? Or can they perhaps work together? If they work together, are they doing so as part of a larger theory of addiction? Well, there is little implication in the passage that a general theory of addiction exists. The author states in the first paragraph: "There are several theories that model addiction." That doesn't really sound as if these theories are just parts of a big theory, so you can eliminate **J**. Do the models seem mutually exclusive to you? Some cover psychological responses to addiction and some biological. Some say addictions are inherited, some say they occur from regular introduction to the body. These two theories do not contradict each other, but they aren't saying the same thing, either. It is safest to assume that these models map different responses and different causes of addiction, but just because one model works in one case doesn't mean that it will always work or that the other models are wrong. So the best inference you can make in this case is **H**.

Science Reasoning Test

Passage I

1. **B** *Read the Chart*

The passage states that the hydrides not in row 2 are attracted to each other through van der Waals forces. These forces are responsible for boiling points, since molecules require a higher temperature to boil when their forces of attraction are stronger. **A** is incorrect, since only row 2 hydrides have hydrogen bonding. **B** is correct, because the higher boiling point of H_2Se is due to greater van der Waals forces. **C** is incorrect, because while an increase in temperature may create enough energy to boil an element, temperature itself does not affect the boiling point of a substance. **D** is incorrect, because the hydrogen atoms themselves are not the reason for the higher boiling points—the weak van der Waals forces between molecules are.

2. **H** *Handle Graphs*

The strength of the hydrogen bond depends on molecular composition and shape, not on temperature. **F** is incorrect, since it shows bond strength increasing with temperature. **G** is incorrect because it shows bond strength decreasing with temperature. **H** is correct, because it shows bond strength remaining unaffected by temperature. **J** is incorrect since it shows bond strength increasing, staying constant, and then increasing again as temperature steadily rises.

3. **D** *Use the Chart*

The key factor determining the strength of hydrogen bonds is the number of hydrogen atoms that are next to highly electronegative atoms. **A** is incorrect, because kinetic energy is dependent on temperature, and does not directly affect molecular properties. **B** is incorrect, because propanol molecules are smaller and less massive, and would therefore have fewer van der Waals forces than diethyl ether molecules. **C** is incorrect, since the passage does not state that size of valence orbitals plays a role in molecular bonding strength. **D** is correct, because it is feasible that propanol has more hydrogen atoms next to highly electronegative atoms than diethyl ether does.

4. **G** *Use The Chart*

The passage states that hydrogen bonds are approximately 10 times stronger than van der Waals forces, which explains why H_2O, HF, and NH_3 have higher boiling points than H_2S, HCl, and PH_3, respectively. But CH_4 has a lower boiling point than SiH_4, so its molecules cannot be held together by hydrogen bonds. **F** is incorrect, because if CH_4 molecules were attracted by hydrogen bonds, we would expect CH_4 to have a higher boiling point than SiH_4. **G** is correct, since CH_4 exhibits van der Waals forces like all other hydrides. **H** is incorrect, since the kinetic energy of molecules is variable and does not affect the attractive force of the molecules in general, which is fixed. **J** is incorrect because the melting of hydrides is not a cause of the CH_4 molecules' attraction to each other.

5.   **B**   *Take the Next Step*

This question tests your total understanding of the passage and figure. **A** is incorrect, because the passage states that only row 2 molecules exhibit hydrogen bonds. **B** is correct, since the passage states that van der Waals forces increase as the number of electrons in a molecule increases, and the figure shows an increase in van der Waals forces as row number increases because the boiling points of the molecules increase from left to right (as long as you exclude row 2 because those molecules exhibit hydrogen bonds). **C** is incorrect because the boiling points of molecules with the same number of hydrogen atoms are not the same. **D** is incorrect because that hypothesis has no support anywhere in either the passage or the figure.

Passage II

6.   **F**   *Read the Chart*

The passage states that a comet whose period is less than 200 years is called periodic. Since Halley's Comet's period is 76 years, it is periodic, so **F** is correct. **G** is incorrect, since the comet is periodic, and **H** and **J** are incorrect because it is impossible for a comet to be both periodic and non-periodic, or to be neither.

7.   **A**   *Handle Graphs*

From Figure 5, you can see that period length happens to correspond to comet size. **A** is correct, because it shows period length increasing with comet size. **B** is incorrect, since it shows period length decreasing with comet size. **C** is incorrect, because it shows period length remaining constant as comet size increases. **D** is incorrect, because it shows period length as unrelated to comet size.

8.   **H**   *Use the Chart*

For this question, you need to read each answer to see which one matches up with the data. **F** is incorrect, because there is no clear relationship in Table 1 between eccentricity and period length. **G** is incorrect, because even though comet C travels nearly twice as close to the sun as comet A, there is no mention of what the relationship between distance from the sun and comet temperature might be. **H** is correct, because the first three orbits have comparable sizes, but wildly different period lengths. **J** is incorrect, because comet *C* has far greater eccentricity than comet *B*, but also travels much slower.

9. **C**   *Take the Next Step*

Each of the answers needs to be checked to see if it's correct, and if it answers the question. **A** is incorrect, because the orbits of comets stay constant. **B** is incorrect, because the speed of comets does not change from revolution to revolution. **C** is correct, because the passage does not contradict that comets orbit in different planes (it turns out to be correct) and this fact can explain why the paths of comets across the Earth sky are different from those of planets. **D** is incorrect, because even though it is true it does not explain why the paths of comets would look different from Earth.

10. **F**   *Take the Next Step*

If nuclear reactions occur each time the comet approaches the sun, we might expect that the material available inside the comet for this reaction would eventually disappear. After many passes by the sun, the comet would progressively "burn out," and thus have a shorter tail. **F** is correct, because it is plausible to suggest that comet *B* might be older and therefore have a shorter tail. **G** is incorrect, because the eccentricity of the orbit is unrelated to the length of its tail. **H** is incorrect, because we would expect a larger comet to have a longer tail, if all other conditions are equal. **J** is incorrect, because the passage does not state any relationship between comet speed and tail length.

Passage III

11. **C**   *Comparison*

Both theories support the notion that the universe is expanding, so both would allow for very distant galaxies moving away. Thus, **C** is correct, and **A**, **B**, and **D** are incorrect.

12. **F**   *Comparison*

The big bang theory states that all galaxies were created at the same time, whereas the steady state theory maintains that galaxies were created at various points in time. Thus, if a lot of galaxies were found to be the same age, it would support the big bang theory. Thus, **F** is correct, and **G**, **H**, and **J** are incorrect.

13. **A**   *Detail*

The big bang theory states that the slight discrepancies in the initial distribution of highly dense matter caused the eventual clumping of matter, which led to stars and then galaxies. **A** is correct, since it correctly states this. **B** is incorrect, since the expansion was a result of the initial force of the explosion. **C** is incorrect, since background radiation was the result of matter being too thinly spread in space for radiation energy to interact with. **D** is incorrect, since radiation waves moving backwards in time have nothing to do with the initial discrepancy in matter distribution (they are only seen as a possible argument for the steady state theory).

14. **H**   *Comparison*

Here, you need to look at all the answers and compare them to the theories. **F** is incorrect, because both theories agree that matter is distributed in the form of stars and galaxies. **G** is incorrect, since both theories agree that the universe is expanding. **H** is correct, because only the steady state theory claims that matter is continuously created. **J** is incorrect, because neither theory states that matter travels backwards in time.

15. **C**   *Comparison*

Each answer needs to be compared with the passages. **A** is incorrect, since only the big bang theory states that matter is the result of quantum fluctuation. **B** is incorrect, since the big bang theory states that the universe is about 15 billion years old, and thus could not have always existed. **C** is correct, because both theories accept that matter is grouped together in stars and galaxies, as opposed to being formlessly spread throughout the universe. **D** is incorrect, since neither theory claims that cosmic radiation causes expansion.

16. **J**   *Detail*

There are many unexplained aspects to the steady state theory, so you need to look at all the answers. **F** is incorrect, because the steady state theory explicitly claims that the universe has always existed. **G** is incorrect since cosmic background radiation does not confirm the steady state theory (it supports the big bang theory). **H** is incorrect, because the speed of galaxies' movement is not relevant to the theory. **J** is correct, because the steady state theory relies on the existence of an unexplained "unknown energy source."

17. B *Inference*

For this question, you need to compare the First Law in the question with the big bang theory passage. **A** is incorrect, because even though it is true, plasma is matter, so it does not explain where the matter came from. **B** is correct, because the passage states that very little is known about the very first part of the tremendous explosion. **C** is incorrect, because it does not explain where matter came from. **D** is incorrect, since the background radiation came as a result of the explosion, and thus could not have caused the initial creation of matter.

Passage IV

18. H *Read the Chart*

The chart contains samples of frisbees of three masses, and each of these different masses comes in a variety of lip heights. This allows a person looking at the chart to analyze the effects of both frisbee mass and frisbee lip height on flight length, so **H** is correct. **F** and **G** are incorrect because they are incomplete. **J** is incorrect because flight height is dependent on mass and lip height; it is not a deciding factor in flight length, though it may correspond to flight length.

19. D *Use the Chart*

This question requires you to find the column on the table where values increase every time the flight length of the frisbee increases. **A** is incorrect because the angle at which the frisbees are thrown never changes. **B** is incorrect, because reducing the lip height sometimes makes a frisbee go farther, but sometimes not as far. **C** is incorrect, because increasing the lip height also sometimes makes the frisbee travel farther, and other times not as far. **D** is correct, since whenever you look at frisbees with different masses but equal lip heights, the lighter one travels farther.

20. H *Handle Graphs*

To answer this question, you need to look at the table to see how flight distance is affected as lip height increases. For each of the three frisbee weights, when lip height increases, flight distance first increases, then decreases. **F** is incorrect because it suggests that flight distance always decreases when lip height increases. **G** is incorrect because it suggests that flight distance always increases when lip height increases. **H** is correct, since it shows flight distance first increasing, then decreasing as lip height increases. **J** is incorrect, because it suggests flight distance decreases, then increases as lip height increases.

21. **B** *Handle Graphs*

Here, you need to find the answer that corresponds to data in the table and would likely increase frisbee flights' maximum height. **A** is incorrect, because there is no data available to suggest what effect greater frisbee diameter might have on flight height. **B** is correct, because the data show that for each of the three types of frisbee, increasing the lip height led to a greater maximum flight height. **C** is incorrect, since there are no data suggesting that a greater rate of rotation would make frisbees fly higher. **D** is incorrect, because the heavier frisbees did not consistently fly higher than lighter ones.

22. **G** *Take the Next Step*

In order to determine the relationship between mass and maximum height of flight, you should keep all the factors in the experiment besides mass at a constant. **F** is incorrect, because you want to test different masses, and changing the angle would not help. **G** is correct, because you want to keep lip height constant while changing the masses. **H** is incorrect, because lip height varies along with mass, and you don't want an additional variable. **J** is incorrect, since you want to vary the masses while keeping other variables constant.

23. **A** *Take the Next Step*

The passage before the table states that a frisbee gets its lift from air pressure on the bottom of the frisbee. If there's a hole in the middle, there is less surface area on the frisbee for the air to push up on, and there is less lift. Thus, the frisbee does not fly as high. **A** is correct because it predicts the maximum height will be lower. **B** is incorrect since it predicts the new frisbees will have more lift and fly higher. **C** is incorrect, since the data does not indicate whether the newer frisbees will fly farther than the old ones. **D** is incorrect, for the same reason as **C**.

Passage V

24. **F** *Read the Chart*

The passage states that photons, when traveling over atoms with a particular frequency, will force excited electrons to a lower energy level, and release yet another photon. Therefore, **F** is correct, and **G**, **H**, and **J** are incorrect.

25. D *Handle Graphs*

The table shows three different sizes of ruby rod. For each size, as reflectivity increases, power output increases, and then decreases. **A** is incorrect, because it shows power output decreasing steadily with reflectivity. **B** is incorrect, because it shows power output increasing as reflectivity increases. **C** is incorrect, because it shows power output first decreasing, and then increasing as reflectivity increases. **D** is correct, because it shows power output increasing and then decreasing as reflectivity increases.

26. H *Use the Chart*

If you look carefully at Figure 1, you can see that to the left of the vertical line there is no power output by the laser at all. Thus, the line marks the point in time when the laser first begins to emit power. In addition, since the top half shows the amount of stimulation on the rod, the vertical line is measuring how much stimulation is required for a burst to overcome the reflectivity of the emitting end of the rod. **F** is incorrect, because the line marks the beginning of the power output in time, not its maximum. **G** is incorrect, because the line is only a moment in time, and does not measure a duration. **H** is correct, because the line marks the point when the photons have sufficient intensity to escape the rod. **J** is incorrect, because the first graph shows that stimulation increased after the time marked by the line.

27. C *Use the Chart*

Here, you need to look at Table 1 and see which of the answers corresponds to a guaranteed increase in power output. You also need to remember the key comment in the passage that rod volume is proportional to the length of the rod times the diameter of the rod. **A** is incorrect, because decreasing the length would likely decrease the power output. **B** is incorrect, because nothing in the passage suggests that rod density affects the power output. **C** is correct, because for every measurement, a rod with a greater volume will have a higher power output than one with a lower volume. **D** is incorrect, because increasing reflectivity of the emitting end does not always lead to a power increase.

28. J *Take the Next Step*

Here, you need to find the answer best supported by data in the passage. **F** is incorrect, because there is no information suggesting that stray photons would affect the reflectivity of either end of the rod. **G** is incorrect, because there is also no information to suggest that photons not in line with those bouncing back and forth in the rod will somehow decrease the amount of energy in the burst. **H** is incorrect, because there is nothing suggesting that photons can be turned into electrons. **J** is correct, because the passage states that only those photons that are traveling lengthwise along the rod end up in the burst, which means that those that don't bounce against reflective surfaces might just leave through the non-reflective sides.

29. **A**   *Take the Next Step*

One of the key properties of laser light is that it remains extremely focused—a laser beam seen thousands of yards away will remain almost exactly the same width as it is when it emerges from the laser device. **A** is correct, because such a focused light could be used to pinpoint signals between satellites at tremendous distances. **B** is incorrect, because a large pool of light would require an equally large laser. **C** is incorrect, because the laser produces a tight beam, and would thus not illuminate dark areas very well. **D** is incorrect, because car headlights should ideally light up as wide an area as possible, a task ill-suited for a laser.

Passage VI

30. **G**   *Read the Chart*

From Table 1, you can see that yellow light has a wavelength of 635 nanometers. For this question, you need to find where on the two tables of data the wavelength of light closest to 635 nm occurs. The closest place is the bottom half of Table 2, where the combination of 70% ester/dye solution #1 and 30% hydrogen peroxide gives a light of wavelength 630 nm at a temperature of 20°C. **F** is incorrect, since the closest wavelength is 700 nm. **G** is correct, since the wavelengths are closest to 635 nm. **H** is incorrect, because its wavelength is longer than yellow, and **J** is incorrect, because its wavelength is shorter than yellow.

31. **A**   *Handle Graphs*

It is fairly obvious from Tables 2 and 3 that as temperature increases, reaction time decreases. It's important to note, however, that for each increase in temperature, reaction time decreases less, which means that the decrease in time is slowing down. **A** is correct, because it shows the reaction time decreasing, and the decrease is also slowing down as temperature increases. **B** is incorrect, because even though it shows reaction time decreasing, the changes in reaction time are increasing as temperature increases. **C** is incorrect, since it shows reaction time increasing, then decreasing. **D** is incorrect because it shows reaction time decreasing, then increasing.

32. J *Use the Chart*

Each answer involves slightly different data from the graphs, so you need to look at each choice carefully. **F** is incorrect, because changing the ester/dye solution concentration has a noticeable effect on the wavelengths of the emitted light. **G** is incorrect because even though the charts show longer reaction times when the concentration of hydrogen peroxide is larger, there is not enough evidence to know whether this is always the case. (In fact, it is probably not the case, since it is doubtful that a solution of 100% hydrogen peroxide would have any reaction at all.) **H** is incorrect, because in Experiment 2, reducing the amount of hydrogen peroxide made the light less blue. **J** is correct, because in both experiments there was a larger difference in reaction times as temperature increased when there was more hydrogen peroxide. This suggests that the effectiveness of hydrogen peroxide is altered more by temperature than the effectiveness of the ester/dye solution.

33. A *Use the Chart*

There are several differences between the two ester/dye solutions, so all the answers need to be looked at. **A** is correct, because reaction times for ester/dye solution #2 vary less with temperature than the ones for solution #1. **B** is incorrect because the passage does not list any data for how visible different light colors are. **C** is incorrect, since solution #2 does not always react for a longer time than solution #1 (for instance, they react for the same time at 15°C when there is 70% ester/dye solution and 30% hydrogen peroxide). **D** is incorrect because according to Table 1, all the light wavelengths emitted in the tests qualify as visible light.

34. H *Take the Next Step*

The graphs illustrate that a lower temperature will make the reaction longer. **F** and **G** are incorrect, because the graphs do not indicate that external light conditions make any difference to the reaction. **H** is correct, because the data suggest that the reaction proceeds slower at lower temperatures. **J** is incorrect since increasing temperature will increase reaction rate.

35. C *Take the Next Step*

For this experiment, the key is to keep all factors constant except for the concentration of hydrogen peroxide. **A** is incorrect, because if each concentration is tested at a different temperature, no conclusions can be drawn. **B** is incorrect because the hydrogen peroxide concentration never changes during the experiment. **C** is correct because all factors except hydrogen peroxide concentration remain constant during the experiment. **D** is incorrect, because there are too many variables in the experiment to learn anything directly about hydrogen peroxide.

Passage VII

36. **G**   *Read the Chart*

The passage states that sublimation is the process of a substance moving from a solid phase to a vapor phase. Figure 2 shows that above 3886 mm Hg of pressure, carbon dioxide moves from a solid to a liquid before it can become a vapor. **F** is incorrect, because 55480 mm Hg is much too high a pressure for carbon dioxide to sublimate. **G** is correct because it is the very highest pressure where carbon dioxide can go directly from solid to vapor. **H** is incorrect, because carbon dioxide can sublimate at higher pressures than 760 mm Hg (air pressure at sea level). **J** is incorrect, because carbon dioxide can sublimate at pressures higher than 0 mm Hg.

37. **B**   *Handle Graphs*

The passage states that when a substance undergoes a phase change, there is a period when the substance does not change temperature. Once the entire phase change is complete, the substance increases in temperature until the next phase change. **A** is incorrect, because it does not show the substance keeping the same temperature during a phase change. **B** is correct, because it properly shows the substance increasing in temperature between phase changes, and remaining constant in temperature during them. **C** is incorrect, since it does not show proper phase changes at all. **D** is incorrect, since it shows the phase changes in the wrong order (at that pressure, water will not sublimate).

38. **J**   *Use the Chart*

Since a higher pressure means that a substance will eventually enter its densest phase at any given temperature, you need see which answer matches what happens when you trace a vertical line going up on the figures. **F** is incorrect, because carbon dioxide liquid will revert to carbon dioxide solid when pressure goes up. **G** is incorrect, since helium will revert to a solid under high pressure. **H** is incorrect for the same reason as **G**. **J** is correct, because ice reverts to water as pressure increases, which means that ice is less dense than water.

39. **C**   *Use the Chart*

The passage states that a triple point is a particular temperature and pressure where solid, liquid, and vapor phases come together. Figure 3 shows that these three phases never meet at the same point. **A** is incorrect, because there is not a point in the graph where the three phases meet. **B** is incorrect, because even though there are two points where three regions of the graph meet, they do not each represent unique phases. **C** is correct, since helium does not have a triple point. **D** is incorrect, since the graph shows the phase relationships, and it can be determined that there is no triple point.

40. **G**   *Take the Next Step*

The ice skates exert pressure on the ice, and Figure 1 shows that as pressure increases, ice turns to water. This water results in a slick surface. **F** is incorrect because it is not based on any information in the passage. **G** is correct, since it correctly suggests that pressure will melt the part of the ice that touches the skate. **H** is incorrect because it is impossible for an increase in pressure to cause sublimation from ice to water vapor. **J** is incorrect, because only a liquid can go to a critical point.